LITERATU

```
MW00981089
```

For additional information on Intel products in the U.S. [...], call Intel's Literature Center at (800) 548-4725 or write to:

INTEL LITERATURE SALES
P.O. Box 7641
Mt. Prospect, IL 60056-7641

To order literature outside of the U.S. and Canada contact your local sales office.

Additional information about Intel products is available on Intel's web site: http://www.intel.com.

CURRENT DATABOOKS

Product line databooks contain datasheets, application notes, article reprints, and other design information. All databooks can be ordered individually, and most are available in a pre-packaged set in the U.S. and Canada. Databooks can be ordered in the U.S. and Canada by calling TAB/McGraw-Hill at 1-800-822-8158; outside of the U.S. and Canada contact your local sales office.

Title	Intel Order Number	ISBN
SET OF NINE DATABOOKS (Available in U.S. and Canada)	**231003**	**N/A**
CONTENTS LISTED BELOW FOR INDIVIDUAL ORDERING:		
EMBEDDED MICROCONTROLLERS	270646	1-55512-248-5
EMBEDDED MICROPROCESSORS	272396	1-55512-249-3
FLASH MEMORY (2 volume set)	210830	1-55512-250-7
i960® PROCESSORS AND RELATED PRODUCTS	272084	1-55512-252-3
NETWORKING	297360	1-55512-256-6
OEM BOARDS, SYSTEMS AND SOFTWARE	280407	1-55512-253-1
PACKAGING	240800	1-55512-254-X
PENTIUM® AND PENTIUM PRO PROCESSORS AND RELATED PRODUCTS	241732	1-55512-251-5
PERIPHERAL COMPONENTS	296467	1-55512-255-8
ADDITIONAL LITERATURE: (Not included in databook set)		
AUTOMOTIVE PRODUCTS	231792	1-55512-257-4
COMPONENTS QUALITY/RELIABILITY	210997	1-55512-258-2
EMBEDDED APPLICATIONS (1995/96)	270648	1-55512-179-9
MILITARY	210461	N/A
SYSTEMS QUALITY/RELIABILITY	231762	1-55512-046-6

A complete set of this information is available on CD-ROM through Intel's Data on Demand program, order number 240897. For information about Intel's Data on Demand ask for item number 240952.

January 1996
Order Number: 000900-001

Intel Application Support Services

World Wide Web [URL: http://www.intel.com/]
Intel's Web site now contains technical and product information that is available 24 hours a day! Also visit Intel's site for financials, history, current news and events, job opportunities, educational news and much, much more!

FaxBack*
Technical and product information are available 24 hours a day! Order documents containing:

- Product Announcements
- Product Literature
- Intel Device Characteristics
- Design/Application Recommendations
- Stepping/Change Notifications
- Quality and Reliability Information

Information on the following subjects are available:

- Microcontroller and Flash
- OEM Branded Systems
- Multibus and iRMX Software/BBS listing
- Multimedia
- Development Tools
- Quality and Reliability/Change Notification
- Microprocessor/PCI/Peripheral
- Intel Architecture Labs

To use FaxBack (for Intel components and systems), dial **(800) 628-2283** or 916-356-3105 (U.S./Canada/APAC/Japan) *or +44{0} 1793-496646 (Europe)* and follow the automated voice-prompt. Document orders will be faxed to the fax number you specify. For information on how the Intel Application Support team can help you, order our Customer Service Agreement, document #1201. Catalogs are updated as needed, so call for the latest information!

Bulletin Board System (BBS)
To use the Intel Application BBS (components and systems), dial **(503) 264-7999** or **(916) 356-3600** (U.S./Canada/APAC/Japan) *or +44{0} 1793-432955 (Europe)*. The BBS will support 1200-19200 baud rate modem. *Typical modem configuration: 14.4K baud rate, No Parity, 8 Data Bits, 1 Stop Bit.*

CompuServe *Just type* 'Go Intel'
Intel maintains several forums where people come together to meet their peers, gather information, share discoveries and debate issues. For more information about service fees and access, call CompuServe at 1-800-848-8199 or 614-529-1340 (outside the U.S.). The INTELC forum is set up to support designers using various Intel components.

General Information Help Desk
Dial 1-800-628-8686 or 916-356-7599 (U.S. and Canada) between 5 a.m. and 5 p.m. PST for help with Intel products. For customers not in the U.S. or Canada, please contact your local distributor.

Intel Literature Centers

U.S.	+1-800-548-4725	France	+44{0} 1793 421777
U.S. (from overseas)	+1-708-296-9333	Germany	+44{0} 1793 421333
England	+44{0} 1793 431 155	Japan (fax only)	+81{0} 120 47 88 32

Intel Distributors
Check the back of an Intel data book or request one of the following distributor listing FaxBack documents: #4083 (U.S. Eastern Time Zone), #4084 (U.S. Central Time Zone), #4085 (Mountain Time Zone), #4086 (U.S. Alaska/Pacific Time Zone), #4209 (Europe) or #4403 (Canada).

Other brands and names are the property of their respective owners.

January 1996
Order Number: 000901-001

int_el_®

Pentium® Pro Family Developer's Manual

Volume 3:
Operating System Writer's Guide

NOTE: The *Pentium® Pro Family Developer's Manual* consists of three books: *Specifications*, Order Number 242690; *Programmer's Reference Manual*, Order Number 242691; and the *Operating System Writer's Guide*, Order Number 242692.
Please refer to all three volumes when evaluating your design needs.

1996

intͺͺ.

TABLE OF CONTENTS

APPENDIX B
PERFORMANCE MONITORING COUNTERS

APPENDIX C
MODEL-SPECIFIC REGISTERS (MSRS)

TABLE OF FIGURES

intel.

TABLE OF TABLES

intel®

1

About This Manual

CHAPTER 1
ABOUT THIS MANUAL

The *Pentium® Pro Family Developer's Manual, Volume 3: Operating System Writer's Guide* (Order Number 242692) is part of a three-volume set that describes the architecture, programming environment, and hardware features of the Pentium® Pro processor. The other two manuals in this set are as follows:

- *Pentium® Pro Family Developer's Manual, Volume 2: Programmer's Reference Manual,* (Order Number 242691)

- *Pentium® Pro Family Developer's Manual, Volume 1: Specifications* (Order Number 242690)

The *Pentium® Pro Family Developer's Manual, Volume 2* and the *Pentium® Pro Family Developer's Manual, Volume 3* describe the architecture and programming environment of the Pentium Pro processor. The *Pentium® Pro Family Developer's Manual, Volume 2* describes the basic programming environment and the instructions set of the processor. It is aimed at application programmers who are writing programs to run under existing operating systems or executives. The *Pentium® Pro Family Developer's Manual, Volume 3* describes the operating system support environment of the processor, including memory management, protection, task management, interrupt and exception handling, and system management mode. Both manuals provide Intel Architecture compatibility information.

1.1. OVERVIEW OF THE PENTIUM® PRO FAMILY DEVELOPER'S MANUAL, VOLUME 3

The contents of this manual are as follows:

Chapter 1 — About the Manual. Gives an overview of this manual and the *Pentium® Pro Family Developer's Manual, Volume 2*. It also describes the notational conventions in these manuals and lists related Intel manuals and documentation of interest to programmers and hardware designers.

Chapter 2 — System Architecture Overview. Describes the modes of operation of the Pentium Pro processor and those processor features used to build operating systems and executives, including the system-oriented registers and data structures and the system-oriented instructions. The steps necessary for switching between real-address and protected modes are also identified.

Chapter 3 — Protected-Mode Memory Management. Describes the data structures, registers, and instructions that support segmentation and paging and explains how they can be used to implement a "flat" (unsegmented) memory model or a segmented memory model.

Chapter 4 — Protection. Describes the Pentium Pro processor's support for page and segment protection. This chapter also explains the implementation of privilege rules, stack switching, pointer validation, user and supervisor modes.

Chapter 5 — Interrupt and Exception Handling. Describes the basic interrupt mechanisms of the Pentium Pro processor, shows how interrupts and exceptions relate to protection, and describes how the processor handles each exception type.

Chapter 6 — Task Management. Describes how the Pentium Pro processor supports multi-tasking with context-switching operations and inter-task protection.

Chapter 7 — Multiple Processor Management. Describes the instructions and flags that support multiple processors with shared memory, memory ordering, and the advanced programmable interrupt controller (APIC).

Chapter 8 — Processor Management and Initialization. Defines the state of the processor and floating-point unit after reset initialization. This chapter also explains how to set up the processor for real-address mode operation and protected mode operation, and how to switch between modes.

Chapter 9 — System Management Mode (SMM). Describes the Pentium Pro processor's implementation of system management mode (SMM), which can be used to implement power management functions.

Chapter 10 — Debugging and Performance Monitoring. Describes the debugging registers and other debug features of the Pentium Pro processor. This chapter also describes the time-stamp counter and the performance monitoring counters.

Chapter 11 — Memory Cache Control. Describes the general concept of caching and the specific mechanisms used by the Pentium Pro processor's internal caches. This chapter also describes the memory type range registers (MTRRs) and how they can be used to map memory types of physical memory.

Chapter 12 — 8086 Emulation. Describes the real-address and virtual-8086 modes of the Pentium Pro processor.

Chapter 13 — Mixing 16-Bit and 32-Bit Code. Describes how to mix 16-bit and 32-bit code modules within the same program or task.

Chapter 14 — Code Optimization. Discusses general optimization techniques for programming in the Intel Architecture environment.

Chapter 15 — Intel Architecture Compatibility. Describes the differences between 8086, the Intel 286, Intel386™, Intel486™, Pentium, and Pentium Pro processors. This chapter covers the system architecture of the Intel Architecture processors.

Chapter 16 — Machine Check Architecture. Describes the processor's machine check architecture.

Appendix A — Opcode Map. Gives an opcode map for the Pentium Pro processor instruction set.

Appendix B — Performance-Monitoring Counters. Lists the events that can be counted with the performance-monitoring counters and the codes used to select these events.

Appendix C — Model Specific Registers (MSRs). Lists the MSRs available in the Pentium Pro processor and their functions.

1.2. OVERVIEW OF THE PENTIUM® PRO PROGRAMMER'S REFERENCE MANUAL

The contents of the *Pentium® Pro Family Developer's Manual, Volume 2* are as follows:

Chapter 1 — About the Manual. Gives an overview of the *Pentium® Pro Family Developer's Manual, Volume 2* and the *Pentium® Pro Family Developer's Manual, Volume 3*. It also describes notation conventions used in these manuals and lists related Intel manuals and documentation of interest to programmers and hardware designers.

Chapter 2 — Introduction to the Intel Pentium® Pro Processor Family. Introduces the Intel Pentium Pro processor family and gives an overview of the new features found in these processors.

Chapter 3 — Program Execution Environment. Introduces the models of memory organization, defines the data types, presents the register set used by applications, introduces the stack, explains string operations, defines the parts of an instruction, explains address calculations, and introduces interrupts and exceptions as they apply to application programming.

Chapter 4 — Procedure Calls, Interrupts, and Exceptions. Describes the mechanisms provided for making procedure calls and for servicing interrupts and exceptions.

Chapter 5 — Data Types and Addressing Modes. Describes the data types and addressing modes recognized by the processor.

Chapter 6 — Instruction Set Summary. Gives an overview of all the Pentium Pro processor instructions except those executed by the processor's floating-point unit. The instructions are presented in functionally related groups. This chapter also gives an overview of the instruction format commonly used by assemblers.

Chapter 7 — Floating-Point Unit. Gives an overview of the Pentium Pro processor's floating-point unit, including the floating-point registers and data types; gives an overview of the floating-point instruction set; and describes the processor's floating-point arithmetic facilities.

Chapter 8 — Input/Output. Describes the processor's I/O architecture, including I/O port addressing, the I/O instructions, and the I/O protection mechanism.

Chapter 9 — Processor Identification and Feature Determination. Describes how to determine the CPU type and the features that are available in the processor.

Chapter 10 — Intel Architecture Compatibility. Describes the programming differences between the Intel 286, Intel386, Intel486, Pentium, and Pentium Pro processors.

Chapter 11 — Instruction Set Reference. Describes each of the Pentium Pro processor instructions in detail, including an algorithmic description of operations, the effect on flags, the effect of operand- and address-size attributes, and the exceptions that may be generated. The instructions are arranged in alphabetical order.

Appendix A — EFLAGS Cross Reference. Summaries how the Pentium Pro processor instructions affect the flags in the EFLAGS register.

Appendix B — EFLAGS Condition Codes. Summarizes how the conditional jump, move, and byte set on condition code instructions use the condition code flags (OF, CF, ZF, SF, and PF) in the EFLAGS register.

Appendix C — Floating-Point Exceptions Summary. Summarizes the exceptions that can be raised by floating-point instructions.

1.3. NOTATIONAL CONVENTIONS

This manual uses special notation for data-structure formats, for symbolic representation of instructions, and for hexadecimal numbers. A review of this notation makes the manual easier to read.

1.3.1. Bit and Byte Order

In illustrations of data structures in memory, smaller addresses appear toward the bottom of the figure; addresses increase toward the top. Bit positions are numbered from right to left. The numerical value of a set bit is equal to two raised to the power of the bit position. The Pentium Pro processor is a "little endian" machine; this means the bytes of a word are numbered starting from the least significant byte. Figure 1-1 illustrates these conventions.

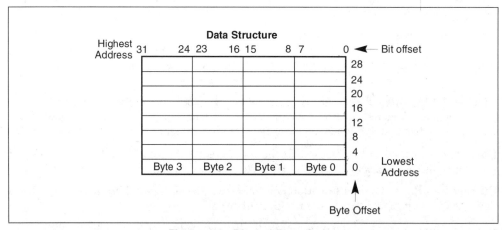

Figure 1-1. Bit and Byte Order

1.3.2. Reserved Bits and Software Compatibility

In many register and memory layout descriptions, certain bits are marked as *reserved*. When bits are marked as reserved, it is essential for compatibility with future processors that software treat these bits as having a future, though unknown, effect. The behavior of reserved bits should be regarded as not only undefined, but unpredictable. Software should follow these guidelines in dealing with reserved bits:

- Do not depend on the states of any reserved bits when testing the values of registers which contain such bits. Mask out the reserved bits before testing.

- Do not depend on the states of any reserved bits when storing to memory or to a register.

- Do not depend on the ability to retain information written into any reserved bits.

- When loading a register, always load the reserved bits with the values indicated in the documentation, if any, or reload them with values previously read from the same register.

NOTE

Avoid any software dependence upon the state of reserved Pentium Pro processor register bits. Depending upon the values of reserved register bits will make software dependent upon the unspecified manner in which the processor handles these bits. Depending upon reserved values risks incompatibility with future processors.

1.3.3. Instruction Operands

When instructions are represented symbolically, a subset of the assembly language for the Pentium Pro processor is used. In this subset, an instruction has the following format:

```
label: mnemonic argument1, argument2, argument3
```

where:

- A *label* is an identifier which is followed by a colon.

- A *mnemonic* is a reserved name for a class of instruction opcodes which have the same function.

- The operands *argument1*, *argument2*, and *argument3* are optional. There may be from zero to three operands, depending on the opcode. When present, they take the form of either literals or identifiers for data items. Operand identifiers are either reserved names of registers or are assumed to be assigned to data items declared in another part of the program (which may not be shown in the example).

When two operands are present in an arithmetic or logical instruction, the right operand is the source and the left operand is the destination.

For example:

```
LOADREG: MOV EAX, SUBTOTAL
```

In this example LOADREG is a label, MOV is the mnemonic identifier of an opcode, EAX is the destination operand, and SUBTOTAL is the source operand. Some assembly languages put the source and destination in reverse order.

1.3.4.   Hexadecimal and Binary Numbers

Base 16 (hexadecimal) numbers are represented by a string of hexadecimal digits followed by the character H (for example, F82EH). A hexadecimal digit is a character from the following set: 0, 1, 2, 3, 4, 5, 6, 7, 8, 9, A, B, C, D, E, and F.

Base 2 (binary) numbers are represented by a string of 1s and 0s, sometimes followed by the character B (for example, 1010B). The "B" designation is only given in situations where confusion as to the type of number might arise.

1.3.5.   Segmented Addressing

The processor uses byte addressing. This means memory is organized and accessed as a sequence of bytes. Whether one or more bytes are being accessed, a byte address is used to address memory. The memory that can be addressed with a byte address is called an *address space*.

The processor also supports segmented addressing. This is a form of addressing where a program may have many independent address spaces, called *segments*. For example, a program can keep its code (instructions) and stack in separate segments. Code addresses would always refer to the code space, and stack addresses would always refer to the stack space. The following notation is used to specify a byte address within a segment:

```
Segment-register:Byte-address
```

For example, the following segment address identifies the byte at offset FF79H in the segment pointed by the DS register:

```
DS:FF79H
```

The following segment address identifies an instruction address in the code segment. The CS register points to the code segment and the EIP register contains the offset of the instruction in the segment.

```
CS:EIP
```

1.3.6.   Exceptions

An exception is an event that typically occurs when an instruction causes an error. For example, an attempt to divide by zero generates an exception. However, some exceptions, such as breakpoints, occur under other conditions. Some types of exceptions may provide error codes. An error code reports additional information about the error. An example of the notation used to show an exception and error code is shown below.

```
#PF(fault code)
```

This example refers to a page-fault exception under conditions where an error code naming a type of fault is reported. Under some conditions, exceptions which produce error codes may not be able to report an accurate code. In this case, the error code is zero, as shown below for a general-protection exception.

```
#GP(0)
```

See Chapter 5, *Interrupt and Exception Handling*, for a list of exception mnemonics and their descriptions.

1.4. RELATED LITERATURE

The following books contain additional material related to Intel processors:

- *Pentium® Processor BIOS Writer's Guide*, Order Number 242692.
- AP-485, *Intel Processor Identification with the CPUID Instruction*, Order Number 241618.
- *Pentium® Processor Data Book*, Order Number 241428.
- *82496 Cache Controller and 82491 Cache SRAM Data Book For Use With the Pentium® Processor*, Order Number 241429.
- *Intel486™ Microprocessor Data Book*, Order Number 240440.
- *Intel486™ Processor Hardware Reference Manual*, Order Number 240552.
- *Intel486™ DX Processor Programmer's Reference Manual*, Order Number 240486.
- *Intel486™ SX CPU/Intel487™ SX Math CoProcessor Data Book*, Order Number 240950.
- *Intel486™ DX2 Microprocessor Data Book*, Order Number 241245.
- *Intel486™ Microprocessor Product Brief Book*, Order Number 240459.
- *Intel386™ Processor Hardware Reference Manual*, Order Number 231732.
- *Intel386™ DX Processor Programmer's Reference Manual*, Order Number 230985.
- *Intel386™ SX Processor Programmer's Reference Manual*, Order Number 240331.
- *Intel386™ Processor System Software Writer's Guide*, Order Number 231499.
- *Intel386™ High-Performance 32-Bit CHMOS Microprocessor with Integrated Memory Management*, Order Number 231630.
- *376 Embedded Processor Programmer's Reference Manual*, Order Number 240314.
- *80387 DX User's Manual Programmer's Reference*, Order Number 231917.
- *376 High-Performance 32-Bit Embedded Processor*, Order Number 240182.
- *Intel386™ SX Microprocessor*, Order Number 240187.
- *Microprocessor and Peripheral Handbook* (Vol. 1), Order Number 230843.
- AP-500, *Optimizations for Intel's 32-Bit Processors*, Order number 241799.

intel®

2

System Architecture Overview

The Pentium Pro processor (like the other 32-bit members of the Intel Architecture family of processors) provides extensive support for operating-system and system-development software. This support is part of the processor's system-level architecture and includes features to assist in the following operations:

- Memory management

- Protection of software modules

- Multitasking

- Exception and interrupt handling

- Multiprocessing

- Cache management

- Hardware resource and power management

- Debugging and performance monitoring

This chapter provides a brief overview of the processor's system-level architecture; a detailed description of each part of this architecture given in the following chapters. This chapter also describes the system registers that are used to set up and control the processor at the system level and gives a brief overview of the processor's system-level (operating system) instructions.

Many of the system-level architectural features of the processor are used only by system programmers. Application programmers may need to read this chapter, and the following chapters which describe the use of these features, in order to understand the hardware facilities used by system programmers to create a reliable and secure environment for application programs.

2.1. OVERVIEW OF THE SYSTEM-LEVEL ARCHITECTURE

The Pentium Pro processor's system architecture consists of a set of registers, data structures, and instructions designed support basic system-level operations such as memory management, interrupt and exception handling, task management, and control of multiple processors (multiprocessing). Figure 2-1 provides a generalized summary of the system registers and data structures.

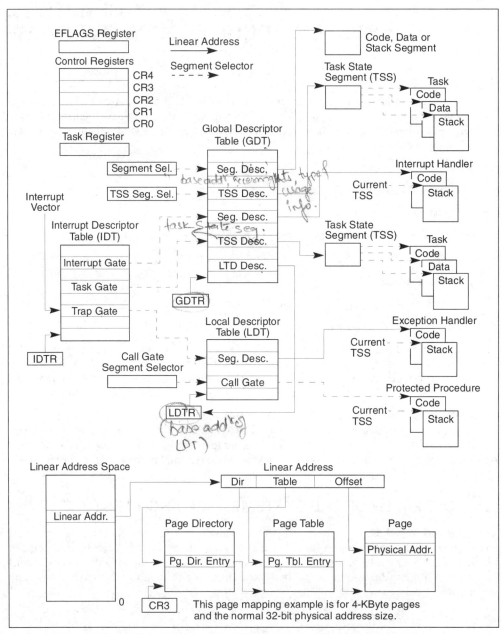

Figure 2-1. System-Level Registers and Data Structures

2.1.1. Global and Local Descriptor Tables

When operating in protected mode, all memory accesses pass through either the global descriptor table (GDT) or the (optional) local descriptor table (LDT). These tables contain entries called segment descriptors. A segment descriptor provides the base address of a segment and access rights, type, and usage information. Each segment descriptor has a segment selector associated with it. The segment selector provides an index into the GDT or LDT (to its associated segment descriptor), a global/local bit (that determines whether the segment selector points to the GDT or the LDT), and access rights information.

To access a byte in a segment, both a segment selector and an offset must be supplied. The segment selector provides access to the segment descriptor for the segment (in the GDT or LDT). From the segment descriptor, the processor obtains the base address of the segment in the linear address space. The offset then provides the location of the byte relative to the base address. This mechanism can be used to access any valid code, data, or stack segment in the GDT or LDT, provided the segment is accessible from the current privilege level (CPL) at which the processor is operating. (The CPL is defined as the protection level of the currently executing code segment.)

In Figure 2-1 the solid arrows indicate a linear address and the dashed lines indicate a segment selector. For simplicity, many of the segment selectors are shown as direct pointers to a segment. However, the actual path from a segment selector to its associated segment is always through the GDT or LDT.

The linear address of the base of the GDT is contained in the GDT register (GDTR); the linear address of the LDT is contained in the LDT register (LDTR).

2.1.2. System Segments, Segment Descriptors, and Gates

Besides the code, data, and stack segments that make up the execution environment of a program or procedure, the system architecture also defines two system segments: the task state segment (TSS) and the LDT. (The GDT is not considered a segment because it is not accessed by means of a segment selector and segment descriptor.) Each of these segment types has a segment descriptor defined for it.

The system architecture also defines a set of special segment descriptors called gates (the call gate, interrupt gate, trap gate, and task gate) that provide protected gateways to system procedures and handlers that operate at different privilege levels than application programs and procedures. For example, a CALL to a call gate provides access to a procedure in a code segment that is at the same or numerically lower privilege level (more privileged) than the current code segment. To access a procedure through a call gate, the calling procedure must supply the segment selector of the call gate. The processor than performs an access rights check on the call gate, comparing the CPL with the privilege level of the call gate and destination code segment. If access to the destination call gate is allowed, the processor gets the segment selector for the destination code segment and an offset into that code segment from the call gate. If the call requires a change in privilege level, the processor also switches to the stack for that privilege level. (The segment selector for the new stack is obtained from the TSS for the currently running task.) Gates also facilitate transitions between 16-bit and 32-bit code segments, and vice versa.

compare CPL with privilege level of call gate — same privilege level or numerically lower value (more privileged)

2.1.3.   Task State Segments and Task Gates

The TSS defines the state of the execution environment for a task. It includes the state of the general-purpose registers, the segment registers, the EFLAGS register, the EIP register, and segment selectors and stack pointers for three stack segments (one stack each for privilege levels 0, 1, and 2). It also includes the segment selector for the LDT associated with the task and the page table base address.

All program execution in protected mode happens within the context of a task, called the current task. The segment selector for the TSS for the current task is stored in the task register. The simplest method of switching to a task is to make a call or jump to the task. Here, the segment selector for the TSS of the new task is given in the CALL or JMP instruction. In switching tasks, the processor performs the following actions:

1.   Stores the state of the current task in the current TSS.

2.   Loads the task register with the segment selector for the new task.

3.   Accesses the new TSS through a segment descriptor the GDT.

4.   Loads the state of the new task from the new TSS into the general-purpose, segment, LDTR, CR3 (page table base address), EFLAGS, and EIP registers.

5.   Begins execution of the new task.

A task can also be accessed through a task gate. A task gate is similar to a call gate, except that it provides access (through a segment selector) to a TSS rather than a code segment.

2.1.4.   Interrupt and Exception Handling

External interrupts, software interrupts, and exceptions are handled thorough the interrupt descriptor table (IDT). The IDT contains a collection of segment descriptors, which provide access to interrupt and exception handlers. Like the GDT, the IDT is not a segment. The linear address of the base of the IDT is contained in the IDT register (IDTR).

The segment descriptors in the IDT can be of the interrupt-, trap-, or task-gate type. To access an interrupt or exception handler, the processor must first receive an interrupt vector (interrupt number) from internal hardware, an external interrupt controller, or from software by means of an INT, INTO, INT3, or BOUND instruction. The interrupt vector provides an index into the IDT to a segment descriptor. If the selected segment descriptor is an interrupt gate or a trap gate, the associate handler procedure is accessed in a manner very similar to calling a procedure through a call gate. If the descriptor is a task gate, the handler is accessed through a task switch.

2.1.5.   Memory Management

The system architecture supports either direct physical addressing of memory or virtual memory (through paging). When physical addressing is used, a linear address is treated as a physical address. When paging is used, all the code, data, stack, and system segments and the GDT and IDT can be paged, with only the most recently accessed pages being held in physical memory.

The location of pages (or page frames as they are sometimes called in the Intel Architecture) in physical memory is contained in two system data structures (a page directory and a page table), both of which reside in physical memory (see Figure 2-1). An entry in a page directory contains the physical address of the base of a page table, access rights, and memory management information. An entry in a page table contains the physical address of a page frame, access rights, and memory management information. The base physical address of the page directory is contained in control register CR3.

To use this paging mechanism, a linear address is broken into three parts, providing separate offsets into the page directory, the page table, and the page frame.

A system can have a single page directory or several. For example, each task can have its own page directory.

2.1.6. System Registers

To assist in initializing the processor and controlling system operations, the system architecture provides system flags in the EFLAGS register and several system registers:

- The system flags and IOPL field in the EFLAGS register control task and mode switching, interrupt handling, instruction tracing, and access rights. See Section 2.3., "System Flags and Fields in the EFLAGS Register" for a description of these flags.

- The control registers (CR0, CR2, CR3, and CR4) contain a variety of flags and data fields for controlling system-level operations. See Section 2.5., "Control Registers" for a description of these flags.

- The debug registers (not shown in Figure 2-1) allow the setting of breakpoints for use in debugging programs and systems software. See Chapter 10, *Debugging and Performance Monitoring*, for a description of these registers.

- The GDTR, LDTR, and IDTR registers contain the linear addresses and sizes (limits) of their respective tables. See Section 2.4., "Memory-Management Registers" for a description of these registers.

- The task register contains the linear address and size of the TSS for the current task. See Section 2.4., "Memory-Management Registers" for a description of this register.

- Model specific registers (not shown in Figure 2-1).

The model-specific registers (MSRs) are a group of registers available primarily to operating-system or executive procedures (that is, code running at privilege level 0). These registers control items such as the debug extensions, the performance monitoring counters, the machine check architecture, and the memory type ranges (MTRRs). The number and functions of these registers may change, depending on the model of the processor in the Pentium Pro processor family. See Section 8.4., "Model Specific Registers (MSRs)" for more information about the MSRs and Appendix C, *Model-Specific Registers (MSRs)*, for a complete list of the MSRs.

Most systems restrict access to all system registers (other than the EFLAGS register) by application programs. Systems can be designed, however, where all programs and procedures run at the most privileged level (privilege level 0), in which case application programs are allowed to modify the system registers.

2.1.7. Other System Resources

Besides the system registers and data structures described in the previous sections, the system architecture provides the following additional resources:

- Operating system instructions (see Section 2.6., "System Instruction Summary").

- Performance monitoring counters (not shown in Figure 2-1).

- Internal caches and buffers (not shown in Figure 2-1).

The performance monitoring counters are event counters that can be programmed to count processor events such as the number of instructions decoded, the number of interrupts received, or the number of cache loads. See Section 10.6., "Performance Monitoring Counters", for more information about these counters.

The processor provides several internal caches and buffers. The caches are used to store both data and instructions. The buffers are used to store things like decoded addresses to system and application segments and write operations waiting to be performed. See Chapter 11, *Memory Cache Control*, for a detailed discussion of the processor's caches and buffers.

2.2. MODES OF OPERATION

The Pentium Pro processor supports three operating modes and one quasi-operating mode:

- **Protected mode.** This is the native operating mode of the processor. In this mode all instructions and architectural features are available, providing the highest performance and capability. This is the recommended mode for all new applications and operating systems.

- **Real-address mode.** This operating mode provides the programming environment of the Intel 8086 processor, with a few extensions (such as the ability to switch to protected or system management mode).

- **System management mode (SMM).** The system management mode (SMM) is a standard architectural feature in all Intel Architecture processors, beginning with the Intel386 SL processor. This mode provides an operating system or executive with a transparent mechanism for implementing power management and OEM differentiation features. SMM is entered through activation of an external system interrupt pin (SMI#), which generates a system management interrupt (SMI). In SMM, the processor switches to a separate address space while saving the context of the currently running program or task. SMM-specific code may then be executed transparently. Upon returning from SMM, the processor is placed back into its state prior to the SMI.

- **Virtual-8086 mode.** In protected mode, the processor supports a quasi-operating mode known as *virtual-8086 mode*. This mode allows the processor execute 8086 software in a protected, multi-tasking environment.

Figure 2-2 shows how the processor moves among these operating modes.

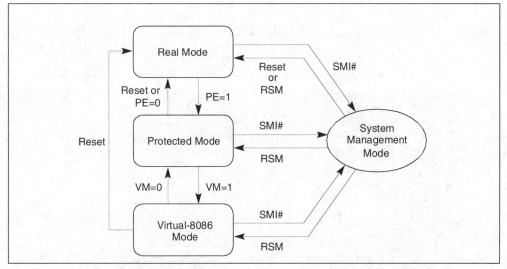

Figure 2-2. Transitions Among the Processor's Operating Modes

The processor is placed in real-address mode following power-up or a reset. Thereafter, the PE flag in control register CR0 controls whether the processor is operating in real-address or protected mode (see Section 2.5., "Control Registers"). Only a single instruction (one that loads the CR0 register) is required to switch between real-address mode and protected mode.

The VM flag in the EFLAGS register determines whether the processor is operating in protected mode or virtual-8086 mode. Transitions between protected mode and virtual-8086 mode are generally carried out as part of a task switch or a return from and interrupt or exception handler (see Section 12.2.5., "Entering Virtual-8086 Mode").

The processor switches to SMM whenever it receives an SMI while the processor is in real-address, protected, or virtual-8086 modes. Upon execution of the RSM instruction, the processor always returns to the mode it was in when the SMI occurred.

2.3. SYSTEM FLAGS AND FIELDS IN THE EFLAGS REGISTER

The system flags and IOPL field of the EFLAGS register control I/O, maskable interrupts, debugging, task switching, and the virtual-8086 mode (see Figure 2-3). An application program should ignore these system flags and should not attempt to change their state.

The functions of the status flags and IOPL are as follows:

TF   **Trap (bit 8).** Set to enable single-step mode for debugging; clear to disable single-step mode. In single-step mode, the processor generates a debug exception after each instruction, which allows the execution state of a program to be inspected after each instruction. If an application program sets the TF flag using a POPF, POPFD, or IRET instruction, a debug exception is generated after the instruction that follows the POPF, POPFD, or IRET instruction.

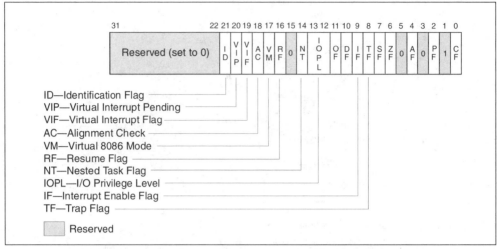

Figure 2-3. System Flags in the EFLAGS Register

IF   **Interrupt enable (bit 9).** Controls the response of the processor to maskable interrupt requests. Set to respond to maskable interrupts; cleared to inhibit maskable interrupts. The IF flag does not effect the generation of exceptions or nonmaskable interrupts (NMI interrupts). The CPL, IOPL, and the state of the VME flag in control register CR4 determine whether the IF flag can be modified by the CLI, STI, POPF, POPFD, and IRET instructions.

IOPL   **I/O privilege level field (bits 12 and 13).** Indicates the I/O privilege level (IOPL) of the currently running program or task. The CPL of the currently running program or task must be less than or equal to the IOPL to access the I/O address space. This field can only be modified by the POPF and IRET instructions when operating at a CPL of 0. See Chapter 8 in the *Pentium® Pro Family Developer's Manual, Volume 2* for more information on the relationship of the IOPL to I/O operations.

          The IOPL is also one of the mechanisms that controls the modification of the IF flag and the handling of interrupts in virtual-8086 mode when the virtual mode extensions are in effect (the VME flag in control register CR4 is set).

NT   **Nested task (bit 14).** Controls the chaining of interrupted and called tasks. The processor sets this flag on calls to a task initiated with a CALL instruction, an interrupt, or an exception. It examines and modifies this flag on returns from a task initiated with the IRET instruction. The flag can be explicitly set or cleared with the POPF/POPFD instructions; however, changing to the state of this flag can generate unexpected exceptions in application programs. See Section 6.4., "Task Linking" for more information on nested tasks.

RF   **Resume (bit 16).** Controls the processor's response to instruction-breakpoint conditions. When set, this flag temporarily disables debug exceptions (#DE) from being generated for instruction breakpoints detected for the next instruction; although, other exception conditions can cause an exception to be generated. The processor automatically clears this flag after the instruction has been successfully executed, except after an IRET instruction and a JMP, CALL, or INT*n* instructions that cause a task switch. The processor sets this flag prior to calling an exception handler for any exception except a debug exception and prior to calling an interrupt handler when a string instruction has been interrupted. Software can also set this flag by setting it in the EFLAGS image saved on the stack and then executing an IRET instruction. The RF flag is not affected by the POPF and POPFD instructions.

The primary function of the RF flag is to allow the restarting of an instruction following a debug exception that was caused by an instruction breakpoint condition. Here, debugger software sets this flag in the EFLAGS image on the stack prior to returning to the interrupted program, to prevent the instruction breakpoint from causing another debug exception. See Section 10.3.1.1., "Instruction-Breakpoint Exception Condition" for more information on the use of this flag.

VM **Virtual 8086 mode (bit 17).** Set to enable virtual-8086 mode; clear to return to protected mode. See Section 12.2.1., "Enabling Virtual-8086 Mode" for a detailed description of the use of this flag to switch to virtual-8086 mode.

AC **Alignment check (bit 18).** Set this flag and the AM bit in the CR0 register to enable alignment checking of memory references; clear the AC flag and/or the AM bit to disable alignment checking. An alignment-check exception is generated when reference is made to an unaligned operand, such as a word at an odd byte address or a doubleword at an address which is not an integral multiple of four. Alignment-check exceptions are generated only in user mode (privilege level 3). Memory references that default to privilege level 0, such as segment descriptor loads, do not generate this exception even when caused by instructions executed in user-mode.

The alignment-check exception can be used to check alignment of data. This is useful when exchanging data with other processors, which require all data to be aligned. The alignment-check exception can also be used by interpreters to flag some pointers as special by misaligning the pointer. This eliminates overhead of checking each pointer and only handles the special pointer when used.

VIF **Virtual Interrupt (bit 19).** Contains a virtual image of the IF flag. The processor only recognizes this flag when the VME flag in control register CR4 is set and the IOPL is less than 3. See Section 12.3.5., "Method 6 Interrupt and Exception Handling" for detailed information about the use of this flag.

VIP **Virtual interrupt pending (bit 20).** Set by software to indicate that an interrupt is pending; cleared to indicate that no interrupt is pending. This flag is used in conjunction with the VIF flag. The processor reads this flag but never modifies it. The processor only recognizes this flag when the VME flag in control register CR4 is set and the IOPL is less than 3. See Section 12.3.5., "Method 6 Interrupt and Exception Handling" for detailed information about the use of this flag.

ID **Identification (bit 21).** The ability of a program or procedure to set or clear this flag indicates support for the CPUID instruction.

2.4. MEMORY-MANAGEMENT REGISTERS

The processor provides four memory-management registers (GDTR, LDTR, IDTR, and TR) that specify the locations of the data structures which control segmented memory management (see Figure 2-4). Special instructions are provided for loading and storing these registers.

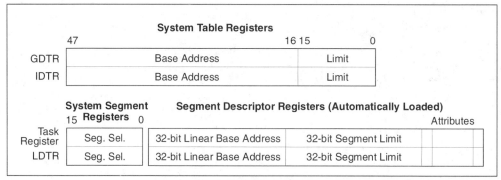

Figure 2-4. Memory Management Registers

2.4.1. Global Descriptor Table Register (GDTR)

The GDTR register holds the 32-bit base address and 16-bit segment limit for the GDT. The base address specifies the linear address of byte 0 of the GDT; the segment limit specifies the number of bytes in the table. The LGDT and SGDT instructions load and store the GDTR register, respectively. On power up or reset of the processor, the base address is set to the default value of 0 and the limit is set to FFFFH. A new base address must be loaded into the GDTR as part of the processor initialization process for protected mode operation. See Section 3.5.1., "Segment Descriptor Tables" for more information on the base address and limit fields.

2.4.2. Local Descriptor Table Register (LDTR)

The LDTR register holds the 16-bit segment selector, 32-bit base address, 32-bit segment limit, and descriptor attributes for the LDT. The base address specifies the linear address of byte 0 of the LDT segment; the segment limit specifies the number of bytes in the segment. See Section 3.5.1., "Segment Descriptor Tables" for more information on the base address and limit fields.

The LLDT and SLDT instructions load and store the segment selector part of the LDTR register, respectively. The segment that contains the LDT must have a segment descriptor in the GDT. When the LLDT instruction loads a segment selector in the LDTR, the base address, limit, and descriptor attributes from the LDT descriptor are automatically loaded into the LDTR.

When a task switch occurs, the LDTR is automatically loaded with the segment selector and descriptor for the LDT for the new task. The contents of the LDTR are not automatically saved prior to writing the new LDT information into the register.

On power up or reset of the processor, the segment selector and base address are set to the default value of 0 and the limit is set to FFFFH.

2.4.3. IDTR Interrupt Descriptor Table Register

The IDTR register holds the 32-bit base address and 16-bit segment limit for the IDT. The base address specifies the linear address of byte 0 of the IDT; the segment limit specifies the number of bytes in the table. The LIDT and SIDT instructions load and store the IDTR register, respectively. On power up or reset of the processor, the base address is set to the default value of 0 and the limit is set to FFFFH. The base address and limit in the register can then be changed as part of the processor initialization process. See Section 5.7., "Interrupt Descriptor Table (IDT)" for more information on the base address and limit fields.

2.4.4. Task Register (TR)

The task register holds the 16-bit segment selector, 32-bit base address, 32-bit segment limit, and descriptor attributes for the TSS of the current task. It references a TSS descriptor in the GDT. The base address specifies the linear address of byte 0 of the TSS; the segment limit specifies the number of bytes in the TSS. (See Section 6.2.3., "Task Register" for more information about the task register.)

The LTR and STR instructions load and store the segment selector part of the task register, respectively. When the LTR instruction loads a segment selector in the task register, the base address, limit, and descriptor attributes from the TSS descriptor are automatically loaded into the task register. On power up or reset of the processor, the base address is set to the default value of 0 and the limit is set to FFFFH.

2.5. CONTROL REGISTERS

The control registers (CR0, CR1, CR2, CR3, and CR4) determine operating mode of the processor and the characteristics of the currently executing task (see Figure 2-5).

- CR0—Contains system control flags that control operating mode and states of the processor.

- CR1—Reserved.

- CR2—Contains the page fault linear address (the linear address that caused a page fault).

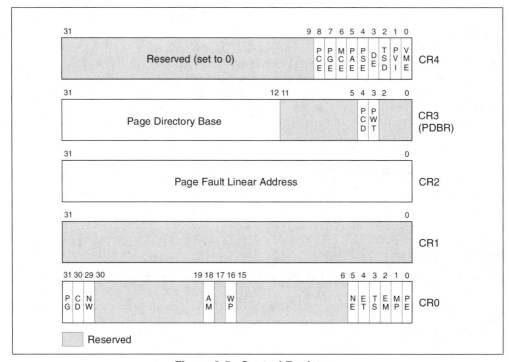

Figure 2-5. Control Registers

- CR3—Contains the physical address of the base of the page directory and two flags (PCD and PWT). This register is also known as the page directory base register (PDBR). Only the 20 most-significant bits of the page directory base address are specified; the lower 12 bits of the address are assumed to be 0. The page directory must thus be aligned to a page (4-KByte) boundary. The PCD and PWT flags control caching of the page directory in the processor's internal data caches (they do not control TLB caching of page directory information.)

  When using the physical address extension, the CR3 register contains the base address of the page directory pointer table (see Section 3.8., "Physical Address Extension").

- CR4—Contains a group of flags that enable several architectural extensions.

When operating in protected mode, application programs (running at privilege levels 1, 2, or 3) are prevented from loading the control registers. Application programs can read these registers, however. For example, an application might need to read register CR0 to determine if an FPU is present. Forms of the MOV instruction allow these registers to be loaded from or stored to the general-data registers.

A program should not attempt to change any of the reserved bit positions. Reserved bits should always be set to the value previously read.

The functions of the flags in the control registers are as follows:

PG **Paging (bit 31 of CR0).** Enables paging when set; disables paging when clear. When paging is disabled, all linear addresses are treated as physical addressed. The PG flag has no effect if the PE flag (bit 0 of register CR0) is not also set; in fact, setting the PG flag when the PE flag is clear causes a general-protection exception (#GP) to be generated. See Section 3.6., "Paging (Virtual Memory)" for a detailed description of the processor's paging mechanism.

CD **Cache Disable (bit 30 of CR0).** Prevents caching for the whole of physical memory in the processor's internal caches (L1 and L2) when set; enables caching when clear. When this flag is set, cache read misses do not cause cache line fills, but cache read hits result in reads from the cache; cache write misses do not result in cache writes, but cache write hits cause a write-back to memory and corresponding cache line invalidation. To prevent the processor from accessing its caches, the caches must be invalidated so that no cache hits can occur (see Section 11.5.2., "Preventing Caching"). When this flag is set, the PCD and PWT flags in register CR3 and in page-directory and page-table entries are ignored; when the CD flag is clear, the PCD and PWT flags in control register CR3 and the in the page-directory and page-table entries can override caching of pages, page tables, and page directories. See Chapter 11, *Memory Cache Control*, for detailed information on caching.

NW **Not Write-through (bit 29 of CR0).** Disables write-throughs and cache invalidation cycles when clear; enables write-throughs that hit the cache and invalidation cycles when set. See Chapter 11, *Memory Cache Control*, for detailed information on caching.

AM **Alignment Mask (bit 18 of CR0).** Enables automatic alignment checking when set; disables alignment checking when clear. Alignment checking is performed only when the AM flag is set, the AC flag in the EFLAGS register is set, the CPL is 3, and the processor is operating in either protected or virtual-8086 mode.

WP **Write Protect (bit 16 of CR0).** Inhibits supervisor-level procedures from writing into user-level pages when set; allows supervisor-level procedures to write into read-only user-level pages when clear. This flag facilitates implementation of the copy-on-write method of creating a new process (forking) used by operating systems such as UNIX.

NE **Numeric Error (bit 5 of CR0).** Enables the standard mechanism for reporting FPU errors when set; disables the standard mechanism when clear. When the NE flag is clear and the IGNNE# input is asserted, FPU errors are ignored. When the NE flag is clear and the IGNNE# input is deasserted, an unmasked FPU error causes the processor to stop instruction execution immediately before executing the next waiting floating-point instruction or WAIT/FWAIT instruction and assert the FERR# pin to generate an external interrupt. The FERR# pin is intended to drive an input to an external interrupt controller (the FERR# pin emulates the ERROR# pin of the Intel287™ and Intel387™ DX math coprocessors). The NE flag, IGNNE# pin, and FERR# pin are used with external logic to implement PC-style error reporting. (See "Software Exception Handling" in Chapter 7, *Floating-Point Unit*, of the *Pentium® Pro Family Developer's Manual, Volume 2* for more information about this flag.)

ET   **Extension Type (bit 4 of CR0).** Reserved in the Pentium Pro and Pentium processors. (In the Pentium Pro processor, this flag is hardcoded to 1.) In the Intel386 and Intel486 processors, setting this flag indicates support of Intel387 DX math coprocessor instructions when set.

TS   **Task Switched (bit 3 of CR0).** Allows the saving of FPU context on a task switch to be delayed until the FPU is actually accessed by the new task. The processor sets this flag on every task switch and tests it when interpreting floating-point arithmetic instructions.

- If the TS flag is set, a device-not-available exception (#NM) is raised prior to the execution of a floating-point instruction.

- If the TS flag and the MP flag (also in the CR0 register) are both set, an #NM exception is raised prior to the execution of floating-point instruction or a WAIT/FWAIT instruction.

Table 2-1 shows the actions taken for floating-point and WAIT/FWAIT instructions based on the settings of the TS, EM, and MP flags.

Table 2-1. Action Taken for Different Combinations of EM, MP and TS

CR0 Flags			Instruction Type	
EM	MP	TS	Floating-Point	WAIT/FWAIT
0	0	0	Execute	Execute
0	0	1	#NM Exception	Execute
0	1	0	Execute	Execute
0	1	1	#NM Exception	#NM Exception
1	0	0	#NM Exception	Execute
1	0	1	#NM Exception	Execute
1	1	0	#NM Exception	Execute
1	1	1	#NM Exception	#NM Exception

The processor does not automatically save the context of the FPU on a task switch. Instead it sets the TS flag, which causes the processor to raise an #NM exception whenever it encounters a floating-point instruction in the instruction stream for the new task. The fault handler for the #NM exception can then be used to save the context of the FPU and clear the TS flag with the CLTS instruction. If the task never encounters a floating-point instruction, the FPU context is never saved.

EM   **Emulation (bit 2 of CR0).** Indicates that the processor does not have an internal or external FPU when set; indicates an FPU is present when clear. When the EM flag is set, execution of a floating-point instruction generates a device-not-available exception (#NM). This flag must be set when the processor does not have an internal FPU or is not connected to a math coprocessor. If the processor does have an internal FPU, setting this flag would force all floating-point instructions to be handled by software emulation. Table 8-3 shows the recommended setting of this flag, depending on the Intel Architecture processor and FPU or math coprocessor present in the system. Table 2-1 shows the interaction of the EM, MP, and TS flags.

MP   **Monitor Coprocessor (bit 1 of CR0).** Controls the interaction of the WAIT (or FWAIT) instruction with the TS flag (bit 3 of CR0). If the MP flag is set, a WAIT instruction generates a device-not-available exception (#NM) if the TS flag is set. If the MP flag is clear, the WAIT instruction ignores the setting of the TS flag. Table 8-3 shows the recommended setting of this flag, depending on the Intel Architecture processor and FPU or math coprocessor present in the system. Table 2-1 shows the interaction of the MP, EM, and TS flags.

PE   **Protection Enable (bit 0 of CR0).** Enables protected mode when set; enables real-address mode when clear. This flag does not enable paging directly. It only enables segment-level protection. To enable paging, both the PE and PG flags must be set. See Section 8.8., "Mode Switching" for information using the PE flag to switch between real and protected mode.

PCD   **Page-level Cache Disable (bit 4 of CR3).** Controls caching of the current page directory. When the PCD flag is set, caching of the page-directory is prevented; when the flag is clear, the page-directory can be cached. This flag affects only the processor's internal caches (both L1 and L2). The processor ignores this flag if paging is not used (the PG flag in register CR0 is clear) or the CD (cache disable) flag in CR0 is set. See Chapter 11, *Memory Cache Control*, for more information about the use of this flag. See Section 3.6.4., "Page-Directory and Page-Table Entries" for a description of a companion PCD flag in the page-directory and page-table entries.

PWT   **Page-level Writes Transparent (bit 3 of CR3).** Controls the write-through or write-back caching policy of the current page directory. When the PWT flag is set, write-through caching is enabled; when the flag is clear, write-back caching is enabled. This flag affects only the internal caches (both L1 and L2). The processor ignores this flag if paging is not used (the PG flag in register CR0 is clear) or the CD (cache disable) flag in CR0 is set. See Section 11.5., "Cache Control" for more information about the use of this flag. See Section 3.6.4., "Page-Directory and Page-Table Entries" for a description of a companion PCD flag in the page-directory and page-table entries.

VME   **Virtual-8086 Mode Extensions (bit 0 of CR4).** Enables interrupt- and exception-handling extensions in virtual-8086 mode when set; disables the extensions when clear. Use of the virtual mode extensions can improve the performance of virtual-8086 applications by eliminating the overhead of calling the virtual-8086 monitor to handle interrupts and exceptions that occur while executing an 8086 program and, instead, redirecting the interrupts and extensions back to the 8086 programs handlers. It also provides hardware support for a virtual interrupt flag (VIF) to improve reliability of running 8086 programs in multitasking and multiple processor environments. See Section 12.3., "Interrupt and Exception Handling in Virtual-8086 Mode" for detailed information about the use of this feature.

PVI   **Protected-Mode Virtual Interrupts (bit 1 of CR4).** Enables hardware support for a virtual interrupt flag (VIF) in protected mode when set; disables the VIF flag in protected mode when clear. See Section 12.4., "Protected Mode Virtual Interrupts" for detailed information about the use of this feature.

TSD **Time Stamp Disable (bit 2 of CR4).** Restricts the execution of the RDTSC instruction to procedures running at privilege level 0 when set; allows RDTSC instruction to be executed at any privilege level when clear.

DE **Debugging Extensions (bit 3 of CR4).** References to debug registers DR4 and DR5 cause an undefined opcode (#UD) exception to be generated when set; when clear, processor aliases references to registers DR4 and DR5 for compatibility with software written to run on earlier Intel Architecture processors. See Section 10.2.2., "Debug Registers DR4 and DR5" for more information on the function of this flag.

PSE **Page Size Extensions (bit 4 of CR4).** Enables 4-MByte pages when set; restricts pages to 4 KBytes when clear. See Section 3.6.1., "Paging Options" for more information about the use of this flag.

PAE **Physical Address Extension (bit 5 of CR4).** Enables paging mechanism to reference 36-bit physical addresses when set; restricts physical addresses to 32 bits when clear. See Section 3.8., "Physical Address Extension" for more information about the physical address extension.

MCE **Machine Check Enable (bit 6 of CR4).** Enables the machine check exception when set; disables the machine check exception when clear. See Chapter 16, *Machine Check Architecture*, for more information about the machine check exception and machine check architecture.

PGE **Page Global Enable (bit 7 of CR4).** Enables the global page feature when set; disables the global page feature when clear. The global page feature allows frequently used or shared pages to be marked as global to all users (done with the global flag, bit 8, in a page-directory or page-table entry). Global pages are not flushed from the translation-lookaside buffer (TLB) on a task switch or a write to register CR3. See Section 3.7., "Translation Lookaside Buffers (TLBs)" for more information on the use of this bit.

PCE **Performance-monitoring Counter Enable (bit 8 of CR4).** Enables execution of the RDPMC instruction for programs or procedures running at any protection level when set; RDPMC instruction can be executed only at protection level 0 when clear.

2.5.1. CPUID Qualification of Control Register Flags

The VME, PVI, TSD, DE, PSE, PAE, MCE, PGE, and PCE flags in control register CR4 are model specific. All of these flags (except the PCE flag) can be qualified with the CPUID instruction to determine if they are implemented on the processor before they are used.

2.6. SYSTEM INSTRUCTION SUMMARY

The system instructions handle system-level functions such as loading system registers, managing the cache, managing interrupts, or setting up the debug registers. Many of these instructions can be executed only by operating-system or executive procedures (that is, procedures running at privilege level 0). Others can be executed at any privilege level and are thus available to application programs. Table 2-2 lists the system instructions and indicates whether they are available and useful for application programs.

These instructions are describe in detail in Chapter 11 of the *Pentium® Pro Family Developer's Manual, Volume 2.*

2.6.1. Loading and Storing System Registers

The GDTR, LDTR, IDTR, and TR registers each have a load and store instruction for loading data into and storing data from the register:

LGDT (Load GDTR Register)	Loads the GDT base address and limit into the GDTR register.
SGDT (Store GDTR Register)	Stores the GDT base address and limit in memory.
LIDT(Load IDTR Register)	Loads the IDT base address and limit into the IDTR register.
SIDT(Load IDTR Register	Stores the IDT base address and limit in memory.
LLDT (Load LDT Register)	Loads the LDT segment selector and segment descriptor into the LDTR.
SLDT (StoreLDT Register)	Stores the LDT segment selector in memory.
LTR (Load Task Register)	Loads segment selector and segment descriptor for a TSS into the task register.
STR (Store Task Register)	Store the segment selector for the current task in memory.

The LMSW (load machine status word) and SMSW (store machine status word) instructions operate on bits 0 through 15 of control register CR0. These instructions are provided for compatibility with the 16-bit Intel 286 processor. Program written to run on 32-bit Intel Architecture processors should not use these instructions. Instead, they should access the control register CR0 using the MOV instruction.

The CLTS (clear TS bit in CR0) instruction is provided for use in handling a device-not-available exception (#NM) that occurs when the processor attempts to execute a floating-point instruction when the TS flag is set. This instruction allows the TS flag to be cleared after the FPU context has been saved, preventing further #NM exceptions. See Section 2.5., "Control Registers" for more information about the TS flag.

The control registers (CR0, CR1, CR2, CR3, and CR4) are loaded with the MOV instruction. This instruction can load a control register from a general-purpose register or store the contents of the control register in a general-purpose register.

2.6.2. Verifying of Access Privileges

The processor provides several instructions for examining segment selectors and segment descriptors to determine if access to their associated segments is allowed. These instructions duplicate some of the automatic access rights and type checking done by the processor, thus allowing operating-system or executive software to prevent exceptions from being generated.

Table 2-2. Summary of System Instructions

Instruction	Description	Useful to Application?	Protected from Application?
LLDT	Load LDT Register	No	Yes
SLDT	Store LDT Register	No	No
LGDT	Load GDT Register	No	Yes
SGDT	Store GDT Register	No	No
LTR	Load Task Register	No	Yes
STR	Store Task Register	No	No
LIDT	Load IDT Register	No	Yes
SIDT	Store IDT Register	No	No
MOV	Load and store control registers	No	Yes
SMSW	Store MSW	Yes	No
LMSW	Load MSW	No	Yes
CLTS	Clear TS bit in CR0	No	Yes
ARPL	Adjust RPL	Yes[1]	No
LAR	Load Access Rights	Yes	No
LSL	Load Segment Limit	Yes	No
VERR	Verify for Reading	Yes	No
VERW	Verify for Writing	Yes	No
MOV	Load and store debug registers	No	Yes
INVD	Invalidate cache, no writeback	No	Yes
WBINVD	Invalidate cache, with writeback	No	Yes
INVLPG	Invalidate TLB entry	No	Yes
HLT	Halt Processor	No	Yes
LOCK (Prefix)	Bus Lock	Yes	No
RSM	Return from system management mode	No	Yes
RDMSR	Read Model-Specific Registers	No	Yes
WRMSR	Write Model-Specific Registers	No	Yes
RDPMC	Read Performance Monitoring Counter	Yes	Yes[2]
RDTSC	Read Time Stamp Counter	Yes	Yes[2]

NOTES:

1. Useful to application programs running at a CPL of 1 or 2.
2. The TSD and PCE flags in control register CR4 control access to these instructions by application programs running at a CPL of 3.

The ARPL (adjust RPL) instruction adjusts the RPL (requestor privilege level) of a segment selector to match that of the procedure or program that supplied the segment selector. See Section 4.10.4., "Checking Caller Access Privileges" for a detailed explanation of the function and use of this instruction.

The LAR (load access rights) instruction verifies the accessibility of a specified segment and loads the access rights information from the segment's segment descriptor into a general-purpose register. Software can then examine the access rights to determine if the segment type is compatible with its intended use. See Section 4.10.1., "Checking Segment Type Compatibility (Access Rights)" for a detailed explanation of the function and use of this instruction.

The LSL (load segment limit) instruction verifies the accessibility of a specified segment and loads the segment limit from the segment's segment descriptor into a general-purpose register. Software can then compare the segment limit with an offset into the segment to determine whether the offset lies within the segment. See Section 4.10.3., "Checking That the Pointer Offset Is Within Limits" for a detailed explanation of the function and use of this instruction.

The VERR (verify for reading) and VERW (verify for writing) instructions verify if a selected segment is readable or writable, respectively, at the CPL. See Section 4.10.2., "Checking Read/Write Rights" for a detailed explanation of the function and use of this instruction.

2.6.3. Loading and Storing Debug Registers

The internal debugging facilities in the processor are controlled by a set of 8 debug registers (DR0 through DR7). The MOV instruction allows setup data to be loaded into and stored from these registers.

2.6.4. Invalidating Caches and TLBs

The processor provides several instructions for use in explicitly invalidating its caches and TLB entries. The INVD (invalidate cache with no writeback) instruction invalidates all data and instruction entries in the internal caches and TLBs and sends a signal to the external caches indicating that they should be invalidated also.

The WBINVD (invalidate cache with writeback) instruction performs the same function as the INVD instruction, except that it writes back any modified lines in its internal caches to memory before it invalidates the caches. After invalidating the internal caches, it signals the external caches to write back modified data and invalidate their contents.

The INVLPG (invalidate TLB entry) instruction invalidates (flushes) the TLB entry for a specified page.

2.6.5. Controlling the Processor

The HLT (halt processor) instruction stops the processor until an enabled interrupt, BINIT, or RESET signal is received. (The NMI and SMI interrupts are always enabled.) The processor generates a special bus cycle to indicate that the halt mode has been entered. Hardware may respond to this signal in a number of ways. An indicator light on the front panel may be turned on. An NMI interrupt for recording diagnostic information may be generated. Reset initialization may be invoked.

The LOCK prefix invokes a locked (atomic) read-modify-write operation when modifying a memory operand. This mechanism is used to allow reliable communications between processors in multiprocessor systems. In the Pentium Pro processor, the locking operation is handled with either a cache lock or bus lock. If a memory access is cacheable and affects only a single cache line, a cache lock is invoked and the system bus and the actual memory location in system memory are not locked during the operation. Here, other Pentium Pro processors on the bus write-back any modified data and invalidate their caches as necessary to maintain system memory coherency. If the memory access is not cacheable and/or it crosses a cache line boundary, the processor's LOCK# signal is asserted and the processor does not respond to requests for bus control during the locked operation.

The RSM (return from SMM) instruction restores the processor (from a context dump) to the state it was in prior to an system management mode (SMM) interrupt.

2.6.6. Reading Performance Monitoring and Time Stamp Counters

The RDPMC (read performance monitoring counter) and RDTSC (read time-stamp counter) instructions allow an application program to read the processors performance monitoring and time-stamp counters, respectively.

The processor has two 40-bit performance counters that record either the occurrence of events or the duration of events. The events that can be monitored include the number of instructions decoded, number of interrupts received, of number of cache loads. Each counter can be set up to monitor a different event, using the system instruction WRMSR to set up values in the model-specific registers PerfEvtSel0 and PerfEvtSel1. The RDPMC instruction loads the current count in counter 0 or 1 into the EDX:EAX registers.

The time-stamp counter is a model specific 64-bit counter that is reset to zero each time the processor is reset. If not reset, the counter is guaranteed to not wrap around for 10 years. The RDTSC instruction loads the current count of the time-stamp counter into the EDX:EAX registers.

See Section 10.6., "Performance Monitoring Counters" and Section 10.5., "Time-Stamp Counter" for more information about the performance monitoring and time stamp counters.

2.6.7. Reading and Writing Model-Specific Registers

The RDMSR (read model-specific register) and WRMSR (write model-specific register) allow the processor's 64-bit model-specific registers (MSRs) to be read and written to, respectively. The MSR to be read or written to is specified by the value in the ECX register. The RDMSR instructions reads the value from the specified MSR into the EDX:EAX registers; the WRMSR writes the value in the EDX:EAX registers into the specified MSR. See Section 8.4., "Model Specific Registers (MSRs)" for more information about the MSRs.

intel®

3

Protected-Mode Memory Management

CHAPTER 3
PROTECTED-MODE MEMORY MANAGEMENT

This chapter describes the Pentium Pro processor's protected-mode memory management facilities, including the physical memory requirements, the segmentation mechanism, and the paging mechanism. See Chapter 4, *Protection*, for a description of the processor's protection mechanism. See Chapter 12, *8086 Emulation*, for a description of memory addressing protection in real-address and virtual-8086 modes.

3.1. MEMORY MANAGEMENT OVERVIEW

The memory management facilities of the Pentium Pro processor are divided into two parts: segmentation and paging. Segmentation provides a mechanism of isolating individual code, data, and stack modules so that multiple programs (or tasks) can run on the same processor without interfering with one another. Paging provides a mechanism for implementing a conventional demand-paged, virtual-memory system where sections of a program's execution environment are mapped into physical memory as needed. When operating in protected mode, some form of segmentation must be used. **There is no mode bit to disable segmentation.** The use of paging, however, is optional.

These two mechanisms (segmentation and paging) can be configured to support simple single-program (or single-task) systems, multitasking systems, or multiple processor systems that used shared memory.

As shown in Figure 3-1, segmentation provides a mechanism for dividing the processor's address space (called the *linear address space*) into smaller protected address spaces called *segments*. Segments can be used to hold the code, data, and stack for a program or to hold system data structures (such as a TSS or LDT). If more than one program is running on a processor, each program can be assigned its own set of segments. The processor then enforces the boundaries between these segments and insures that one program does not interfere with the execution of another program by writing into the other program's segments. The segmentation mechanism also allows typing of segments so that the operations that may be performed on a particular type of segment can be restricted.

All of the segments within a system are contained in the processor's linear address space. To locate a byte in a particular segment, a *logical address* (sometimes called a far pointer) must be provided. A logical address consists of a segment selector and an offset. The segment selector is a unique identifier for a segment. Among other things it provides an offset into a descriptor table (such as the global descriptor table, GDT) to a data structure called a segment descriptor. Each segment has a segment descriptor, which specifies the size of the segment, the access rights and privilege level for the segment, the segment type, and the location of the first byte of the segment in the linear address space (called the base address of the segment). The offset part of the logical address is added to the base address for the segment to locate a byte within the segment. The base address plus the offset thus forms a *linear address* in the processor's linear address space.

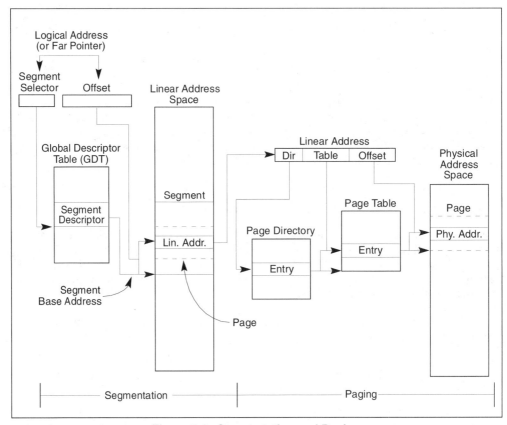

Figure 3-1. Segmentation and Paging

If paging is not used, the linear address space of the processor is mapped directly into the physical address space of processor. The physical address space is defined as the range of addresses that the processor can generate on its address bus.

Because multitasking computing systems commonly define a linear address space much larger than it is economically feasible to contain all at once in physical memory, some method of "virtualizing" the linear address space is needed. This virtualization of the linear address space is handled through the processor's paging mechanism.

Paging supports a "virtual memory" environment where a large linear address space is simulated with a small amount of physical memory (RAM and ROM) and some disk storage. When using paging, each segment is divided into pages (ordinarily 4 KBytes each in size), which are stored either in physical memory or on the disk. The operating system or executive maintains a page directory and a set of page tables to keep track of the pages. When a program (or task) attempts to access an address location in the linear address space, the processor uses the page directory and page tables to translate the linear address into a physical address and then performs the requested operation (read or write) on the memory location. If the page being accessed is not currently in physical memory, the processor interrupts execution of the program, reads the page into physical memory from the disk, and then continues executing the program.

When paging is implemented properly in the operating-system or executive, the swapping of pages between physical memory and the disk is transparent to the correct execution of a program. Even programs written for 16-bit Intel Architecture processors can be paged (transparently) when they are run in virtual-8086 mode.

3.2. USING SEGMENTS

The segmentation mechanism provided in the Pentium Pro processor can be used to implement a wide variety of system designs. These designs range from flat models that make only minimal use of segmentation to protect programs to multi-segmented models that employ segmentation to create a robust operating environment in which multiple programs and tasks can be executed reliably.

The following sections give several examples of how segmentation can be employed in a system to improve memory management performance and reliability.

3.2.1. Flat Model

The simplest memory model for a system is the "flat model," in which the operating system and application programs have access to a continuous, unsegmented address space. To implement a flat model with the Pentium Pro processor, at least two segment descriptors must be created, one for code references and one for data references (see Figure 3-2). Both of these segments, however, are mapped to the entire linear address space: that is, both segment descriptors have the same base address value of 0 and the same segment limit of 4 GBytes. By setting the segment limit to 4 GBytes, the segmentation mechanism is kept from generating exceptions for out of limit memory references, even if no physical memory resides at a particular address. ROM (EPROM) is generally located at the top of the physical address space, because the processor begins execution at FFFF_FFF0H. RAM (DRAM) is placed at the bottom of the address space because the initial base address for the DS data segment after reset initialization is 0.

To the greatest extent possible, this flat model hides the segmentation mechanism of the architecture from both the system designer or the application programmer. This model might be used when porting a UNIX-type operating system to a Pentium Pro processor, because UNIX operating systems commonly implement protection through the paging mechanism and do not use segmentation.

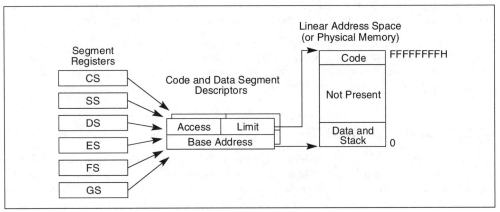

Figure 3-2. Flat Model

3.2.2. Protected Flat Model

The protected flat model is like the flat model, except the segment limits are set to include only the range of addresses for which physical memory actually exists (see Figure 3-3). A general-protection exception (#GP) is then generated on any attempt to access non-existent memory. This model provides a minimum level of hardware protection against some kinds of program bugs.

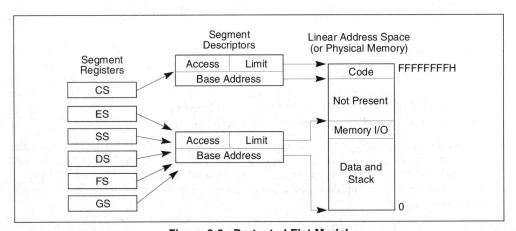

Figure 3-3. Protected Flat Model

3.2.3. Multi-Segment Model

A multi-segment model (such as the one shown in Figure 3-4) uses the full capabilities of the segmentation mechanism to provided hardware enforced protection of code, data structures, and programs and tasks. Here, each program (or task) is given its own table of segment descriptors and its own segments. The segments can be completely private to their assigned programs or shared among programs. Access to all segments and to the execution environments of individual programs running on the system is controlled by hardware.

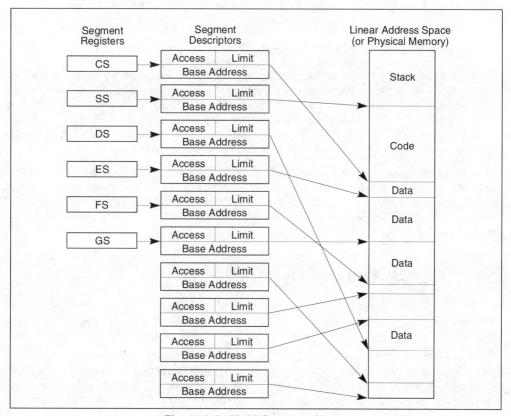

Figure 3-4. Multi-Segment Model

Here, access checks used can protect not only against referencing an address outside the limit of a segment, but also against performing disallowed operations in certain segments. For example, if code segments can be designated as read-only segments, hardware can be used to prevent writes into code segments. The access rights information created for segments can also be used to set up protection rings or levels. Protection levels can be used to protect operating-system procedures from unauthorized access by application programs.

3.2.4. Paging and Segmentation

Paging can be used with any of the segmentation models described in Figures 3-2 and 3-3. When paging is used, the linear address space in which segments are mapped is mapped to physical memory through the processor's paging mechanism (as shown in Figure 3-1) instead of directly.

The paging mechanism offers several page-level protection facilities that can be used with or instead of the segment-protection facilities. For example, when using paging, read-write protection can be enforced on a page-by-page basis. The paging mechanism also provides two-level user-supervisor protection that can also be specified on a page-by-page basis.

3.3. PHYSICAL ADDRESS SPACE

In protected mode, the Pentium Pro processor provides a normal physical address space of 4 GBytes (2^{32} bytes). This is the address space that the processor can address on its address bus. This address space is flat (unsegmented), with addresses ranging continuously from 0 to FFFFFFFFH. This physical address space can be mapped to read-write memory, read-only memory, and memory mapped I/O. The memory mapping facilities describe in this chapter can be used to divide this physical memory up into segments and/or pages.

The Pentium Pro processor also supports an extension of the physical address space to 2^{36} bytes (64 GBytes), with a maximum physical address of FFFFFFFFFH. This extension is invoked with the physical address extension (PAE) flag, located in bit 5 of control register CR4. (See Section 3.8., "Physical Address Extension" for more information about extended physical addressing.)

3.4. LOGICAL AND LINEAR ADDRESSES

At the system-architecture level in protected mode, the processor uses two stages of address translation to arrive at a physical address: logical-address translation and linear address space paging.

Even with the minimum use of segments, every byte in the processor's address space is accessed with a logical address. A logical address consists of a 16-bit segment selector and a 32-bit offset (see Figure 3-5). The segment selector identifies the segment the byte is located in and the offset specifies the location of the byte in the segment relative to the base address of the segment.

The processor translates every logical address into a linear address. A linear address is a 32-bit address in the processor's linear address space. Like the physical address space, the linear address space is a flat (unsegmented), 2^{32}-byte address space, with addresses ranging from 0 to FFFFFFFFH. The linear address space contains all the segments and system tables defined for a system.

To translate a logical address into a linear address, the processor does the following:

1. Uses the offset in the segment selector to locate the segment descriptor for the segment in the GDT or LDT.

2. Checks the access rights and range of the segment to insure that the segment is accessible and that the offset is within the limits of the segment.

3. Adds the base address of the segment from the segment descriptor to the offset to form a linear address.

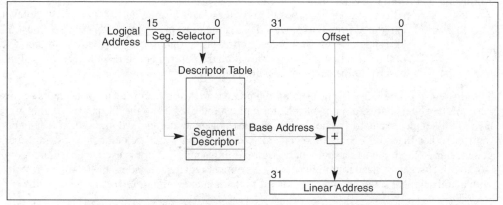

Figure 3-5. Logical Address to Linear Address Translation

If paging is not used, the processor maps the linear address directly to a physical address (that is, the linear address goes out on the processors address bus). If the linear address space is paged, a second level of address translation is used to translate the linear address into a physical address. Page translation is described in Section 3.6., "Paging (Virtual Memory)".

3.4.1. Segment Selectors

A segment selector is a 16-bit identifier for a segment (see Figure 3-6). It does not point directly to the segment, but instead points to the segment descriptor that defines the segment. A segment selector contains the following items:

Index   (Bits 3 through 15). Selects one of 8192 descriptors in the GDT or LDT. The processor multiplies the index value by 8 (the number of bytes in a segment descriptor) and adds the result to the base address of the GDT or LDT (from the GDTR or LDTR register, respectively).

TI (table indicator) flag

         (Bit 2). Specifies the descriptor table to use: clearing this flag selects the GDT; setting this flag selects the current LDT.

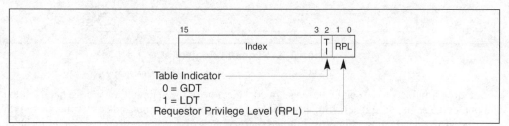

Figure 3-6. Segment Selector

Requestor Privilege Level (RPL)

(Bits 0 and 1). Specifies the privilege level of the selector. The privilege level can range from 0 to 3, with 0 being the most privileged level. See Section 4.5., "Privilege Levels" for a description of the relationship of the RPL to the CPL of the executing program or task and the descriptor privilege level (DPL) of the descriptor the segment selector points to.

The first entry of the GDT is not used by the processor. A segment selector that points to this entry of the GDT (that is, a segment selector with an index of 0 and the TI flag set to 0) is used as a "null segment selector." The processor does not generate an exception when a segment register (other than the CS or SS registers) is loaded with a null selector. It does, however, generate an exception when a segment register holding a null selector is used to access memory. A null selector can be used to initialize unused segment registers. Loading the CS or SS register with a null segment selector causes a general-protection exception (#GP) to be generated.

Segment selectors are visible to application programs as part of a pointer variable, but the values of selectors are usually assigned or modified by link editors or linking loaders, not application programs.

3.4.2. Segment Registers

To reduce address translation time and coding complexity, the processor provides registers for holding up to 6 segment selectors (see Figure 3-7). Each of these segment registers support a specific kind of memory reference (code, stack, or data). For virtually any kind of program execution to take place, at least the code segment (CS), data segment (DS), and stack segment (SS) registers must be loaded with valid segment selectors. The processor also provides three additional data segment registers (ES, FS, and GS), which can be used to make additional data segments available to the currently executing program or task.

Visible Part	Hidden Part	
Segment Selector	Base Address, Limit, Access Information	CS
		SS
		DS
		ES
		FS
		GS

Figure 3-7. Segment Registers

For a program to access a segment, the segment selector for the segment must have been loaded in one of the segment registers. So, although a system can define thousands of segments, only 6 can be available for immediate use. Other segments can be made available by loading their segment selectors into these registers during program execution.

Every segment register has a "visible" part and a "hidden" part. When a segment selector is loaded into the visible part of a segment register, the processor also loads the hidden part of the segment register with the base address, segment limit, and access control information from the segment descriptor pointed to by the segment selector into. The information cached in the segment register (visible and hidden) allows the processor to translate addresses without taking extra bus cycles to read the base address and limit from the segment descriptor. In systems in which multiple processors have access to the same descriptor tables, it is the responsibility of software to reload the segment registers when the descriptor tables are modified. If this is not done, an old segment descriptor cached in a segment register might be used after its memory-resident version has been modified.

Two kinds of load instructions are provided for loading the segment registers:

1. Direct load instructions such as the MOV, POP, LDS, LES, LSS, LGS, and LFS instructions. These instructions explicitly reference the segment registers.

2. Implied load instructions such as the far pointer versions of the CALL, JMP, and RET instructions and the IRET, INT*n*, INTO and INT3 instructions. These instructions change the contents of the CS register (and sometimes other segment registers) as an incidental part of their operation.

The MOV instruction can also be used to store visible part of a segment register in a general-purpose register.

3.4.3.   Segment Descriptors

A segment descriptor is a data structure in a GDT, LDT, or IDT that provides the processor with the size and location of a segment, as well as access control and status information. Segment descriptors are typically created by compilers, linkers, loaders, or the operating system or executive, but not application programs. Figure 3-8 illustrates the general descriptor format for all types of segment descriptors.

The flags and fields in a segment descriptor are as follows:

Segment limit field

Specifies the size of the segment. The processor puts together the two segment limit fields to form a 20-bit value. The processor interprets the segment limit in one of two ways, depending on the setting of the G (granularity) flag:

- If the granularity flag is clear, the segment size can range from 1 byte to 1 MByte, in byte increments.

- If the granularity flag is set, the segment size can range from 4 KBytes to 4 GBytes, in 4-KByte increments.

The processor uses the segment limit in two different ways, depending on whether the segment is an expand-up or an expand-down segment. See Section 3.4.3.1., "Code and Data Segment-Descriptor Types" for more information about segment types. For expand-up segments, the offset in a logical address can range from 0 to the segment limit. Offsets greater than the segment limit generate general-protection exceptions (#GP). For expand-down segments, the segment limit has the reverse function; the offset can range from the segment limit to the FFFFFFFFH or FFFFH, depending on the setting of the B flag. Offsets less than the segment limit generate general-protection exceptions. Decreasing the value segment limit field for an expand-down segment allocates new memory at the bottom of the segment's address space, rather than at the top.

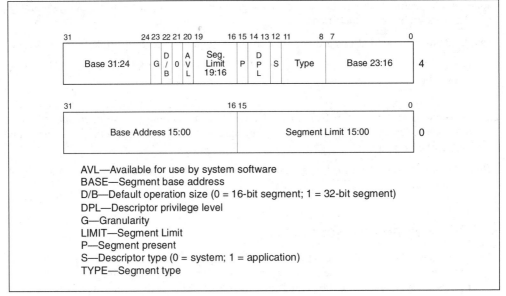

Figure 3-8. Segment Descriptor

Base address fields

Defines the location of byte 0 of the segment within the 4-GByte linear address space. The processor puts together the three base address fields to form a single 32-bit value. Segment base addresses should be aligned to 16-byte boundaries to allow programs to maximize performance by aligning code and data on 16-byte boundaries; however, such alignment is not required.

Type field

Indicates the segment or gate type and specifies the kinds of access that can be made to the segment and the direction of growth. The interpretation of this field depends on whether the descriptor type flag specifies an application (code or data) descriptor or a system descriptor. The encoding of the type field is different for code, data, and system descriptors (see Figure 4-1). See Section 3.4.3.1., "Code and Data Segment-Descriptor Types" for a description of how this field is used to specify code and data segment types.

S (descriptor type) flag

Specifies whether the segment descriptor is for a system segment (S flag is clear) or a code or data segment (S flag is set).

DPL (descriptor privilege level) field

Specifies the privilege level of the segment. The privilege level can range from 0 to 3, with 0 being the most privileged level. The DPL is used to control access to the segment. See Section 4.5., "Privilege Levels" for a description of the relationship of the DPL to the CPL of the executing program or task and the RPL of a segment selector.

P (segment-present) flag

Indicates whether the segment is present in memory (set) or not present (clear). If this bit is clear, the processor generates a segment-not-present exception (#NP) when a segment selector that points to the segment descriptor is loaded into a segment register. Memory management software can use this bit to control which segments are actually loaded into physical memory at a given time. It offers a control in addition to paging for managing virtual memory.

Figure 3-9 shows the format of a segment descriptor when the segment-present flag is clear. When this bit is clear, the operating system or executive is free to use the locations marked "Available" to store its own data, such as information regarding the whereabouts of the missing segment.

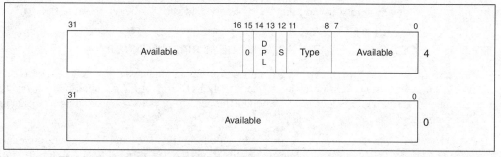

Figure 3-9. Segment Descriptor When Segment-Present Flag Is Clear

D (default operation size)/B (default stack size) flag

Performs different functions depending on whether the segment descriptor is an executable code segment, an expand-down data segment, or a data segment used as a procedure stack. (This flag should always be set to 1 for 32-bit code and data segments and to 0 for 16-bit code and data segments.)

• **Executable code segment.** The D flag indicates the default length for linear addresses and operands. If the flag is set, 32-bit addresses and 32-bit or 8-bit operands are assumed; if it is clear, 16-bit addresses and 16-bit or 8-bit operands are assumed. An instruction prefix can be used to select an operand size other than the default.

- **Expand-down data segment.** The D flag specifies the upper bound of the segment. If the flag is set, the upper bound is FFFFFFFFH (4 GBytes); if the flag is clear, the upper bound is FFFFH (64 KBytes).

- **Data segment used as a stack segment (pointed to by the SS register).** For stack segments this flag is called the B (default stack size) flag. The B flag specifies the size of the stack pointer register (ESP), which implicit stack operations use to address the stack. If the flag is set, the 32-bit ESP register is used, allowing stack pointers of up to 32-bit; if the flag is clear, the 16-bit SP register is used, allowing stack pointers of up to 16-bits. The operand-size of an instruction (such as a MOV instruction) determines the size of the ESP register when writing directly to the register.

G (granularity) flag

Determines the scaling of the segment limit field. When the granularity flag is clear, the segment limit is interpreted in byte units; when flag is set, the segment limit is interpreted in 4-KByte units. (This flag does not affect the granularity of the base address; it is always byte granular.) When the granularity bit is set, the twelve least significant bits of an offset are not tested when checking the offset against the segment limit. For example, when the granularity bit is set, a limit of 0 results in valid offsets from 0 to 4095.

Available and reserved bits

Bit 20 of the second doubleword of the segment descriptor is available for use by system software; bit 21 is reserved and should always be set to 0.

3.4.3.1. CODE AND DATA SEGMENT-DESCRIPTOR TYPES

When the S (descriptor type) flag in a segment descriptor is set, the descriptor is for either a code or a data segment. The highest order bit of the type field (bit 11 of the second double word of the segment descriptor) then determines whether the descriptor is for a data segment (clear) or a code segment (set).

For data segments, the three low-order bits of the type field (bits 8, 9, and 10) are interpreted as accessed (A), write-enable (W), and expansion-direction (E). See Table 3-1 for a description of the encoding of the bits in the type field for code and data segments. Data segments can be read-only or read/write segments, depending on the setting of the write-enable bit.

Stack segments are data segments which must be read/write segments. Loading the SS register with a segment selector for a non-writable data segment generates a general-protection exception (#GP). If the size of a stack segment needs to be changed dynamically, the stack segment can be an expand-down data segment (expansion-direction flag set). Here, dynamically changing the segment limit causes stack space to be added to the bottom of the stack. If the size of a stack segment is intended to remain static, the stack segment may be either an expand-up or expand-down type.

The accessed bit indicates whether the segment has been accessed since the last time the operating-system or executive cleared the bit. The processor sets this bit whenever it loads a segment selector for the segment into a segment register. The bit remains set until explicitly cleared. This bit can be used both for virtual memory management and for debugging.

Table 3-1. Code and Data Segment Types

Type Field						
Decimal	11	10 E	9 W	8 A	Descriptor Type	Description
0	0	0	0	0	Data	Read-Only
1	0	0	0	1	Data	Read-Only, accessed
2	0	0	1	0	Data	Read/Write
3	0	0	1	1	Data	Read/Write, accessed
4	0	1	0	0	Data	Read-Only, expand-down
5	0	1	0	1	Data	Read-Only, expand-down, accessed
6	0	1	1	0	Data	Read/Write, expand-down
7	0	1	1	1	Data	Read/Write, expand-down, accessed
		C	R	A		
8	1	0	0	0	Code	Execute-Only
9	1	0	0	1	Code	Execute-Only, accessed
10	1	0	1	0	Code	Execute/Read
11	1	0	1	1	Code	Execute/Read, accessed
12	1	1	0	0	Code	Execute-Only, conforming
13	1	1	0	1	Code	Execute-Only, conforming, accessed
14	1	1	1	0	Code	Execute/Read-Only, conforming
15	1	1	1	1	Code	Execute/Read-Only, conforming, accessed

For code segments, the three low-order bits of the type field are interpreted as accessed (A), read enable (R), and conforming (C). Code segments can be execute-only or execute/read, depending on the setting of the read-enable bit. An execute/read segment might be used, when constants or other static data have been placed with instruction code in a ROM. Here, data can be read from the code segment either by using an instruction with a CS override prefix or by loading a segment selector for the code segment in a data-segment register (the DS, ES, FS, or GS registers). In protected mode, code segments are not writable.

Code segments can be either conforming or non-conforming. A transfer of execution into a more-privileged conforming segment allows execution to continue at the current privilege level. A transfer into a non-conforming segment at a different privilege level results in a general-protection exception (#GP), unless a call gate or task gate is used (see Section 4.8.1., "Direct Calls or Jumps to Code Segments" for more information on conforming and non-conforming code segments). System utilities that do not access protected facilities and handlers for some types of exceptions (such as, divide error or overflow) may be loaded in conforming code segments. Utilities that need to be protected from less privileged programs and procedures should be placed in non-conforming code segments.

All data segments are nonconforming, but unlike code segments, data segments can be accessed by procedures or programs operating at numerically higher privilege levels (less privileged) without using a call or task gate.

The processor may update the Type field when a segment is accessed, even if the access is a read cycle. If the descriptor tables have been put in ROM, it may be necessary for hardware to prevent the ROM from being enabled onto the data bus during a write cycle. It also may be necessary to return the READY# signal to the processor when a write cycle to ROM occurs, otherwise the cycle will not terminate. These features of the hardware design are necessary for using ROM-based descriptor tables with the Intel386 DX processor, which always sets the Accessed bit when a segment descriptor is loaded. The Pentium Pro, Pentium, and Intel486 processors, however, only set the accessed bit if it is not already set. Writes to descriptor tables in ROM can be avoided by setting the accessed bits in every descriptor.

3.5. SYSTEM SEGMENT-DESCRIPTOR TYPES

When the S (descriptor type) flag in a segment descriptor is clear, the descriptor type is a system descriptor. The processor recognizes the following types of system descriptors:

- Local descriptor table (LDT) segment descriptor.

- Task state segment (TSS) descriptor.

- Call gate descriptor.

- Task gate descriptor.

- Interrupt gate descriptor.

- Trap gate descriptors.

These descriptor types fall into two categories: system segment descriptors and gate descriptors. System segment descriptors point to system segments (LDT and TSS segments); gate descriptors point to gates (call, task, interrupt, and trap), which hold pointers to procedure entry points in code segments. Table 3-2 shows the encoding of the type field for system segment and gate descriptors.

For more information on the system segment descriptors, see Section 3.5.1., "Segment Descriptor Tables" and Section 6.2.2., "TSS Descriptor"; for more information on the gate descriptors, see Section 4.8.2., "Gate Descriptors", Section 5.8., "IDT Descriptors", and Section 6.2.4., "Task Gate Descriptor".

Table 3-2. System Segment and Gate Descriptor Types

Decimal	11	10	9	8	Description
	Type Field				
0	0	0	0	0	Reserved
1	0	0	0	1	16-Bit TSS (Available)
2	0	0	1	0	LDT
3	0	0	1	1	16-Bit TSS (Busy)
4	0	1	0	0	16-Bit Call Gate
5	0	1	0	1	Task Gate
6	0	1	1	0	16-Bit Interrupt Gate
7	0	1	1	1	16-Bit Trap Gate
8	1	0	0	0	Reserved
9	1	0	0	1	32-Bit TSS (Available)
10	1	0	1	0	Reserved
11	1	0	1	1	32-Bit TSS (Busy)
12	1	1	0	0	32-Bit Call Gate
13	1	1	0	1	Reserved
14	1	1	1	0	32-Bit Interrupt Gate
15	1	1	1	1	32-Bit Trap Gate

3.5.1. Segment Descriptor Tables

A segment descriptor table is an array of segment descriptors (see Figure 3-10). A descriptor table is variable in length and can contain up to 8192 (213) 8-byte descriptors. There are two kinds of descriptor tables:

- The global descriptor table (GDT)
- The local descriptor tables (LDT)

There is one GDT for all programs and tasks in the system and one LDT for each separate task being run. If the operating system allows, some or all tasks can share the same LDT. The system also can be set up with no LDTs; all programs and tasks will then use the GDT.

The GDT is not a segment itself; instead, it is a data structure in the linear address space. The base linear address and limit of the GDT must be loaded into the GDTR register (see Section 2.4., "Memory-Management Registers"). The base addresses of the GDT should be aligned on an eight-byte boundary to yield the best processor performance. The limit value for the GDT is expressed in bytes. As with segments, the limit value is added to the base address to get the address of the last valid byte. A limit value of 0 results in exactly one valid byte. Because segment descriptors are always 8 bytes long, the GDT limit should always be one less than an integral multiple of eight (that is, $8N - 1$).

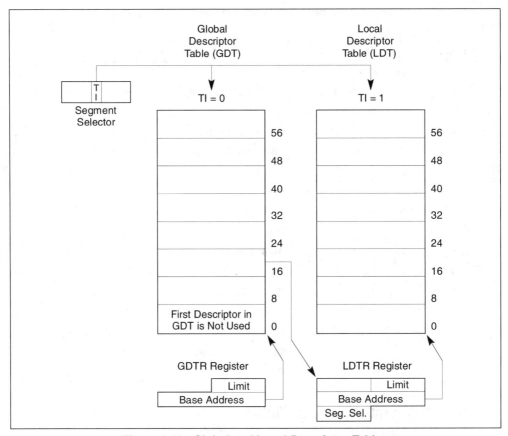

Figure 3-10. Global and Local Descriptor Tables

The first descriptor in the GDT is not used by the processor. A segment selector to this "null descriptor" does not generate an exception when loaded into a data segment register (DS, ES, FS, or GS), but it always generates a general-protection exception (#GP) when an attempt is made to access memory using the descriptor. By initializing the segment registers with this segment selector, accidental reference to unused segment registers can be guaranteed to generate an exception.

The LDT is located in a system segment of the LDT type. The GDT must contain a segment descriptor for the LDT segment. If the system supports multiple LDTs, each must have a separate segment selector and segment descriptor in the GDT. The segment descriptor for an LDT can be located anywhere in the GDT. See Section 3.5., "System Segment-Descriptor Types" information on the LDT segment descriptor type.

An LDT is accessed with its segment selector. To eliminate address translations when accessing the LDT, the segment selector, base linear address, limit, and access rights of the LDT are stored in the LDTR register (see Section 2.4., "Memory-Management Registers").

When the GDTR register is stored (using the SGDT instruction), a 48-bit "pseudo-descriptor" is stored in memory (see Figure 3-11). To avoid alignment check faults in user mode (privilege level 3), the pseudo-descriptor should be located at a doubleword address (that is, an address that is 0 MOD 4). This causes the processor to store an aligned word, followed by an aligned doubleword. User-mode programs normally do not store pseudo-descriptors, but the possibility of generating an alignment check fault can be avoided by aligning pseudo-descriptors in this way. The same alignment should be used when storing the IDTR register using the SIDT instruction. When storing the LDTR or task register (using the SLTR or STR instruction, respectively), the pseudo-descriptor should be located at an odd word address (that is, an address that is 2 MOD 4).

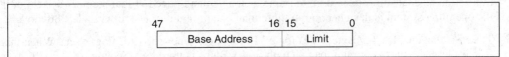

Figure 3-11. Pseudo-Descriptor Format

3.6. PAGING (VIRTUAL MEMORY)

When operating in protected mode, the Pentium Pro processor can map a linear address directly into a large physical address space (for example, an address space composed of several gigabytes of RAM) or indirectly (using paging) into a smaller physical address space (RAM) and disk storage. This latter method of mapping linear addresses is commonly referred to as virtual memory or demand-paged virtual memory.

When paging is used, the processor divides the linear address space into fixed-size pages (generally 4 KBytes in length) that can be mapped into physical memory and/or disk storage. When a program or task references a logical address in memory, the processor translates the address into a linear address and then uses its paging mechanism to translate the linear address into a corresponding physical address. If the page containing the linear address is not currently in physical memory, the processor generates a page-fault exception (#PF). This exception directs the operating system to load the page from disk storage into physical memory (perhaps writing different page from physical memory out to disk in the process), then restart the instruction that generated the exception. The information that the processor uses to map linear addresses into the physical address space and to generate page fault exceptions (when necessary) is contained in page directories and page tables stored in memory.

Paging is different from segmentation through its use of fixed-size pages. Unlike segments, which usually are the same size as the code or data structures they hold, pages have a fixed size. If segmentation is the only form of address translation which is used, a data structure which is present in physical memory will have all of its parts in memory. If paging is used, a data structure can be partly in memory and partly in disk storage.

To minimize the number of bus cycles required for address translation, the most recently accessed page-directory and page-table entries are cached in the processor in devices called translation lookaside buffers (TLBs). The TLBs satisfy most requests for reading the current page directory and page tables without requiring a bus cycle. Extra bus cycles occur only when the TLBs do not contain a page table entry, which typically happens when a page has not been accessed for a long time. See Section 3.7., "Translation Lookaside Buffers (TLBs)" for more information on the TLBs.

3.6.1.   Paging Options

Paging is controlled by three flags in the processor's control registers:

- PG (paging) flag, bit 31 of CR0.

- PSE (page size extensions) flag, bit 4 of CR4.

- PAE (physical address extension) flag, bit 5 of CR4).

The PG flag enables the page-translation mechanism. The operating system or executive usually sets this flag during processor initialization. The PG flag must be set if the processor's page-translation mechanism is to be used to implement a demand-paged virtual memory system or if the operating system is designed to run more than one program or task in virtual-8086 mode.

The PSE flag enables 4-MByte pages (or 2-MByte pages when the PAE flag is set). When this flag is clear, the more common page length of 4 KBytes is used. See Section 3.6.2.2., "Linear Address Translation (4-MByte Pages)" and Section 3.8.2., "Linear Address Translation With Extended Addressing Enabled (2-MByte Pages)" for more information about the use of the PSE flag.

The PAE flag enables 36-bit physical addresses. This physical address extension can only be used when paging is enabled. It relies on page directories and page tables to reference physical addresses above FFFFFFFFH. See Section 3.8., "Physical Address Extension" for more information about the physical address extension.

3.6.2.   Page Tables and Directories

The information that the processor uses to translate linear addresses into physical addresses (when paging is enabled) is contained in four data structures:

- Page directory—An array of 32-bit page-directory entries contained in a 4-KByte page. Up to 1024 page-directory entries can be held in a page directory.

- Page table—An array of 32-bit page-table entries contained in a 4-KByte page. Up to 1024 page-table entries can be held in a page table. (Page tables are not used for 2-MByte or 4-MByte pages. These page sizes are mapped directly from one or more page directories.)

- Page—A 4-KByte, 2-MByte, or 4-MByte flat address space.

- Page Directory Pointer Table—An array of four 64-bit entries, each of which points to a page directory. This data structure is only used when the physical address extension is enabled (see Section 3.8., "Physical Address Extension").

These tables provide access to either 4-KByte or 4-MByte pages when normal 32-bit physical addressing is being used and to either 4-KByte or 2-MByte pages when extended (36-bit) physical addressing is being used. Table 3-3 shows the page size and physical address size obtained from various settings of the paging control flags.

Table 3-3. Page Sizes and Physical Address Sizes

PG Flag, CR0	PAE Flag, CR4	PSE Flag, CR4	PS Flag, PDE	Page Size	Physical Address Size
0	X	X	X	—	Paging Disabled
1	0	0	X	4 KBytes	32 Bits
1	0	1	0	4 KBytes	32 Bits
1	0	1	1	4 MBytes	32 Bits
1	1	X	0	4 KBytes	36 Bits
1	1	X	1	2 MBytes	36 Bits

3.6.2.1. LINEAR ADDRESS TRANSLATION (4-KBYTE PAGES)

Figure 3-12 shows the page directory and page table hierarchy when mapping linear addresses to 4-KByte pages. The entries in the page directory point to page tables, and the entries in a page table point to pages in physical memory. This paging method can be used to address up to 2^{20} pages, which spans a linear address space of 2^{32} bytes (4 GBytes).

To select the various table entries, the linear address is divided into three sections:

- Page directory entry—Bits 22 through 31 provide an offset to an entry in the page directory. The selected entry provides the base physical address of a page table.

- Page table entry—Bits 12 through 21 of the linear address provide an offset to an entry in the selected page table. This entry provides the base physical address of a page in physical memory.

- Page offset—Bits 0 through 11 provides an offset to a physical address in the page.

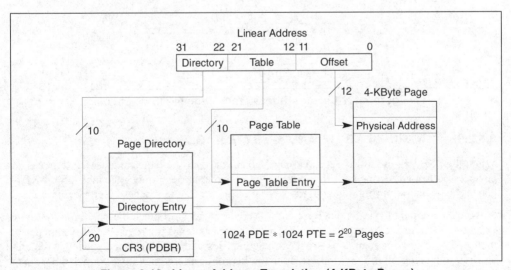

Figure 3-12. Linear Address Translation (4-KByte Pages)

Memory management software has the option of using one page directory for all programs and tasks, one page directory for each task, or some combination of the two.

3.6.2.2.   LINEAR ADDRESS TRANSLATION (4-MBYTE PAGES)

Figure 3-12 shows how a page directory can be used to map linear addresses to 4-MByte pages. The entries in the page directory point to page tables, and the entries in a page table point to pages in physical memory. This paging method can be used to map up to 1024 pages into a 4-GByte linear address space.

The 4-MByte page size is selected by setting the PSE flag in control register CR4 and setting the page size (PS) flag in a page-directory entry (see Figure 3-14). With these flags set, the linear address is divided into two sections:

- Page directory entry—Bits 22 through 31 provide an offset to an entry in the page directory. The selected entry provides the base physical address of a 4-MByte page.

- Page offset—Bits 0 through 21 provides an offset to a physical address in the page.

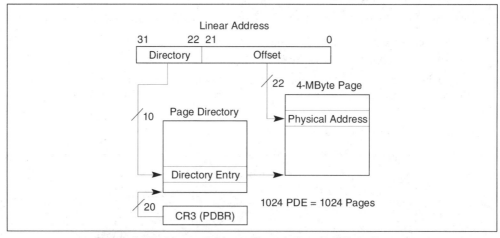

Figure 3-13. Linear Address Translation (4-MByte Pages)

3.6.2.3.   MIXING 4-KBYTE AND 4-MBYTE PAGES

When the PSE flag in CR4 is set, both page tables for 4-KByte pages and 4-MByte pages can be accessed from the same page directory. If the PSE flag is clear, only page tables for 4-KByte pages can be accessed (regardless of the setting of the PS flag in a page-directory entry).

A typical example of mixing 4-KByte and 4-MByte pages is to place the operating system or executive's kernel in a large page to reduce TLB misses and thus improve overall system performance. The processor maintains 4-MByte page entries and 4-KByte page entries in separate TLBs. So, placing often used code such as the kernel in a large page, frees up 4-KByte-page TLB entries for application programs and tasks and for infrequently used utilities.

3.6.3. Base Address of the Page Directory

The physical address of the current page directory is stored in the CR3 register (also called the page directory base register or PDBR). (See Figure 2-5 and Section 2.5., "Control Registers" for more information on the PDBR.) If paging is to be used, the PDBR must be loaded as part of the processor initialization process (prior to enabling paging). The PDBR can then be changed either explicitly by loading a new value in CR3 with a MOV instruction or implicitly as part of a task switch. (See Section 6.2.1., "Task State Segment (TSS)" for a description of how the contents of the CR3 register is set for a task.)

There is no present bit in the PDBR for the page directory. The page directory may be not-present (paged out of physical memory) while its associated task is suspended, but the operating system must ensure that the page directory indicated by the PDBR image in a task's TSS is present in physical memory before the task is dispatched. The page directory must also remain in memory as long as the task is active.

3.6.4. Page-Directory and Page-Table Entries

Figure 3-14 shows the format for the page-directory and page-table entries when 4-KByte pages and 32-bit physical addresses are being used. Figure 3-14 shows the format for the page-directory entries when 4-MByte pages and 32-bit physical addresses are being used. See Section 3.8., "Physical Address Extension" for the format of page-directory and page-table entries when the physical address extension is being used.

The functions of the flags and fields in these entries are as follows:

Page base address, bits 12 through 32

> (Page-table entries for 4-KByte pages.) Specifies the physical address of the first byte of a 4-KByte page. The bits in this field are interpreted as the 20 most-significant bits of the physical address, which forces pages to be aligned on 4-KByte boundaries.

> (Page-directory entries for 4-KByte page tables.) Specifies the physical address of the first byte of a page table. The bits in this field are interpreted as the 20 most-significant bits of the physical address, which forces page tables to be aligned on 4-KByte boundaries.

> (Page-directory entries for 4-MByte pages.) Specifies the physical address of the first byte of a 4-MByte page. Only bits 22 through 32 of this field are used (and bits 12 through 21 are reserved). The base address bits are interpreted as the 11 most-significant bits of the physical address, which forces pages to be aligned on 4-MByte boundaries.

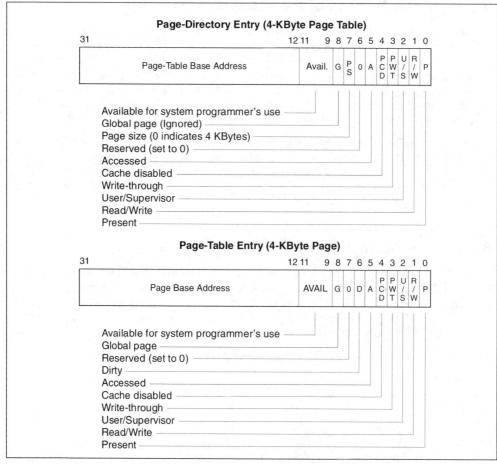

Figure 3-14. Format of Page-Directory and Page-Table Entries for 4-KByte Pages and 32-Bit Physical Addresses

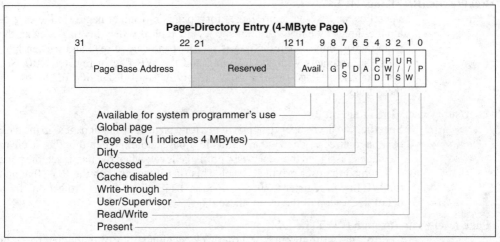

Figure 3-15. Format of Page-Directory Entries for 4-MByte Pages and 32-Bit Addresses

Present (P) flag, bit 0

Indicates whether the page or page table being pointed to by the entry is currently loaded in physical memory. When the flag is set, the page is in physical memory and address translation is carried out. When the flag is clear, the page is not in memory and, if the processor attempts to access the page, it generates a page fault exception (#PF).

The processor does not set or clear this flag; it is up to the operating system or executive to maintain the state of the flag.

If the processor generates a page-fault exception, the operating system generally needs to carry out the following operations:

1. Copy the page from disk storage into physical memory.

2. Load the page address into the page-table or page-directory entry and set its present flag. Other bits, such as the dirty and accessed bits, may also be set at this time.

3. Invalidate the current page table entry in the TLB (see Section 3.7., "Translation Lookaside Buffers (TLBs)" for a discussion of TLBs and how to invalidate them).

4. Return from the page fault handler to restart the interrupted program or task.

Read/write (R/W) flag, bit 1

Specifies the read-write privileges for a page or group of pages (in the case of a page-directory entry that points to a page table). When this flag is clear, the page is read only; when the flag is set, the page can be read and written into. This flag interacts with the U/S flag and the WP flag in register CR0. See Section 4.11., "Page-Level Protection" for a detail discussion of the use of these flags.

User/supervisor (U/S) flag, bit 2

Specifies the user-supervisor privileges for a page or group of pages (in the case of a page-directory entry that points to a page table). When this flag is clear, the page is assigned the supervisor privilege level; when the flag is set, the page is assigned the user privilege level. This flag interacts with the R/W flag and the WP flag in register CR0. See Section 4.11., "Page-Level Protection" for a detail discussion of the use of these flags.

Page-level write-through (PWT) flag, bit 3

Controls the write-through or write-back caching policy of individual pages or page tables. When the PWT flag is set, write-through caching is enabled for the associated page or page table; when the flag is clear, write-back caching is enabled for the associated page or page table. The processor ignores this flag if paging is not used (the PG flag in register CR0 is clear) or the CD (cache disable) flag in CR0 is set. See Section 11.5., "Cache Control" for more information about the use of this flag. See Section 2.5., "Control Registers" for a description of a companion PWT flag in control register CR3.

Page-level cache disable (PCD) flag, bit 4

Controls the caching of individual pages or page tables. When the PCD flag is set, caching of the associated page or page table is prevented; when the flag is clear, the page or page table can be cached. This flag permits caching to be disabled for pages that contain memory-mapped I/O ports or that do not provide a performance benefit when cached. The processor ignores this flag (assumes it is set) if paging is not used (the PG flag in register CR0 is clear) or the CD (cache disable) flag in CR0 is set. See Chapter 11, *Memory Cache Control*, for more information about the use of this flag. See Section 2.5., "Control Registers" for a description of a companion PCD flag in control register CR3.

Accessed (A) flag, bit 5

Indicates whether a page or page table has been accessed (read from or written to) when set. Memory management software typically clears this flag when a page or page table is initially loaded into physical memory. The processor then sets this flag the first time a page or page table is accessed. This bit is a "sticky" flag, meaning that once set, the processor does not implicitly clear it. Only software can clear this flag. The accessed and dirty flags are provided for use by memory management software to manage the transfer of pages and page tables into and out of physical memory.

Dirty (D) flag, bit 6

Indicates whether a page has been written to when set. (This flag is not used in page-directory entries.) Memory management software typically clears this flag when a page is initially loaded into physical memory. The processor then sets this flag the first time a page is accessed for a write operation. This bit is "sticky," meaning that once set, the processor does not implicitly clear it. Only software can clear this bit. The dirty and accessed flags are provided for use by memory management software to manage the transfer of pages and page tables into and out of physical memory.

Page size (PS) flag, bit 7

Determines the page size. This flag is only used in page-directory entries. When this flag is clear, the page size is 4 KBytes and the page-directory entry points to a page table. When the flag is set, the page size is 4 MBytes for normal 32-bit addressing (and 2 MBytes if extended physical addressing is enabled) and the page-directory entry points to a page. If the page-directory entry points to a page table, all the pages associated with that page table will be 4-KByte pages.

Global (G) flag, bit 8

Indicates a global page when set. When a page is marked global and the page global enable (PGE) flag in register CR4 is set, the page-table or page-directory entry for the page is not invalidated in the TLB when register CR3 is loaded or a task switch occurs. This flag is provided to prevent frequently used pages (such as pages that contain kernel or other operating system or executive code) from being flushed from the TLB. Only software can set or clear this flag. For page-directory entries that point to page tables, this bit is ignored and the global characteristics of a page are set in the page table entries. See Section 3.7., "Translation Lookaside Buffers (TLBs)" for more information about the use of this flag.

Reserved and available-to-software bits

In a page-table entry, bit 7 is reserved and should be set to 0; in a page-directory entry that points to a page table, bit 6 is reserved and should be set to 0. For both types of entries, bits 9, 10, and 11 are available for use by software. (When the present bit is clear, bits 1 through 31 are available to software.) When the PSE and PAE flags in control register CR4 are set, the processor generates a page fault if reserved bits are not set to 0.

3.6.5. Not Present Page-Directory and Page-Table Entries

When the present flag is clear for a page-table or page-directory entry, the operating system or executive may use the rest of the entry for storage of information such as the location of the page (see Figure 3-16).

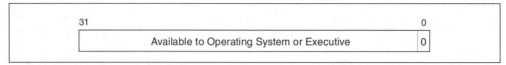

Figure 3-16. Format of a Page-Table or Page-Directory Entry for a Not-Present Page

3.7. TRANSLATION LOOKASIDE BUFFERS (TLBS)

The processor stores the most recently used page-directory and page-table entries in on-chip caches called translation lookaside buffers or TLBs. The Pentium Pro and Pentium processors have separate TLBs for the data and instruction caches. Also, the Pentium Pro processor maintains separate TLBs for 4-KByte and 4-MByte page sizes. The CPUID instruction can be used to determine the sizes of the TLBs provided in the Pentium Pro processor.

Most paging is performed using the contents of the TLBs. Bus cycles to the page directory and page tables in memory are performed only when the TLBs do not contain the translation information for a requested page.

The TLBs are inaccessible to application programs and tasks (privilege level greater than 0); that is, they cannot invalidate TLBs. Only, operating system or executive procedures running at privilege level of 0 can invalid TLBs or selected TBL entries. Whenever a page-directory or page-table entry is changed (including when the present bit is set to zero), the operating-system must immediately invalidate the corresponding entry in the TLB so that it can be updated the next time the entry is referenced.

All of the TLBs are automatically invalidated any time the CR3 register loaded. The CR3 register can be loaded in either of two ways:

*   Explicitly, using the MOV instruction, for example:

    ```
    MOV CR3, EAX
    ```

    where the EAX register contains an appropriate page directory base address.

*   Implicitly by executing a task switch, which automatically changes the contents of the CR3 register.

The INVLPG instruction is provided to invalidate a specific page-table entry. Normally, this instruction invalidates only an individual TLB entry; however, in some cases, it may invalidate more than the selected entry and may even invalidate all of the TLBs.

The page global enable (PGE) flag in register CR4 and the global (G) flag in a page-directory or page-table entry (bit 8) can be used to prevent frequently used pages from being automatically invalidated in the TLBs on a task switch or a load of register CR3. (See Section 3.6.4., "Page-Directory and Page-Table Entries" for more information about the global flag.) When the processor loads a page-directory or page-table entry for a global page into a TLB, the entry will remain in the TLB indefinitely. The only way to deterministically invalidate global page entries is to clear the PGE flag and then invalidate the TLBs.

3.8. PHYSICAL ADDRESS EXTENSION

The physical address extension (PAE) flag in register CR4 enables an extension of physical addresses in the Pentium Pro processor from 32 bits to 36 bits. The processor provides 4 additional address line pins to accommodate the additional address bits. This option can only be used when paging is enabled (that is, when both the PG flag in register CR0 and the PAE flag in register CR4 are set).

When the physical address extension is enabled, the processor allows two sizes of pages: 4-KByte and 2-MByte. As with 32-bit addressing, both page sizes can be addressed within the same set of paging tables (that is, a page-directory entry can point to either a 2-MByte page or a page table that in turn points to 4-KByte pages). To support the 36-bit physical addresses, the following changes are made to the paging data structures:

- The paging table entries are increased to 64 bits to accommodate 36-bit base physical addresses. Each 4-KByte page directory and page table can thus have up to 512 entries.

- A new table, called the page directory pointer table, is added to the linear-address translation hierarchy. This table has 4 entries of 64-bits each, and it lies above the page directory in the hierarchy. With the physical address extension mechanism enabled, the processor supports up to 4 page directories.

- The 20-bit page-directory base address in register CR3 is replaced with a 27-bit page-directory-pointer-table base address (see Figure 3-17). This field provides the 27 most-significant bits of the physical address of the first byte of the page directory pointer table, which forces the table to be located on a 32-byte boundary.

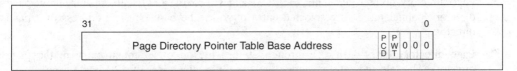

Figure 3-17. Register CR3 Format When the Physical Address Extension is Enabled

- Linear address translation is changed to allow mapping 32-bit linear addresses into the larger physical address space.

3.8.1. Linear Address Translation With Extended Addressing Enabled (4-KByte Pages)

Figure 3-12 shows the page-directory-pointer, page-directory, and page-table hierarchy when mapping linear addresses to 4-KByte pages with extended physical addressing enabled. This paging method can be used to address up to 2^{20} pages, which spans a linear address space of 2^{32} bytes (4 GBytes).

To select the various table entries, the linear address is divided into three sections:

- Page-directory-pointer-table entry—Bits 30 and 31 provide an offset to one of the 4 entries in the page directory pointer table. The selected entry provides the base physical address of a page directory.

- Page-directory entry—Bits 21 through 29 provide an offset to an entry in the selected page directory. The selected entry provides the base physical address of a page table.

- Page-table entry—Bits 12 through 21 provide an offset to an entry in the selected page table. This entry provides the base physical address of a page in physical memory.

- Page offset—Bits 0 through 11 provide an offset to a physical address in the page.

3.8.2. Linear Address Translation With Extended Addressing Enabled (2-MByte Pages)

Figure 3-12 shows how a page-directory-pointer table and page directories can be used to map linear addresses to 2-MByte pages. This paging method can be used to map up to 2048 pages (4 page-directory-pointer-table entries times 512 page-directory entries) into a 4-GByte linear address space.

The 2-MByte page size is selected by setting the PSE flag in control register CR4 and setting the page size (PS) flag in a page-directory entry (see Figure 3-14). With these flags set, the linear address is divided into three sections:

- Page-directory-pointer-table entry—Bits 30 and 31 provide an offset to an entry in the page directory pointer table. The selected entry provides the base physical address of a page directory.

- Page directory entry—Bits 21 through 29 provide an offset to an entry in the page directory. The selected entry provides the base physical address of a 2-MByte page.

- Page offset—Bits 0 through 20 provides an offset to a physical address in the page.

3.8.3. Accessing the Full Extended Physical Address Space With the Extended Page Table Structure

The page table structure described in the previous two sections allows up to 4 GBytes of the 64 GByte extended physical address space to be addressed at one time. Additional 4-GByte sections of physical memory can be addressed in either of two way:

- Change the pointer in register CR3 to point to another the page directory pointer table, which in turn points to another set of page directories and page tables.

- Change entries in the page directory pointer table to point to other page directories, which in turn point to other sets of page tables.

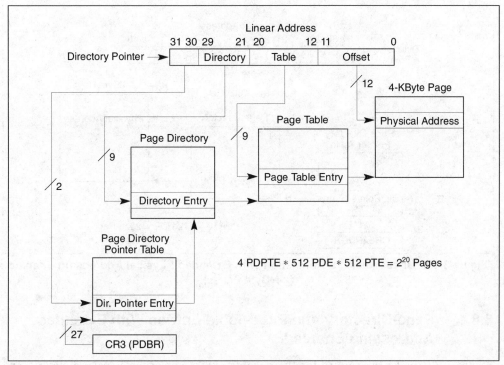

Figure 3-18. Linear Address Translation With Extended Physical Addressing Enabled (4-KByte Pages)

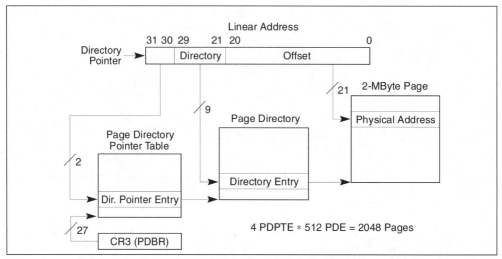

Figure 3-19. Linear Address Translation With Extended Physical Addressing Enabled (2-MByte Pages)

3.8.4. Page-Directory and Page-Table Entries With Extended Addressing Enabled

Figure 3-20 shows the format for the page-directory-pointer-table, page-directory, and page-table entries when 4-KByte pages and 36-bit extended physical addresses are being used. Figure 3-21 shows the format for the page-directory-pointer-table and page-directory entries when 2-MByte pages and 36-bit extended physical addresses are being used. The functions of the flags in these entries are the same as described in Section 3.6.4., "Page-Directory and Page-Table Entries". The major differences in these entries are as follows:

- A page-directory-pointer-table entry is added.

- The size of the entries are increased from 32 bits to 64 bits.

- The maximum number of entries in a page directory or page table is 512.

- The base physical address field in each entry is extended to 24 bits.

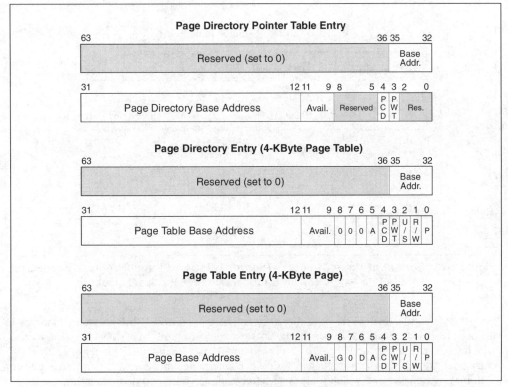

Figure 3-20. Format of Page Directory Pointer Table, Page Directory, and Page Table Entries for 4-KByte Pages and 36-Bit Extended Physical Addresses

The base physical address in an entry specifies the following, depending on the type of entry:

- Page-directory-pointer-table entry—the physical address of the first byte of a 4-KByte page directory

- Page-directory entry—the physical address of the first byte of a 4-KByte page table or a 2-MByte page.

- Page-table entry—the physical address of the first byte of a 4-KByte page.

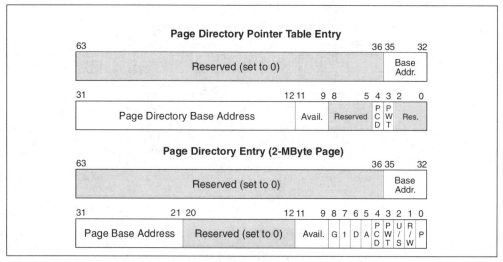

Figure 3-21. Format of Page Directory Pointer Table and Page Directory Entries for 2-MByte Pages and 36-Bit Extended Physical Addresses

For all table entries (except for page-directory entries that point to 2-MByte pages), the bits in the page base address are interpreted as the 24 most-significant bits of a 36-bit physical address, which forces page tables and pages to be aligned on 4-KByte boundaries. When a page-directory entry points to a 2-MByte page, the base address is interpreted as the 15 most-significant bits of a 36-bit physical address, which forces pages to be aligned on 2-MByte boundaries.

The page size (PS) flag (bit 7) in a page-directory entry determines if the entry points to a page table or a 2-MByte page. When this flag is clear, the entry points to a page table; when the flag is set, the entry points to a 2-MByte page. This bit allows 4-KByte and 2-MByte pages to be mixed within one set of paging tables.

Access (A) and dirty (D) flags (bits 5 and 6) are provided for table entries that point to pages.

Bits 9, 10, and 11 in all the table entries for the physical address extension are available for use by software. (When the present bit is clear, bits 1 through 63 are available to software.) All bits in Figure 3-14 that are marked reserved or 0 should be set to 0 by software and not accessed by software. When the PSE and PAE flags in control register CR4 are set, the processor generates a page fault (#PF) if reserved bits in page-directory and page-table entries are not set to 0, and it generates a general-protection exception (#GP) if reserved bits in a page-directory-pointer-table entry are not set to 0.

3.9. MAPPING SEGMENTS TO PAGES

The segmentation and paging mechanisms provide in the Pentium Pro processor support a wide variety of approaches to memory management. When segmentation and paging is combined, segments can be mapped to pages in several ways. To implement a flat (unsegmented) addressing environment, for example, all the code, data, and stack modules can be mapped to one or more large segments (up to 4-GBytes) that share same range of linear addresses (see Figure 3-2). Here, segments are essentially invisible to applications and the operating-system or executive. If paging is used, the paging mechanism can map a single linear address space (contained in a single segment) into virtual memory. Or, each program or task can have its own large linear address space (contained in its own segment), which is mapped into virtual memory through its own page directory and set of page tables.

Segments can be smaller than the size of a page. If one of these segments is placed in a page which is not shared with another segment, the extra memory is wasted. For example, a small data structure, such as a 1-byte semaphore, occupies 4K bytes if it is placed in a page by itself. If many semaphores are used, it is more efficient to pack them into a single page.

The Intel Architecture does not enforce correspondence between the boundaries of pages and segments. A page can contain the end of one segment and the beginning of another. Likewise, a segment can contain the end of one page and the beginning of another.

Memory-management software may be simpler and more efficient if it enforces some alignment between page and segment boundaries. For example, if a segment which can fit in one page is placed in two pages, there may be twice as much paging overhead to support access to that segment.

One approach to combining paging and segmentation that simplifies memory-management software is to give each segment its own page table, as shown in Figure 3-22. This convention gives the segment a single entry in the page directory which provides the access control information for paging the entire segment.

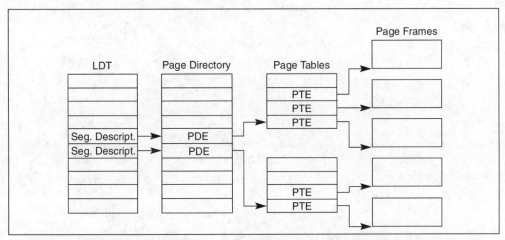

Figure 3-22. Memory Management Convention That Assigns a Page Table to Each Segment

intel®

4

Protection

CHAPTER 4
PROTECTION

In protected mode, the Pentium Pro processor provides a protection mechanism that operates at both the segment level and the page level. This protection mechanism provides the ability to limit access to certain segments or pages based on privilege levels (four privilege levels for segments and two privilege levels for pages). For example, critical operating-system code and data can be protected by placing them in more privileged segments than those that contain applications code. The processor's protection mechanism will then prevent application code from accessing the operating-system code and data in any but a controlled, defined manner.

Segment and page protection can be used at all stages of software development to assist in localizing and detecting design problems and bugs. It can also be incorporated into end-products to offer added robustness to operating systems, utilities software, and applications software.

When the protection mechanism is used, each memory reference is checked to verify that it satisfies various protection checks. All checks are made before the memory cycle is started; any violation results in an exception. Because checks are performed in parallel with address translation, there is no performance penalty. The protection checks that are performed fall into the following categories:

- Limit checks.
- Type checks.
- Restriction of addressable domain.
- Restriction of procedure entry-points.
- Restriction of instruction set.

All protection violation results in an exception being generated. See Chapter 5, *Interrupt and Exception Handling*, for an explanation of the exception mechanism. This chapter describes the protection mechanism and the violations which lead to exceptions.

The following sections describe the protection mechanism available in protected mode. See Chapter 12, *8086 Emulation*, for information on protection in real-address and virtual-8086 mode.

4.1. ENABLING AND DISABLING SEGMENT AND PAGE PROTECTION

Setting the PE flag in register CR0 causes the processor to switch to protected mode, which in turn enables the segment protection mechanism. Once in protected mode, there is no control bit for turning the protection mechanism on or off. The part of the segment protection mechanism that is based on privilege levels can be disabled while still in protected mode by assigning a privilege level of 0 (most privileged) to all segment selectors and segment descriptors. This action disables the privilege level protection barriers between segments, but other protection checks such as limit checking and type checking are still carried out.

Page level protection is automatically enabled when paging is enabled (by setting the PG flag in register CR0). Here again there is no mode bit for turning off page-level protection once paging is enabled. However, page level protection can be disabled by performing the following operations:

- Clear the WP flag in control register CR0.

- Set the read/write (R/W) and user/supervisor (U/S) flags for each page-directory and page-table entry.

This action makes each page a writable, user page, which in effect disables page-level protection.

4.2. FIELDS AND FLAGS USED FOR SEGMENT-LEVEL AND PAGE-LEVEL PROTECTION

The processor's protection mechanism uses the following fields and flags in the system data structures to control access to segments and pages:

- System/application (S) flag—(Bit 12 in the second doubleword of a segment descriptor.) Determines if the segment descriptor is for an application segment (code or data) or a system segment.

- Type field—(Bits 8 through 11 in the second doubleword of a segment descriptor.) Determines the type of code, data, or system segment.

- Limit field—(Bits 0 through 15 of the first doubleword and bits 16 through 19 of the second doubleword of a segment descriptor.) Determines the size of the segment.

- Descriptor privilege level (DPL) field—(Bits 13 and 14 in the second doubleword of a segment descriptor.) Determines the privilege level and accessibility of the segment.

- RPL field. (Bits 0 and 1 of any segment selector). Determines the privilege level of a segment selector.

- CPL field. (Bits 0 and 1 of the CS segment register). Indicates the privilege level of the currently executing program or procedure. The term current privilege level (CPL) refers to the setting of this field.

- User/supervisor (U/S) flag. (Bit 2 of a page-directory or page-table entry). Determines the type of page: user or supervisor.

- Read/write (R/W) flag. (Bit 1 of a page-directory or page-table entry). Determines the type of access allowed to a page: read only or read-write.

Figure 4-1 shows the location of the S flag, type field, limit field, and DPL field in the data, code, and system segment descriptors; Figure 3-6 shows the location of the RPL (or CPL) field in a segment selector (or the CS register); and Figure 3-14 shows the location of the U/S and R/W flags in the page-directory and page-table entries.

Many different styles of protection schemes can be implemented with these fields and flags. When the operating system creates a descriptor, it places values in these fields and flags in keeping with the particular protection style chosen for an operating system or executive. Application program do not generally access or modify these fields and flags.

The following sections describe how the processor uses these fields and flags to perform the various categories of checks described in the introduction to this chapter.

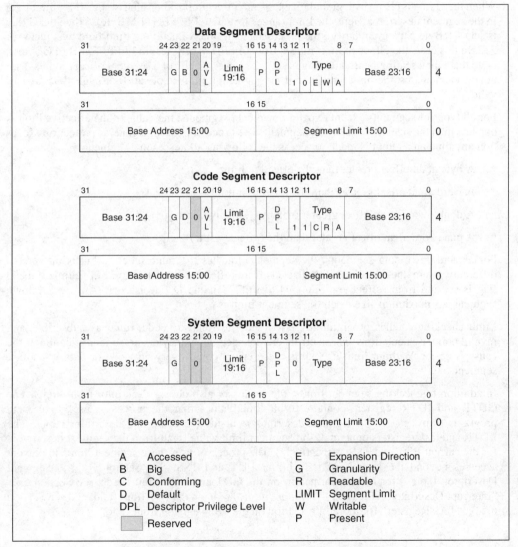

Figure 4-1. Descriptor Fields Used for Protection

4.3. LIMIT CHECKING

The limit field of a segment descriptor prevents programs or procedures from addressing memory locations outside the segment. The effective value of the limit depends on the setting of the G (granularity) flag (see Figure 4-1). For data segments, the limit also depends on the E (expansion direction) flag and the D (default address and operand size) flag. The E flag is one of the bits in the type field when the segment descriptor is for a data segment type.

When the G flag is clear (byte granularity), the effective limit is the value of the 20-bit limit field in the segment descriptor. Here, the limit ranges from 0 to FFFFFH (1 MByte). When the G flag is set (4-KByte page granularity), the processor scales the value in the limit field by a factor of 212. In this case, the effective limit ranges from 0FFFH (4 KBytes) to FFFFFFFFH (4 GBytes). Note that when scaling is used (G flag is set), the lower 12 bits of a segment offset (address) are not checked against the limit; however, if the segment limit is 0, offsets 0 through 4095 are still valid.

For all types of segments except expand-down data segments, the value of the effective limit is one less than the size, in bytes, of the segment. The processor causes a general-protection exception any time an attempt is made to access the following addresses in a segment:

- A byte at an offset greater than the effective limit.

- A word at an offset greater than the (effective-limit − 1)

- A doubleword at an offset greater than the (effective-limit − 3)

- A quadword at an offset greater than the (effective-limit − 7)

For expand-down data segments, the segment limit has the same function but is interpreted differently. Here, the range of valid offsets is from (effective-limit + 1) to FFFFFFFFH if the D flag is set and from (effective-limit + 1) to FFFFH if the D flag is clear. An expand-down segment has maximum size when the segment limit is 0.

Limit checking catches programming errors such as runaway code, runaway subscripts, and invalid pointer calculations. These errors are detected when they occur, so identification of the cause is easier. Without limit checking, these errors could overwrite code or data in another segment.

In addition to checking segment limits, the processor also checks descriptor table limits. The GDTR and IDTR registers contain 16-bit limit values that the processor uses to prevent programs from selecting a segment descriptors outside the respective descriptor tables. The LDTR and task registers contain 32-bit segment limit value (read from the segment descriptors for the current LDT and TSS, respectively). The processor uses these segment limits to prevent accesses beyond the bounds of the current LDT and TSS. See Section 3.5.1., "Segment Descriptor Tables" for more information on the GDT and LDT limit fields; see Section 5.7., "Interrupt Descriptor Table (IDT)" for more information on the IDT limit field; and see Section 6.2.3., "Task Register" for more information on the TSS segment limit field.

4.4. TYPE CHECKING

Segment descriptors contain type information in two places:

- The S (system/application) flag.
- The type field.

The processor uses this information to detect programming errors that result in a program or procedure's attempt to use a segment or gate in an incorrect or unintended manner.

The S flag indicates whether a segment descriptor is an application type or a system type. The type field provides 4 additional bits for use in defining various types of code, data, and system descriptors. Table 3-1 shows the encoding of the type field for code and data descriptors; Table 3-2 shows the encoding of the field for system descriptors.

The processor examines type information at various times while operating on segment selectors and segment descriptors. The following list gives examples of typical operations where type checking is performed. This list is not exhaustive.

- **When a segment selector is loaded into a segment register.** Certain segment registers can contain only certain descriptor types, for example:

    — The CS register only can be loaded with a selector for a code segment.

    — Segment selectors for code segments that are not readable or for system segments cannot be loaded into data-segment registers (DS, ES, FS, and GS).

    — Only segment selectors of writable data segments can be loaded into the SS register.

- **When a segment selector is loaded into the LDTR or task registers.**

- **When instructions access segments whose descriptors are already loaded into segment registers.** Certain segments can be used by instructions only in certain predefined ways, for example:

    — No instruction may write into an executable segment.

    — No instruction may write into a data segment if it is not writable.

    — No instruction may read an executable segment unless the readable flag is set.

- **When an instruction operand contains a segment selector.** Certain instructions can access segment or gates of only a particular type, for example:

    — A far CALL or far JMP instruction can only access a segment descriptor for a conforming code segment, nonconforming code segment, call gate, task gate, or TSS.

    — The LLDT instruction must reference a segment descriptor for an LDT.

    — The LTR instruction must reference a segment descriptor for a TSS.

    — The LAR instruction must reference a segment descriptor for an LDT, TSS, call gate, task gate, code segment, or data segment.

— The LSL instruction must reference a segment descriptor for a LDT, TSS, code segment, or data segment.

— IDT entries must be interrupt or trap gates.

5. **During certain internal operations.** For example:

— On a task switch, the processor automatically checks that the segment descriptor for the task being switched to is a TSS or task gate descriptor.

— On a procedure call through a call gate, trap gate, or interrupt gate, the processor automatically checks that the segment descriptor being pointed to by the gate is a code segment.

— On a jump through a call gate, the processor checks the segment selector in the call gate descriptor to insure that it is for a code segment.

— On a call or jump through a task gate, the processor checks the segment selector in the task gate descriptor to insure that it is for a TSS.

— On an IRET return from a task, the processor checks the back link field in the current TSS (a segment selector) to ensure that it points to a TSS.

4.4.1. Null Segment Selector Checking

Attempting to load a null segment selector (see Section 3.4.1., "Segment Selectors") into the CS or SS segment register generates a general-protection exception (#GP). A null segment selector can be loaded into the DS, ES, FS, or GS register, but any attempt to access a segment through one of these registers when it is loaded with a null segment selector results in a #GP exception being generated. Loading unused data-segment registers with a null segment selector is a useful method of detecting accesses to unused registers and/or preventing unwanted accesses to data segments.

4.5. PRIVILEGE LEVELS

The processor's segment protection mechanism recognizes 4 privilege levels, numbered from 0 to 3. The greater numbers mean lesser privileges. Figure 4-2 shows how these levels of privilege can be interpreted as rings of protection. The center (reserved for the most privileged code, data, and stacks) is used for the segments containing the critical software, usually the kernel of an operating system. Outer rings are used for less critical software. (Systems that use only 2 of the 4 possible privilege levels should use levels 0 and 3.)

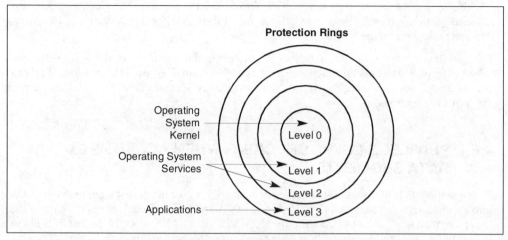

Figure 4-2. Protection Rings

The processor uses privilege levels to prevent a program or task operating at a lesser privilege level from accessing a segment with a greater privilege, except under controlled situations. When the processor detects a privilege level violation, it generates a general-protection exception (#GP).

To carry out privilege-level checks between code modules and data segments, the processor recognizes the following three types of privilege levels:

- **Current privilege level (CPL).** The CPL is the privilege level of the currently executing program or task. It is stored in bits 0 and 1 of the CS and SS segment registers. Normally, the CPL is equal to the privilege level of the code segment from which instructions are being fetched. The processor changes the CPL when program control is transferred to a code segment with a different privilege level. The CPL is treated slightly differently when accessing conforming code segments. Conforming code segments can be accessed from any privilege level, and the CPL is not changed when the processor accesses a conforming code segment that has a different privilege level than the CPL.

- **Descriptor privilege level (DPL).** The DPL is the privilege level of a segment or gate. It is stored in the DPL field of the segment descriptor for the segment or gate. The DPL generally is interpreted as the numerically lowest privilege level that a program or task can have to be allowed to access the segment. For example, if the DPL of a segment is 1, only programs running at a CPL of 0 or 1 can access the segment. For call gates, the DPL is interpreted as the numerically highest privilege level the currently executing program or task can be at and still be able to access call gate.

- **Requestor privilege level (RPL).** The RPL is an override privilege level that is assigned to segment selectors. It is stored in bits 0 and 1 of the segment selector. The processor checks the RPL along with the CPL to determine if access to a segment is allowed. Even if the program or task requesting access to a segment has sufficient privilege to access the segment, access is denied if the RPL is not of sufficient privilege level. That is, if the RPL of a segment selector is greater than the CPL, the RPL overrides the CPL, and vice versa. See Section 4.10.4., "Checking Caller Access Privileges" for a description of the purpose and typical use of the RPL.

Privilege levels are checked when the segment selector of a segment descriptor is loaded into a segment register. The checks used for data access differ from those used for transfers of program control among code segments; therefore, the two kinds of accesses are considered separately in the following sections.

4.6. PRIVILEGE LEVEL CHECKING WHEN ACCESSING DATA SEGMENTS

To access operands in a data segment, the segment selector for the data segment must be loaded into the data-segment registers (DS, ES, FS, or GS) and into the stack segment register (SS). (Segment registers can be loaded with the MOV, POP, LDS, LES, LFS, LGS, and LSS instructions). Before the processor loads a segment selector into a segment register, it performs a privilege check (see Figure 4-3) by comparing the privilege levels of the currently running program or task (the CPL), the RPL of the segment selector, and the DPL of the segment's segment descriptor. The processor loads the segment selector into the segment register if the DPL is greater than or equal to both the CPL and the RPL. Otherwise, a general-protection fault is generated and the segment register is not loaded.

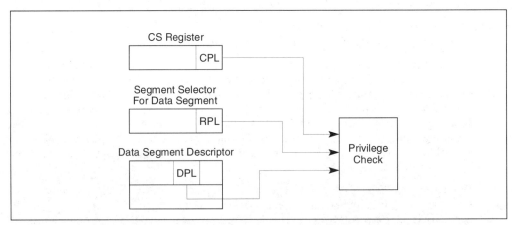

Figure 4-3. Privilege Check for Data Access

Figure 4-4 shows three programs, running at different privilege levels, each attempting to access the same data segment.

* Program A is able to access the data segment using segment selector A, because the CPL of program A and the RPL of segment selector A are both numerically lower than (more privileged) than the DPL of the data segment.

- Program B is not able to access the data segment using segment selector B (dotted line), because the CPL of program B and the RPL of segment selector B are both numerically greater than (less privileged) than the DPL of the data segment.

- Program C should be able to access the data segment because its CPL is numerically less than the DPL of the data segment. However, the RPL of segment selector B is numerically greater than the DPL of the data segment, so access is not allowed. If program C were to use segment selector A to access the data segment, access would be allowed.

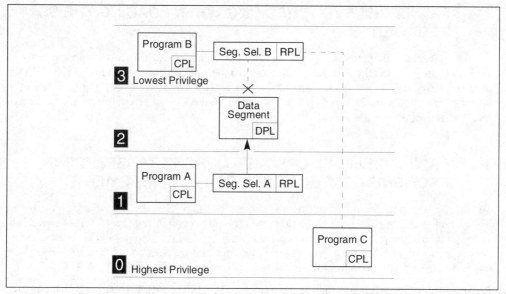

Figure 4-4. Examples of Accessing Data Segments From Various Privilege Levels

As demonstrated in the previous examples, the addressable domain of a program or task varies as its CPL changes. When the CPL is 0, data segments at all privilege levels are accessible; when the CPL is 1, only data segments at privilege levels 1 through 3 are accessible; when the CPL is 3, only data segments at privilege level 3 are accessible. The RPL of a segment selector can always override the addressable domain of a program or task.

4.6.1. Accessing Data in Code Segments

In some instances it may be desirable to access data structures that are contained in a code segment. The following methods of accessing data in code segments are possible:

- Load a data-segment register with a segment selector for a nonconforming, readable, code segment.

- Load a data-segment register with a segment selector for a conforming, readable, code segment.

- Use a code-segment override prefix (CS) to read a readable, code segment whose selector is already loaded in the CS register.

The same rules for access to data segments apply to method 1. Method 2 is always valid because the privilege level of a conforming code segment is effectively the same as the CPL, regardless of its DPL. Method 3 is always valid because the DPL of the code segment selected by the CS register is the same as the CPL.

4.7. PRIVILEGE LEVEL CHECKING WHEN LOADING THE SS REGISTER

Privilege level checking also occurs when the SS register is loaded with the segment selector for a stack segment. Here all privilege levels related to the stack segment must match the CPL; that is, the CPL, the RPL of the stack segment selector, and the DPL of the stack segment descriptor must be the same. If the RPL and DPL are not equal to the CPL, a general-protection exception (#GP) is generated.

4.8. PRIVILEGE LEVEL CHECKING WHEN TRANSFERRING PROGRAM CONTROL BETWEEN CODE SEGMENTS

To transfer program control from one code segment to another, the segment selector for the destination code segment must be loaded into the code-segment register (CS). As part of this loading process, the processor performs various limit, type, and privilege checks. If these checks are successful, the CS register is loaded, program control is transferred to the new code segment, and program execution begins at the instruction pointed to by the EIP register.

Program control transfers are carried out with the JMP, CALL, RET, INT*n*, and IRET instructions, as well as by the exception and interrupt mechanisms. Exceptions and interrupts are special cases discussed in Chapter 5, *Interrupt and Exception Handling*. This chapter discusses only the JMP, CALL, and RET instructions.

A JMP or CALL instruction can reference another code segment in any of four ways:

- The target operand points the segment descriptor of another code segment.

- The target operand points to a call gate descriptor, which in turn points to a segment selector for another code segment.

- The target operand points to a TSS, which in turn points to a segment selector for another code segment.

- The target operand points to a task gate, which turn points to a TSS, which in turn points to a segment selector for another code segment.

The following sections describe first two types of references. See Section 6.3., "Task Switching" for information on transferring program control through a task gate and/or TSS.

4.8.1. Direct Calls or Jumps to Code Segments

The near forms of the JMP, CALL, and RET instructions transfer program control within the current code segment, so privilege-level checks are not performed. The far forms of the JMP and CALL instruction transfer control to other code segments, so the processor does perform privilege-level checks.

When transferring program control to another code segment without going through a call gate, the processor examines four kinds of privilege level and type information (see Figure 4-5):

- The CPL (privilege level of the calling procedure, that is, the procedure making the call or jump).

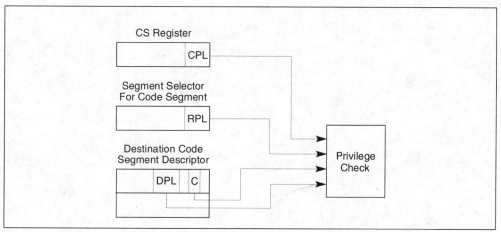

Figure 4-5. Privilege Check for Control Transfer Without Using a Gate

- The DPL of the segment descriptor for the destination code segment that contains the called procedure.

- The RPL of the segment selector of the destination code segment

- The conforming (C) flag in the segment descriptor for the destination code segment, which determines whether the segment is a conforming (C flag is set) or nonconforming (C flag is clear) code segment. (See Section 3.4.3.1., "Code and Data Segment-Descriptor Types" for more information about this flag.)

The rules that the processor uses to check the CPL, RPL, and DPL depends on the setting of the C flag, as described in the following sections.

4.8.1.1. ACCESSING NONCONFORMING CODE SEGMENTS

When accessing nonconforming code segments, the CPL of the calling procedure must be equal to the DPL of the destination code segment; otherwise, the processor generates a general-protection exception (#GP).

For, example, in Figure 4-4, code segment B is a nonconforming code segment. Therefore, a procedure in code segment A can call a procedure in code segment B, because they are at the same privilege level (the CPL of code segment A is equal to the DPL of code segment B). However, a procedure in code segment C cannot call a procedure in code segment B, because the two code segments are at different privilege levels.

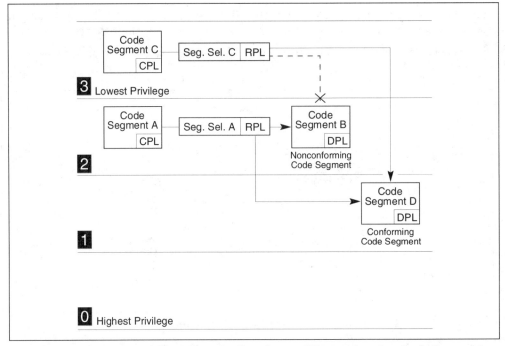

Figure 4-6. Examples of Accessing Conforming and Nonconforming Code Segments From Various Privilege Levels

The RPL of the segment selector that points to a nonconforming code segment has a limited effect on the privilege check. The RPL must be less than or equal to the CPL of the calling procedure for a successful control transfer to occur. So, in the example in Figure 4-4, the RPL of segment selector A could legally be set to 0, 1, or 2, but not to 3.

When the segment selector of a nonconforming code segment is loaded into the CS register, the privilege level field is not changed; that is, it remains at the CPL (which is the privilege level of the calling procedure). This is true, even if the RPL of the segment selector is different from the CPL.

4.8.1.2. ACCESSING CONFORMING CODE SEGMENTS

When accessing conforming code segments, the CPL of the calling procedure may be equal to or greater than the DPL of the destination code segment; the processor generates a general-protection exception (#GP) only if the CPL is less than the DPL. (The segment selector RPL for the destination code segment is not checked if the segment is a conforming code segment.)

In the example in Figure 4-4, code segment D is a conforming code segment. Therefore, calling procedures in both code segment A and C can access code segment D, because they both have CPLs that are greater than or equal to the DPL of the conforming code segment. **For conforming code segments, the DPL represents the numerically lowest privilege level that a calling procedure may be at to successfully make a call to the code segment.**

When program control is transferred to a conforming code segment, the CPL does not change, even if the DPL of the destination code segment is less than the CPL. This situation is the only one where the CPL may be different from the DPL of the current code segment. Also, since the CPL does not change, no stack switch occurs.

Conforming segments are used for code modules such as math libraries and exception handlers, which support applications but do not require access to protected system facilities. These modules are part of the operating system or executive software, but they can be executed at numerically higher privilege levels (less privileged levels). Keeping the CPL at the level of a calling code segment when switching to a conforming code segment prevents an application program from accessing nonconforming code segments while at the privilege level (DPL) of a conforming code segment.

Most code segments are nonconforming. For these segments, program control can be transferred only to code segments at the same level of privilege, unless the transfer is carried out through a call gate, as described in the following sections.

4.8.2. Gate Descriptors

To provide controlled access to code segments with different privilege levels, the processor provides special set of descriptors called gate descriptors. There are four kinds of gate descriptors:

* Call gates

* Trap gates

* Interrupt gates

* Task gates

Task gates are used for task switching and are discussed in Chapter 6, *Task Management*. Trap and interrupt gates are special kinds of call gates used for calling exception and interrupt handlers. The are described in Chapter 5, *Interrupt and Exception Handling*. This chapter is concerned only with call gates.

4.8.3. Call Gates

Call gates facilitate controlled transfers of program control between different privilege levels. They are typically used only in operating systems or executives that use the privilege-level protection mechanism. Call gates are also useful for transferring program control between 16-bit and 32-bit code segments, as described in Section 13.4., "Transferring Control Among Mixed-Size Code Segments".

Figure 4-7 shows the format of a call gate descriptor. A call gate descriptor may reside in the GDT or in an LDT, but not in the interrupt descriptor table (IDT). It performs five functions:

- It specifies the code segment to be accessed.

- It defines an entry point for a procedure in the specified code segment.

- It specifies the privilege level required to access a procedure.

- If a stack switch occurs, it specifies the number of optional parameters to be copied between stacks.

- If defines the size of values to be pushed onto the target stack: 16-bit gates force 16-bit pushes and 32-bit gates force 32-bit pushes.

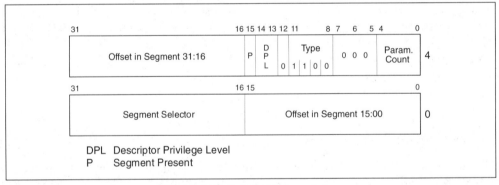

Figure 4-7. Call Gate Descriptor

The segment selector field in a call gate specifies the code segment to be accessed. The offset field specifies the entry point in the code segment. This entry point is generally to the first instruction of a specific procedure. The DPL field indicates the privilege level of the call gate, which in turn is the privilege level required to access the selected procedure. The P flag indicates whether or not the code segment being pointed to by the call gate is present in memory. The parameter count field indicates the number of parameters to copy from the calling procedures stack to the new stack if a stack switch occurs (see Section 4.8.5., "Stack Switching"). The parameter count specifies the number of words for 16-bit call gates and doublewords for 32-bit call gates.

4.8.4. Accessing a Code Segment Through a Call Gate

To access a call gate, a far pointer to the gate is provided as a target operand in a CALL or JMP instruction. The segment selector from this pointer identifies the call gate (see Figure 4-8); the offset from the pointer is required, but not used or checked by the processor. (The offset can be set to any value.)

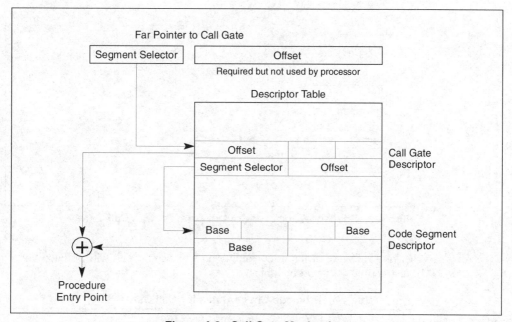

Figure 4-8. Call Gate Mechanism

When the processor has accessed the call gate, it uses the segment selector from the call gate to locate the segment descriptor for the destination code segment. (This segment descriptor can be in the GDT or the LDT.) It then combines the base address from the code segment descriptor with the offset from the call gate to form the linear address of the procedure entry point in the code segment.

As shown in Figure 4-9, four different privilege levels are used to check the validity of a program control transfer through a call gate:

- The CPL (current privilege level).

- The RPL (requestor's privilege level) of the call gate's segment selector.

- The DPL (descriptor privilege level) of the call gate descriptor.

- The DPL of the segment descriptor of the destination code segment.

The C flag (conforming) in the segment descriptor for the destination code segment is also checked.

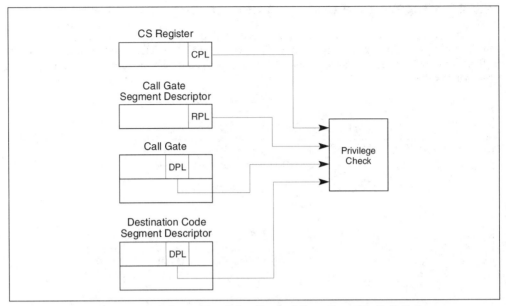

Figure 4-9. Privilege Check for Control Transfer with Call Gate

The privilege checking rules are different depending on whether the call was initiated with a CALL or a JMP instruction, as shown in Table 4-1.

Table 4-1. Privilege Check Rules for Call Gates

Instruction	Privilege Check Rules
CALL	CPL ≤ call gate DPL; RPL ≤ call gate DPL
	Destination conforming code segment DPL ≤ CPL
	Destination nonconforming code segment DPL ≤ CPL
JMP	CPL ≤ call gate DPL; RPL ≤ call gate DPL
	Destination conforming code segment DPL ≤ CPL
	Destination nonconforming code segment DPL = CPL

The DPL field of the call gate descriptor specifies the numerically highest privilege level from which a calling procedure can access the call gate; that is, to access a call gate, the CPL of a calling procedure must be equal to or less than the DPL of the call gate. orexample, in Figure 4-12, call gate A has a DPL of 3. So calling procedures at all CPLs (0 through 3) can access this call gate, which includes calling procedures in code segments A and B. Call gate B has a DPL of 2, so only calling procedures at a CPL or 0, 1, or 2 can access call gate B. The dotted line shows that a calling procedure in code segment A cannot access call gate B.

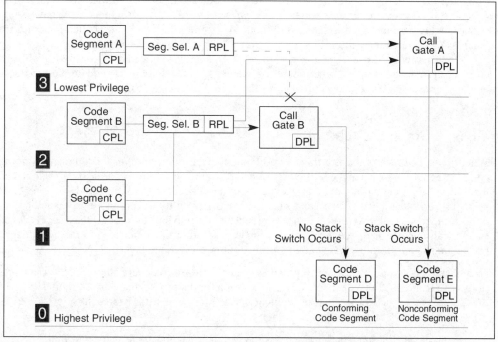

Figure 4-10. Example of Accessing Call Gates At Various Privilege Levels

The RPL of the segment selector to a call gate must satisfy the same test as the CPL of the calling procedure; that is, the RPL must be less than or equal to the DPL of the call gate. In the example in Figure 4-12, a calling procedure in code segment C can access either call gate A or call gate B using segment selector B. However, if segment selector A was used, only call gate A could be accessed.

If the privilege checks between the calling procedure and call gate are successful, the processor then checks the DPL of the code segment descriptor against the CPL of the calling procedure. Here, the privilege check rules vary between CALL and JMP instructions. Only CALL instructions can use call gates to transfer program control more privileged (numerically lower privilege level) nonconforming code segments; that is, to nonconforming code segments with a DPL less than the CPL. A JMP instruction can use a call gate only to transfer program control to a nonconforming code segment with a DPL equal to the CPL. CALL and JMP instruction can both transfer program control to a more privileged conforming code segment; that is, to a conforming code segment with a DPL less than or equal to the CPL.

If a call is made to a more privileged (numerically lower privilege level) nonconforming destination code segment, the CPL is lowered to the DPL of the destination code segment and a stack switch occurs (see Section 4.8.5., "Stack Switching"). If a call or jump is made to a more privileged conforming destination code segment, the CPL is not changed and no stack switch occurs.

Call gates allow a single code segment to have procedures that can be accessed at different privilege levels. For example, an operating system located in a code segment may have some services which are intended to be used by both the operating system and application software (such as procedures for handling character I/O). Call gates for these procedures can be set up that allow access at all privilege levels (0 through 3). More privileged call gates (with DPLs of 0 or 1) can then be set up for other operating system services that are intended to be used only by the operating system (such as procedures that initialize device drivers).

4.8.5. Stack Switching

Whenever a call gate is used to transfer program control to a more privileged nonconforming code segment (that is, when the DPL of the nonconforming destination code segment is less than the CPL), the processor automatically switches to the procedure stack for the destination code segment's privilege level. This stack switching is carried out to prevent more privileged procedures from crashing due to insufficient stack space. It also prevents the data on the less privileged (numerically higher privilege level) stack from being read or manipulated by a more privileged procedure (a procedure operating at a numerically lower privilege level).

Each task running on a Pentium Pro processor must define 4 procedure stacks: one for applications code (running at privilege level 3) and one each for the privilege levels 2, 1, and 0. Each of these stacks is located in a separate segment and is identified with a segment selector and an offset into the stack segment (a stack pointer).

The segment selector and stack pointer for the privilege level 3 stack is located in the SS and ESP registers, respectively, when privilege-level-3 code is being executed and is automatically stored on the called procedure's stack when a stack switch occurs.

Pointers to the privilege level 0, 1, and 2 stacks are stored in the TSS for the currently running task (see Figure 6-2). Each of these pointers consists of a segment selector and a stack pointer (loaded into the ESP register). These initial pointers are strictly read-only values. The processor does not change them while the task is running. They are used only to create new stacks when calls are made to more privileged levels (numerically lower privilege levels). These stacks are disposed of when a return is made from the called procedure. The next time the procedure is called, a new stack is created using the initial stack pointer. (The TSS does not specify a stack for privilege level 3 because the processor does not allow a transfer of program control from a procedure running at a CPL of 0, 1, or 3 to a procedure running at a CPL of 3, except on a return.)

The operating system is responsible for creating stacks and stack-segment descriptors for all the privilege levels to be used and for loading initial pointers for these stacks into the TSS. Each stack must be read/write accessible (as specified in the type field of its segment descriptor) and must contain enough space (as specified in the limit field) to hold the following items:

- The contents of the SS, ESP, CS, and EIP registers for the calling procedure.

- The parameters and temporary variables required by the called procedure.

- The EFLAGS register and error code, when implicit calls are made to an exception or interrupt handler.

(If the operating system does not use the processor's multitasking mechanism, it still must create at least one TSS for this stack-related purpose.)

When a procedure call through a call gate results in a change in privilege level, the processor performs the following steps to switch stacks and begin execution of the called procedure at a new privilege level (see Figure 4-11):

1. Uses the DPL of the destination code segment (the new CPL) to select a pointer to the new stack (segment selector and stack pointer) from the TSS.

2. Reads the segment selector and stack pointer for the stack to be switched to from the current TSS. Any limit violations detected while reading the stack segment selector, stack pointer, or stack segment descriptor cause a TSS exception to be generated.

3. Temporarily saves the current values of the SS and ESP registers.

4. Loads the segment selector and stack pointer for the new stack in the SS and ESP registers.

5. Pushes the temporarily saved values for the SS and ESP registers (for the calling procedure onto the new stack.

6. Copies the number of parameter specified in the parameter count field of the call gate from the calling procedure's stack to the new stack.

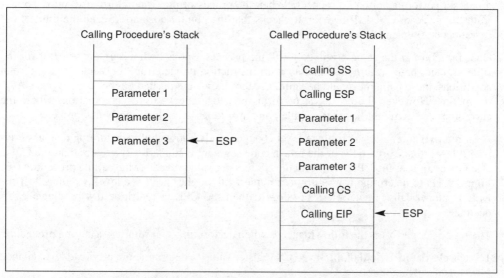

Figure 4-11. Stack Switching During an Interprivilege-Level Call

7. Pushes the return instruction pointer (the current contents of the CS and EIP registers) onto the new stack. If the count is 0, no parameters are copied.

8. Loads the segment selector for the new code segment and the new instruction pointer from the call gate into the CS and EIP registers, respectively, and begins execution of the called procedure.

See the description of the CALL instruction in Chapter 11, *Instruction Set Reference*, in the *Pentium® Pro Family Developer's Manual, Volume 2* for a detailed description of the privilege level checks and other protection checks that the processor performs on a far call through a call gate.

The parameter count field in a call gate specifies the number of data items (up to 31) that the processor should copy from the calling procedure's stack to the stack of the called procedure. If more than 31 data items need to be passed to the called procedure, one of the parameters can be a pointer to a data structure, or the saved contents of the SS and ESP registers may be used to access parameters in the old stack space. The size of the data items passed to the called procedure depends on the call gate size, as described in Section 4.8.3., "Call Gates".

4.8.6. Returning from a Called Procedure

The RET instruction can be used to perform a near return, a far return at the same privilege level, and a far return to a different privilege level. This instruction is intended to execute returns from procedures that were called with a CALL instruction. It does not support returns from a JMP instruction.

A near return only transfers program control within the current code segment; therefore, the processor performs only a limit check. When the processor pops the return instruction pointer from the stack into the EIP register, it checks that the pointer does not exceed the limit of the current code segment.

On a far return at the same privilege level, the processor pops both a segment selector for the code segment being returned to and a return instruction pointer from the stack. Under normal conditions, these pointers should be valid, because they were pushed on the stack by the CALL instruction. However, the processor performs privilege checks to detect situations where the current procedure might have altered the pointer or failed to maintain the stack properly.

A far return that requires a privilege-level change is only allowed when returning to a less privileged level (that is, the DPL of the return code segment is numerically greater than the CPL). The processor uses the RPL field from the CS register value saved for the calling procedure (see Figure 4-11) to determine if a return to a numerically higher privilege level is required. If the RPL is numerically greater (less privileged) than the CPL, a return across privilege levels occurs.

The processor performs the following steps when performing a far return to a calling procedure:

1. Checks the RPL field of the saved CS register value to determine if a privilege level change is required on the return.

2. Loads the CS and EIP registers with the values on the called procedure's stack.

3. (If the return requires a privilege level change.) Loads the SS and ESP registers with the values on the called procedure's stack. The values of the SS and ESP registers for the called procedure are discarded. Any limit violations detected while loading the stack segment selector or stack pointer cause a general-protection exception (#GP) to be generated.

4. Adjusts the value in the ESP registers by the number of bytes indicated in the RET instruction. The resulting ESP value is not checked against the limit of the stack segment. If the ESP value is beyond the limit, that fact is not recognized until the next stack operation.

5. (If the return requires a privilege level change.) Checks the contents of the DS, ES, FS, and GS segment registers. If any of these registers refer to segments whose DPL is less than the new CPL (excluding conforming code segments), the segment register is loaded with a null segment selector.

See the description of the RET instruction in Chapter 11, *Instruction Set Reference*, of the *Pentium® Pro Family Developer's Manual, Volume 2* for a detailed description of the privilege level checks and other protection checks that the processor performs on a far return.

4.9. PRIVILEGED INSTRUCTIONS

Some of the system instructions (called "privileged instructions" are protected from use by application programs. The privileged instructions control system functions (such as the loading of system registers). They can be executed only when the CPL is 0 (most privileged). If one of these instructions is executed when the CPL is not 0, a general-protection exception (#GP) is generated. The following system instructions are privileged instructions:

- LGDT—Load GDT register.
- LLDT—Load LDT register.
- LTR—Load task register.
- LIDT—Load IDT register.
- MOV CR*n*—Load and store control registers.
- LMSW—Load machine status word.
- CLTS—Clear task-switched flag in register CR0.
- MOV DR*n*—Load and store debug registers.
- INVD—Invalidate cache, without writeback.
- WBINVD—Invalidate cache, with writeback.
- INVLPG—Invalidate TLB entry.
- HLT—Halt processor.
- RDMSR—Read Model-Specific Registers
- WRMSR—Write Model-Specific Registers
- RDPMC—Read Performance Monitoring Counter
- RDTSC—Read Time Stamp Counter

The PCE and TSD flags in register CR4 (bits 4 and 2, respectively) enable to RDPMC and RDTSC instructions, respectively, to be read at any CPL.

The LLDT, SLDT, LTR, STR, LSL, LAR, VERR, VERW, and ARPL instructions can only be executed in protected mode. Attempting to execute these instructions while in real-address or virtual-8086 mode will result in an invalid opcode (#UD) exception being generated.

4.10. POINTER VALIDATION

When operating in protected mode, the processor validates all pointers to enforce protection between segments and maintain isolation between privilege levels. Pointer validation consists of the following checks:

1. Checking if the segment type is compatible with its use.

2. Checking read/write rights

3. Checking if the pointer offset exceeds the segment limit.

4. Checking if the supplier of the pointer is allowed to access the segment.

5. Checking the offset alignment.

The processor automatically performs first, second, and third checks during instruction execution; software must assist in performing the fourth check. The fifth check (offset alignment) is performed automatically if alignment checking is turned on. Offset alignment does not affect isolation of privilege levels.

4.10.1. Checking Segment Type Compatibility (Access Rights)

When the processor accesses a segment using a far pointer, it performs an access rights check on the segment descriptor pointed to by the far pointer. This check is performed to determine if type and privilege level (DPL) of the segment descriptor are compatible with the operation to be performed. For example, when making a far call in protected mode, the segment descriptor type must be for a conforming or nonconforming code segment, a call gate, a task gate, or a TSS. Then, if the call is to a non-conforming code segment, the DPL of the code segment must be equal to the CPL, and the RPL of the code segment's segment selector must be less than or equal to the DPL. If type or privilege level are found to be incompatible, the appropriate exception is generated.

To prevent type incompatibility exceptions from being generated, software can check the access rights of a segment descriptor using the LAR (load access rights) instruction. The LAR instruction specifies the segment selector for the segment descriptor whose access rights are to be checked and a destination register. If the segment descriptor is readable, the LAR instruction performs the following operations:

1. If the segment selector points to a segment descriptor that is beyond descriptor table limit (GDT or LDT), the destination register is not modified and the ZF flag is cleared.

2. Determines if the segment selector is null.

3. Checks that the segment descriptor is a code, data, LDT, call gate, task gate, or TSS segment descriptor type.

4. If the segment is not a conforming code segment, checks if the segment descriptor is visible at the CPL (that is, if the CPL and the RPL of the segment selector are less than or equal to the DPL).

5. If the privilege level and type checks are true, loads the second doubleword of the segment descriptor into the destination register (masked by the value 00FxFF00H) and sets the ZF flag in the EFLAGS register. If the segment selector is not visible at the current privilege level or is an invalid type for the LAR instruction, the instruction does not modify the destination register and clears the ZF flag.

Once loaded in the destination register, software can preform additional checks on the access rights information.

4.10.2. Checking Read/Write Rights

The VERR (verify for reading) and VERW (verify for writing) instructions determine whether a code or data segment can be read or written to, respectively. These instructions perform the same operation that the processor performs when it loads the DS, ES, FS or GS register.

Both these instructions specify the segment selector for the segment being checked. The VERR instruction sets the ZF flag in the EFLAGS register if the segment is visible at the CPL and readable; the VERW sets the ZF flag if the segment is visible and writable. (Code segments are never writable.) If the segment selector points to a segment descriptor that is beyond its descriptor table limit (GDT or LDT), the ZF flag is cleared.

4.10.3. Checking That the Pointer Offset Is Within Limits

When the processor accesses any segment it performs a limit check to insure that the offset is within the limit of the segment. Software can perform this limit check using the LSL (load segment limit) instruction. Like the LAR instruction, the LSL instruction specifies the segment selector for the segment descriptor whose limit is to be checked and a destination register. If the segment descriptor is readable, the LSL instruction performs the following operations:

1. If the segment selector points to a segment descriptor that is beyond its descriptor table limit (GDT or LDT), the destination register is not modified and the ZF flag is cleared.

2. Checks that the segment descriptor is a code, data, LDT, or TSS segment descriptor type.

3. If the segment is not a conforming code segment, checks if the segment descriptor is visible at the CPL (that is, if the CPL and the RPL of the segment selector less than or equal to the DPL).

4. If the privilege level and type checks are true, loads the unscrambled limit from the segment selector into the destination register and sets the ZF flag in the EFLAGS register. (If the segment selector is not visible at the current privilege level or is an invalid type for the LSL instruction, the instruction does not modify the destination register and clears the ZF flag.

Once loaded in the destination register, software can compare the segment limit with the offset of a pointer.

4.10.4. Checking Caller Access Privileges

The requestor's privilege level (RPL) field of a segment selector is intended to carry the privilege level of a calling procedure (the calling procedure's CPL) to a called procedure. The called procedure then uses the RPL to determine if access to a segment is allowed. The RPL is said to "weaken" the privilege level of the called procedure to that of the RPL.

Operating-system procedures typically use the RPL to prevent less privileged application programs from accessing data located in more privileged segments. When an operating-system procedure (the called procedure) receives a segment selector from an application program (the calling procedure), it sets the segment selector's RPL to the privilege level of the calling procedure. Then, when the operating system uses the segment selector to access its associated segment, the processor performs privilege checks using the calling procedure's privilege level (stored in the RPL) rather than the numerically lower privilege level (the CPL) of the operating-system procedure. The RPL thus insures that the operating system does not access a segment on behalf of an application program unless that program itself has access to the segment.

Figure 4-12 shows an example of how the processor uses the RPL field. In this example, an application program (located in code segment A) passes segment selector B (which points to a data segment B) to the operating system (located in code segment C). The segment selector is passed as a parameter on the stack. Before passing the segment selector, the application program sets the RPL of the segment selector to its current privilege level (which in this example is 2). To determine whether the operating system can access data segment B, the processor compares the CPL (taken from code segment C's DPL), the RPL of segment selector B, and the DPL of data segment B. Since the RPL is greater than the DPL, access to data segment B is denied. The processor's protection mechanism thus protects data segment B from access by the operating system, because application program's privilege level (represented by the RPL of segment selector B) is greater than the DPL of data segment B.

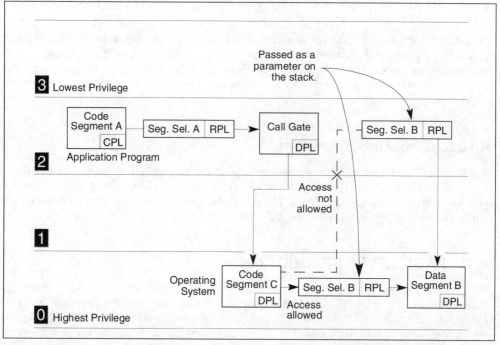

Figure 4-12. Use of RPL to Weaken Privilege Level of Called Procedure

Now assume that instead of setting the RPL of segment selector B to 2, the application program sets the RPL to 0. The operating system can now access data segment B, because its CPL and the RPL of segment selector B are both equal to the DPL of data segment B. Because the application program is able to change the RPL of a segment selector to any value, it can potentially use a procedure operating at a numerically lower privilege level to access a protected data structure. This ability to lower the RPL of a segment selector breaches the processor's protection mechanism.

Because a called procedures cannot rely on the calling procedure to set the RPL correctly, operating-system procedures (executing at numerically lower privilege-levels) that receive segment selectors from numerically higher privilege-level procedures need to test the RPL of the segment selector to determine if it is at the appropriate level. The ARPL (adjust requested privilege level) instruction is provided for this purpose. This instruction adjusts the RPL of one segment selector to match that of another segment selector.

The example in Figure 4-12 demonstrates how the ARPL instruction is intended to be used. When the operating-system receives segment selector B from the application program, it uses the ARPL instruction to compare the RPL of the segment selector with the privilege level of the application program. If the RPL is less than application program's privilege level, the ARPL instruction changes the RPL of the segment selector to match the privilege level of the application program. Using this instruction thus prevents a procedure running at a numerically higher privilege level from accessing numerically lower privilege-level (more privileged) segments by lowering the RPL of a segment selector.

Note that the privilege level of the application program can be determined by reading the RPL field of the segment selector for the application-program's code segment. This segment selector is stored on the stack as part of the call to the operating system. The operating system can copy the segment selector from the stack into a register for use as an operand for the ARPL instruction.

4.10.5. Checking Alignment

When the CPL is 3, alignment of memory references can be checked by setting the AM flag in the CR0 register and the AC flag in the EFLAGS register. Unaligned memory references generate alignment exceptions (#AC). The processor does not generate alignment exceptions when operating at privilege level 0, 1, or 2.

4.11. PAGE-LEVEL PROTECTION

Page-level protection can be used alone or applied to segments. When page-level protection is used with the flat memory model, it allows supervisor code and data (the operating system or executive) to be protected from user code and data (application programs). It also allows pages containing code to be write protected. When the segment- and page-level protection are combined, page-level read/write protection allows more protection granularity within segments.

With page-level protection (as with segment-level protection) each memory reference is checked to verify that protection checks are satisfied. All checks are made before the memory cycle is started, and any violation prevents the cycle from starting and results in a page-fault exception being generated. Because checks are performed in parallel with address translation, there is no performance penalty.

The processor performs two page-level protection checks:

• Restriction of addressable domain (supervisor and user modes).

• Page type (read only or read/write).

Violations of either of these checks results in a page-fault exception being generated. See Chapter 5, "Interrupt 14—Page Fault Exception (#PF)" for an explanation of the page-fault exception mechanism. This chapter describes the protection violations which lead to page-fault exceptions.

4.11.1. Page Protection Flags

Protection information for pages is contained in two flags in a page-directory or page-table entry (see Figure 3-14): the read/write flag (bit 1) and the user/supervisor flag (bit 2). The protection checks are applied to both first- and second-level page tables (that is page directories and page tables).

4.11.2. Restricting Addressable Domain

The page-level protection mechanism allows restricting access to pages based on two privilege levels:

* Supervisor mode (U/S flag is 0)—(Most privileged) For the operating system or executive, other system software (such as device drivers), and protected system data (such as page tables).

* User mode (U/S flag is 1)—(Least privileged) For application code and data.

The segment privilege levels map to the page privilege levels as follows. If the processor is currently operating at a CPL of 0, 1, or 2, it is in supervisor mode; if it is operating at a CPL of 3, it is in user mode. When the processor is in supervisor mode, it can access all pages; when in user mode, it can access only user-level pages.

4.11.3. Page Type

The page-level protection mechanism recognizes two page types:

* Read-only access (R/W flag is 0).

* Read/write access (R/W flag is 1).

When the processor is in supervisor mode and the WP flag in register CR0 is clear (its state following reset initialization), all pages are both readable and writable (write-protection is ignored). When the processor is in user mode, it can write only to user-mode pages that are read/write accessible. User-mode pages which are read/write or read-only are readable; supervisor-mode pages are neither readable nor writable from user mode. A page-fault exception is generated on any attempt to violate the protection rules.

The Pentium Pro, Pentium, and Intel486 processors allow user-mode pages to be write-protected against supervisor-mode access. Setting the WP flag in register CR0 enables supervisor-mode sensitivity to user-mode, write-protected pages.

The supervisor write-protect feature is also useful for implementing the copy-on-write strategy used by some operating systems, such as UNIX, for task creation (also called forking or spawning). When a new task is created, it is possible to copy the entire address space of the parent task. This gives the child task a complete, duplicate set of the parent's segments and pages. An alternative strategy, copy-on-write, saves memory space and time by mapping the child's segments and pages to the same segments and pages used by the parent task. A private copy of a page gets created only when one of the tasks writes to the page. By using the WP flag, the supervisor can detect an attempt to write to a user-level page, and can copy the page at that time.

4.11.4. Combining Protection of Both Levels of Page Tables

For any one page, the protection attributes of its page-directory entry (first-level page table) may differ from those of its page-table entry (second-level page table). The processor checks the protection for a page in both its page-directory and the page-table entries. Table 4-2 shows the protection provided by the possible combinations of protection attributes when the WP flag is clear.

Table 4-2. Combined Page Directory and Page Table Protection

Page Directory Entry		Page Table Entry		Combined Effect	
Privilege	**Access Type**	**Privilege**	**Access Type**	**Privilege**	**Access Type**
User	Read-Only	User	Read-Only	User	Read-Only
User	Read-Only	User	Read-Write	User	Read-Only
User	Read-Write	User	Read-Only	User	Read-Only
User	Read-Write	User	Read-Write	User	Read/Write
User	Read-Only	Supervisor	Read-Only	Supervisor	Read/Write*
User	Read-Only	Supervisor	Read-Write	Supervisor	Read/Write*
User	Read-Write	Supervisor	Read-Only	Supervisor	Read/Write*
User	Read-Write	Supervisor	Read-Write	Supervisor	Read/Write
Supervisor	Read-Only	User	Read-Only	Supervisor	Read/Write*
Supervisor	Read-Only	User	Read-Write	Supervisor	Read/Write*
Supervisor	Read-Write	User	Read-Only	Supervisor	Read/Write*
Supervisor	Read-Write	User	Read-Write	Supervisor	Read/Write
Supervisor	Read-Only	Supervisor	Read-Only	Supervisor	Read/Write*
Supervisor	Read-Only	Supervisor	Read-Write	Supervisor	Read/Write*
Supervisor	Read-Write	Supervisor	Read-Only	Supervisor	Read/Write*
Supervisor	Read-Write	Supervisor	Read-Write	Supervisor	Read/Write

NOTE:

* If the WP flag of CR0 is set, the access type is determined by the R/W flags of the page-directory and page-table entries.

4.11.5. Overrides to Page Protection

The following types of memory accesses are checked as if they are privilege-level 0 accesses, regardless of the CPL at which the processor is currently operating:

* Access to segment descriptors in the GDT, LDT, or IDT.

* Access to an inner-privilege-level stack during an inter-privilege-level call or a call to in exception or interrupt handler, when a change of privilege level occurs.

4.12. COMBINING PAGE AND SEGMENT PROTECTION

When paging is enabled, the processor evaluates segment protection first, then evaluates page protection. If the processor detects a protection violation at either the segment level or the page level, the memory access is not carried out and an exception is generated. If an exception is generated by segmentation, no paging exception is generated.

Page-level protections cannot be used to override segment-level protection. For example, a code segment is by definition not writable. If a code segment is paged, setting the R/W flag for the pages to read-write does not make the pages writable. Attempts to write into the pages will be blocked by segment-level protection checks.

Page-level protection can be used to enhance segment-level protection. For example, if a large read-write data segment is paged, the page-protection mechanism can be used to write-protect individual pages.

intel®

5

Interrupt and
Exception Handling

CHAPTER 5
INTERRUPT AND EXCEPTION HANDLING

This chapter describes the processor's interrupt and exception handling mechanism, when operating in protected mode. Most of the information provided here also applies to the interrupt and exception mechanism used in real-address or virtual-8086 mode. See Chapter 12, *8086 Emulation*, for a description of the differences in the interrupt and exception mechanism for real-address and virtual-8086 mode.

5.1. INTERRUPT AND EXCEPTION OVERVIEW

Interrupts and exceptions are forced transfers of execution to a procedure or task. The procedure or task is called a *handler*. Interrupts typically occur at random times during the execution of a program, in response to signals from hardware. They are used to handle events external to the processor, such as requests to service peripheral devices. Software can also generate interrupts by executing the INT *n* instruction. Exceptions occur when the processor detects an error condition while executing an instruction, such as division by zero. The processor detects a variety of error conditions including protection violations, page faults, and internal machine faults.

The processor's interrupt and exception handling mechanism allows interrupts and exceptions to be handled transparently to application programs and the operating system or executive. When an interrupt is received or an exception is detected, the currently running procedure or task is automatically suspended while the processor executes an interrupt or exception handler. When execution of the handler is complete, the processor resumes execution of the interrupted procedure or task. The resumption of the interrupted procedure or task happens without loss of program continuity, unless recovery from an exception was not possible or an interrupt caused the currently running program to be terminated.

The processor receives interrupts from three sources and exceptions from two sources:

- Interrupts

    — **Non-maskable interrupts (NMIs).** These interrupts are received on the processor's NMI# input pin. The processor does not provide a mechanism to prevent non-maskable interrupts.

    — **Maskable interrupts.** These interrupts are received either at the processor's INTR# (interrupt) pin from an external, system-based interrupt controller (8259A) or as a serial message on the LINT[1:0] pins from a system-based I/O APIC. The processor does not act on maskable interrupts unless the IF (interrupt-enable) flag in the EFLAGS register is set.

    — **Software-generated interrupts.** These are generated by INT *n* instruction. The processor does not provide a mechanism for masking interrupts generated in this manner.

- Exceptions

  — **Processor-detected exceptions.** These are generated when the processor detects program and machine errors. They are further classified as *faults*, *traps*, and *aborts*.

  — **Software-generated exceptions.** The INTO, INT3, BOUND, and INT*n* instructions generate exceptions. (The INT*n* instruction generates an exception when an exception vector number as an operand.) These instructions allow checks for specific exception conditions to be performed a specific points in the instruction stream. For example, the INT3 instruction causes a breakpoint exception to be generated.

This chapter describes the processor's interrupt and exception handling mechanism, when operating in protected mode. A detailed description of the exceptions and the conditions that cause them to be generated is given at the end of this chapter. See Chapter 12, *8086 Emulation*, for a description of the interrupt and exception mechanism for real-address and virtual-8086 mode.

5.2. EXCEPTION AND INTERRUPT VECTORS

The processor associates an identification number, called a *vector*, with each interrupt and exception. Table 5-1 shows the assignment of exception and interrupt vectors. This table also gives the interrupt or exception type of each exception, indicates whether an error code is saved on the stack for an exception, and gives the source of the exception or interrupt.

The NMI interrupt and the exceptions are assigned vectors in the range 0 through 31. Not all of these vectors are currently used by the processor. Unassigned vectors in this range are reserved for possible future uses. Do not use the reserved vectors.

The vectors in the range 32 to 255 are provided for maskable interrupts, generated either by asserting the INTR pin or by sending interrupt messages over the APIC bus. External interrupt controllers (such as Intel's 8259A Programmable Interrupt Controller) deliver one of these vectors to the processor on the system bus during its interrupt-acknowledge cycle. Any vectors in the range 32 through 255 are legal.

The INT *n* instruction can be used to generate an interrupt or exception from within software, by using a vector number as an operand. For example, the INT 35 instruction forces an implicit call to the interrupt handler for interrupt 35.

Table 5-1. Protected Mode Exceptions and Interrupts

Vector No.	Description	Interrupt or Exception Type	Error Code	Source
0	Divide Error (#DE)	Fault	No	DIV and IDIV instructions.
1	Debug (#DB)	Fault/ Trap	No	Any code or data reference.
2	NMI Interrupt	Non-Maskable	No	External interrupt.
3	Breakpoint (#BP)	Trap	No	INT3 instruction.
4	Overflow (#OF)	Trap	No	INTO instruction.
5	BOUND Range Exceeded (#BR)	Fault	No	BOUND instruction.
6	Invalid Opcode (#UD)	Fault	No	UD2 instruction or reserved opcode.
7	Device Not Available (#NM)	Fault	No	Floating-point or WAIT/FWAIT instruction.
8	Double Fault (#DF)	Abort	Yes (Zero)	Any instruction that can generate an exception, an NMI, or an INTR.
9	CoProcessor Segment Overrun (reserved)	Fault	No	Floating-point instruction. Pentium® Pro processor does not generate this exception.
10	Invalid TSS (#TS)	Fault	Yes	Task switch or TSS access.
11	Segment Not Present (#NP)	Fault	Yes	Loading segment registers or accessing system segments.
12	Stack Fault (#SS)	Fault	Yes	Stack operations and SS register loads.
13	General Protection (#GP)	Fault/Trap	Yes	Any memory reference and other protection checks.
14	Page Fault (#PF)	Fault	Yes	Any memory reference.
15	(Intel reserved. Do not use.)		No	
16	Floating-Point Error (#MF)	Fault	No	Floating-point or WAIT/FWAIT instruction.
17	Alignment Check (#AC)	Fault	Yes (Zero)	Any data reference in memory.
18	Machine Check (#MC)	Abort	Model Dependent	Model dependent.
19-31	(Intel reserved. Do not use.)			
32-255	Maskable Interrupts	Maskable		External interrupt or INT *n* instruction.

5.3. EXCEPTION CLASSIFICATIONS

Exceptions are classified as *faults*, *traps*, or *aborts* depending on the way they are reported and whether the instruction that caused the exception can be restarted with no loss of program or task continuity.

Faults
A fault is an exception that can generally be corrected and that, once corrected, allows the program to be restarted with no loss of continuity. When a fault is reported, the processor restores the machine state to the state prior to the beginning of execution of the faulting instruction. The return address (saved contents of the CS and EIP registers) for the fault handler points to the faulting instruction, rather than the instruction following the faulting instruction.

Traps
A trap is an exception that is reported immediately following the execution of the trapping instruction. Some traps allow execution of a program or task to be continued without loss of program continuity; others do not. The return address for the trap handler points to the instruction to be executed after the trapping instruction.

Aborts
An abort is an exception that does not always report the precise location of the instruction causing the exception and does not allow restart of the program or task that caused the exception. Aborts are used to report severe errors, such as hardware errors and inconsistent or illegal values in system tables.

5.4. PROGRAM OR TASK RESTART

To allow restarting of program or task following the handling of an exception or an interrupt, all exceptions except aborts are guaranteed to report the exception on a precise instruction boundary, and all interrupts are guaranteed to be taken on an instruction boundary.

For fault-class exceptions, the return instruction pointer that the processor saves when it generates the exception points to the faulting instruction. So, when a program or task is restarted following the handling of a fault, the faulting instruction is restarted (re-executed). Restarting the faulting instruction is commonly used to handle exceptions that are generated when access to an operand is blocked. The most common example of a fault is a page-fault exception(#PF) that occurs when a program or task references an operand in a page that is not in memory. When a page-fault exception occurs, the exception handler can load the page into memory and resume execution of the program or task by restarting the faulting instruction. To insure that this instruction restart is handled transparently to the currently executing program or task, the processor saves the necessary registers and stack pointers to allow it to restore itself to its state prior to the execution of the faulting instruction.

For trap-class exceptions, the return instruction pointer points to the instruction following the trapping instruction. If a trap is detected during an instruction which transfers execution, the return instruction pointer reflects the transfer. For example, if a trap is detected while executing a JMP instruction, the return instruction pointer points to the destination of the JMP instruction, not to the next address past the JMP instruction. Most trap exceptions allow program or task restart with no loss of continuity. For example, the overflow exception is a trapping exception. Here, the return instruction pointer points to the instruction following the INTO instruction that tested the OF (overflow) flag in the EFLAGS register. The trap handler for this exception resolves the overflow condition. Upon return from the trap handler, program or task execution continues at the next instruction following the INTO instruction.

The abort-class exceptions do not support reliable restarting of the program or task. Abort handlers generally are designed to collect diagnostic information about the state of the processor when the abort exception occurred and then perform a graceful system shutdown.

Interrupts rigorously support restarting of interrupted programs and tasks without loss of continuity. The return instruction pointer saved for an interrupt points to the next instruction to be executed at the instruction boundary where the processor took the interrupt. If the instruction just executed has a repeat prefix, the interrupt is taken at the end of the current iteration with the registers set to execute the next iteration.

The ability of the processor to speculatively execute instructions does not affect the taking of interrupts by the processor. Interrupts are taken at instruction boundaries located during the retirement phase of instruction execution; so, they are always taken in the "in-order" instruction stream. See Chapter 2, *Introduction to the Intel Pentium® Pro Processor*, in the *Pentium® Pro Family Developer's Manual, Volume 2* for more information about the Pentium Pro processor's microarchitecture and its support for out-of-order instruction execution.

5.5.   ENABLING AND DISABLING INTERRUPTS

The processor inhibits the generation of some interrupts, depending on the state of processor and of the IF and RF flags in the EFLAGS register, as described in the following sections.

5.5.1.   Handling Multiple NMIs

While an NMI interrupt handler is executing, the processor disables additional calls to the NMI handler until the next IRET instruction is executed. This blocking of subsequent NMIs prevents stacking up calls to the NMI handler. It is recommended that the NMI interrupt handler be accessed through an interrupt gate to disable maskable interrupts (see Section 5.5.2., "Masking Maskable Interrupts").

5.5.2.   Masking Maskable Interrupts

The IF flag can disable the servicing of maskable interrupts received on the processor's INTR# pin or through the local APIC (see Section 5.1., "Interrupt and Exception Overview"). When the IF flag is clear, maskable interrupts are ignored; when the IF flag is set, maskable interrupts are serviced. As with the other flags in the EFLAGS register, the processor clears the IF flag in response to a hardware reset.

The IF flag can be set or cleared with the STI (set interrupt-enable flag) and CLI (clear interrupt-enable flag) instructions, respectively. These instructions may be executed only if the CPL is an equal to or less than the IOPL. A general-protection exception (#GP) is generated if they are executed when the CPL is greater than the IOPL. (The effect of the IOPL on these instructions is modified slightly when the virtual mode extension is enabled by setting the VME flag in control register CR4, see Section 12.3., "Interrupt and Exception Handling in Virtual-8086 Mode".)

The IF flag is also affected by the following operations:

- The PUSHF instruction stores all flags on the stack, where they can be examined and modified. The POPF instruction can be used to load the modified form back into the EFLAGS register.

- Task switches and the POPF and IRET instructions load the EFLAGS register; therefore, they can be used to modify the setting of the IF flag.

- When an interrupt is handled through an interrupt gates, the IF flag is automatically clear, which disables maskable interrupts.

See the descriptions of the CLI, STI, PUSHF, POPF, and IRET instructions in Chapter 11, *Instruction Set Reference*, of the *Pentium® Pro Family Developer's Manual, Volume 2* for a detailed description of the operations these instructions are allowed to perform on the IF flag.

5.5.3. Masking Debug Exceptions

The RF (resume) flag in the EFLAGS register controls the response of the processor to instruction-breakpoint conditions (see the description of the RF flag in Section 2.3., "System Flags and Fields in the EFLAGS Register"). Its primary function is to prevent the processor from generating a debug exception (#DB) due to an instruction-breakpoint condition on a return from an exception or interrupt handler. When an exception occurs (other than a debug exception caused by an instruction-breakpoint condition) or when an interrupt occurs during a string instruction, the processor sets the RF flag in the EFLAGS image it that stores on the exception or interrupt handler's stack. Upon returning from the exception or interrupt handler and restoring the EFLAGS register from the image on the stack, the processor ignores instruction-breakpoint conditions for the duration of the next instruction (although it does respond to other debug exception conditions).

(The processor clears the RF flag following the successful completion of every instruction, except after the IRET instruction and after JMP, CALL, or INT *n* instructions that cause a task switch. Therefore, the RF flag remains set for no more than one instruction, the one executed immediately after the IRET or the task switch.)

When the processor generates a debug exception in response to an instruction-breakpoint condition, it does not set the RF flag in the EFLAGS image that it pushes onto the exception handler's stack. This action gives the exception handler the option of disabling the instruction breakpoint or setting the RF flag in the EFLAGS image on the stack to cause the instruction breakpoint to be ignored on a return from the exception handler. If the handler neither disables the instruction breakpoint nor sets the RF flag in the EFLAGS image, the processor will respond to the same instruction-breakpoint condition and generate another debug exception upon returning from the exception handler. This time, however, the processor automatically sets the RF flag to prevent further looping on the instruction-breakpoint condition.

5.5.4. Masking Exceptions and Interrupts When Switching Stacks

To switch to a different stack segment, software often uses a pair of instructions, for example:

```
MOV SS, AX
MOV ESP, StackTop
```

If an interrupt or exception occurs after the segment selector has been loaded into the SS register but before the ESP register has been loaded, these two parts of the logical address into the stack space are inconsistent for the duration of the interrupt or exception handler.

To prevent this situation, the processor inhibits interrupts, debug exceptions, and single-step trap exceptions after either a MOV to SS instruction or a POP to SS instruction, until the instruction boundary following the next instruction is reached. General-protection faults may still be generated. If the LSS instruction is used to modify the contents of the SS register (which is the recommended method of modifying this register), this problem does not occur.

5.6. PRIORITY AMONG SIMULTANEOUS EXCEPTIONS AND INTERRUPTS

If more than one exception or interrupt is pending at an instruction boundary, the processor services them in a predictable order. Table 5-2 shows the priority among classes of exception and interrupt sources. While priority among these classes is consistent throughout the architecture, exceptions within each class are implementation-dependent and may vary from processor to processor. The processor first services a pending exception or interrupt from the class which has the highest priority, transferring execution to the first instruction of the handler. Lower priority exceptions are discarded; lower priority interrupts are held pending. Discarded exceptions are re-generated when the interrupt handler returns execution to the point in the program or task where the exceptions and/or interrupts occurred.

5.7. INTERRUPT DESCRIPTOR TABLE (IDT)

The interrupt descriptor table (IDT) associates each exception or interrupt vector with a gate descriptor for the procedure or task used to services the associated exception or interrupt. Like the GDT and LDTs, the IDT is an array of 8-byte gate descriptors (in protected mode). Unlike the GDT, the first entry of the IDT may contain a descriptor. To form an index into the IDT, the processor scales the exception or interrupt vector by eight (the number of bytes in a gate descriptor). Because there are only 256 interrupt or exception vectors, the IDT need not contain more than 256 descriptors. It can contain fewer than 256 descriptors, because descriptors are required only for the interrupt and exception vectors that may occur.

Table 5-2. Priority Among Simultaneous Exceptions and Interrupts

Priority	Descriptions
1 (Highest)	Hardware Reset and Machine Checks - RESET - Machine Check
2	Trap on Task Switch - T flag in TSS is set
3	External Hardware Interventions - FLUSH - STOPCLK - SMI - INIT
4	Traps on the Previous Instruction - Breakpoints - Debug Trap Exceptions (TF flag set or data/I-O breakpoint)
5	External Interrupts - NMI Interrupts - Maskable Interrupts
6	Faults from Fetching Next Instruction - Code Breakpoint Fault - Code Segment Limit Violation - Code Page Fault
7	Faults from Decoding the Next Instruction - Instruction length > 15 bytes - Illegal Opcode - Coprocessor Not Available
8 (Lowest)	Faults on Executing an Instruction - Floating-point exception - Overflow - Bound error - Invalid TSS - Segment Not Present - Stack fault - General Protection - Data Page Fault - Alignment Check

The base addresses of the IDT should be aligned on an 8-byte boundary to maximize performance of cache line fills. The limit value is expressed in bytes and is added to the base address to get the address of the last valid byte. A limit value of 0 results in exactly 1 valid byte. Because IDT entries are always eight bytes long, the limit should always be one less than an integral multiple of eight (that is, $8N - 1$).

The IDT may reside anywhere in the linear address space. As shown in Figure 5-1, the processor locates the IDT using the IDTR register. This register holds both a 32-bit base address and 16-bit limit for the IDT.

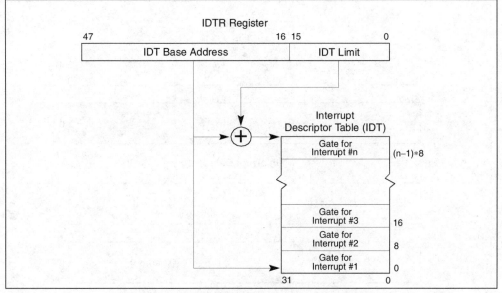

Figure 5-1. Relationship of the IDTR and IDT

The LIDT (load IDT register) and SIDT (store IDT register) instructions load and store the contents of the IDTR register, respectively. The LIDT instruction loads the IDTR register with the base address and limit held in a memory operand. This instruction can be executed only when the CPL is 0. It normally is used by the initialization code of an operating system when creating an IDT. An operating system also may use it to change from one IDT to another. The SIDT instruction copies the base and limit value stored in IDTR to memory. This instruction can be executed at any privilege level.

If a vector references a descriptor beyond the limit of the IDT, a general-protection exception ((#GP) is generated.

5.8. IDT DESCRIPTORS

The IDT may contain any of three kinds of gate descriptors:

- Task gate descriptor
- Interrupt gate descriptor
- Trap gate descriptor

Figure 5-2 shows the format of task gate, interrupt gate, and trap gate descriptors. The task gate in an IDT is the same as the task gate in the GDT or an LDT. An interrupt and task gates are very similar to call gates, and they are used for the same purpose.

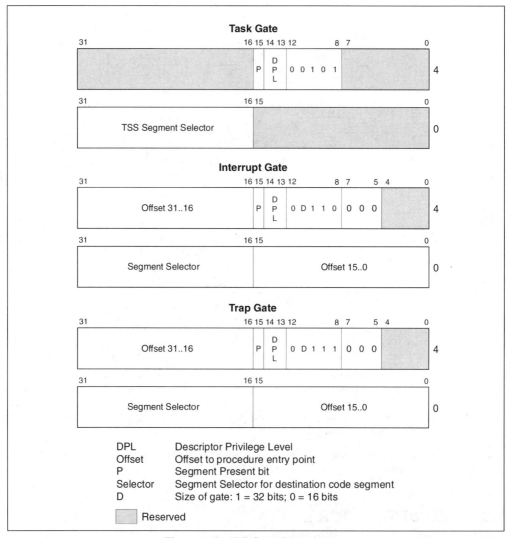

Figure 5-2. IDT Gate Descriptors

Calls to exception- or interrupt-handler procedures through an interrupt or trap gate are handled the same, except for the way the processor handles the IF flag in the EFLAGS register (see Section 5.9.1.1., "Flag Usage By Exception- or Interrupt-Handler Procedure").

5.9.   EXCEPTION- AND INTERRUPT HANDLING

The processor handles calls to exception- and interrupt-handlers the same way that it handles calls with a CALL instruction to a procedure or a task. When responding to an exception or interrupt, the processor uses the exception or interrupt vector as an index to a descriptor in the IDT. If the index points to an interrupt gate or trap gate, the processor calls the exception or interrupt handler in a manner similar to a CALL to a call gate. If index points to a task gate, the processor executes a task switch to the exception- or interrupt-handler task in a manner similar to a CALL to a task gate.

5.9.1.   Exception- or Interrupt-Handler Procedures

An interrupt gate or trap gate references an exception- or interrupt-handler procedure that runs in the context of the currently executing task (see Figure 5-3). The segment selector for the gate points to a segment descriptor for an executable code segment in either the GDT or the current LDT. The offset field of the gate descriptor points to the beginning of the exception- or interrupt-handling procedure.

When the processor performs a call to the exception- or interrupt-handler procedure, it saves the current states of the EFLAGS register, CS register, and EIP register on the stack (see Figure 5-4). (The CS and EIP registers provide a return instruction pointer for the handler.) If an exception causes an error code to be saved, it is pushed on the stack after the EIP value.

If the handler procedure is going to be executed at the same privilege level as the interrupted procedure, the handler uses the current stack.

If the handler procedure is going to be executed at a numerically lower privilege level, a stack switch occurs. When a stack switch occurs, a stack pointer for the stack to be returned to is also saved on the stack. (The SS and ESP registers provide a return stack pointer for the handler.) The segment selector and stack pointer for the stack to be used by the handler is obtained from the TSS for the currently executing task. The processor copies the EFLAGS, SS, ESP, CS, EIP, and error code information from the interrupted procedure's stack to the handler's stack.

To return from an exception- or interrupt-handler procedure, the handler must use the IRET (or IRETD) instruction. The IRET instruction is similar to the RET instruction except that it restores the saved flags into the EFLAGS register. The IOPL field of the EFLAGS register is restored only if the CPL is 0. The IF flag is changed only if the CPL is less than or equal to the IOPL. See "IRET/IRETD—Interrupt Return" in Chapter 11, *Instruction Set Reference*, of the *Pentium® Pro Family Developer's Manual, Volume 2* for the complete operation performed by the IRET instruction.

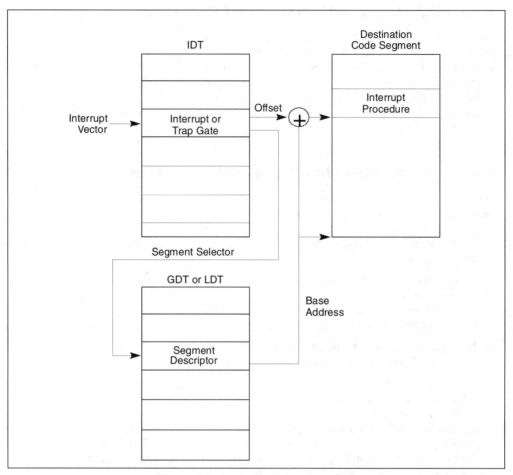

Figure 5-3. Interrupt Procedure Call

If a stack switch occurred when calling the handler procedure, the IRET instruction switches back to the interrupted procedures stack on the return.

5.9.1.1.　FLAG USAGE BY EXCEPTION- OR INTERRUPT-HANDLER PROCEDURE

When accessing an exception- or interrupt handler through either an interrupt gate or a trap gate, the processor clears the TF flag in the EFLAGS register after it saves the contents of the EFLAGS register on the stack. (On calls to exception and interrupt handlers, the processor also clears the VM, RF, and NT flags in the EFLAGS register.) Clearing the TF flag prevents instruction tracing from affecting interrupt response. A subsequent IRET instruction restores the TF (and VM, RF, and NT) flags to the values in the saved contents of the EFLAGS register on the stack.

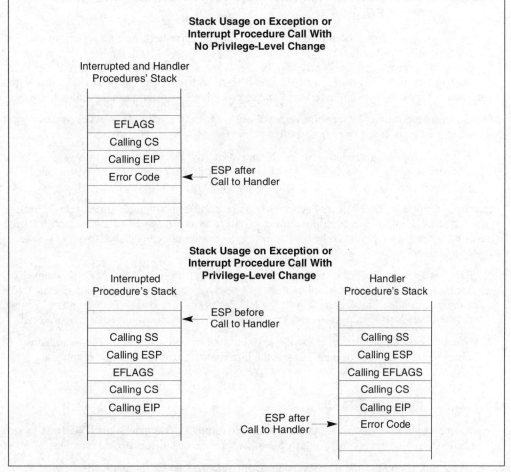

Figure 5-4. Stack Usage on Calls to Interrupt and Exception Handling Routines

The only difference between an interrupt gate and a trap gate is the way the processor handles the IF flag in the EFLAGS register. When accessing an exception- or interrupt-handling procedure through an interrupt gate, the processor clears the IF flag to prevents other interrupts from interfering with the current interrupt handler. A subsequent IRET instruction restores the IF flag to its value in the saved contents of the EFLAGS register on the stack. Accessing a handler procedure through a trap gate does not affect the IF flag.

5.9.1.2.   PROTECTION OF EXCEPTION- AND INTERRUPT-HANDLER PROCEDURES

The privilege-level protection for exception- and interrupt-handler procedures is similar to that for ordinary procedure calls. The processor does not permit an exception or interrupt to transfer execution to a procedure in a less privileged code segment (numerically greater privilege level). An attempt to violate this rule results in a general-protection exception (#GP). The protection mechanism for exception- and interrupt-handler procedures is different in the following ways:

- Because interrupt and exception vectors have no RPL, the RPL is not checked on implicit calls to exception and interrupt handlers.

- If an interrupt is generated with an INTn instruction, the interrupt or trap gate privilege level must allow access to the gate at the current privilege level. That is, for the INTn, INT3, and INTO instruction, CPL must be less than or equal to the DPL of the gate.

Because exceptions and interrupts generally do not occur at predictable times, these privilege rules effectively imposes restrictions on the privilege levels at which exception and interrupt handling procedures can run. Either of the following techniques can be used to avoid privilege-level violations.

- The exception or interrupt handler can be placed in a conforming code segment. This technique can be used for handlers that only need to access data available on the stack (for example, divide error exceptions). If the handler needs data from a data segment, the data segment needs to be accessible from privilege level 3, which would make it unprotected.

- The handler can be placed in a code segment with privilege level 0. This handler would always run, regardless of the CPL that the interrupted program or task is running at.

5.9.2.   Interrupt Tasks

When an exception- or interrupt handler is accessed through a task gate in the IDT, a task switch results. Handling an exception or interrupt with a separate task offers two advantages:

- The entire context of the interrupted program or task is saved automatically.

- The handler can be isolated from other tasks by giving it a separate address space. This is done by giving it a separate LDT.

A task gate in the IDT references a TSS descriptor in the GDT (see Figure 5-5). A switch to the handler task is handled in the same manner as an ordinary task switch (see Section 6.3., "Task Switching"). The link between the handler task and the interrupted task is stored in the link field of the handler task's TSS. If an exception caused an error code to be generated, this error code is copied to the stack of the new task.

When exception- or interrupt-handler tasks are used in an operating system, there are actually two mechanisms that can be used to dispatch tasks: the software scheduler (part of the operating system) and the hardware scheduler (part of the processor's interrupt mechanism). The software scheduler needs to accommodate interrupt tasks which may be dispatched when interrupts are enabled.

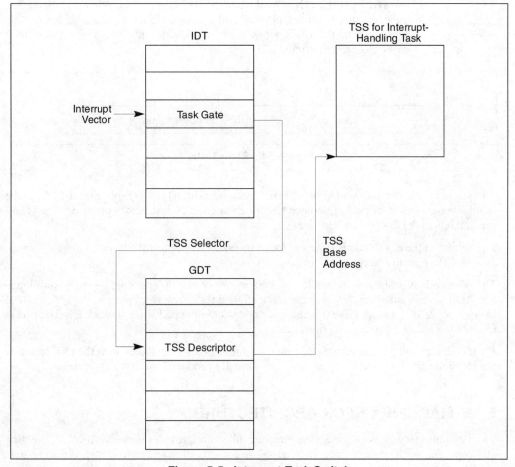

Figure 5-5. Interrupt Task Switch

5.10. ERROR CODE

When an exception condition is related to a specific segment, the processor pushes an error code onto the stack of the exception handler (whether it is a procedure or task). The error code has the format shown in Figure 5-6. The error code resembles a segment selector; however, instead of a TI flag and RPL field, the error code contains 3 flags:

EXT   **External event (bit 0).** When set, indicates that an event external to the program caused the exception.

IDT   **Descriptor location (bit 1).** When set, indicates that the index portion of the error code refers to a gate descriptor in the IDT; when clear, indicates that the index refers to a descriptor in the GDT or the current LDT.

TI   **GDT/LDT (bit 2).** Only used when the IDT flag is clear. When set, the TI flag indicates that the index portion of the error code refers to a segment or gate descriptor in the LDT; when clear, it indicates that the index refers to a descriptor in the current GDT.

Figure 5-6. Error Code

The segment selector index field provide an index into the IDT, GDT, or current LDT to the segment or gate selector being referenced by the error code. In some cases the error code is null (i.e., all bits in the lower word are clear).

The format of the error code is different for page-fault exceptions (#PF), see Chapter 5, "Interrupt 14—Page Fault Exception (#PF)".

The error code is pushed on the stack as a doubleword or word (depending on the default interrupt, trap, or task gate size). To keep the stack aligned for doubleword pushes, the upper half of the error code is reserved. Note that the error code is not popped when the IRET instruction is executed to return from an exception handler.

Error codes are not pushed on the stack for exceptions that are generated with the INTR# pin or the INTn instruction, even if an error code is normally produced for those exceptions.

5.11. MACHINE CHECK ARCHITECTURE

The Pentium Pro processor's machine check architecture provides a mechanism for detecting and reporting on hardware (machine) errors. It consists of a set of model-specific registers (MSRs) for setting up machine checking and recording any machine-check errors that are detected. The processor signals the detection of a machine check error by generating a machine-check exception (#MC). Chapter 16, *Machine Check Architecture*, gives a detailed description of the machine check architecture. See Chapter 5, "Interrupt 18—Machine Check Exception (#MC)" for information about the machine-check exception.

5.12. EXCEPTION REFERENCE

The following sections describe conditions which generate exceptions. They are arranged in the order of vector numbers. The information contained in these sections are as follows:

Exception Class	Indicates whether the exception class is a fault, trap, or abort type. Some exceptions can be either a fault or trap type, depending on the when the error condition is detected.
Description	Gives a general description of the purpose of the exception type. It also describes how the processor handles the exception.
Error Code	Indicates whether an error code is saved for the exception. If one is saved, the contents of the error code are described.
Saved Instruction Pointer	Describes which instruction the saved (or return) instruction pointer points to. It also indicates whether the pointer can be used to restart a faulting instruction.
Program State Change	Describes the effects of the exception on the state of the currently running program or task and the possibilities of restarting the program or task without loss of continuity.

Interrupt 0—Divide Error Exception (#DE)

Exception Class   Fault.

Description

Indicates the divisor operand for a DIV or IDIV instruction is 0 or that the result cannot be represented in the number of bits specified for the destination operand.

Error Code

None.

Saved Instruction Pointer

Saved contents of CS and EIP registers point to the instruction that generated the exception.

Program State Change

A program-state change does not accompany the divide error, because the exception occurs before the faulting instruction is executed.

Interrupt 1—Debug Exception (#DB)

Exception Class   Trap or Fault. The exception handler can distinguish between traps or faults by examining the contents of the DR6 register and other debug registers.

Description

Indicates that one or more of several debug-exception conditions has been detected. Whether the exception is a fault or a trap depends on the condition, as shown below:

Exception Condition	Exception Class
Instruction fetch breakpoint	Fault
Data write breakpoint	Trap
Data read or write breakpoint	Trap
I/O read or write breakpoint	Trap
General detect condition (in conjunction with in-circuit emulation)	Fault
Single-step	Trap
Task-switch	Trap

See Chapter 10, *Debugging and Performance Monitoring*, for detailed information about the debug exceptions.

Error Code

None. An exception handler can examine the debug registers to determine which condition caused the exception.

Saved Instruction Pointer

Fault—Saved contents of CS and EIP registers point to the instruction that generated the exception.

Trap—Saved contents of CS and EIP registers point to the instruction following the instruction that generated the exception.

Program State Change

Fault—A program-state change does not accompany the debug exception, because the exception occurs before the faulting instruction is executed.

Trap—A program-state change does not accompany the debug exception, because the exception occurs before the faulting instruction is executed. Here, all of the program-state changes required by the instruction do occur before the exception is generated.

Interrupt 2—NMI Interrupt

Exception Class   Trap.

Description

The non-maskable interrupt (NMI) is generated externally by asserting the processor's NMI# pin. This interrupt causes the NMI interrupt handler to be called.

Error Code

None.

Saved Instruction Pointer

The processor always takes an NMI interrupt on an instruction boundary. The saved contents of CS and EIP registers point to the next instruction to be executed at the point the interrupt is taken. See Section 5.4., "Program or Task Restart" for more information about when the processor takes NMI interrupts.

Program State Change

The instruction executing when an NMI interrupt is received is completed before the NMI is generated. A program or task can thus be restarted upon returning from an interrupt handler without loss of continuity, providing the interrupt handler saves the state of the processor before handling the interrupt restores the processor's state prior to a return.

Interrupt 3—Breakpoint Exception (#BP)

Exception Class   Trap.

Description

Indicates that a breakpoint instruction (INT3) was executed, causing a breakpoint trap to be generated. Typically, a debugger sets a breakpoint by replacing the first opcode byte of an instruction with the opcode for the INT3 instruction. (The INT3 instruction is one byte long, which makes it easy to replace an opcode in a code segment in RAM with the breakpoint opcode.) The operating system or a debugging tool can use a data segment mapped to the same physical address space as the code segment to place an INT3 instruction in places where it is desired to call the debugger.

With the Pentium Pro, Pentium, Intel486, and Intel386 processors, it is more convenient to set breakpoints with the debug registers. See Section 10.3.2., "Breakpoint Exception (#BP)—Interrupt Vector 3", for information about the breakpoint exception.

The breakpoint (#BP) exception can also be generated by executing the INT*n* instruction with an operand of 3. The action of this instruction (INT 3) is slightly different than that of the INT3 instruction (see "INTn/INTO/INT3—Call to Interrupt Procedure" in Chapter 11, *Instruction Set Reference*, of the *Pentium® Pro Family Developer's Manual, Volume 2*).

Error Code

None.

Saved Instruction Pointer

Saved contents of CS and EIP registers point to the instruction following the INT3 instruction.

Program State Change

Even though the EIP points to the instruction following the breakpoint instruction, the state of the program is essentially unchanged because the INT 3 instruction does not affect any register or memory locations. The debugger can thus resume the suspended program by replacing the INT 3 instruction that caused the breakpoint with the original opcode and decrementing the saved contents of the EIP register. Upon returning from the debugger, program execution resumes with the replaced instruction.

Interrupt 4—Overflow Exception (#OF)

Exception Class   Trap.

Description

Indicates that an overflow trap occurred when an INTO instruction was executed. The INTO instruction checks the state of the OF flag in the EFLAGS register. If the OF flag is set, an overflow trap is generated.

Some arithmetic instructions (such as the ADD and SUB) perform both signed and unsigned arithmetic. These instructions set the OF and CF flags in the EFLAGS register to indicate signed overflow and unsigned overflow, respectively. When performing arithmetic on signed operands, the OF flag can be tested directly or the INTO instruction can be used. The benefit of using the INTO instruction is that if the overflow exception is detected, an exception handler can be called automatically to handle the overflow condition.

Error Code

None.

Saved Instruction Pointer

The saved contents of CS and EIP registers point to the instruction following the INTO instruction.

Program State Change

Even though the EIP points to the instruction following the INTO instruction, the state of the program is essentially unchanged because the INTO instruction does not affect any register or memory locations. The debugger can thus resume the program execution upon returning from the overflow exception handler.

Interrupt 5—BOUND Range Exceeded Exception (#BR)

Exception Class   Fault.

Description

Indicates that a BOUND-range-exceeded fault occurred when a BOUND instruction was executed. The BOUND instruction checks a signed array index against signed limits upper and lower bounds of the array. If the array index is not within the bounds of the array, a BOUND-range-exceeded fault is generated.

Error Code

None.

Saved Instruction Pointer

The saved contents of CS and EIP registers point to the BOUND instruction that generated the exception.

Program State Change

A program-state change does not accompany the bounds-check fault, because the operands for the BOUND instruction are not modified. Returning from the BOUND-range-exceeded exception handler causes the BOUND instruction to be restarted.

Interrupt 6—Invalid Opcode Exception (#UD)

Exception Class   Fault.

Description

Indicates that the processor did one of the following things:

- Attempted to execute an invalid or reserved opcode.

- Attempted to execute an instruction with an operand type that is invalid for its accompanying opcode; for example, the source operand for a LES instruction is not a memory location.

- Executed a UD2 instruction.

- Detected a LOCK prefix that precedes an instruction that may not be locked or one that may be locked but the destination operand is not a memory location.

- Attempted to execute an LLDT, SLDT, LTR, STR, LSL, LAR, VERR, VERW, or ARPL instruction while in real-address or virtual-8086 mode.

- Attempted to execute the RSM instruction when not in SMM mode.

This exception is not generated until an attempt is made to retire the result of executing the invalid instruction; that is, decoding and speculatively attempting to execute of an invalid opcode does not generate this exception.

The opcodes D6 and F1 are undefined opcodes that are reserved by Intel. These opcodes, even though undefined, do not generate an invalid opcode exception.

The UD2 instruction is guaranteed to generate an invalid opcode exception.

Error Code

None.

Saved Instruction Pointer

The saved contents of CS and EIP registers point to the instruction that generated the exception.

Program State Change

A program-state change does not accompany an invalid-opcode fault, because the invalid instruction is not executed.

Interrupt 7—Device Not Available Exception (#NM)

Exception Class   Fault.

Description

Indicates one of the following things:

The device-not-available fault is generated by either of two conditions:

- The processor executed a floating-point instruction while the EM flag of register CR0 was set.

- The processor executed a floating-point instruction while the TS flag of register CR0 was set.

- The processor executed a WAIT or FWAIT instruction while the MP and TS flags of register CR0 were set.

The EM flag is set when the processor does not have an internal floating-point unit. An exception is then generated each time a floating-point instruction is encounter, allowing an exception handler to call floating-point instruction emulation routines.

The TS flag indicates that a context switch (task switch) has occurred since the last time a floating-point instruction was executed, but that the context of the FPU was not saved. When the TS flag is set, the processor generates a device-not-available exception each time a floating-point instruction is encountered. The exception handler can then save the context of the FPU before it executes the instruction. See Section 2.5., "Control Registers" for more information about the TS flag.

The MP flag in control register CR0 is used along with the TS bit to determine if WAIT or FWAIT instructions should generate a device-not-available exception. It extends the function of the TS flag to the WAIT and FWAIT instructions, giving the exception handler an opportunity to save the context of the FPU before the WAIT or FWAIT instruction is executed. This flag is provided primarily for use with the Intel 286 and Intel386 DX processors. For programs running on the Pentium Pro, Pentium, or Intel486 DX processors, or the Intel487 SX coprocessors, the MP flag should always be set; for programs running on the Intel486 SX processor, the MP flag should be clear.

Error Code

None.

Saved Instruction Pointer

The saved contents of CS and EIP registers point to the floating-point instruction or the WAIT/FWAIT instruction that generated the exception.

Program State Change

A program-state change does not accompany a device-not-available fault, because the instruction that generated the exception is not executed.

If the EM flag is set, the exception handler can then read the floating-point instruction pointed to by the EIP and call the appropriate emulation routine.

If the MP and TS flags are set or the TS flag alone is set, the exception handler can save the context of the FPU, clear the TS flag, and continue execution at the interrupted floating-point or WAIT/FWAIT instruction.

Interrupt 8—Double Fault Exception (#DF)

Exception Class   Abort.

Description

Indicates that the processor detected a second exception while calling an exception handler for a prior exception. Normally, when the processor detects another exception while trying to call an exception handler, the two exceptions can be handled serially. If, however, the processor cannot handle them serially, it signals the double-fault exception. To determine when two faults need to be signalled as a double fault, the processor divides the exceptions into three classes: benign exceptions, contributory exceptions, and page faults (see Table 5-3).

Table 5-3. Interrupt and Exception Classes

Class	Vector Number	Description
Benign Exceptions and Interrupts	1	Debug Exception
	2	NMI Interrupt
	3	Breakpoint
	4	Overflow
	5	BOUND Range Exceeded
	6	Invalid Opcode
	7	Device Not Available
	9	Coprocessor Segment Overrun
	16	Floating-Point Error
	17	Alignment Check
	18	Machine Check
	All	INTn
	All	INTR#
Contributory Exceptions	0	Divide Error
	10	Invalid TSS
	11	Segment Not Present
	12	Stack Fault
	13	General Protection
Page Faults	14	Page Fault

Table 5-4 shows the various combinations of exception classes that cause a double fault to be generated. A double-fault exception falls in the abort class of exceptions. The program or task cannot be restarted or resumed. The double-fault handler can be used to collect diagnostic information about the state of the machine and/or, when possible, to shut the machine down gracefully or restart the machine.

Table 5-4. Conditions for Generating a Double Fault

First Exception	Second Exception		
	Benign	Contributory	Page Fault
Benign	Handle Exceptions Serially	Handle Exceptions Serially	Handle Exceptions Serially
Contributory	Handle Exceptions Serially	Generate a Double Fault	Handle Exceptions Serially
Page Fault	Handle Exceptions Serially	Generate a Double Fault	Generate a Double Fault

An segment or page fault encountered while prefetching instructions is outside the domain of Table 5-4.

If another exception occurs while attempting to call the double-fault handler, the processor enters shutdown mode. This mode is similar to the state following execution of an HLT instruction. In this mode, the processor stops executing instructions until an NMI interrupt, hardware reset, or INIT is received. The processor generates a special bus cycle to indicate that it has entered shutdown mode. Software designers may need to be aware of the response of hardware to receiving this signal. For example, hardware may turn on an indicator light on the front panel, generate an NMI interrupt to record diagnostic information, or invoke reset initialization.

If the shutdown occurs while the processor is executing an NMI interrupt handler, then only a hardware reset can restart the processor.

Error Code

Zero. The processor always pushes an error code of 0 onto the stack of the double-fault handler.

Saved Instruction Pointer

The saved contents of CS and EIP registers are undefined.

Program State Change

A program-state following a double-fault exception is undefined. The program or task cannot be resumed or restarted. The only available action of the double-fault exception handler is to collect context information for use in diagnostics and shut down or reset the processor.

Interrupt 9—CoProcessor Segment Overrun

Exception Class   Abort. (**Intel reserved; do not use. The processor does not generate this exception.**)

Description

Indicates that an Intel386 CPU-based systems with an Intel387 math coprocessor detected a page or segment violation while transferring the middle portion of an Intel387 math coprocessor operand. The Pentium Pro, Pentium, and Intel486 processors do not generate this exception; instead, this condition is detected with a general protection exception (#GP), interrupt 13.

Error Code

None.

Saved Instruction Pointer

The saved contents of CS and EIP registers point to the instruction that generated the exception.

Program State Change

A program-state following a coprocessor segment-overrun exception is undefined. The program or task cannot be resumed or restarted. The only available action of the double-fault exception handler is to save the instruction pointer and reinitialize the FPU using the FNINIT instruction.

Interrupt 10—Invalid TSS Exception (#TS)

Exception Class   Fault.

Description

Indicates that a task switch was attempted that referenced an invalid TSS. It also indicates that a stack segment selector obtained from a TSS was beyond the GDT or LDT limit, did not point to a writable data segment, did not have the proper RPL value, or did not reference a segment descriptor with the proper DPL value. Table 5-5 shows the conditions that will cause an invalid-TSS exception to be generated. In general, these invalid conditions result from protection violations for the TSS descriptor, the LDT that contains the TSS descriptor, or the stack, code, or data segments referenced by the TSS.

Table 5-5. Invalid TSS Conditions

Error Code Index	Invalid Condition
TSS segment selector index	TSS segment limit less than 67H
LDT segment selector index	Invalid LDT or LDT not present
Stack segment selector index	Stack segment selector exceeds descriptor table limit
Stack segment selector index	Stack segment is not writable
Stack segment selector index	Stack segment DPL not compatible with CPL
Stack segment selector index	Stack segment selector RPL not compatible with CPL
Code segment selector index	Code segment selector exceeds descriptor table limit
Code segment selector index	Code segment is not executable
Code segment selector index	Non-conforming code segment DPL not equal to CPL
Code segment selector index	Conforming code segment DPL greater than CPL
Data segment selector index	Data segment selector exceeds descriptor table limit
Data segment selector index	Data segment not readable

This exception can generated either in the context of the original task or in the context of the new task. Until the processor has completely verified the presence of the new TSS, the exception is generated in the context of the original task. Once the existence of the new TSS is verified, the task switch is considered complete. Any invalid-TSS conditions detected after this point are handled in the context of the new task. (A task switch is considered complete when the TR register is loaded with the segment selector for the new TSS and, if the switch is due to a procedure call or interrupt, the link field of the new TSS references the old TSS.)

To insure that a TSS is available to process the exception, the invalid-TSS exception handler must be a task called using a task gate.

Error Code

An error code containing the segment selector index for the segment descriptor that caused the violation is pushed onto the stack of the exception handler. If the EXT flag is set, it indicates that the exception was caused by an event external to the currently running program (for example, if an external interrupt handler using a task gate attempted a task switch to an invalid TSS).

Saved Instruction Pointer

If the exception condition was detected before the task switch was carried out, the saved contents of CS and EIP registers point to the instruction that invoked the task switch. If the exception condition was detected after the task switch was carried out, the saved contents of CS and EIP registers point to the first instruction of the new task.

Program State Change

The ability of the invalid-TSS handler to recover from the fault depends on the error condition than causes the fault. See Section 6.3., "Task Switching" for more information on the task switch process and the possible recovery actions that can be taken.

If an invalid TSS exception occurs during a task switch, it can occur before or after the commit-to-new-task point. If it occurs before the commit point, no program state change occurs. If it occurs after the commit point (when segment descriptor information for the new segment selectors have been loaded in the segment registers), the processor will load all the state information from the new TSS before it generates the exception. During a task switch, the processor first loads all the segment registers with segment selectors from the TSS, then checks their contents for validity. If an invalid TSS exception is discovered, the remaining segment registers are loaded but not checked for validity and therefore may not be usable for referencing memory. The invalid TSS handler should not rely on being able to use the segment selectors found in the CS, SS, DS, ES, FS, and GS registers without causing another exception. The exception handler should load all segment registers before trying to resume the new task; otherwise, general-protection exceptions (#GP) may result later under conditions that make diagnosis more difficult. There are three ways to handle this situation:

- Handle the invalid TSS exception with a task. The task switch back to the interrupted task causes the processor to check the registers as it loads them from the TSS.

- Use the MOV or the PUSH and POP instructions on all data segment registers. Each POP instruction causes the processor to check the new contents of the segment register.

- Check the saved contents of each data segment register in the TSS, simulating the test that the processor makes when it loads a segment register.

Interrupt 11—Segment Not Present (#NP)

Exception Class   Fault.

Description

Indicates that the present flag of a segment or gate descriptor is clear. The processor can generate this exception during any of the following operations:

- While attempting to load CS, DS, ES, FS, or GS registers. [Detection of a not-present segment while loading the SS register causes a stack fault exception (#SS) to be generated.] This situation can occur while performing a task switch.

- While attempting to load the LDTR using an LLDT instruction. Detection of a not-present LDT while loading the LDTR during a task switch operation causes an invalid-TSS exception (#TS) to be generated.

- When executing the LTR instruction and the TSS is marked not present.

- While attempting to use a gate descriptor or TSS that is marked segment-not-present, but is otherwise valid.

An operating system typically uses the segment-not-present exception to implement virtual memory at the segment level. If the exception handler loads the segment and returns, the interrupted program or task resumes execution.

A not-present indication in a gate descriptor, however, does not indicate that a segment is not present (because gates do not correspond to segments). The operating system may use the present flag for gate descriptors to trigger exceptions of special significance to the operating system.

Error Code

An error code containing the segment selector index for the segment descriptor that caused the violation is pushed onto the stack of the exception handler. If the EXT flag is set, it indicates that the exception resulted from an external event (NMI or INTR) that caused an interrupt, which subsequently referenced a not-present segment. The IDT bit is set if the error code refers to an IDT entry (e.g., an INT instruction referencing a not-present gate).

Saved Instruction Pointer

The saved contents of CS and EIP registers normally point to the instruction that generated the exception. If the exception occurred while loading segment descriptors for the segment selectors in a new TSS, the CS and EIP registers point to the first instruction in the new task. If the exception occurred while accessing a gate descriptor, the CS and EIP registers point to the instruction that invoked the access (for example a CALL instruction that references a call gate).

Program State Change

If the segment-not-present exception occurs as the result of loading a register (CS, DS, SS, ES, FS, GS, or LDTR), a program-state change does accompany the exception, because the register is loaded. Recovery from this exception is possible by simply loading the missing segment into memory and setting the present flag in the segment's segment descriptor.

If the segment-not-present exception occurs while accessing a gate descriptor, a program-state change does not accompany the exception. Recovery from this exception is possible merely by setting the present flag in the segment's segment descriptor.

If a segment-not-present exception occurs during a task switch, it can occur before or after the commit-to-new-task point. If it occurs before the commit point, no program state change occurs. If it occurs after the commit point, the processor will load all the state information from the new TSS (without performing any additional limit, present, or type checks) before it generates the exception. The segment-not-present exception handler should thus not rely on being able to use the segment selectors found in the CS, SS, DS, ES, FS, and GS registers without causing another exception. (See the Program State Change Chapter 5, "Interrupt 10—Invalid TSS Exception (#TS)" for additional information on how to handle this situation.)

Interrupt 12—Stack Fault Exception (#SS)

Exception Class   Fault.

Description

Indicates that one of the following stack related conditions was detected:

- A limit violation is detected during an operation that refers to the SS register. Operations that can cause a limit violation include stack-oriented instructions such as POP, PUSH, CALL, RET, IRET, ENTER, and LEAVE, as well as other memory references which implicitly or explicitly use the SS register (for example, MOV AX, [BP+6] or MOV AX, SS:[EAX+6]). The ENTER instruction generates this exception when there is not enough stack space for allocating local variables.

- A not-present stack segment is detected when attempting to load the SS register. This violation can occur during the execution of a task switch, a CALL instruction to a different privilege level, a return to a different privilege level, an LSS instruction, or a MOV or POP instruction to the SS register.

Recovery from this fault is possible by either extending the limit of the stack segment (in the case of a limit violation) or loading the missing stack segment into memory (in the case of a not-present violation.

Error Code

If the exception is caused by a not-present stack segment or by overflow of the new stack during an inter-privilege-level call, the error code contains a segment selector to the segment which caused the exception. Here, the exception handler can test the present flag the segment descriptor pointed to determine the cause of the exception. For a normal limit violation (on a stack segment already in use) the error code is set to 0.

Saved Instruction Pointer

The saved contents of CS and EIP registers generally point to the instruction that generated the exception. However, when the exception results from attempting to load a not-present stack segment during a task switch, the CS and EIP registers point to the first instruction of the new task.

Program State Change

A program-state change does not generally accompany a stack-fault exception, because the instruction that generated the fault is not executed. Here, the instruction can be restarted after the exception handler has corrected the stack fault condition.

When a stack-fault exception occurs during a task switch, the segment registers may not be usable for addressing memory. During a task switch, the selector values are loaded before the descriptors are checked. If a stack exception is generated, the remaining segment registers not have been checked. The stack fault handler should not expect to use the segment selectors found in the CS, SS, DS, ES, FS, and GS registers following a stack-fault exception without causing another exception. The exception handler should check all segment registers before trying to resume the new task; otherwise, general protection faults may result later under conditions that are more difficult to diagnose.

If a stack fault occurs during a task switch, it can occur before or after the commit-to-new-task point. If it occurs before the commit point, no program state change occurs. If it occurs after the commit point, the processor will load all the state information from the new TSS (without performing any additional limit, present, or type checks) before it generates the exception. The stack fault handler should thus not rely on being able to use the segment selectors found in the CS, SS, DS, ES, FS, and GS registers without causing another exception. (See Chapter 5, "Interrupt 10—Invalid TSS Exception (#TS)" for additional information on how to handle this situation.)

Interrupt 13—General Protection Exception (#GP)

Exception Class   Fault.

Description

Indicates that the processor detected one of a class of protection violations called "general-protection violations." The conditions that cause this exception to be generated comprise all the protection violations that do not cause other exceptions to be generated (such as, invalid-TSS, segment-not-present, stack-fault, or page-fault exceptions). The following conditions cause general-protection exceptions to be generated:

- Exceeding the segment limit when accessing the CS, DS, ES, FS, or GS segments.

- Exceeding the segment limit when referencing a descriptor table.

- Transferring execution to a segment that is not executable.

- Writing to a code segment or a read-only data segment.

- Reading from an execute-only code segment.

- Loading the SS register with a segment selector for a read-only segment (unless the selector comes from a TSS during a task switch, in which case an invalid-TSS exception occurs).

- Loading the SS, DS, ES, FS, or GS register with a segment selector for a system segment.

- Loading the DS, ES, FS, or GS register with a segment selector for an execute-only code segment.

- Loading the SS register with the segment selector of an executable segment or a null segment selector.

- Loading the CS register with a segment selector for a data segment or a null segment selector

- Accessing memory using the DS, ES, FS, or GS register when it contains a null segment selector.

- Switching to a busy task during a call or jump to a TSS or a return to a TSS initiated with an IRET instruction.

- Using a segment selector on task switch that points to a TSS descriptor in the current LDT. TSS descriptors can only reside in the GDT.

- Violating any of the privilege rules described in Chapter 4, *Protection*.

- Exceeding the instruction length limit of 15 bytes (this only can occur when redundant prefixes are placed before an instruction).

- Loading the CR0 register with a set PG flag (paging enabled) and a clear PE flag (protection disabled).

- Loading the CR0 register with a set NW flag and a clear CD flag.

- Referencing an entry in the IDT (following an interrupt or exception) that is not an interrupt, trap, or task gate.

- Attempting to access an interrupt or exception handler through an interrupt or trap gate from virtual-8086 mode when the handler's DPL is greater than 0.

- Attempting to write a 1 into a reserved bit of CR4.

- Attempting to execute a privileged instruction when the CPL is not equal to 0 (see Section 4.9., "Privileged Instructions" for a list of privileged instructions).

- Writing to a reserved bit in an MSR.

- Accessing a gate that contains a null segment selector.

- Executing the INTn instruction when the CPL is greater than the DPL of the referenced interrupt, trap, or task gate.

- The segment selector in a call, interrupt, or trap gate does not point to a code segment.

- The segment selector operand in the LLDT instruction is a local type (TI flag is set) or does not point to a segment descriptor of the LDT type.

- The segment selector operand in the LTR instruction is local or points to a TSS that is not available.

- The target code segment selector for a call, jump, or return is null.

- If the PAE flag in control register CR4 is set and the processor detects any reserved bits in a page-directory-pointer-table entry set to 1. These bits are checked during a write to control registers CR0, CR3, or CR4 that causes a reloading of the page-directory-pointer-table entry.

A program or task can be restarted following any general-protection exception. If the exception occurs while attempting to call an interrupt handler, the interrupted program can be restartable, but the interrupt may be lost.

Error Code

The processor pushes an error code onto the exception handler's stack. If the fault condition was detected while accessing a segment descriptor, the error code contains a segment selector to the descriptor; otherwise, the error code is 0. The source of the selector in an error code may be any of the following:

- An operand of the instruction.

- A selector from a gate which is the operand of the instruction.

- A selector from a TSS involved in a task switch.

Saved Instruction Pointer

The saved contents of CS and EIP registers point to the instruction that generated the exception.

Program State Change

In general, a program-state change does not accompany a general-protection exception, because the invalid instruction or operation is not executed. An exception handler can be designed to correct all of the conditions that cause general-protection exceptions and restart the program or task without any loss of program continuity.

If a general-protection exception occurs during a task switch, it can occur before or after the commit-to-new-task point. If it occurs before the commit point, no program state change occurs. If it occurs after the commit point, the processor will load all the state information from the new TSS (without performing any additional limit, present, or type checks) before it generates the exception. The general-protection exception handler should thus not rely on being able to use the segment selectors found in the CS, SS, DS, ES, FS, and GS registers without causing another exception. (See the Program State Change section of Chapter 5, "Interrupt 10—Invalid TSS Exception (#TS)" for additional information on how to handle this situation.)

Interrupt 14—Page Fault Exception (#PF)

Exception Class   Fault.

Description

Indicates that, with paging enabled (the PG flag in the CR0 register is set), the processor detected one of the following conditions while using the page-translation mechanism to translate a linear address to a physical address:

- The P (present) flag in a page-directory or page-table entry needed for the address translation is clear, indicating that a page table or the page containing the operand is not present in physical memory.

- The procedure does not have sufficient privilege to access the indicated page (for example, a procedure running in user mode attempts to access a supervisor-mode page).

The exception handler can recover from page-not-present conditions and restart the program or task without any loss of program continuity. It can also restart the program or task after a privilege violation, but the problem that caused the privilege violation may be uncorrectable.

Error Code

Yes (special format). The processor provides the page fault handler with two items of information to aid in diagnosing the exception and recovering from it:

- An error code on the stack. The error code for a page fault has a format different from that for other exceptions (see Figure 5-7). The error code tells the exception handler three things:

  - The P flag indicates whether the exception was due to a not-present page (0) or to either an access rights violation or the use of a reserved bit (1).

  - The W/R flag indicates whether the memory access that caused the exception was a read (0) or write (1).

  - The U/S flag indicates whether the processor was executing at user mode (1) or supervisor mode (0) at the time of the exception.

  - The RSVD flag indicates that the processor detected 1s in reserved bits of the page directory, when the PSE or PAE flags in control register CR4 are set to 1.

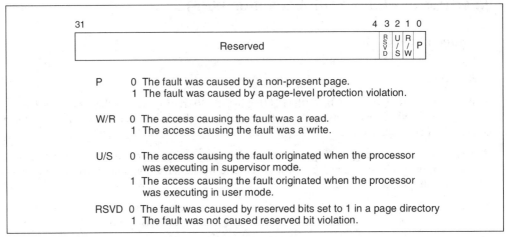

Figure 5-7. Page Fault Error Code

- The contents of the CR2 register. The processor loads the CR2 register with the 32-bit linear address that generated the exception. The page-fault handler can use this address to locate the corresponding page directory and page table entries. If another page fault occurs during execution of the page fault handler, the handler will push the contents of the CR2 register onto the stack.

If a page fault is caused by a page-level protection violation, the access and dirty flags in the page directory are set when the fault occur. The access flag in the page table is only set if there are no page-level protection violations or if a read/write violation occurs.

Saved Instruction Pointer

The saved contents of CS and EIP registers generally point to the instruction that generated the exception. If the page-fault exception occurred during a task switch, the CS and EIP registers may point to the first instruction of the new task (as described in the following "Program State Change" section).

Program State Change

A program-state change does not normally accompany a page-fault exception, because the instruction that causes the exception to be generated is not executed. After the page-fault exception handler has corrected the violation (for example, loaded the missing page into memory), execution of the program or task can be resumed.

When a page-fault exception is generated during a task switch, the program-state may change, as follows. During a task switch, a page-fault exception can occur during any of following operations:

- While writing the state of the original task into the TSS of that task.

- While reading the GDT to locate the TSS descriptor of the new task.

- While reading the TSS of the new task to check the types of segment descriptors from the TSS.

- While reading the LDT of the new task to verify the segment registers stored in the new TSS.

In the last two cases the exception occurs in the context of the new task. The instruction pointer refers to the first instruction of the new task, not to the instruction which caused the task switch (or the last instruction to be executed, in the case of an interrupt). If the design of the operating system permits page faults to occur during task-switches, the page-fault handler should be called through a task gate.

If a page fault occurs during a task switch, it can occur before or after the commit-to-new-task point. If it occurs before the commit point, no program state change occurs. If it occurs after the commit point, the processor will load all the state information from the new TSS (without performing any additional limit, present, or type checks) before it generates the exception. The page fault handler should thus not rely on being able to use the segment selectors found in the CS, SS, DS, ES, FS, and GS registers without causing another exception. (See the Program State Change section in Chapter 5, "Interrupt 10—Invalid TSS Exception (#TS)" for additional information on how to handle this situation.)

Additional Exception Handling Information

Special care should be taken to ensure that a page fault does not cause the processor to use an invalid stack pointer (SS:ESP). Software written for 16-bit Intel Architecture processors often use a pair of instructions to change to a new stack, for example:

```
MOV SS, AX
MOV SP, StackTop
```

When executing this code on one of the 32-bit Intel Architecture processors, it is possible to get a page fault after the segment selector has been loaded into the SS register but before the ESP register has been loaded. At this point, the two parts of the stack pointer (SS:ESP) are inconsistent. The new stack segment is being used with the old stack pointer.

The processor does not use the inconsistent stack pointer if the page-fault handler switches to a well defined stack (that is, the handler is a task or a more privileged procedure). However, if the page fault occurs at the same privilege level and in the same task as the page-fault handler, the processor will attempt to use the stack indicated by the inconsistent stack pointer.

In systems that use paging and handle page faults within the faulting task (with trap or interrupt gates), software executing at the same privilege level as the page fault handler should initialize a new stack by using the LSS instruction rather than a pair of MOV instructions, as describe earlier in this note. When the page fault handler is running at privilege level 0 (the normal case), the problem is limited to procedures or tasks that run at privilege level 0, typically the kernel of the operating system.

Interrupt 16—Floating-Point Error Exception (#MF)

Exception Class   Fault.

Description

Indicates that the FPU has detected a floating-point-error exception. The NE flag in the register CR0 must be set for an interrupt 16, floating-point-error exception to be generated. (See Section 2.5., "Control Registers" for a detailed description of the NE flag.)

While executing floating-point instructions, the FPU detects and reports six types of floating-point errors:

- Invalid operation (#I)

  — Stack overflow or underflow (#IS)

  — Invalid arithmetic operation (#IA)

- Divide-by-zero (#Z)

- Denormalized operand (#D)

- Numeric overflow (#O)

- Numeric underflow (#U)

- Inexact result (precision) (#P)

For each of these error types, the FPU provides a flag in the FPU status register and a mask bit in the FPU control register. If the FPU detects a floating-point error and the mask bit for the error is set, the FPU handles the error automatically by generating a predefined (default) response and continuing program execution. The default responses have been designed to provide a reasonable result for most floating-point applications.

If the mask for the error is clear and the NE flag in register CR0 is set, the FPU does the following:

1. Sets the necessary flag in the FPU status register

2. Waits until the next "waiting" floating-point instruction or WAIT/FWAIT instruction is encountered in the program's instruction stream. (The FPU checks for pending floating-point exceptions on "waiting" instructions prior to executing them. All the floating-point instructions except the FNINIT, FNCLEX, FNSTSW, FNSTSW AX, FNSTCW, FNSTENV, and FNSAVE instructions are "waiting" instructions.)

3. Generates an internal error signal that cause the processor to generate a floating-point-error exception.

All of the floating-point-error conditions can be recovered from. The floating-point-error exception handler can determine the error condition that caused the exception from the settings of the flags in the FPU status word. See Section 7.7.3., "Software Exception Handling" in Chapter 7, *Floating-Point Unit*, of the *Pentium® Pro Family Developer's Manual, Volume 2* for more information on handling floating-point-error exceptions.

Error Code

None. The FPU provides its own error information.

Saved Instruction Pointer

The saved contents of CS and EIP registers point to the floating-point or WAIT/FWAIT instruction that was about to be executed when the floating-point-error exception was generated. This is not the faulting instruction in which the error condition was detected. The address of the faulting instruction is contained in the FPU instruction pointer register. See Section 7.3.7., "The Floating-Point Instruction and Data Pointers" in Chapter 7, *Floating-Point Unit*, of the *Pentium® Pro Family Developer's Manual, Volume 2* for more information about information the FPU saves for use in handling floating-point-error exceptions.

Program State Change

A program-state change generally accompanies a floating-point-error exception because the handling of the exception is delayed until the next waiting floating-point or WAIT/FWAIT instruction following the faulting instruction. The FPU, however, saves sufficient information about the error condition to allow recovery from the error and re-execution of the faulting instruction if needed.

In situations where non-floating-point instructions depend on the results of a floating-point instruction, a WAIT or FWAIT instruction can be inserted in front of a dependent instruction to force a pending floating-point-error exception to be handled before the dependent instruction is executed. See Section 7.9., "Floating-Point Exception Synchronization" in Chapter 7, *Floating-Point Unit*, of the *Pentium® Pro Family Developer's Manual, Volume 2* for more information about synchronization of floating-point-error exceptions.

Interrupt 17—Alignment Check Exception (#AC)

Exception Class   Fault.

Description

Indicates that the processor detected an unaligned memory operand when alignment checking was enabled. Alignment checks are only carried out in data (or stack) segments (not in code or system segments). An example of an alignment-check violation is a word stored at an odd byte address, or a doubleword stored at an address that is not an integer multiple of 4. Table 5-6 lists the alignment requirements various data types recognized by the processor.

Table 5-6. Alignment Requirements by Data Type

Data Type	Address Must Be Divisible By
Word	2
Doubleword	4
Single Real	4
Double Real	8
Extended Real	8
Segment Selector	2
32-bit Far Pointer	2
48-bit Far Pointer	4
32-bit Pointer	4
GDTR, IDTR, LDTR, or Task Register Contents	4
FSTENV/FLDENV Save Area	4 or 2, depending on operand size
FSAVE/FRSTOR Save Area	4 or 2, depending on operand size
Bit String	2 or 4 depending on the operand-size attribute.

To enable alignment checking, the following conditions must be true:

- AM flag in CR0 register is set.
- AC flag in the EFLAGS register is set.
- The CPL is 3 (protected mode or virtual-8086 mode).

Alignment-check faults are generated only when operating at privilege level 3 (user mode). Memory references that default to privilege level 0, such as segment descriptor loads, do not generate alignment-check faults, even when caused by a memory reference made from privilege level 3.

Storing the contents of the GDTR, IDTR, LDTR, or task register in memory while at privilege level 3 can generate an alignment-check fault. Although application programs do not normally store these registers, the fault can be avoided by aligning the information stored on an odd word-address.

FSAVE and FRSTOR instructions generate unaligned references which can cause alignment-check faults. These instructions are rarely needed by application programs.

Error Code

Yes (always zero).

Saved Instruction Pointer

The saved contents of CS and EIP registers point to the instruction that generated the exception.

Program State Change

A program-state change does not accompany an alignment-check fault, because the instruction is not executed.

Interrupt 18—Machine Check Exception (#MC)

Exception Class   Abort.

Description

Indicates that the processor detected an internal machine error. The machine check exception is model-specific, available only on the Pentium Pro and Pentium processors. The implementation of the machine check exception is different on the Pentium Pro and Pentium processors, may not be compatible with future Intel Architecture processors. (Use the CPUID instruction to determine whether this feature is present.)

The machine check exception and machine check architecture is discussed in detail in Chapter 16, *Machine Check Architecture*.

Error Code

None. Error information is provide by machine-check MSRs.

Saved Instruction Pointer

If the EIPV flag in the MCG_STATUS MSR is set, the saved contents of CS and EIP registers are directly associated with the error that caused the machine-check exception to be generated; if the flag is clear, the saved instruction pointer may not be associated with the error (see Section 16.3.1.2., "MCG_STATUS MSR").

Program State Change

A program-state change always accompanies a machine-check exception. If the machine-check mechanism is enabled (the MCE flag in control register CR4 is set), a machine-check exception results in an abort; that is, information about the exception can be collected from the machine check MSRs, but the program cannot be restarted. If the machine-check mechanism is not enabled, a machine-check exception causes the processor to enter the shutdown state.

Interrupts 32 to 255—Software Interrupts or Responses to the INTR# Signal

Exception Class   No applicable.

Description

Indicates that the processor did one of the following things:

* Executed an INT*n* instruction, where the instruction operand is one of the vector numbers from 32 through 255.

* Responded to an interrupt request at the INTR# pin, when the pin is associated with one of the interrupt vectors from 32 through 255.

Error Code

None.

Saved Instruction Pointer

The saved contents of CS and EIP registers point to the instruction that follows the INT*n* instruction or instruction following the instruction on which the INTR# signal occurred.

Program State Change

A program-state change does not accompany interrupts generated by the INT*n* instruction or the INTR# signal. The INT*n* instruction generates the interrupt within the instruction stream. When the processor receives an INTR# signal, it commits all state changes for all previous instructions before it responds to the interrupt; so, program execution can resume upon returning from the interrupt handler.

intel®

6

Task Management

CHAPTER 6
TASK MANAGEMENT

This chapter describes the Pentium Pro processor's task management facilities. These facilities are only available when the processor is running in protected mode.

6.1. TASK-MANAGEMENT OVERVIEW

A task is a unit of work that a processor can dispatch, execute, and suspend. It can be used to execute a program, a task or process, an operating-system service utility, an interrupt or exception handler, or a kernel or executive utility.

The Pentium Pro processor provides a mechanism for saving the state of a task, for dispatching tasks for execution, and for switching from one task to another. When operating in protected mode, all processor execution takes place from within a task. Even simple applications must define at least one task. More complex systems can use the processor's task management facilities to support multitasking applications.

6.1.1. Task Structure

A task is made up of two parts: a task execution space and a task state segment (TSS). The task execution space consists of a code segment, a stack segment, and one or more data segments (see Figure 6-1). If an operating system or executive uses the processor's privilege-level protection mechanism, the task execution space also provides a separate stack for each privilege level.

The TSS specifies the segments that make up the task execution space and provides a storage place for task state information. In multitasking systems, the TSS also provides a mechanism for linking tasks.

A task is identified by the segment selector for its TSS. When a task is loaded into the processor for execution, the task's segment selector and the base address and limit for the TSS are loaded into the task register (see Section 2.4.4., "Task Register (TR)").

If paging is implemented for the task, the base address of the page directory used by the task is loaded into control register CR3.

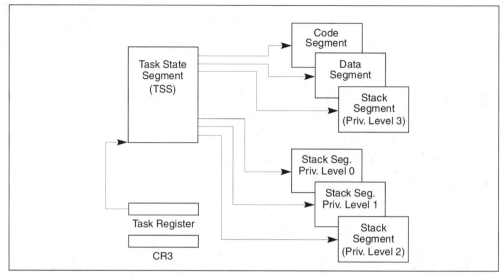

Figure 6-1. Structure of a Task

6.1.2. Task State

The following items define the state of the currently executing task:

- The task's current execution space, defined by the segment selectors in the segment registers (CS, DS, SS, ES, FS, and GS).

- The state of the general-purpose registers.

- The state of the EFLAGS register.

- The state of the EIP register.

- The state of control register CR3.

- The state of the task register.

- The state of the LDTR register.

- The I/O map base address and I/O map (contained in the TSS).

- Stack pointers to the privilege 0, 1, and 2 stacks (contained in the TSS).

- Link to previously executed task (contained in the TSS).

Prior to dispatching a task, all of these items are contained in the task's TSS, except the state of the task register. Also, the complete contents of the LDTR register are not contained in the TSS, only the segment selector for the LDT.

6.1.3.   Executing a Task

Software or the processor can dispatch a task for execution in one of the following ways:

* A explicit call to a task with the CALL instruction.

* A explicit jump to a task with the JMP instruction.

* An implicit call (by the processor) to an interrupt-handler task.

* An implicit call to an exception-handler task.

All of these methods of dispatching a task identify the task to be dispatched with a segment selector that points either to a task gate or the TSS for the task.

When a task is dispatched for execution, a task switch automatically occurs between the currently running task and the dispatched task. During a task switch, the execution environment of the currently executing task (called the task's state or *context*) is saved in its TSS and execution of the task is suspended. The context for the dispatched task is then loaded into the processor and execution of that task begins as the instruction pointed to by the newly loaded EIP register.

If the currently executing task (the calling task) called the task being dispatched (the called task), the segment selector for the calling task is stored in the TSS of the called task to provide a link back to the calling task.

For all Intel architecture processors, tasks are not recursive. A task cannot call or jump to itself.

Interrupts and exceptions can be handled with a task switch to a handler task. Here, the processor not only can perform a task switch to handle the interrupt or exception, but it can automatically switch back to the interrupted task upon returning from the interrupt- or exception-handler task. This mechanism can handle interrupts that occur during interrupt tasks.

As part of task switch, the processor can also switch to another LDT, allowing each task to have a different logical-to-physical address mapping. This protection facility helps isolate tasks and prevents them from interfering with one another. The page directory base register (CR3) also is reloaded on a task switch, allowing each task to have its own set of page tables.

Use of task management facilities for handling multitasking applications is optional. Multitasking can be handled in software, with each software defined task executed in the context of a single Pentium Pro processor task.

6.2.   TASK MANAGEMENT DATA STRUCTURES

The processor defines four data structures for handling task related activities:

* Task state segment (TSS).

* Task gate descriptor.

* TSS descriptor.

* Task register.

When operating in protected mode, a TSS and TSS descriptor must be created for at least one task, and the segment selector for the TSS must be loaded into the task register (using the LTR instruction).

6.2.1. Task State Segment (TSS)

The processor state information needed to restore a task is saved in a system segment called the task state segment (TSS). Figure 6-2 shows the format of a TSS for tasks designed for 32-bit CPUs. (Compatibility with 16-bit Intel 286 processor tasks is provided by a different kind of TSS, see Figure 6-9). The fields of a TSS are divided into two main categories: dynamic fields and static fields.

The processor updates the dynamic fields when a task is suspended during a task switch. The following are dynamic fields:

General-purpose register fields
> State of the EAX, ECX, EDX, EBX, ESP, EBP, ESI, and EDI registers prior to the task switch.

Segment selector fields
> State of the ES, CS, SS, DS, FS, and GS registers prior to the task switch.

EFLAGS register field
> State of the EFAGS register prior to the task switch.

EIP (instruction pointer) field
> State of the EIP register prior to the task switch.

Link (to previous task) field
> Contains the segment selector for the TSS of the previous task (updated on a task switch only when a return is expected).

The processor reads the static fields, but does not normally change them. These fields are set up when a task is created. The following are static fields:

LDT segment selector field
> Contains the segment selector for the task's LDT.

CR3 control register field
> Contains the base physical address of the page directory to be used by the task. Control register CR3 is also known as the page directory base register (PDBR).

Privilege level-0, -1, and -2 stack pointer fields
> These stack pointers consist of a logical address made up of the segment selector for the stack segment (SS0, SS1, and SS2) and an offset into the stack (ESP0, ESP1, and ESP2).

T (debug trap) flag (byte 100, bit 0)
> When set, the T flag causes the processor to raise a debug exception when a task switch occurs (see Section 10.3.1.5., "Task-Switch Exception Condition").

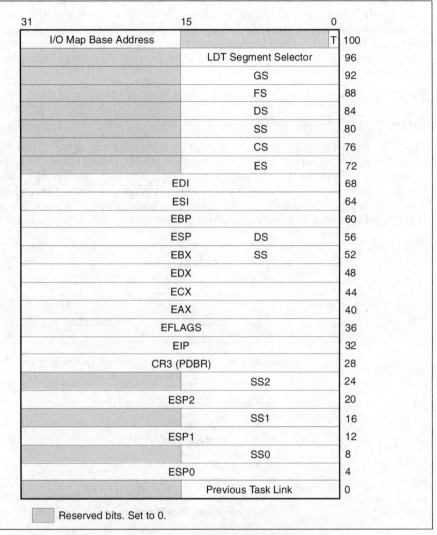

Figure 6-2. 32-Bit Task State Segment (TSS)

I/O map base address field

Contains a 16-bit offset from the base of the TSS to the I/O permission bit map and interrupt redirection bitmap. When present, these maps are stored in the TSS at higher addresses. The I/O map base address points to the beginning of the I/O permission bit map and the end of the interrupt redirection bit map. See Chapter 8, *Input/Output*, in the *Pentium® Pro Family Developer's Manual, Volume 2* for more information about the I/O permission bit map. See Section 12.3., "Interrupt and Exception Handling in Virtual-8086 Mode" for a detailed description of the interrupt redirection bit map.

If paging is used, care should be taken to avoid placing a page boundary within the part of the TSS that the processor reads during a task switch (the first 104 bytes). If a page boundary is placed within this part of the TSS, the pages on either side of the boundary must be present at the same time. Also, if paging is used, the pages corresponding to the previous task's TSS, the current task's TSS, and the descriptor table entries for each should be marked as present and read/write.

6.2.2. TSS Descriptor

The TSS, like all other segments, is defined by a segment descriptor. Figure 6-3 shows the format of a TSS descriptor. TSS descriptors may only be placed in the GDT; they cannot be placed in an LDT or the IDT. An attempt to access a TSS using a segment selector with its TI flag set (which indicates the current LDT) causes a general-protection exception (#GP) to be generated. A general-protection exception is also generated if an attempt is made to load a segment selector for a TSS into a segment register.

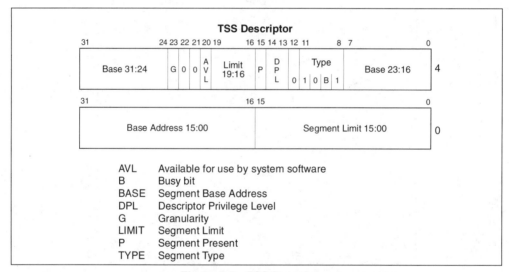

Figure 6-3. TSS Descriptor

The busy flag (B) in the type field indicates whether the task is busy. A busy task is currently running or waiting to run. A type field with a value of 1001B indicates an inactive task; a value of 1011B indicates a busy task. Tasks are not recursive. The processor uses the busy flag to detect an attempt to call a task whose execution has been interrupted. To insure that there is only one busy flag is associated with a task, each TSS should have only one TSS descriptor that points to it.

The base, limit, and DPL fields and the granularity and present flags have functions similar to their use in data-segment descriptors (see Section 3.4.3., "Segment Descriptors"). The limit field must have a value equal to or greater than 67H, one byte less than the minimum size of a TSS.

Attempting to switch to a task whose TSS descriptor has a limit less than 67H generates an invalid-TSS exception (#TS). A larger limit is required if an I/O permission bit map is included in the TSS. An even larger limit would be required if the operating system stores additional data in the TSS. The processor does not check for a limit greater than 67H on a task switch; however, it does when accessing the I/O permission bit map or interrupt redirection bit map.

Any program or procedure with access to a TSS descriptor (that is, whose CPL is equal to or less than the DPL of the TSS descriptor) can dispatch the task with a call or a jump. In most systems, the DPLs of TSS descriptors should be set to values less than 3, so that only privileged software can perform task switching. However, in multitasking applications, DPLs for some TSS descriptors can be set to 3 to allow task switching at the application (or user) privilege level.

6.2.3.   Task Register

The task register holds the 16-bit segment selector, 32-bit base address, 32-bit segment limit, and descriptor attributes for the TSS of the current task (see Figure 2-4). It references a TSS descriptor in the GDT. Figure 6-4 shows the path the processor uses to accesses the TSS.

The task register has both a visible part (that can be read and changed by software) and an invisible part (that is maintained by the processor and is inaccessible by software). The segment selector in the visible portion points to a TSS descriptor in the GDT. The processor uses the invisible portion of the TR register to cache the base linear address, limit value, and segment attributes from the TSS descriptor. Caching these values in a register makes execution of the task more efficient, because the processor does not need to fetch these values from memory to reference the TSS of the current task.

The LTR (load task register) and STR (store task register) instructions load and read the visible portion of the task register. The LTR instruction loads a segment selector (source operand) into the task register that points to a TSS descriptor in the GDT, and then loads the invisible portion of the task register with information from the TSS descriptor. This instruction is a privileged instruction that may be executed only when the CPL is 0. The LTR instruction generally is used during system initialization to put an initial value in the task register. Afterwards, the contents of the task register are changed implicitly when a task switch occurs.

The STR (store task register) instruction stores the visible portion of the task register in a general-purpose register or memory.

On power up or reset of the processor, the segment selector and base address are set to the default value of 0 and the limit is set to FFFFH.

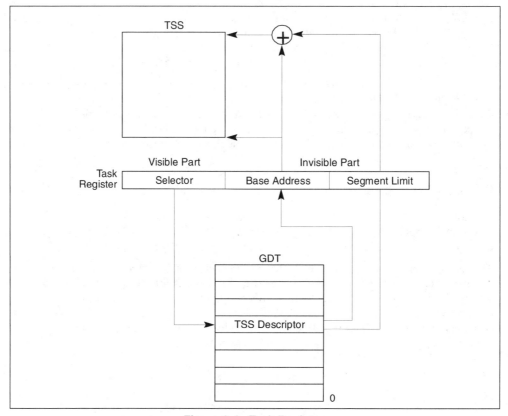

Figure 6-4. Task Register

6.2.4. Task Gate Descriptor

A task gate descriptor provides an indirect, protected reference to a task. Figure 6-5 shows the format of a task gate descriptor. A task gate descriptor can be placed in the GDT, an LDT, or the IDT.

The TSS segment selector field of a task gate descriptor points to a TSS descriptor in the GDT. The RPL in this segment selector is not used.

The DPL of a task gate descriptor controls access to the descriptor during a task switch. When a program or procedure makes a call or jump to a task through a task gate, the CPL and the RPL of the task gate's segment selector must be less than or equal to the DPL of the task gate descriptor. (Note that when a task gate is used, the DPL of the destination TSS descriptor is not used.)

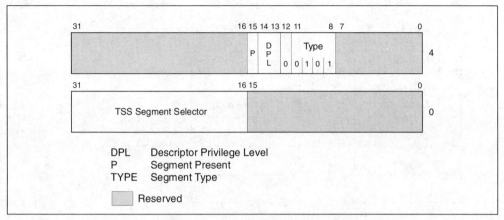

Figure 6-5. Task Gate Descriptor

A task can be accessed either through a task gate descriptor or a TSS descriptor. Both of these structures are provided to satisfy the following needs:

- The need for a task to have only one busy flag. Because the busy flag for a task is stored in the TSS descriptor, each task should have only one TSS descriptor. There may, however, be several task gates that reference the same TSS descriptor.

- The need to provide selective access to tasks. Task gates fill this need, because they can reside in an LDT and can have a DPL that is different from the TSS descriptor's DPL. A program or procedure that does not have sufficient privilege to access the TSS descriptor for a task in the GDT (which usually has a DPL of 0) may be allowed access to the task through a task gate with a higher DPL. Task gates give the operating system greater latitude for limiting access to specific tasks.

- The need for an interrupt or exception to be handled by an independent task. Task gates may also reside in the IDT, which allows interrupts and exceptions to be handled by handler tasks. When an interrupt or exception vector points to a task gate, the processor switches to the specified task.

Figure 6-6 illustrates how a task gates in an LDT and a task gate in the IDT can both point to the same task.

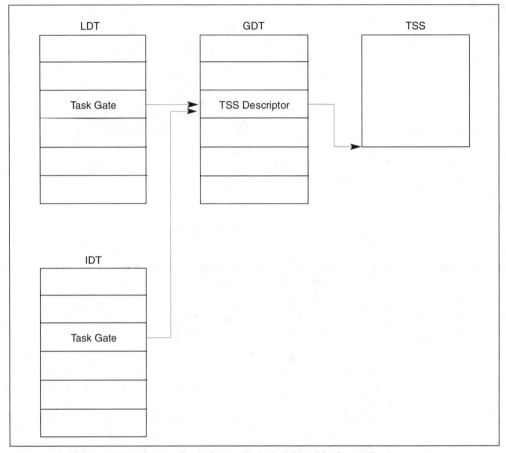

Figure 6-6. Task Gates Referencing the Same Task

6.3.   TASK SWITCHING

The processor transfers execution to another task in any of four cases:

- The current program, task, or procedure executes a JMP or CALL instruction to a TSS descriptor in the GDT.

- The current program, task, or procedure executes a JMP or CALL instruction to a task gate descriptor in the GDT or the current LDT.

- An interrupt or exception vector points to a task gate descriptor in the IDT.

- The current task executes an IRET when the NT flag in the EFLAGS register is set.

The JMP, CALL, and IRET instructions, as well as interrupts and exceptions, are all generalized mechanisms for redirecting a program. The referencing of a TSS descriptor or a task gate (when calling or jumping to a task) or the state of the NT flag (on a task return) determines whether a task switch occurs.

The processor performs the following operations when switching to a new task:

1. Checks that the current task is allowed to switch to the new task. Data-access privilege rules apply to JMP and CALL instructions. The CPL of the current task and the RPL of the segment selector for the new task must be less than or equal to the DPL of the TSS descriptor or the task gate being referenced. Exceptions, interrupts, and the IRET instruction are permitted to switch tasks regardless of the DPL of the destination task gate or TSS descriptor.

2. Checks that the TSS descriptor of the new task is marked present and has a valid limit (greater than or equal to 67H). Errors restore any changes made in the processor state when an attempt is made to execute the error-generating instruction. This lets the return address for the exception handler point to the error-generating instruction, rather than the instruction following the error-generating instruction. The exception handler can fix the condition which caused the error, and restart the task. The intervention of the exception handler can be completely transparent to the application program.

3. Checks that the old TSS, new TSS, and all segment descriptors used in the task switch are paged into system memory.

4. Saves the state of the current task. The processor finds the base address of the current TSS in the task register and then copies the states of the following registers into the current TSS: all the general-purpose registers, all the segment registers, the EFLAGS register, and the instruction pointer register (EIP).

NOTE

At this point, if all checks and saves have been carried out successfully, the processor commits to the task switch. If an unrecoverable error occurs in steps 1 through 4, the processor does not complete the task switch. If an unrecoverable error occurs after the commit point (in steps 6 and 7), the processor completes the task switch (without performing additional access and segment availability checks) and generates the appropriate exception prior to beginning execution of the new task. If exceptions occur after the commit point, the exception handler must finish the task switch itself before allowing the processor to begin executing the task. See Chapter 5, "Interrupt 10—Invalid TSS Exception (#TS)" for more information about the affect of exceptions on a task when they occur after the commit point of a task switch.

5. Loads the task register with the segment selector to the new task's TSS descriptor, sets the new task's busy flag, and sets the TS flag in control register CR0. The segment selector is obtained either as the operand of the JMP or CALL instruction or from a task gate.

6. Loads the new task's state from its TSS and begins executing the new task. The registers loaded are the LDTR register, the PDBR (control register CR3), the EFLAGS register, the EIP register, the general-purpose registers, and the segment registers are all loaded with the state of the new task. Any errors detected in this step occur in the context of the new task. To an exception handler, the first instruction of the new task appears not to have been executed.

The state of the currently executing task is always saved when a successful task switch occurs. If the task is resumed, execution starts with the instruction pointed to by the saved EIP value, and the registers are restored to the values they held when the task was suspended.

When switching tasks, the privilege level of the new task does not inherit its privilege level from the suspended task. The new task begins executing at the privilege level specified in the CPL field of the CS register, which is loaded from the TSS. Because the tasks are isolated by their separate address spaces and TSSs and because privilege rules control access to a TSS, software does not need to perform explicit privilege checks on a tasks switch.

Table 6-1 shows the exception conditions that the processor checks for when switching tasks. It also shows the exception that is generated for each check if an error is detected and the segment that the error code references. (The order of the check in the table is the order used in the Pentium Pro processor. This order is model specific and may be different for other Intel Architecture processors.) Exception handlers designed to handle these exceptions may be subject to recursive calls if they attempt to reload the segment selector that generated the exception. The cause of the exception (or the first of multiple causes) should be fixed before reloading the selector.

The TS (task switched) flag in the control register CR0 is set every time a task switch occurs. System software uses the TS flag to coordinate the operations of the integer unit with the floating-point unit. The TS flag indicates that the context of the floating-point unit may be different from that of the current task. See Section 2.5., "Control Registers" for a detailed description of the function and use of the TS flag.

Table 6-1. Exception Conditions Checked During a Task Switch

Condition Checked	Exception[1]	Error Code Reference[2]
Segment selector for a TSS descriptor references the GDT.	#GP	New Task's TSS
TSS descriptor is present in memory.	#NP	New Task's TSS
TSS descriptor is not busy.	#TS (for IRET); #GP (for JMP, CALL, INT)	Task's back-link TSS
TSS segment limit greater than or equal to 108.	#TS	New Task's TSS
Registers are loaded from the values in the TSS		
LDT segment selector of new task is valid [3].	#TS	New Task's LDT
Code segment DPL matches segment selector RPL.	#TS	New Code Segment
SS segment selector is valid [2]	#TS	New Stack Segment
Stack segment is present in memory	#SF	New Stack Segment

Table 6-1. Exception Conditions Checked During a Task Switch (Contd.)

Stack segment DPL matches CPL	#TS	New stack segment
LDT of new task is present in memory	#TS	New Task's LDT
CS segment selector is valid [3].	#TS	New Code Segment
Code segment is present in memory	#NP	New Code Segment
Stack segment DPL matches selector RPL	#TS	New Stack Segment
DS, ES, FS, and GS segment selectors are valid [3].	#TS	New Data Segment
DS, ES, FS, and GS segments are readable	#TS	New Data Segment
DS, ES, FS, and GS segments are present in memory	#NP	New Data Segment
DS, ES, FS, and GS segment DPL greater than or equal to CPL (unless these are conforming segments)	#TS	New Data Segment

NOTES:

1. #NP is segment-not-present exception, #GP is general-protection exception, #TS is invalid-TSS exception, and #SF is stack-fault exception.

2. The error code contains an index to the segment descriptor referenced in this column.

3. A segment selector is valid if it is in a compatible type of table (GDT or LDT), occupies an address within the table's segment limit, and refers to a compatible type of descriptor (for example, a segment selector in the CS register only is valid when it points to a code segment descriptor).

6.4. TASK LINKING

The link field of the TSS and the NT flag in the EFLAGS register are used to return execution to the previous task. The NT flag indicates whether the currently executing task is nested within the execution of another task, and the link field of the current task's TSS holds the TSS selector for the higher-level task in the nesting hierarchy, if there is one (see Figure 6-7).

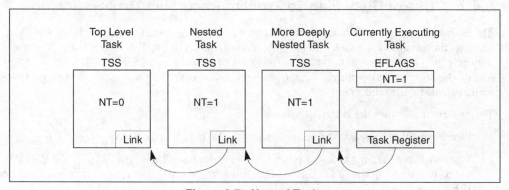

Figure 6-7. Nested Tasks

When a call, jump, interrupt, exception causes a task switch, the processor copies the segment selector for the current TSS into the link field of the TSS for the new task, and then sets the NT flag in the EFLAGS register. The NT flag indicates that the link field of the TSS has been loaded with a saved TSS segment selector. If software uses an IRET instruction to suspend the new task, the processor uses the value in the link field and the NT flag to return to the previous task; that is, if the NT flag is set, the processor performs a task switch task specified in the link field.

Table 6-2 summarizes the uses of the busy flag (in the TSS segment descriptor), the NT flag, and the link field during task switching. Note that the NT flag may be modified by software executing at any privilege level. It is possible for a program to set its NT flag and execute an IRET instruction, which would have the effect of invoking the task specified in the link field of the current task's TSS. To keep spurious task switches from succeeding, the operating system should initialize the link field for every TSS it creates.

Table 6-2. Effect of a Task Switch on Busy Flag, NT Flag, and Link Field

Field	Effect of JMP instruction	Effect of CALL Instruction or Interrupt	Effect of IRET Instruction
Busy flag of new task	Flag is set. Must have been clear before.	Flag is set. Must have been clear before.	No change. Must be set.
Busy flag of old task	Flag is cleared.	No change. Flag is currently set.	Flag is cleared.
NT flag of new task	No change.	Flag is set.	No change.
NT flag of old task	No change.	No change.	Flag is cleared.
Link field of new task.	No change.	Loaded with selector for old task's TSS.	No change.
Link field of old task.	No change.	No change.	No change.

6.4.1. Use of Busy Flag To Prevent Recursive Task Switching

The B (busy) flag in the TSS segment descriptor prevents re-entrant task switching. Only one context can be saved for a task (which is the context saved in the TSS); therefore, a task may only be called once before it terminates. The chain of nested suspended tasks may grow to any length, due to multiple interrupts, exceptions, jumps, and calls. The B flag prevents a task from being called if it is in this chain.

The processor manages the B flag as follows:

1. When switching to a task, the processor sets the B flag of the new task.

2. When switching from a task, the processor clears the busy flag of the old task if that task is not to be placed in the chain that is, the instruction causing the task switch is a JMP or IRET instruction). If the task is placed in the chain, its busy flag remains set.

3. When switching to a task, the processor generates a general-protection exception (#GP) if the busy flag of the new task is already set.

In this manner the processor prevents recursive task switching by preventing a task from switching to itself or to any task in a nested chain of tasks.

The B flag may be used in multiprocessor configurations, because the processor asserts a bus lock when it sets or clears the B flag. This lock keeps two processors from invoking the same task at the same time. (See Section 7.1.2.1., "Automatic Bus Locking" for more information about setting the B flag in a multiprocessor applications.)

6.4.2.   Modifying Task Linkages

In situations where it is necessary to remove a task from a chain of linked tasks, use the following procedure to remove the task:

1. Disable interrupts.

2. Change the link field in the TSS of the pre-empting task (that is, the task that suspended the task to be removed). It is assumed that the pre-empting task is the next task (newer task) in the chain from the task to be removed. The link field should be changed to point to the TSS of the next oldest task in the chain or to an even older task in the chain.

3. Clear the B flag in the TSS segment descriptor for the task being removed from the chain. If more than one task is being removed from the chain, the busy flag for each task being remove must be cleared.

4. Enable interrupts.

6.5.   TASK ADDRESS SPACE

The address space for a task consists of the segments that the task can access. These segments include the code, data, stack, and system segments referenced in the TSS and any other segments accessed by the task code. These segments are mapped into the processor's linear address space, which is in turn mapped into the processor's physical address space (either directly or through paging).

The LDT segment field in the TSS can be used to give each task its own LDT. Giving a task its own LDT allows the task address space to be isolated from other tasks by placing the segment descriptors for all the segments associated with the task in the tasks LDT.

It also is possible for several tasks to use the same LDT. This is a simple and memory-efficient way to allow some tasks to communicate with or control each other, without dropping the protection barriers for the entire system.

Because all tasks have access to the GDT, it also is possible to create shared segments accessed through segment descriptors in this table.

If paging is enabled, the CR3 register (PDBR) field in the TSS allows each task can also have its own set of page tables for mapping linear addresses to physical addresses. Or, several tasks can share the same set of page tables.

6.5.1. Mapping Tasks to the Linear and Physical Address Spaces

Tasks can be mapped to the linear address space and physical address space in either of two ways:

- One linear-to-physical address space mapping is shared among all tasks. When paging is not enabled, this is the only choice. Without paging, all linear addresses map to the same physical addresses. When paging is enabled, this form of linear-to-physical address space mapping is obtained by using one page directory for all tasks. The linear address space may exceed the available physical space if demand-paged virtual memory is supported.

- Each task has its own linear address space that is mapped to the physical address space. This form of mapping is accomplished by using a different page directory for each task. Because the PDBR (control register CR3) is loaded on each task switch, each task may have a different page directory.

The linear address spaces of different tasks may map to completely distinct physical addresses. If the entries of different page directories point to different page tables and the page tables point to different pages of physical memory, then the tasks do not share any physical addresses.

With either method of mapping task linear address spaces, the TSSs for all tasks must lie in a shared area of the physical space, which is accessible to all tasks. This mapping is required so that the mapping of TSS addresses does not change while the processor is reading and updating the TSSs during a task switch. The linear address space mapped by the GDT also should be mapped to a shared area of the physical space; otherwise, the purpose of the GDT is defeated. Figure 6-8 shows how the linear address spaces of two tasks can overlap in the physical space by sharing page tables.

6.5.2. Task Logical Address Space

Mapping the linear address spaces of tasks to a shared physical address space does not allow sharing of data among tasks. To share data, tasks must also map the logical addresses of the task to the linear addresses that are mapped to the shared physical address space. There are three ways to create shared logical-to-physical address-space mappings:

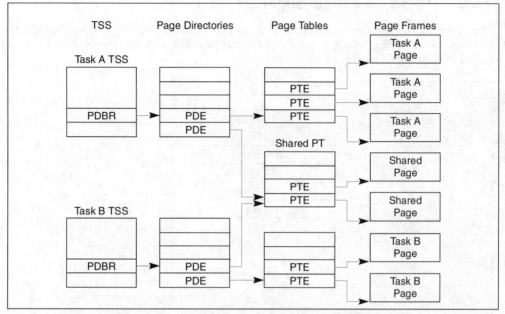

Figure 6-8. Overlapping Linear-to-Physical Mappings

- Through the segment descriptors in the GDT. All tasks must have access to the segment descriptors in the GDT. If some segment descriptors in the GDT point to segments in the linear-address space that are mapped into an area of the physical-address space common to all tasks, then all tasks can share the data and code in those segments.

- Through a shared LDT. Two or more tasks can use the same LDT if the LDT fields in their TSSs point to the same LDT. If some segment descriptors in a shared LDT point to segments that are mapped to a common area of the physical address space, the data and code in those segments can be shared among the tasks that share the LDT. This method of sharing is more selective than sharing through the GDT, because the sharing can be limited to specific tasks. Other tasks in the system may have different LDTs that do not give them access to the shared segments.

- Through segment descriptors in distinct LDTs that are mapped to common addresses in the linear address space. If this common area of the linear address space is mapped to the same area of the physical address space for each task, these segment descriptors permit the tasks to share segments. Such segment descriptors are commonly called aliases. This method of sharing is even more selective than those listed above, because, other segment descriptors in the LDTs may point to independent linear addresses which are not shared.

6.5.3.   16-Bit Task State Segment

The Pentium Pro processor also recognizes a 16-bit TSS format like the one used in Intel 286 processors (see Figure 6-9). It is supported for compatibility with software written to run on earlier Intel Architecture processors.

15	0	
Task LDT Selector		42
DS Selector		40
SS Selector		38
CS Selector		36
ES Selector		34
DI		32
SI		30
BP		28
SP		26
BX		24
DX		22
CX		20
AX		18
FLAG Word		16
IP (Entry Point)		14
SS2		12
SP2		10
SS1		8
SP1		6
SS0		4
SP0		2
Previous Task Link		0

Figure 6-9. 16-Bit TSS Format

intel®

7

Multiple Processor
Management

The Pentium Pro processor provides several mechanisms for managing and improving the performance of multiple processors connected to the same system bus. These mechanisms include:

- A secondary cache (level 2 cache) that is tightly coupled to the processor.

- Bus locking and/or cache coherency management for performing atomic operations on system memory.

- Serializing instructions.

- Advance programmable interrupt controller (APIC) located on the processor chip.

These mechanisms are particularly useful in symmetric-multiprocessing systems; however, they can also be used in applications where a Pentium Pro processor and a special-purpose processor (such as a communications, graphics, or video processor) share the system bus.

The main goals of these multiprocessing mechanisms are as follows:

- To maintain system memory coherency—When two or more processors are attempting simultaneously to access the same address in system memory, some communication mechanism or memory access protocol must be available to promote data coherency and, in some instances, to allow one processor to temporarily lock a memory location.

- To maintain cache consistency—When one processor accesses data cached in another processor, it must not receive incorrect data. If it modifies data, all other processors that access that data must receive the modified data.

- To allow predictable ordering of writes to memory—In some circumstances, it is important that memory writes be observed externally in precisely the same order as programmed.

- To distribute interrupt handling among a group of processors—When several processors are operating in a system in parallel, it is useful to have a centralized mechanism for receiving interrupts and distributing them to available processors for servicing.

Cache consistency is discussed in Chapter 11, *Memory Cache Control*. Bus and memory locking, serializing instructions, memory ordering, and the processor's internal APIC are discussed in the following sections.

7.1. LOCKED ATOMIC OPERATIONS

The Pentium Pro processor, as with earlier 32-bit Intel Architecture processors, supports locked atomic operations on locations in system memory. These operations are typically used to manage shared data structures (such as semaphores, segment descriptors, system segments, or page tables) in which two or more processors may try simultaneously to modify same field or flag. The processor uses three interdependent mechanisms for carrying out locked atomic operations:

- Guaranteed atomic operations.

- Bus locking, using the LOCK# signal and the LOCK instruction prefix.

- Cache coherency protocols that insure that atomic operations can be carried out on cached data structures.

These mechanisms are interdependent in the following ways. Certain basic memory transactions (such as reading or writing a byte in system memory) are always guaranteed to be handled atomically. That is, once started, the processor guarantees that the operation will be completed before another processor or bus agent is allowed access to the memory location. The processor also supports bus locking for performing selected memory operations (such as a read-modify-write operation in a shared area of memory) that typically need to be handled atomically, but are not automatically handled this way. Because frequently used memory locations are often cached in a processor's L1 or L2 caches, atomic operations can often be carried out inside a processor's caches without asserting the bus lock. Here the processor's cache coherency protocols insure that other processors that are caching the same memory locations are managed while atomic operations are performed on cached memory locations.

7.1.1.   Guaranteed Atomic Operations

The Pentium Pro processor guarantees that the following basic memory operations will always be carried out atomically:

- Reading or writing a byte.

- Reading or writing a word aligned on a 16-bit boundary.

- Reading or writing a doubleword aligned on a 32-bit boundary.

- Reading or writing a quadword aligned on a 64-bit boundary.

- 16-bit accesses to uncached memory locations that fit within a 32-bit data bus

- 16-, 32-, and 64-bit accesses to cached memory that fit within a 32-Byte cache line

For compatibility with other 32-bit Intel Architecture processors (the Intel386, Intel486, and Pentium processors), software should assume that only the following memory accesses are guaranteed to be handled atomically:

- 8-bit accesses on any boundary

- 16-bit accesses on a 16-bit boundary

- 32-bit accesses on a 32-bit boundary

Accesses to cacheable memory that are split across bus widths, cache lines, and page boundaries are not guaranteed to be atomic by the Pentium Pro processor. The processor provides bus control signals that permit external memory subsystems to make split accesses atomic; however, non-aligned data accesses will seriously impact the performance of the processor and should be avoided where possible.

7.1.2. Bus Locking

The processor provides a LOCK# signal that it asserts automatically during certain critical memory operations to lock the system bus. While this output signal is asserted, requests from other processor's or bus agents for control of the bus are ignored. It is the responsibility of the hardware designer to make this signal available to control memory accesses among processors.

Software can specify other occasions when the LOCK# signal should be asserted by prepending the LOCK prefix to an instruction. Here, if the area of memory being accessed is cached, the LOCK# signal is generally not asserted; instead, locking is only applied to the processor's cache (see Section 7.1., "Locked Atomic Operations").

7.1.2.1. AUTOMATIC BUS LOCKING

The operations on which the processor automatically asserts the LOCK# signal are as follows:

- **When executing an XCHG instruction that references memory.**

- **When setting the B (busy) flag of a TSS descriptor.** The processor tests and sets the busy flag in the type field of the TSS descriptor when switching to a task. To insure that two processors do not switch to the same task simultaneously, the processor asserts the LOCK# signal while testing and setting this flag.

- **When updating segment descriptors.** When loading a segment descriptor, the processor will set the accessed flag in the segment descriptor if the flag is clear. During this operation, the processor asserts LOCK# so that the descriptor will not be modified by another processor while it is being updated. For this action to be effective, operating-system procedures that update descriptors should use the following steps:

  — Use a locked operation to modify the access-rights byte to indicate that the segment descriptor is not-present, and specify a value for the type field that indicates that the descriptor is being updated.

  — Update the fields of the segment descriptor. (This operation may require several memory accesses; therefore, locked operations cannot be used.)

  — Use a locked operation to modify the access-rights byte to indicate that the segment descriptor is valid and present.

  Note that the Intel386 DX processor always updates the accessed flag in the segment descriptor, whether it is clear or not. The Pentium Pro, Pentium, and Intel486 processors only update this flag if it is not already set.

- **When updating page-directory and page-table entries.** When updating page-directory and page-table entries, the processor uses locked cycles to set the accessed and dirty flag int he page-directory and page-table entries.

7.1.2.2.   SOFTWARE CONTROLLED BUS LOCKING

To explicitly lock the bus, software can use the LOCK prefix with the following instructions when they are used to modify a memory location. An invalid-opcode exception (#UD) is generated when the LOCK prefix is used with any other instruction or when no write operation is made to memory (that is, when the destination operand is in a register).

- The bit test and modify instructions (BTS, BTR, and BTC).

- The exchange instructions (XADD, CMPXCHG, and CMPXCHG8B).

- The LOCK prefix is automatically assumed for XCHG instruction.

- The following single-operand arithmetic and logical instructions: INC, DEC, NOT, and NEG.

- The following two-operand arithmetic and logical: ADD, ADC, SUB, SBB, AND, OR, and XOR.

A locked instruction is guaranteed to lock only the area of memory defined by the destination operand, but may be interpreted by the system as a lock for a larger memory area.

Software should access semaphores (shared memory used for signalling between multiple processors) using identical addresses and operand lengths. For example, if one processor accesses a semaphore using word access, other processors should not access the semaphore using byte access.

The integrity of a bus lock is not affected by the alignment of the memory field. The LOCK# signal is asserted for as many bus cycles as necessary to update the entire operand. However, it is recommend that locked accesses be aligned on their natural boundaries for better system performance:

- Any boundary for an 8-bit access (locked or otherwise).

- 16-bit boundary for locked word accesses.

- 32-bit boundary for locked doubleword access.

- 64-bit boundary for locked quadword access.

Locked operations are serializing. They wait for all previous instructions to complete. Locked operations are atomic with respect to all other memory operations and all externally visible events. Only instruction fetch and page table accesses can pass locked instructions.

Locked instructions can be used to synchronize data written by one processor and read by another processor. Locked instructions cannot be used to insure that data written will be fetched as instructions.

7.1.3. Effects of a Locked Operation on Internal Processor Caches

If the area of memory being locked during a locked operation is cached in the processor that is performing the locking operation as write-back memory and is completely contained in a cache line, the processor may not assert the LOCK# signal on the bus. Instead, it will modify the memory location internally and allow it's cache coherency mechanism to insure that the operation is carried out atomically. The cache coherency mechanism automatically prevents two or more processors that have cached the same area of memory from simultaneously modifying data in that area.

7.2. MEMORY ORDERING

The Pentium Pro processor uses a memory ordering model defined as *processor ordering* to maintain consistency in the order data is read (loaded) and written (stored) in a program and the order the processor actually carries out the reads and writes. Processor ordering is a form of *write ordering* that can be defined as "write ordered with store-buffer forwarding." It can be characterized as follows.

In a single-processor system for memory regions defined as write-back cacheable, the following ordering rules apply:

1. Reads can be carried out speculatively and in any order.

2. Reads can pass buffered writes, but the processor guarantees program correctness if the write is to the same memory location as the read.

3. Writes to memory are always carried out in program order.

4. Writes can be buffered.

5. Writes are not performed speculatively; they are only performed for instructions that have actually been executed.

6. Data writes can be forwarded within the processor.

7. Reads or writes cannot pass (be carried out ahead of) I/O instructions, locked instructions, or serializing instructions.

The second rule allows a read to pass a write. However, if the write is to the same memory location as the read, the processor's internal "snooping" mechanism will detect the conflict and update the already cached read before the processor executes the instruction that uses the value.

The sixth rule constitutes an exception to an otherwise write ordered model. It is provided to improve prefetch accuracy and performance. It is used in situations where the processor is attempting to read a memory location that is currently held in the processor's store buffer, waiting to be written to memory. Here, the processor is allowed to read the value from the store buffer ahead of other writes, even though the processor carries out the actual writes in program order. Another way to view this capability is to say that the Pentium Pro processor is strongly ordered in itself, meaning that if it immediately reads a memory location that it has just written to, it is guaranteed to read the last value that it wrote.

In a multiple-processor system, the following ordering rules apply:

- Individual processors use the same ordering rules as in a single-processor system.

- Writes by a single processor are observed in the same order by all processors.

- Writes from all the processors on the system bus can be observed in different orders.

Figure 7-1 illustrates the latter rule. Here, three processors are all performing three writes to the same memory locations (A, B, and C). Individually, the processors perform the writes in the same program order, but because of bus arbitration and other memory access mechanisms, the order that the three processors write the individual memory locations can differ each time the respective code sequences are executed on the processors.

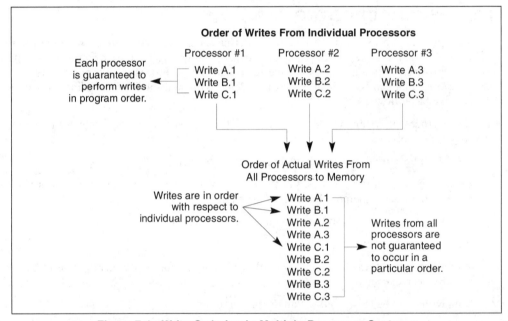

Figure 7-1. Write Ordering in Multiple-Processor Systems

The processor-ordering model described in this section is virtually identical to that used by the Pentium and Intel486 processors. The only enhancement in the Pentium Pro processor is the added support for speculative reads and store-buffer forwarding, when a read passes a write to the same memory location.

intel

7.2.1.   Strengthening or Weakening the Processor-Order Model

The Pentium Pro processor provides several mechanisms for strengthening or weakening the processor-order model to handle special programming situations. These mechanisms include:

- The I/O instructions, locking instructions, the LOCK prefix, and serializing instructions force strong ordering on the processor.

- The memory type range registers (MTRRs) can be used to strengthen or weaken memory ordering for specific area of physical memory.

These mechanisms can be used as follows.

Memory mapped devices and other I/O devices on the bus are often sensitive to the order of writes to their I/O buffers. I/O instructions can be used to (the IN and OUT instructions) impose strong write ordering on such accesses as follows. Prior to executing an I/O instruction, the processor waits for all previous instructions in the program to complete and for all buffered writes to drain to memory. Only instruction fetch and page tables walks can pass I/O instructions on the Pentium Pro processor. Execution of subsequent instructions do not begin until the processor determines that the I/O instruction has been completed.

Synchronization mechanisms in multiple-processor systems may depend upon a strong memory-ordering model. Here, a program can use a locking instruction such as the XCHG instruction or the LOCK prefix to insure that a read-modify-write operation on memory is carried out atomically. Locking operations typically operate like I/O operations in that they wait for all previous instructions to complete and for all buffered writes to drain to memory.

Program synchronization can also be carried out with serializing instructions (see Section 7.3., "Serializing Instructions"). These instructions are typically used at critical procedure or task boundaries to force completion of all previous instructions before a jump to a new section of code or a context switch occurs. Like the I/O and locking instructions, the processor waits until all previous instructions have been completed and all buffered writes have been drained to memory before executing the serializing instruction.

The MTRRs define the cache characteristics for specified areas of physical memory. The following are two examples of how memory types set up with MTRRs can be used strengthen or weaken memory ordering:

- The uncached (UC) memory type forces a strong-ordering model on memory accesses. Here, all reads and writes to the UC memory region appear on the bus and out-of-order or speculative accesses are not performed. This memory type can be applied to an address range dedicated to memory mapped I/O devices to force strong memory ordering.

- For areas of memory where weak ordering is acceptable, the write back (WB) memory type can be chosen. Here, reads can be performed speculatively and writes can be buffered and combined. For this type of memory, cache locking is performed on atomic (locked) operations that do not split across cache lines, which helps to reduce the performance penalty associated with the use of the typical synchronization instructions, such as XCHG, that lock the bus during the entire read-modify-write operation. With the WB memory type, the XCHG instruction locks the cache instead of the bus if the memory access is contained within a cache line.

It is recommended that software written to run on the Pentium Pro processor assume the processor-ordering model or a weaker memory-ordering model. The Pentium Pro processor does not implement stronger memory-ordering models, except when using the UC memory type. Despite the fact that the Pentium Pro, Pentium, and Intel486 processors support processor ordering, Intel does not guarantee that future processors will support this model. To make software portable to future processors, it is recommended I/O, locking, and/or serializing instructions be used to synchronize access to shared areas of memory in multiple-processor systems. Also, software should not depend on processor ordering in situations where the system hardware does not support this memory-ordering model.

7.3. SERIALIZING INSTRUCTIONS

After executing certain instructions the processor serializes instruction execution. Serialization means that all modifications to flags, registers, and memory by previous instructions are completed before the next instruction is fetched and executed and all buffered writes have drained to memory. For example, when a new value is loaded into control register CR0 to enable protected mode, the processor always performs a serialization operation before it fetches and executes subsequent instructions in the instruction stream. This operation insures that subsequent instructions are executed with protection enabled.

It is important to note that executing of serializing instructions on the Pentium Pro processor constrains speculative execution, because the results of speculatively executed instructions are discarded.

The following instructions are serializing instructions:

- Privileged serializing instructions—MOV (to control register), MOV (to debug register), WRMSR, INVD, INVLPG, WBINVD, LGDT, LLDT, LIDT, and LTR.

- Non-privileged serializing instructions—CPUID, IRET, and RSM.

The CPUID instruction can be executed at any privilege level to serialize instruction execution with no effect on program flow, except that the EAX, EBX, ECX, and EDX registers are modified.

Nothing can pass a serializing instruction, and serializing instructions cannot pass any other instruction (read, write, instruction fetch, or I/O).

When the processor serializes instruction execution, it ensures that all pending memory transactions are completed, including writes stored in its store buffer, before it executes the next instruction.

The following additional information is worth noting regarding serializing instructions:

- The processor does not writeback the contents of modified data in its data cache to external memory when it serializes instruction execution. Software can force modified data to be written back by executing the WBINVD instruction, which is a serializing instruction. It should be noted that frequent use of the WBINVD instruction will seriously reduce system performance.

- When an instruction is executed that enables or disables paging (that is, changes the PG flag in control register CR0), the instruction should be followed by a jump instruction. The target instruction of the jump instruction is fetched with the new setting of the PG flag (that is, paging is enabled or disabled), but the jump instruction itself is fetched with the previous setting. The Pentium Pro processor does not require the jump operation following the move to register CR0 (because any use of the MOV instruction in the Pentium Pro processor to write to CR0 is completely serializing). However, to maintain backwards and forward compatibility with code written to run on other Intel architecture processors, it is recommended that the jump operation be performed.

- Whenever an instruction is executed to change the contents of CR3 while paging is enabled, the next instruction is fetched using the translation tables that correspond to the new value of CR3. Therefore the next instruction and the sequentially following instructions should have a mapping based upon the new value of CR3. (Global entries in the TLBs are not invalidated, see Section 11.9., "Invalidating the Translation Lookaside Buffers (TLBs)".)

- The Pentium Pro processor uses branch-prediction techniques to improve performance by prefetching the destination of a branch instruction before the branch instruction is executed. Consequently, instruction execution is not generally serialized when a branch instruction is executed.

7.4. ADVANCED PROGRAMMABLE INTERRUPT CONTROLLER (APIC)

The Pentium Pro processor contains an Advanced Programmable Interrupt Controller (APIC), referred to in the following sections as the *local APIC*. The local APIC performs two main functions for the processor:

- It processes local external interrupts that the processor receives at its interrupt pins and local internal interrupts that software generates.

- In multiple processor systems, it communicates with an external I/O APIC chip. The external I/O APIC receives external interrupt events from the system and interprocessor interrupts from the processors on the system bus and distributes them to the processors on the system bus. The I/O APIC is part of Intel's system chip set.

Figure 7-2 shows the relationship of the local APICs on the processors in a multiple processor (MP) system and the I/O APIC. The local APIC controls the dispatching of interrupts (to its associated processor) that it receives either locally or from the I/O APIC. It provides facilities for queuing, nesting and masking of interrupts. It handles the interrupt delivery protocol with its local processor and accesses to APIC registers, and also manages interprocessor interrupts and remote APIC register reads. A timer on the local APIC allows local generation of interrupts, and local interrupt pins permit local reception of processor-specific interrupts. The local APIC can be disabled (in hardware or software) and used in conjunction with a standard 8259A-style interrupt controller.

The I/O APIC is responsible for receiving interrupts generated by I/O devices and distributing them among the local APICs by means of the APIC Bus. The I/O APIC manages interrupts using either static or dynamic distribution schemes. Dynamic distribution of interrupts allows routing of interrupts to the lowest priority processors. It also handles the distribution of interprocessor interrupts and system-wide control functions such as NMI, INIT, SMI and start-up-interprocessor interrupts. Individual pins on the I/O APIC can be programmed to generate a specific, prioritized interrupt vector when asserted. The I/O APIC also has an 8259A-compatible mode.

The Pentium Pro processor's APIC is an architectural subset of the Intel 82489DX external APIC. The differences are described in Section 7.4.16., "Software Visible Differences Between the Local APIC and the 82489DX".

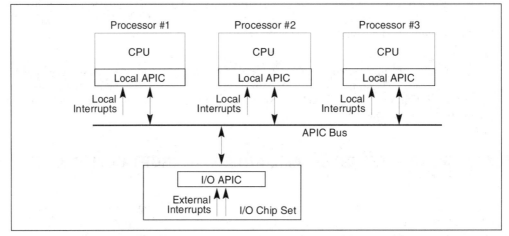

Figure 7-2. I/O APIC and Local APICs in Multiple Processor Systems

The following sections focus on the local APIC, and its implementation in the Pentium Pro processor. Contact Intel for the information on I/O APIC.

7.4.1. APIC Bus

All I/O APIC and local APICs communicate through the APIC bus (a 3-line inter-APIC bus). Two of the lines are open-drain (wired-OR) and are used for data transmission; the third line is a clock. **The bus and its messages are invisible to software and are not classed as architectural (that is, they may change in future implementations without having any effect on software compatibility).**

7.4.2. Valid Interrupts

The local and I/O APICs support 240 distinct vectors in the range of 16 to 255. Interrupt priority is implied by its vector, according to the following relationship:

priority = vector / 16

One is the lowest priority and 15 is the highest. Vectors 16 through 31 are reserved for exclusive use by the processor. The remaining vectors are for general use. The processor's local APIC includes an in-service entry and a holding entry for each priority level. To avoid losing interrupts, software should allocate no more than 2 interrupt vectors per priority.

7.4.3. Interrupt Sources

The local APIC can receive interrupts from the following sources:

- Interrupt pins on the processor chip, driven by locally connected I/O devices.

- A bus message from the I/O APIC, originated by an I/O device connected to the I/O APIC.

- A bus message from another processor's local APIC, originated as an interprocessor interrupt.

- The local APIC's programmable timer or the error register, through the self-interrupt generating mechanism.

- Software, through the self-interrupt generating mechanism.

- The Pentium Pro processor's performance-monitoring counters.

The local APIC services the I/O APIC and interprocessor interrupts according to the information included in the bus message (such as vector, trigger type, interrupt destination, etc.). Interpretation of the processor's interrupt pins and the timer-generated interrupts is programmable, by means of the local vector table (LVT). To generate an interprocessor interrupt, the source processor programs its interrupt command register (ICR). The programming of the ICR causes generation of a corresponding interrupt bus message. See Section 7.4.8., "Local Vector Table" and Section 7.4.9., "Interprocessor and Self Interrupts" for detailed information on programming the LVT and ICR, respectively.

7.4.4. Bus Arbitration Overview

Being connected on a common bus (the APIC bus), the local and I/O APICs have to arbitrate for permission to send a message on the APIC bus. Logically, the APIC bus is a wired-OR connection, enabling more than one local APIC to send messages simultaneously. Each APIC issues its arbitration priority at the beginning of each message, and one winner is collectively selected following an arbitration round. At any given time, a local APIC's the arbitration priority is a unique value from 0 to 15. The arbitration priority of each local APIC is dynamically modified after each successfully transmitted message to preserve fairness. See Section 7.4.13., "APIC Bus Arbitration Mechanism and Protocol" for a detailed discussion of bus arbitration.

Section 7.4.1., "APIC Bus" describes the existing arbitration protocols and bus message formats, while Section 7.4.9., "Interprocessor and Self Interrupts" describes the INIT level de-assert message, used to resynchronize all local APICs' arbitration IDs. Note that except for start-up (see Section 7.4.8., "Local Vector Table"), all bus messages failing during delivery are auto-matically retried. The software should avoid situations in which interrupt messages may be "ignored" by disabled or nonexistent "target" local APICs, and messages are being resent repeatedly.

7.4.5.   The Local APIC Block Diagram

Figure 7-3 gives a functional block diagram for the local APIC. Software interacts with the local APIC by reading and writing its registers. The registers are memory-mapped to the processor's physical address space, and for each processor they have an identical address space of 4 KBytes starting at address FEE00000H. The register address allocation scheme is shown in Table 7-1. Register offsets are aligned on 128-bit boundaries. All registers must be accessed using 32-bit loads and stores. Wider registers (64-bit or 256-bit) are defined and accessed as independent multiple 32-bit registers.

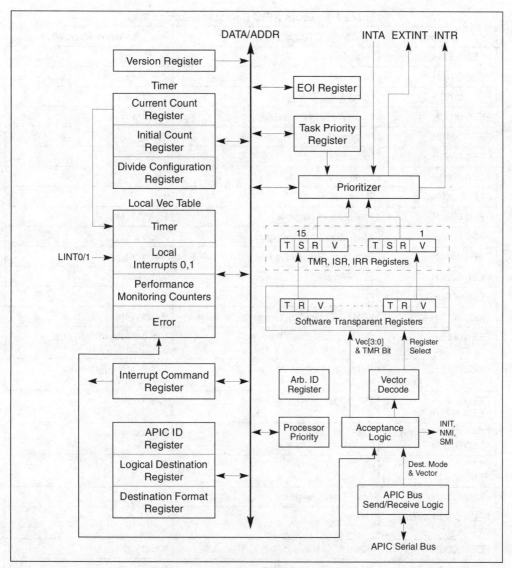

Figure 7-3. Local APIC Structure

Table 7-1. Local APIC Register Address Map

Address	Register Name	Software Read/Write
FEE0 0000H	Reserved	
FEE0 0010H	Reserved	
FEE0 0020H	Local APIC ID Register	Read/write
FEE0 0030H	Local APIC Version Register	Read only
FEE0 0040H	Reserved	
FEE0 0050H	Reserved	
FEE0 0060H	Reserved	
FEE0 0070H	Reserved	
FEE0 0080H	Task Priority Register	Read/Write
FEE0 0090H	Arbitration Priority Register	Read only
FEE0 00A0H	Processor Priority Register	Read only
FEE0 00B0H	EOI Register	Write only
FEE0 00C0H	Reserved	
FEE0 00D0H	Logical Destination Register	Read/Write
FEE0 00E0H	Destination Format Register	Bits 0-27 Read only. Bits 28-31 Read/Write
FEE0 00F0H	Spurious Interrupt Vector Register	Bits 0-3 Read only. Bits 4-9 Read/Write
FEE0 0100H through FEE0 0170H	ISR 0-255	Read only
FEE0 0180H through FEE0 01F0H	TMR 0-255	Read only
FEE0 0200H through FEE0 0270H	IRR 0-255	Read only
FEE0 0280H	Error Status Register	Read only
FEE0 0290H through FEE0 02F0H	Reserved	
FEE0 0300H	Interrupt Command Reg. 0-31	Read/Write
FEE0 0310H	Interrupt Command Reg. 32-63	Read/Write
FEE0 0320H	Local Vector Table (Timer)	Read/Write
FEE0 0330H	Reserved	
FEE0 0340H	Performance Counter LVT	Read/Write
FEE0 0350H	Local Vector Table (LINT0)	Read/Write
FEE0 0360H	Local Vector Table (LINT1)	Read/Write
FEE0 0370H	Local Vector Table (Error)	Read/Write

Table 7-1. Local APIC Register Address Map (Contd.)

Address	Register Name	Software Read/Write
FEE0 0380H	Initial Count Register for Timer	Read/Write
FEE0 0390H	Current Count Register for Timer	Read only
FEE0 03A0H through FEE0 03D0H	Reserved	
FEE0 03E0H	Timer Divide Configuration Register	Read/Write
FEE0 03F0H	Reserved	

7.4.6. Interrupt Destination and APIC ID

The destination of an interrupt can be one, all, or a subset of the processors in the system. The sender specifies the destination of an interrupt in one of two destination modes: physical or logical.

7.4.6.1. PHYSICAL DESTINATION MODE

In physical destination mode, the destination processor is specified by its local APIC ID. This ID is matched against the local APIC's actual physical ID, which is stored in the local APIC ID register (see Figure 7-4). Either a single destination (the ID is 0 through 14) or a broadcast to all (the ID is 15) can be specified in physical destination mode. Note that in this mode, up to 15 the local APICs can be individually addressed. An ID of all 1s denotes a broadcast to all local APICs. The APIC ID register is loaded at power up by sampling configuration data that is driven onto lines A11# and A12# and lines BR0# through BR3# of the system bus. The ID portion can be read and modified by software.

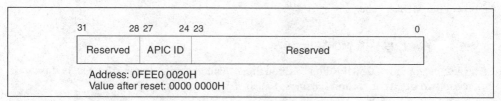

Figure 7-4. Local APIC ID Register

7.4.6.2. LOGICAL DESTINATION MODE

In logical destination mode, message destinations are specified using an 8-bit message destination address (MDA). The MDA is compared against the 8-bit logical APIC ID field of the APIC logical destination register (LDR), see Figure 7-5.

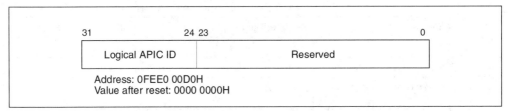

Figure 7-5. Logical Destination Register (LDR)

Destination format register (DFR) defines the interpretation of the logical destination information (see Figure 7-6). The DFR register can be programmed for *flat model* or *cluster model* interrupt delivery modes.

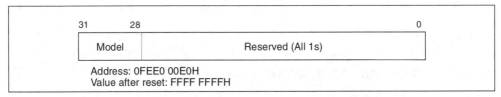

Figure 7-6. Destination Format Register (DFR)

7.4.6.3. FLAT MODEL

For the flat model, bits 28 through 31 of the DFR must be programmed to 1111. The MDA is interpreted as a decoded address. This scheme allows the specification of arbitrary groups of local APICs simply by setting each APIC's bit to 1 in the corresponding LDR. In the flat model, up to 8 local APICs can coexist in the system. Broadcast to all APICs is achieved by setting all 8 bits of the MDA to ones.

7.4.6.4. CLUSTER MODEL

For the cluster model, the DFR bits 28 through 31 should be programmed to 0000. In this model, there are two basic connection schemes: flat cluster and hierarchical cluster.

In the flat cluster connection model, all clusters are assumed to be connected on a single APIC bus. Bits 28 through 31 of the MDA contains the encoded address of the destination cluster. These bits are compared with bits 28 through 31 of the LDR to determine if the local APIC is part of the cluster. Bits 24 through 27 of the MDA are compared with Bits 24 through 27 of the LDR to identify individual local APIC unit within the cluster. Arbitrary sets of processors within a cluster can be specified by writing the target cluster address in bits 28 through 31 of the MDA and setting selected bits in bits 24 through 27 of the MDA, corresponding to the chosen members of the cluster. In this mode, 15 clusters (with cluster addresses of 0 through 14) each having 4 processors can be specified in the message. The APIC arbitration ID, however, supports only 15 agents, and hence the total number of processors supported in this mode is limited to 15.

Broadcast to all local APICs is achieved by setting all destination bits to one. This guarantees a match on all clusters, and selects all APICs in each cluster.

In the hierarchical cluster connection model, an arbitrary hierarchical network can be created by connecting different flat clusters via independent APIC buses. This scheme requires a cluster manager within each cluster, responsible for handling message passing between APIC buses. One cluster contains up to 4 agents. Thus 15 cluster managers, each with 4 agents, can form a network of up to 60 APIC agents. Note that hierarchical APIC networks requires a special cluster manager device, which is not part of the local or the I/O APIC units.

7.4.6.5.   ARBITRATION PRIORITY

Each local APIC is given an arbitration priority of from 0 to 15 upon reset. The I/O APIC uses this priority during arbitration rounds to determine which local APIC should be allowed to transmit a message on the APIC bus when multiple local APICs are issuing messages. The local APIC with the highest arbitration priority wins access to the APIC bus. Upon completion of an arbitration round, the winning local APIC lowers its arbitration priority to 0 and the losing local APICs each raise theirs by 1. In this manner, the I/O APIC distributes message bus-cycles among the contesting local APICs.

The current arbitration priority for a local APIC is stored in a 4-bit, software-transparent arbitration ID (Arb ID) register. During reset, this register is initialized to the APIC ID number (stored in the local APIC ID register). The INIT-deassert command resynchronizes the arbitration priorities of the local APICs by resetting Arb ID register of each agent to its current APIC ID value.

7.4.7.   Interrupt Distribution Mechanisms

The APIC supports two mechanisms for selecting the destination processor for an interrupt: static and dynamic. Static distribution is used to access a specific processor in the network. Using this mechanism, the interrupt is unconditionally delivered to all local APICs that match the destination information supplied with the interrupt. The following delivery modes fall into the static distribution category: fixed, SMI, NMI, EXTINT, and start-up.

Dynamic distribution assigns incoming interrupts to the lowest priority processor, which is generally the least busy processor. It can be programmed in the LVT for local interrupt delivery or the ICR for bus messages. Using dynamic distribution, only the "lowest priority" delivery mode is allowed. From all processors listed in the destination, the processor selected is the one whose current arbitration priority is the lowest. The latter is specified in the arbitration priority register (APR), see Section 7.4.10.4., "Arbitration Priority Register (APR)". If more than one processor shares the lowest priority, the processor with the highest arbitration priority (the unique value in the Arb ID register) is selected.

In lowest priority mode, if a *focus processor* exists, it may accept the interrupt, regardless of its priority. A processor is said to be the focus of an interrupt if it is currently servicing that interrupt or if it has a pending request for that interrupt.

7.4.8. Local Vector Table

The local APIC contains a local vector table (LVT), specifying interrupt delivery and status information for the locally interrupts. The information contained in this table includes the interrupt associated vector, delivery mode, status bits and other data as shown in Figure 7-7. The LVT incorporates four 32-bit entries. Entry 0 corresponds to the timer, entries 1 and 2 belong to the two local interrupt pins, and entry 3 is for the error interrupt.

The fields in the LVT are as follows:

Vector Interrupt vector number.

Delivery Mode Defined only for local interrupt entries 1 and 2 and the performance counter. The timer and the error status register (ESR) generate only edge triggered maskable interrupts to the local processor. The delivery mode field does not exist for the timer and error interrupts. The performance counter LVT may be programmed with a Deliver Mode equal to Fixed or NMI only. Note that certain delivery modes will only operate as intended when used in conjunction with a specific Trigger Mode. The allowable delivery modes are as follows:

000 (Fixed) Delivers the interrupt, received on the local interrupt pin, to the processor as specified in the corresponding LVT entry. The trigger mode can be edge or level. Note, if the processor is not used in conjunction with an I/O APIC, the fixed delivery mode may be software programmed for an edge-triggered interrupt, but the Pentium Pro processor implementation will always operate in a level-triggered mode.

100 (NMI) Delivers the interrupt, received on the local interrupt pin, to the processor as an NMI interrupt. The vector information is ignored. The NMI interrupt is treated as edge-triggered, even if programmed otherwise. Note that the NMI may be masked. It is the software's responsibility to program the LVT mask bit according to the desired behavior of NMI.

111 (ExtINT) Delivers the interrupt, received on the local interrupt pin, to the processor and responds as if the interrupt originated in an externally connected (8259A-compatible) interrupt controller. A special INTA bus cycle corresponding to ExtINT, is routed to the external controller. The latter is expected to supply the vector information. When the delivery mode is ExtINT, the trigger-mode is level-triggered, regardless of how the APIC triggering mode is programmed. The APIC architecture supports only one ExtINT source in a system, usually contained in the compatibility bridge.

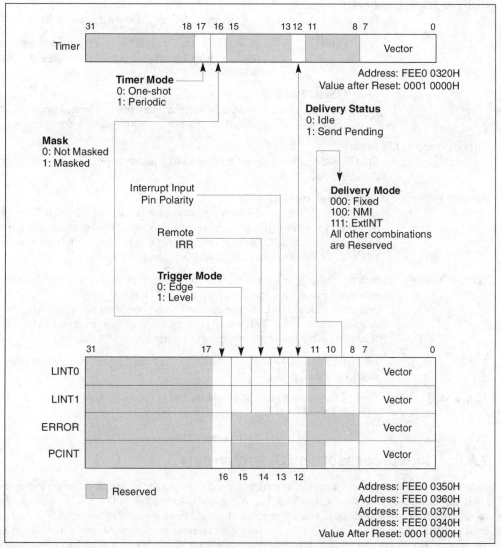

Figure 7-7. Local Vector Table (LVT)

Delivery Status (read only)
Holds the current status of interrupt delivery. Two states are defined:

0 (Idle) There is currently no activity for this interrupt, or the previous interrupt from this source has been accepted.

1 (Send Pending) Indicates that the interrupt has been injected, but the APIC has not yet completely accepted it.

Interrupt Input Pin Polarity
Specifies the polarity of the corresponding interrupt pin: (0) active high or (1) active low.

Remote Interrupt Request Register (IRR) Bit
Used for level triggered interrupts only; its meaning is undefined for edge triggered interrupts. For level triggered interrupts, the bit is set when the logic of the local APIC accepts the interrupt. The remote IRR bit is reset when an EOI command is received from the processor.

Trigger Mode Selects the trigger mode for the local interrupt pins when the delivery mode is Fixed: (0) edge sensitive and (1) level sensitive. When the delivery mode is NMI, the trigger mode is always level sensitive; when the delivery mode is ExtINT, the trigger mode is always level sensitive. The timer and error interrupts are always treated as edge sensitive.

Mask Interrupt mask: (0) enables injection of the interrupt and (1) inhibits injection of the interrupt.

Timer Mode Selects the timer mode: (0) one-shot and (1) periodic (see Section 7.4.15., "Timer").

7.4.9. Interprocessor and Self Interrupts

A processor generates interprocessor interrupts by writing into the interrupt command register (ICR) of its local APIC (see Figure 7-8). The processor may use the ICR for self interrupts or for interrupting other processors (for example, to forward device interrupts originally accepted by it to other processors for service). In addition, special inter-processor interrupts (IPI) such as the start-up IPI message, can only be delivered using the ICR mechanism. ICR-based interrupts are treated as edge triggered even if programmed otherwise.

All fields of the ICR are read-write by software with the exception of the delivery status field, which is read-only. Writing to the 32-bit word that contains the interrupt vector causes the interrupt message to be sent. The ICR consists of the following fields.

Vector The vector identifying the interrupt being sent. If the delivery mode is remote read, then the vector field contains bits 11 through 4 (8 bits) of the register address to be read from the remote local APIC unit. The local-APIC register addresses are summarized in Table 7-1.

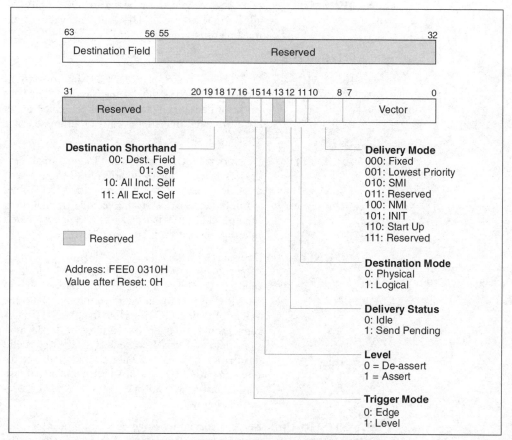

Figure 7-8. Interrupt Command Register (ICR)

Delivery Mode   Specifies how the APICs listed in the destination field should act upon reception of the interrupt. Note that all interprocessor interrupts behave as edge triggered interrupts (except for INIT level de-assert message) even if they are programmed as level triggered interrupts.

        000 (Fixed)   Deliver the interrupt to all processors listed in the destination field according to the information provided in the ICR. The fixed interrupt is treated as an edge-triggered interrupt even if programmed otherwise.

        001 (Lowest Priority)
                Same as fixed mode, except that the interrupt is delivered to the processor executing at the lowest priority among the set of processors listed in the destination.

010 (SMI) (The vector field must be set to 00B.) Only the edge trigger mode is allowed. The vector field must be programmed to zero.

011 (Reserved)

100 (NMI) Delivers the interrupt as an NMI interrupt to all processors listed in the destination field. The vector information is ignored. NMI is treated as an edge triggered interrupt even if programmed otherwise.

101 (INIT) Delivers the interrupt as an INIT signal to all processors listed in the destination field. As a result, all addressed APICs will assume their INIT state. As in the case of NMI, the vector information is ignored, and INIT is treated as an edge triggered interrupt even if programmed otherwise.

101 (INIT Level De-assert)
(The trigger mode must also be set to 1 and level mode to 0.) Sends a synchronization message to all APIC agents to set their arbitration IDs to the values of their APIC IDs. Note that the INIT interrupt is sent to all agents, regardless of the destination field value. However, at least one valid destination processor should be specified. For future compatibility, the software is requested to use a broadcast-to-all ("all-incl-self" shorthand, as described below).

110 (Start-Up) Sends a special message between processors in a multiple-processor system. For details refer to the *Pentium® Pro Family Developer's Manual, Volume 1.* The Vector information contains the start-up address for the multiple-processor boot-up protocol. Start-up is treated as an edge triggered interrupt even if programmed otherwise.

Start-Up Interrupts are not automatically retried by the source APIC upon failure in delivery of the message. It is up to the software to decide whether a retry is needed in the case of failure, and issue a retry message accordingly.

Destination Mode Selects either (0) physical or (1) logical destination mode.

Delivery Status Indicates the delivery status:

> **0 (Idle)** Means that there is currently no activity for this interrupt.
>
> **1 (Send Pending)** Indicates that the interrupt has been injected, but its delivery is temporarily delayed due to APIC bus being busy or the inability of the receiving APIC unit to accept the interrupt at that time.

Level For INIT level de-assert delivery mode the level is 0. For all other modes the level is 1.

Trigger Mode Used for the INIT level de-assert delivery mode only.

Destination Shorthand

Indicates whether a shorthand notation is used to specify the destination of the interrupt and, if so, which shorthand is used. Destination shorthands do not use the 8-bit destination field, and can be sent by software using a single write to the lower 32-bit part of the APIC interrupt command register. Shorthands are defined for the following cases: software self interrupt, interrupt to all processors in the system including the sender, interrupts to all processors in the system excluding the sender.

> **00: (destination field, no shorthand)** The destination is specified in bits 56 through 63 of the ICR.
>
> **01: (self)** The current APIC is the single destination of the interrupt. This is useful for software self interrupts. The destination field is ignored. See Table 7-2 for description of supported modes. Note that self interrupts do not generate bus messages.
>
> **10: (all including self)** The interrupt is sent to all processors in the system including the processor sending the interrupt. The APIC will broadcast a message with the destination field set to FH. See Table 7-2 for description of supported modes.
>
> **11: (all excluding self)** The interrupt is sent to all processors in the system with the exception of the processor sending the interrupt. The APIC will broadcast a message using the physical destination mode and destination field set to FH.

Destination This field is only used when the destination shorthand field is set to "dest field". If the destination mode is physical, then bits 56 through 59 contain the APIC ID. In logical destination mode, the interpretation of the 8-bit destination field depends on the DFR and LDR of the local APIC Units.

Table 7-2 shows the valid combinations for the fields in the interrupt control register.

Table 7-2. Valid Combinations for the APIC Interrupt Command Register

Trigger Mode	Destination Mode	Delivery Mode	Valid/ Invalid	Destination Shorthand
Edge	Physical or Logical	Fixed, Lowest Priority, NMI, SMI, INIT, Start-Up	Valid	Dest. Field
Level	Physical or Logical	Fixed, Lowest Priority, NMI	1	Dest. field
Level	Physical or Logical	INIT	2	Dest. Field
Level	x	SMI, Start-Up	Invalid[3]	x
Edge	x	Fixed	Valid	Self
Level	x	Fixed	1	Self
x	x	Lowest Priority, NMI, INIT, SMI, Start-Up	Invalid[3]	Self
Edge	x	Fixed	Valid	All inc Self
Level	x	Fixed	1	All inc Self
x	x	Lowest Priority, NMI, INIT, SMI, Start-Up	Invalid[3]	All inc Self
Edge	x	Fixed, Lowest Priority, NMI, INIT, SMI, Start-Up	Valid	All excl Self
Level	x	Fixed, Lowest Priority, NMI	1	All excl Self
Level	x	SMI, Start-Up	Invalid[3]	All excl Self
Level	x	INIT	2	All excl Self

NOTES:

1. Valid. Treated as edge triggered if Level = 1 (assert), otherwise ignored.
2. Valid. Treated as edge triggered when Level = 1 (assert); when Level = 0 (deassert), treated as "INIT Level Deassert" message. Only INIT level deassert messages are allowed to have level = deassert. For all other messages the level must be "assert."
3. Invalid. The behavior of the APIC is undefined.

7.4.10. Interrupt Acceptance

Three 256-bit read-only registers (the IRR, ISR, and TMR registers) are involved in the interrupt acceptance logic (see Figure 7-9). The 256 bits represents the 256 possible vectors. Because vectors 0 through 15 are reserved, so are bits 0 through 15 in these registers. The functions of the three registers are as follows:

TMR (trigger mode register)

> Upon acceptance of an interrupt, the corresponding TMR bit is cleared for edge triggered interrupts and set for level interrupts. If the TMR bit is set, the local APIC sends an EOI message to all I/O APICs as a result of software issuing an EOI command (see Section 7.4.10.6., "End-Of-Interrupt (EOI)" for a description of the EOI register).

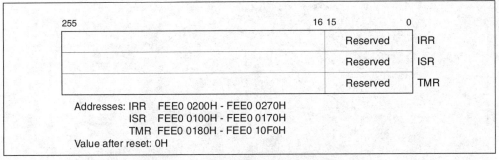

Figure 7-9. IRR, ISR and TMR Registers

IRR (interrupt request register)

> Contains the active interrupt requests that have been accepted, but not yet dispensed by the current local APIC. A bit in IRR is set when the APIC accepts the interrupt. The IRR bit is cleared, and a corresponding ISR bit is set when the INTA cycle is issued.

ISR (in-service register)

> Marks the interrupts that have been delivered to the processor, but have not been fully serviced yet, as an EOI has not yet been received from the processor. The ISR reflects the current state of the processor interrupt queue. The ISR bit for the highest priority IRR is set during the INTA cycle. During the EOI cycle, the highest priority ISR bit is cleared, and if the corresponding TMR bit was set, an EOI message is sent to all I/O APICs.

7.4.10.1. INTERRUPT ACCEPTANCE DECISION FLOW CHART

The process that the APIC uses to accept an interrupt is shown in the flow chart in Figure 7-10. The response of the local APIC to the start-up IPI is explained in the *Pentium® Pro Family Developer's Manual, Volume 1.*

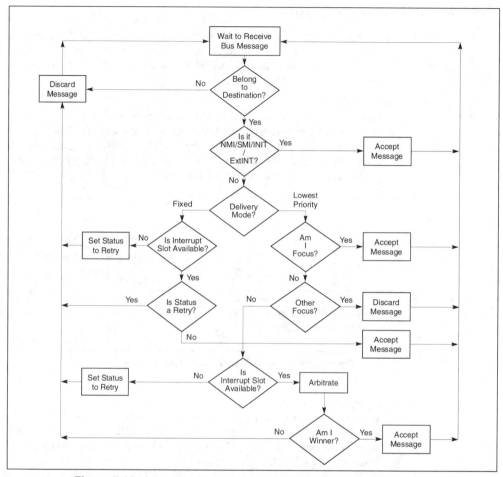

Figure 7-10. Interrupt Acceptance Flow Chart for the Local APIC

7.4.10.2. TASK PRIORITY REGISTER

Task priority register (TPR) provides a *priority threshold* mechanism for interrupting the processor (see Figure 7-11). Only interrupts whose priority is higher than that specified in the TPR will be serviced. Other interrupts are recorded and are serviced as soon as the TPR value is decreased enough to allow that. This enables the operating system to block temporarily specific interrupts (generally low priority) from disturbing high-priority tasks execution. The priority threshold mechanism is not applicable for delivery modes excluding the vector information (that is, for ExtINT, NMI, SMI, INIT, INIT-Deassert, and Start-Up delivery modes).

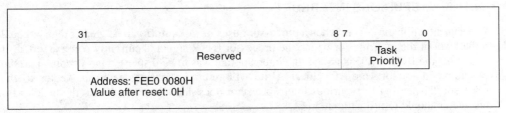

Figure 7-11. Task Priority Register (TPR)

The Task Priority is specified in the TPR. The 4 most-significant bits of the task priority correspond to the 16 interrupt priorities, while the 4 least-significant bits correspond to the sub-class priority. The TPR value is generally denoted as $x{:}y$, where x is the main priority and y provides more precision within a given priority class. When the x-value of the TPR is 15, the APIC will not accept any interrupts.

7.4.10.3.   PROCESSOR PRIORITY REGISTER (PPR)

The processor priority register (PPR) is used to determine whether a pending interrupt can be dispensed to the processor. Its value is computed as follows:

```
IF TPR[7:4] ≥ ISRV[7:4]
    THEN
        PPR[7:0] = TPR[7:0]
    ELSE
        PPR[7:4] = ISRV[7:4] AND PPR[3:0] = 0
```

Where ISRV is the vector of the highest priority ISR bit set, or zero if no ISR bit is set. The PPR format is identical to that of the TPR. The PPR address is FEE000A0H, and its value after reset is zero.

7.4.10.4.   ARBITRATION PRIORITY REGISTER (APR)

Arbitration priority register (APR) holds the current, lowest-priority of the processor, a value used during lowest priority arbitration (see Section 7.4.13., "APIC Bus Arbitration Mechanism and Protocol"). The APR format is identical to that of the TPR. The APR value is computed as the following.

```
IF (TPR[7:4] ≥ IRRV[7:4]) AND (TPR[7:4] > ISRV[7:4])
    THEN
        APR[7:0] = TPR[7:0]
    ELSE
        APR[7:4] = max(TPR[7:4] AND ISRV[7:4], IRRV[7:4]), APR[3:0]=0.
```

Here, IRRV is the interrupt vector with the highest priority IRR bit set or cleared (if no IRR bit is set). The APR address is FEE0 0090H, and its value after reset is 0.

7.4.10.5. SPURIOUS INTERRUPT

A special situation may occur when a processor raises its task priority to be greater than or equal to the level of the interrupt for which the processor INTR signal is currently being asserted. If at the time the INTA cycle is issued, the interrupt that was to be dispensed has become masked (programmed by software), the local APIC will return a spurious interrupt vector to the processor. Dispensing the spurious interrupt vector does not affect the ISR, so the handler for this vector should return without an EOI.

7.4.10.6. END-OF-INTERRUPT (EOI)

During the interrupt serving routine, software should indicate acceptance of lowest-priority, fixed, timer, and error interrupts by writing an arbitrary value into its local APIC end-of-interrupt (EOI) register (see Figure 7-12). This is an indication for the local APIC it can issue the next interrupt, regardless of whether the current interrupt service has been terminated or not. Note that interrupts whose priority is higher than that currently in service, do not wait for the EOI command corresponding to the interrupt in service.

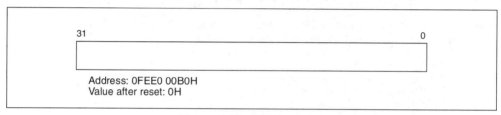

Figure 7-12. EOI Register

Upon receiving end-of-interrupt, the APIC clears the highest priority bit in the ISR and selects the next highest priority interrupt for posting to the CPU. If the terminated interrupt was a level-triggered interrupt, the local APIC sends an end-of-interrupt message to all I/O APICs. Note that EOI command is supplied for the above two interrupt delivery modes regardless of the interrupt source (that is, as a result of either the I/O APIC interrupts or those issued on local pins or using the ICR). For future compatibility, the software is requested to issue the end-of-interrupt command by writing a value of 0H into the EOI register.

7.4.11. Local APIC State

All local APICs are initialized in a software-disabled state after power-up. A software-disabled local APIC unit responds only to self-interrupts and to INIT, NMI, SMI, and start-up messages arriving on the APIC Bus. The operation of local APICs during the disabled state is as follows:

- For the INIT, NMI, SMI, and start-up messages, the APIC behaves normally, as if fully enabled.

- Pending interrupts in the IRR and ISR registers are held and require masking or handling by the CPU.

- A disabled local APIC does not affect the sending of APIC messages. It is software's responsibility to avoid issuing ICR commands if no sending of interrupts is desired.

- Disabling a local APIC does not affect the message in progress. The local APIC will complete the reception/transmission of the current message and then enter the disabled state.

- A disabled local APIC automatically sets all mask bits in the LVT entries. Trying to reset these bits in the local vector table will be ignored.

- A disabled local APIC listens to all bus messages in order to keep its arbitration ID synchronized with the rest of the system.

7.4.11.1. SPURIOUS-INTERRUPT VECTOR REGISTER

Software can enable or disable a local APIC at any time by programming bit 8 of the spurious-interrupt vector register (SVR), see Figure 7-13. The functions of the fields in the SVR are as follows:

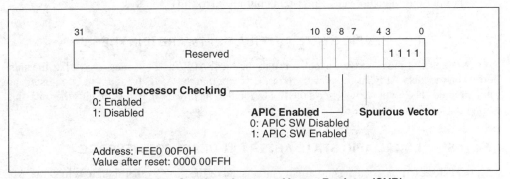

Figure 7-13. Spurious Interrupt Vector Register (SVR)

Spurious Vector | Released during an INTA cycle when all pending interrupts are masked or when no interrupt is pending. Bits 4 through 7 of the this field are programmable by software, and bits 0 through 3 are hardwired to logical ones. Software writes to bits 0 through 3 have no effect.

APIC Enable | Allows software to enable (1) or disable (0) the local APIC.

Focus Processor Checking | Determines if focus processor checking is enabled during the lowest priority delivery: (0) enabled and (1) disabled.

7.4.11.2. LOCAL APIC INITIALIZATION

On a hardware reset, the processor and its local APIC are initialized simultaneously. The local APIC obtains its physical ID at the falling edge of the RESET# signal by sampling 6 lines on the system bus (the BR[3:0]) and cluster ID[1:0] lines) and stores this value into the APIC ID register.

7.4.11.3.   LOCAL APIC STATE AFTER POWER-UP RESET

The state of local APIC registers and state machines after a power-up reset are as follows:

- The following registers are all reset to 0: the IRR, ISR, TMR, ICR, LDR, and TPR registers; the holding registers; the timer initial count and timer current count registers; the remote register; and the divide configuration register.

- The DFR register is reset to all 1s.

- The LVT register entries are reset to 0 except for the mask bits, which are set to 1s.

- The local APIC version register is not affected.

- The local APIC ID and Arb ID registers are loaded from processor input pins (the Arb ID register is set to the APIC ID value for the local APIC).

- All internal state machines are reset.

- APIC is software disabled (that is bit 8 of the SVR register is set to 0).

- The spurious interrupt vector register is initialized to FFH.

7.4.11.4.   LOCAL APIC STATE AFTER A SOFTWARE (INIT) RESET

An INIT reset of the processor is delivered to the local APIC as a bus message. It has the same effect on the local APIC as the power-up reset, except that the APIC ID and Arb ID registers are not affected. The local APIC asserts the INIT signal to its processor, which begins the initialization process in the local APIC.

7.4.11.5.   LOCAL APIC STATE AFTER INIT-DEASSERT MESSAGE

An INIT-disassert message has no affect on the state of the APIC, other than to reload the arbitration ID register with the value in the APIC ID register.

7.4.12. Local APIC Version Register

The local APIC contains a hardwired version register, which software can use to identify the APIC version (see Figure 7-15). In addition, the version register specifies the size of LVT used in the specific implementation. The fields in the local APIC version register are as follows:

Version   The version numbers of the local APIC or an external 82489DX APIC controller:

        1XH   local APIC.

        0XH   82489DX.

        20H through FFH   reserved.

Max LVT Entry   Shows the number of the highest order LVT entry. For the Pentium Pro processor, having 5 LVT entries, the Max LVT number is 4.

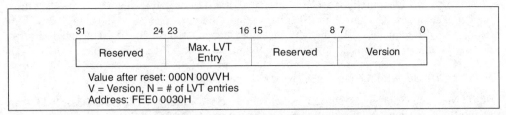

Figure 7-14. Local APIC Version Register

7.4.13. APIC Bus Arbitration Mechanism and Protocol

Because only one message can be sent at a time on the APIC bus, the I/O APIC and local APICs employ a "rotating priority" arbitration protocol to gain permission to send a message on the APIC bus. One or more APICs may start sending their messages simultaneously. At the beginning of every message, each APIC presents the type of the message it is sending and its current arbitration priority on the APIC bus. This information is used for arbitration. After each arbitration cycle (within an arbitration round, only the potential winners keep driving the bus. By the time all arbitration cycles are completed, there will be only one APIC left driving the bus. Once a winner is selected, it is granted exclusive use of the bus, and will continue driving the bus to send its actual message.

After each successfully transmitted message, all APICs increase their arbitration priority by 1. The previous winner (that is, the one that has just successfully transmitted its message) assumes a priority of 0 (lowest). An agent whose arbitration priority was 15 (highest) during arbitration, but did not send a message, adopts the previous winner's arbitration priority, incremented by 1.

Note that the arbitration protocol described above is slightly different if one of the APICs issues a special End-Of-Interrupt (EOI). This high-priority message is granted the bus regardless of its sender's arbitration priority, unless more than one APIC issues an EOI message simultaneously. In the latter case, the APICs sending the EOI messages arbitrate using their arbitration priorities.

If the APICs are set up to use "lowest priority" arbitration (see Section 7.4.7., "Interrupt Distribution Mechanisms") and multiple APICs are currently executing at the lowest priority (the value in the APR register), the arbitration priorities (unique values in the Arb ID register) are used to break ties. All 8 bits of the APR are used for the lowest priority arbitration.

7.4.13.1. BUS MESSAGE FORMATS

The APICs use 4 types of messages: EOI message, short message, non-focused lowest priority message, and remote read message. The purpose of each type of message and its format are described below.

EOI Message. Local APICs send 14-cycle EOI messages to the I/O APIC to indicate that a level triggered interrupt has been accepted by the processor. This interrupt, in turn, is a result of software writing into the EOI register of the local APIC. Table 7-3 shows the cycles in an EOI message.

The checksum is computed for cycles 6 through 9. It is a cumulative sum of the 2-bit (Bit1:Bit0) logical data values. The carry out of all but the last addition is added to the sum. If any APIC computes a different checksum than the one appearing on the bus in cycle 10, it signals an error, driving 11 on the APIC bus during cycle 12. In this case, the APICs disregard the message. The sending APIC will receive an appropriate error indication (see Section 7.4.14., "Error Handling") and resend the message. The status cycles are defined in Table 7-6.

Short Message. Short messages (21-cycles) are used for sending fixed, NMI, SMI, INIT, start-up, ExtINT and lowest-priority-with-focus interrupts. Table 7-4 shows the cycles in a short message.

Table 7-3. EOI Message (14 Cycles)

Cycle	Bit1	Bit0	
1	1	1	11 = EOI
2	ArbID3	0	Arbitration ID bits 3 through 0
3	ArbID2	0	
4	ArbID1	0	
5	ArbID0	0	
6	V7	V6	Interrupt vector V7 - V0
7	V5	V4	
8	V3	V2	
9	V1	V0	
10	C	C	Checksum for cycles 6 - 9
11	0	0	
12	A	A	Status Cycle 0
13	A1	A1	Status Cycle 1
14	0	0	Idle

If the physical delivery mode is being used, then cycles 15 and 16 represent the APIC ID and cycles 13 and 14 are considered don't care by the receiver. If the logical delivery mode is being used, then cycles 13 through 16 are the 8-bit logical destination field. For shorthands of "all-incl-self" and "all-excl-self," the physical delivery mode and an arbitration priority of 15 (D0:D3 = 1111) are used. The agent sending the message is the only one required to distinguish between the two cases. It does so using internal information.

When using lowest priority delivery with an existing focus processor, the focus processor identifies itself by driving 10 during cycle 19 and accepts the interrupt. This is an indication to other APICs to terminate arbitration. If the focus processor has not been found, the short message is extended on-the-fly to the non-focused lowest-priority message. Note that except for the EOI message, messages generating a checksum or an acceptance error (see Section 7.4.14., "Error Handling") terminate after cycle 21.

Table 7-4. Short Message (21 Cycles)

Cycle	Bit1	Bit0	
1	0	1	0 1 = normal
2	ArbID3	0	Arbitration ID bits 3 through 0
3	ArbID2	0	
4	ArbID1	0	
5	ArbID0	0	
6	DM	M2	DM = Destination Mode
7	M1	M0	M2-M0 = Delivery mode
8	L	TM	L = Level, TM = Trigger Mode
9	V7	V6	V7-V0 = Interrupt Vector
10	V5	V4	
11	V3	V2	
12	V1	V0	
13	D7	D6	D7-D0 = Destination
14	D5	D4	
15	D3	D2	
16	D1	D0	
17	C	C	Checksum for cycles 6-16
18	0	0	
19	A	A	Status cycle 0
20	A1	A1	Status cycle 1
21	0	0	Idle

Non-Focused Lowest Priority Message. These 34-cycle messages (see Table 7-5) are used in the lowest priority delivery mode when a focus processor is not present. Cycles 1 through 20 are same as for the short message. If during the status cycle (cycle 19) the state of the (A:A) flags is 10B, a focus processor has been identified, and the short message format is used (see Table 7-4). If the (A:A) flags are set to 00B, lowest priority arbitration is started and the 34-cycles of the non-focused lowest priority message are competed. For other combinations of status flags, refer to Section 7.4.13.2., "APIC Bus Status Cycles".

Table 7-5. Non-Focused Lowest Priority Message (34 Cycles)

Cycle	Bit0	Bit1	
1	0	1	0 1 = normal
2	ArbID3	0	Arbitration ID bits 3 through 0
3	ArbID2	0	
4	ArbID1	0	
5	ArbID0	0	
6	DM	M2	DM = Destination mode
7	M1	M0	M2-M0 = Delivery mode
8	L	TM	L = Level, TM = Trigger Mode
9	V7	V6	V7-V0 = Interrupt Vector
10	V5	V4	
11	V3	V2	
12	V1	V0	
13	D7	D6	D7-D0 = Destination
14	D5	D4	
15	D3	D2	
16	D1	D0	
17	C	C	Checksum for cycles 6-16
18	0	0	
19	A	A	Status cycle 0
20	A1	A1	Status cycle 1
21	P7	0	P7 - P0 = Inverted Processor Priority
22	P6	0	
23	P5	0	
24	P4	0	
25	P3	0	
26	P2	0	
27	P1	0	
28	P0	0	
29	ArbID3	0	Arbitration ID 3 -0
30	ArbID2	0	
31	ArbID1	0	
32	ArbID0	0	
33	A2	A2	Status Cycle
34	0	0	Idle

Cycles 21 through 28 are used to arbitrate for the lowest priority processor. The processors participating in the arbitration drive their inverted processor priority on the bus. Only the local APICs having free interrupt slots participate in the lowest priority arbitration. If no such APIC exists, the message will be rejected, requiring it to be tried at a later time.

Cycles 29 through 32 are also used for arbitration in case two or more processors have the same lowest priority. In the lowest priority delivery mode, all combinations of errors in cycle 33 (A2 A2) will set the "accept error" bit in the error status register (see Figure 7-15). Arbitration priority update is performed in cycle 20, and is not affected by errors detected in cycle 33. Only the local APIC that wins in the lowest priority arbitration, drives cycle 33. An error in cycle 33 will force the sender to resend the message.

7.4.13.2.   APIC BUS STATUS CYCLES

Certain cycles within an APIC bus message are status cycles. During these cycles the status flags (A:A) and (A1:A1) are examined. Table 7-6 shows how these status flags are interpreted, depending on the current delivery mode and existence of a focus processor.

Table 7-6. APIC Bus Status Cycles Interpretation

Delivery Mode	Focus Processor	Status A A	Comments	Status A1 A1	Comments
Fixed, EOI	Not Applicable	0 0	CS OK	1 0 1 1 0 X	Accepted Retry Accept Error
		1 1 1 0 0 1	CS Error Error Error	0 0 0 0 0 0	
NMI, SMI, INIT, ExtINT, Start-Up	Not Applicable	0 0	CS OK	1 0 1 1 0 X	Accepted Error Error
		1 1 1 0 0 1	CS Error Error Error	0 0 0 0 0 0	
Lowest Priority	No	0 0	CS OK, no focus	1 1 1 0 0 X	Do lowest priority arbitration* End and Retry Error
	Yes	1 0 1 1 0 1	CS OK, focus CS Error Error	0 0 0 0 0 0	

NOTE:

*   Status: A2 A2 flags (relevant for lowest priority arbitration only)

    1   0   Accept
    1   1   Error
    0   X   Error

7.4.14. Error Handling

The local APIC sets flags in the error status register (ESR) to record all the errors that is detects (see Figure 7-15). The ESR is a read/write register and is reset after being written to by the processor. A write to the ESR must be done just prior to reading the ESR to allow the register to be updated. An error interrupt is generated when one of the error bits is set. Error bits are cumulative. The ESR must be cleared by software after unmasking of the error interrupt entry in the LVT is performed (by executing back-to-back a writes). If the software, however, wishes to handle errors set in the register prior to unmasking, it should write and then read the ESR prior or immediately after the unmasking.

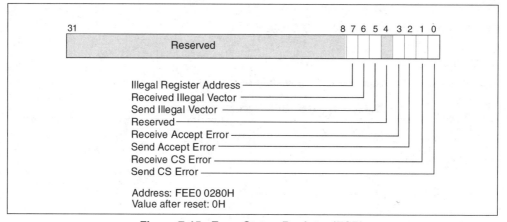

Figure 7-15. Error Status Register (ESR)

The functions of the ESR flags are as follows:

Send CS Error	Set when the local APIC detects a check sum error for a message that was sent by it.
Receive CS Error	Set when the local APIC detects a check sum error for a message that was received by it.
Send Accept Error	Set when the local APIC detects that a message it sent was not accepted by any APIC on the bus.
Receive Accept Error	Set when the local APIC detects that the message it received was not accepted by any APIC on the bus, including itself.
Send Illegal Vector	Set when the local APIC detects an illegal vector in the message that it is sending on the bus.
Receive Illegal Vector	Set when the local APIC detects an illegal vector in the message it received, including an illegal vector code in the local vector table interrupts and self-interrupts from ICR.
Illegal Reg. Address	Set when the processor is trying to access a register that is not implemented in the Pentium Pro processor local APIC register address space (that is, within FEE00000H through FEE003FFH).

7.4.15. Timer

The local APIC unit contains a 32-bit programmable timer for use by the local processor. This timer is configured through the timer register in the local vector table (see Figure 7-7). The time base is derived from the processor's bus clock, divided by a value specified in the divide configuration register (see Figure 7-16). After reset, the timer is initialized to zero. The timer supports one-shot and periodic modes. The timer can be configured to interrupt the local processor with an arbitrary vector.

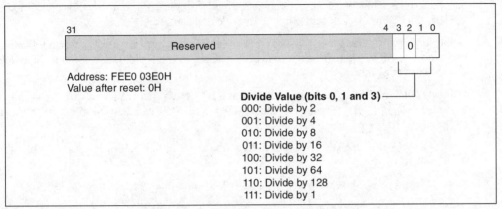

Figure 7-16. Divide Configuration Register

The timer is started by programming its initial-count register, see Figure 7-17. The initial count value is copied into the current-count register and count-down is begun. After the timer reaches zero in one-shot mode, an interrupt is generated and the timer remains at its 0 value until reprogrammed. In periodic mode, the current-count register is automatically reloaded from the initial-count register when the count reaches 0 and the count-down is repeated. If during the count-down process the initial-count register is set, the counting will restart and the new value will be used. The initial-count register is read-write by software, while the current-count register is read only.

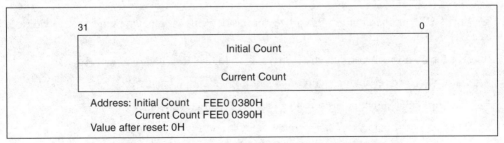

Figure 7-17. Initial Count and Current Count Registers

7.4.16. Software Visible Differences Between the Local APIC and the 82489DX

The following local APIC features differ in their definitions from the 82489DX features:

- In the local APIC does not clear any registers. It sets the mask bits in the local vector tables and ceases accepting the bus messages except for INIT, SMI, NMI, remote read and start-up. In the 82489DX, when the local unit is disabled by resetting the bit 8 of the spurious vector register, all the internal registers including the IRR, ISR and TMR are cleared and the mask bits in the local vector tables are set to logical ones. In the disabled mode, 82489DX local unit will accept only the reset deassert message.

- In the local APIC, NMI and INIT (except for INIT deassert) are always treated as edge triggered interrupts, even if programmed otherwise. In the 82489DX these interrupts are always level triggered.

- In local APIC, the interrupts generated through ICR messages are always treated as edge triggered (except INIT Deassert). In the 82489DX, the ICR can be used to generate either edge or level triggered interrupts.

- Logical Destination register the local APIC supports 8 bits, where it supports 32 bits for the 82489DX.

- APIC ID register is 4 bits wide for the local APIC and 8 bits wide for the 82489DX.

7.4.17. Performance Related Differences between the Local APIC and the 82489DX

For the 82489DX, in the lowest priority mode, all the target local APICs specified by the destination field participate in the lowest priority arbitration. Only those local APICs which have free interrupt slots will participate in the lowest priority arbitration.

7.4.18. New Features Incorporated in the Pentium® Pro Processor Local APIC

The local APIC in the Pentium Pro processor has the following new features not found in the 82489DX.

- The local APIC supports cluster addressing in logical destination mode.
- Focus processor checking can be enabled/disabled in the local APIC.
- Interrupt input signal polarity can be programmed in the local APIC.
- The local APIC supports SMI through the ICR and I/O redirection table.
- The local APIC incorporates an error status register to log and report errors to the processor.
- The local APIC incorporates an additional local vector table entry to handle performance counter interrupts.

7.5. MULTIPLE PROCESSOR (MP) INITIALIZATION PROTOCOL

The following sections describe an MP initialization protocol that the Pentium Pro processor executes in both single- or multiple-processor system. The MP protocol uses the message passing capabilities of the processor's local APIC to dynamically determine a boot strap processor (BSP). The algorithm used essentially implements a "race for the flag" mechanism using the APIC bus for atomicity.

7.5.1. MP Protocol Goals

The primary goals of the MP protocol are as follows:

- To permit sequential or controlled booting of multiple processors (from 2 to 4) with no dedicated system hardware. The initialization algorithm is not limited to 4 processors; it can support supports from 1 to 15 processors in a multi-clustered system when the APIC busses are tied together. Larger systems are not supported.

- To be able to initiate the MP protocol without the need for a dedicated signal.

- To provide fault tolerance. No single processor is geographically designated the BSP. The BSP is determined dynamically during initialization.

7.5.2. Protocol Requirements and Restrictions

The MP protocol imposes the following requirements and restrictions on the system:

- An APIC clock (APICLK) must be provided on all system based on the Pentium Pro processor.

- All interrupt mechanisms must be disabled for the duration of the MP protocol algorithm. That is, requests generated by interrupting devices must not be seen by the local APIC unit (on board the processor) until the completion of the algorithm.

- The MP protocol should be initiated only after a hardware reset. After completion of the protocol algorithm, a flag is set in the APIC base MSR of the BSP (APIC_BASE.BSP) to indicate that it is the BSP. This flag is cleared for all other processors. If a processor or the complete system is subject to an INIT sequence (either through the INIT# pin or an INIT IPI), then the MP protocol is not re-executed. Instead, each processor examines its BSP flag to determine whether the processor should boot or wait for a STARTUP IPI.

- If the processor needs to participate in the protocol after an INIT sequence, the APIC should be enabled prior to the INIT. This is not a requirement for the BSP.

7.5.3. MP Protocol Nomenclature

Table 7-7 describes the interrupt-style abbreviations that will be used through out the remaining description of the protocol. These IPIs do not define new interrupt messages. They are messages that are special only by virtue of the time that they exist (that is, before the RESET sequence is complete).

Table 7-7. Types of Boot Phase IPIs

Message Type	Abbreviation	Description
Boot Inter-Processor Interrupt	BIPI	An APIC serial bus message that Symmetric Multi-Processing (SMP) agents use to dynamically determine a BSP after reset.
Final Boot Inter Processor Interrupt	FIPI	An APIC serial bus message that the BSP issues before it fetches from the reset vector. This message has the lowest priority of all boot phase IPIs. When a BSP sees an FIPI that it issued, it fetches the reset vector because no other boot phase IPIs can follow an FIPI.
Startup Inter-Processor Interrupt	SIPI	Used to send a new reset vector to a Application Processor (non-BSP) processor in an MP system.

Table 7-8 describes the various fields of each boot phase IPI.

Table 7-8. Boot Phase IPI Message Format

Type	Destination Field	Destination Shorthand	Trigger Mode	Level	Destination Mode	Delivery Mode	Vector (Hex)
BIPI	Not used	All including self	Edge	Deassert	Don't Care	Fixed (000)	40 to 4E*
FIPI	Not used	All including self	Edge	Deassert	Don't Care	Fixed (000)	10 to 1E
SIPI	Used	All allowed	Edge	Assert	Physical or Logical	StartUp (110)	00 to FF

NOTE:

* For all Pentium® Pro processors.

For BIPI and FIPI messages, the lower 4 bits of the vector field are equal to the APIC ID of the processor issuing the message. The upper 4 bits of the vector field of a BIPI or TIPI can be thought of as the "generation ID" of the message. All processors that run symmetric to a Pentium Pro processor will have a generation ID of 0100B or 4H. BIPIs in a system based on the Pentium Pro processor will therefore use vector values ranging from 40H to 4EH (4FH can not be used because FH is not a valid APIC ID).

7.5.4.   Error Detection During the MP Initialization Protocol

Errors may occur on the APIC bus during the MP initialization phase. These errors may be transient or permanent and can be caused by a variety of failure mechanisms (for example, broken traces, soft errors during bus usage, etc.). All serial bus related errors will result in an APIC checksum or acceptance error.

The occurrence of an APIC error causes a processor shutdown.

7.5.5. Error Handling During the MP Initialization Protocol

The MP initialization protocol makes the following assumptions:

- If any errors are detected on the APIC bus during execution of the MP initialization protocol, all processors will shutdown.

- In a system that conforms to Intel architecture guidelines, a likely error (broken trace, check sum error during transmission) will result in no more than one processor booting.

- The MP initialization protocol will be executed by processors even if they fail their BIST sequences.

7.5.6. MP Initialization Protocol Algorithm

The MP initialization protocol algorithm (using the APIC bus) is based on the fact that one and only one message is allowed to exist on the APIC bus at a given time and that once the message is issued, it will complete (APIC messages are atomic). Another feature of the APIC architecture that is used in the initialization algorithm is the existence of a round-robin priority mechanism between all agents that use the APIC bus.

The MP initialization protocol algorithm performs the following operations in a SMP system (see Figure 7-1):

1. After completing their internal BISTs, all processors start their MP initialization protocol sequence by issuing BIPIs to "all including self" (at time t=0). The four least significant bits of the vector field of the IPI contain each processor's APIC ID. The APIC hardware observes the BNR# (block next request) and BPRI# (priority-agent bus request) pins to guarantee that the initial BIPI is not issued on the APIC bus until the BIST sequence is complete for all processors in the system.

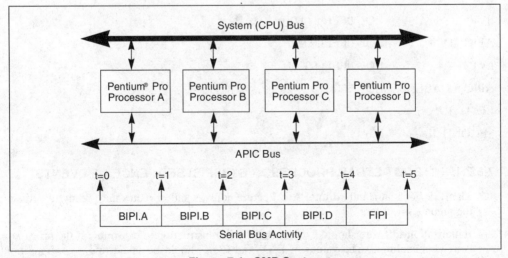

Figure 7-1. SMP System

2. When the first BIPI completes (at time t=1), the APIC hardware (in each processor) propagates an interrupt to the processor core to indicate the arrival of the BIPI.

3. The processor compares the four least significant bits of the BIPI's vector field to the processor's APIC ID. A match indicates that the processor should be the BSP and continue the initialization sequence. If the APIC ID fails to match the BIPIs vector field, the processor is essentially the "loser" or not the BSP. The processor then becomes an application processor and should enter a "wait for SIPI" loop.

4. The winner (the BSP) issues an FIPI. The FIPI is issued to "all including self" and is guaranteed to be the last IPI on the APIC bus during the initialization sequence. This is due to the fact that the round-robin priority mechanism forces the winning APIC agent's (the BSPs) arbitration priority to 0. The FIPI is therefore issued by a priority 0 agent and has to wait until all other agents have issued their BIPI's. When the BSP receives the FIPI that it issued (t=5), it will start fetching code at the reset vector (Intel architecture address).

5. All application processors (non-BSP processors) remain in a halted state until woken up by SIPIs issued by the BSP.

7.5.7. Two-Processor Bootup Handshake Protocol Sequence With Examples

The following example shows the protocol for booting two Pentium Pro processors in a multiple-processor system and initializing their APICs.

The following constants and data definitions are used in this document code examples. They are based on the addresses of the APIC registers as defined in Table 7-1.

ICR_LOW	EQU 0FEE00300H
ICR_HI	EQU 0FEE00310H
SVR	EQU 0FEE000F0H
APIC_ID	EQU 0FEE00020H
LVT3	EQU 0FEE00370H
APIC_ENABLED	EQU 100H
BOOT_ID	DW ?
SECOND_ID	DW ?

7.5.7.1. BOOT STRAP PROCESSOR'S (BSP'S) SEQUENCE OF EVENTS

1. The BSP boots at standard Intel Architecture address and executes until ready to activate the second processor.

2. Initialization software should execute the CPUID instruction to determine if the processor is a "GenuineIntel." The values of EAX and EDX should be saved into a configuration RAM space for use later.

3. The following operation can be used to detect the second processor:

    Set a timer before sending the start-up IPI to the second processor (AP). In the APs initialization routine, it should write a value into memory indicating its presence. The BSP can then use the timer expiration to check if something has been written into memory. If the timer expires and nothing has been written into memory, the AP is not present or some error has occurred.

4. Load start-up code for the AP to execute into a 4-KByte page in the lower 1 MByte of memory.

5. Switch to protected mode (to access APIC address space above 1 MByte) or change the APIC base to less than 1 MByte and insure it is mapped to an uncached (UC) memory type.

6. Determine the BSP's APIC ID from the local APIC ID register.
    ```
    MOV ESI, APIC_ID; address of local APIC ID register
    MOV EAX, [ESI]
    AND EAX, 0F000000H; zero out all other bits except APIC ID
    MOV BOOT_ID, EAX; save in memory
    ```
    Save the ID in the configuration RAM (optional).

7. Determine APIC ID of the AP and save it in the configuration RAM (optional).
    ```
    MOV EAX, BOOT_ID
    XOR EAX, 100000H; toggle lower bit of ID field (bit 24)
    MOV SECOND_ID, EAX
    ```

8. Convert the base address of the 4-KByte page for the AP's bootup code into 8-bit vector. The 8-bit vector defines the address of a 4-KByte page in the real-address mode address space (1-MByte space). For example, a vector of 0BDH specifies a start-up memory address of 000BD000H.

    Steps 9 and 10 are used if the programmer wants to use the LVT APIC error handling entry to deal with unsuccessful delivery of the start-up IPI.

9. Enable the local APIC by writing to spurious vector register (SVR). This is required to do APIC error handling via the local vector table.
    ```
    MOV ESI, SVR    ; address of SVR
    MOV EAX, [ESI]
    OR  EAX, APIC_ENABLED; set bit 8 to enable (0 on reset)
    MOV [ESI], EAX
    ```

10. Program LVT3 (APIC error interrupt vector) of the local vector table with an 8-bit vector for handling APIC errors
    ```
    MOV ESI, LVT3
    MOV EAX, [ESI]
    AND EAX, FFFFFF00H; clear out previous vector
    OR EAX, 000000xxH; xx is the 8-bit vector for APIC error
                    ; handling.
    MOV [ESI], EAX
    ```

11. Write APIC ICRH with address of the AP's APIC.

```
MOV ESI, ICR_HI ; address of ICR high dword
MOV EAX, [ESI]  ; get high word of ICR
AND EAX, 0F0FFFFFFH; zero out ID Bits
 OR  EAX, SECOND_ID; write ID into appropriate bits - don't
                  ; affect reserved bits
MOV [ESI], SECOND_ID; write upgrade ID to destination field
```

12. Initialize the memory location into which the AP will write to signal it's presence.

13. Set the timer with an appropriate value (~100 milliseconds).

14. Write APIC ICRL to send a start-up IPI message via the APIC.

```
MOV ESI, ICR_LOW; write address of ICR low dword
MOV EAX, [ESI]  ; get low dword of ICR
AND EAX, 0FFF0F800H; zero out delivery mode and vector fields
 OR  EAX, 000006xxH; 6 selects delivery mode 110 (StartUp IPI)
                  ; xx should be vector of 4kb page as
                  ; computed in Step 8.
MOV [ESI], EAX
```

15. Wait for timer interrupt or AP signal appearing in memory

16. If necessary, reconfigure the APIC and continue with the remaining system diagnostics as appropriate.

7.5.7.2.   AP'S SEQUENCE OF EVENTS FOLLOWING START-UP IPI

If the AP's APIC is to be used for symmetric multiprocessing, the following steps must be taken (executed by the other processors after receiving SIPIs):

1. Switch to protected mode to access the APIC addresses.

2. Initialize the local APIC by writing to bit 8 of the SVR register and programming its LVT3 for error handling.

3. Configure the APIC as appropriate.

4. Enable interrupts.

5. (Optional) Execute the CPUID instruction and write the results into the configuration RAM or update the multiple-processor specification table entries.

6. Write into the memory location that is being used to signal to the BSP that the AP is executing.

7. Continue execution i.e. self configuration, MP Specification Configuration table completion or execute a HLT instruction and wait for an IPI from the operating system.

7.5.7.3. PROGRAM THE LINT0 AND LINT1 INPUTS

The following procedure describes how to program the LINT0# and LINT1# local APIC pins on a processor after multiple processors have been booted and initialized. In this example, LINT0# is programmed to be an ExtINT pin and LINT1# is programmed to be an NMI pin.

The following constants are defined:

LVT1	EQU 0FEE00350H
LVT2	EQU 0FEE00360H
LVT3	EQU 0FEE00370H
SVR	EQU 0FEE000F0H

1. Mask 8259 interrupts.

2. Enable APIC via SVR (spurious vector register) if not already enabled.

```
MOV ESI, SVR    ; address of SVR
MOV EAX, [ESI]
OR  EAX, APIC_ENABLED; set bit 8 to enable (0 on reset)
MOV [ESI], EAX
```

3. Program LVT1 as an ExtINT which delivers the signal to the INTR signal of all processors cores listed in the destination as an interrupt that originated in an externally connected interrupt controller.

```
MOV ESI, LVT1
MOV EAX, [ESI]
AND EAX, 0FFFE58FFH; mask off bits 8-10, 12, 14 and 16
OR  EAX, 700H   ; Bit 16=0 for not masked, Bit 15=0 for edge
                ; triggered, Bit 13=0 for high active input
                ; polarity, Bits 8-10 are 111b for ExtINT
MOV [ESI], EAX  ; Write to LVT1
```

4. Program LVT2 as NMI which delivers the signal on the NMI signal of all processor cores listed in the destination.

```
MOV ESI, LVT2
MOV EAX, [ESI]
AND EAX, 0FFFE58FFH; mask off bits 8-10 and 15
OR  EAX, 000000400H; Bit 16=0 for not masked, Bit 15=0 edge
                ; triggered, Bit 13=0 for high active input
                ; polarity, Bits 8-10 are 100b for NMI
MOV [ESI], EAX  ; Write to LVT2
;Unmask 8259 interrupts and allow NMI.
```

intel®

8

Processor
Management and
Initialization

This chapter describes the facilities provided for managing processor wide functions and for initializing the processor. The subjects covered include: processor initialization, FPU initialization, processor configuration, feature determination, mode switching, the model-specific registers (MSRs), and the memory type range registers (MTRRs).

8.1. INITIALIZATION OVERVIEW

Following power-up or an assertion of the RESET# pin, the processor performs a hardware initialization of the processor (known as a hardware reset) and an optional built-in self test (BIST). A hardware reset sets the processor's registers to a known state and places the processor in real-address mode. It also invalidates the internal caches, translation lookaside buffers (TLBs) and the branch target buffer (BTB). The processor will then execute the multiple processor initialization protocol across the APIC bus (see Section 7.5., "Multiple Processor (MP) Initialization Protocol" for more details). From this point, the processor that becomes the bootstrap processor (BSP) immediately starts executing software-initialization code the current code segment beginning at the offset in the EIP register. The software-initialization code performs additional system-specific initialization of the processor's registers and loads system data structures such as the IDT and GDT into memory. When the necessary data structures are loaded into memory, the initialization code can then switch the processor to protected mode and begin executing an initial operating-system task and/or an application program.

The floating-point unit (FPU) is also initialized to a known state during hardware reset. FPU software initialization code can then be executed to perform operations such as setting the precision of the FPU and the exception masks. No special initialization of the FPU is required to switch operating modes; the FPU operates the same regardless of whether the processor is operating in protected, real-address, or virtual-8086 mode.

Asserting the INIT# pin on the processor invokes a similar response to a hardware reset. The major difference is that during an INIT, the internal caches, MSRs, or FPU state are left unchanged (although, the TLBs and BTB are invalidated as with a hardware reset). An INIT provides a method for switching from protected to real-address mode while maintaining the contents of the internal caches.

8.1.1. Processor State After Reset

Table 8-1 shows the state of the flags and other registers following power-up. The state of control register CR0 following reset is 60000010H (see Figure 8-1). In this state, the processor is in real-address mode with paging disabled.

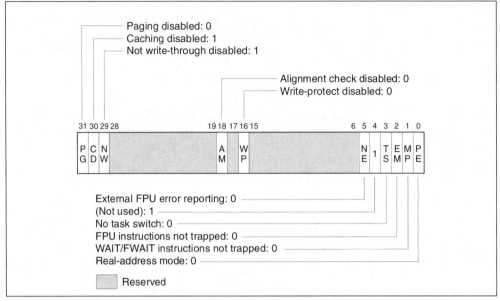

Figure 8-1. Contents of CR0 Register after Reset

8.1.2. Processor Built-In Self Test (BIST)

Hardware may request that the BIST be performed at power-up. If the BIST is performed, it takes about 5.5 million clock periods to complete on the Pentium Pro processor. (This clock count is model-specific and Intel reserves the right to change the exact number of periods without notification.)

The EAX register is clear (0H) if the processor passed the BIST. A non-zero value in the EAX register after the BIST indicates that a processor fault was detected. If the BIST is not requested, the contents of the EAX register after a hardware reset is 0H.

Table 8-1. Pentium® Pro Processor State Following Reset

Register	RESET	INIT
EFLAGS[1]	00000002H	00000002H
EIP	0000FFF0H	0000FFF0H
CR0	60000010H	Note 2
CR2/CR3/CR4	00000000H	00000000H
CS	selector = F000H base = FFFF0000H limit = FFFFH AR = Present, R/W, Accessed	selector = 0F000H base = FFFF000H limit = FFFFH AR = Present, R/W, Accessed

Table 8-1. Pentium® Pro Processor State Following Reset (Contd.)

Register	RESET	INIT
SS, DS, ES, FS, GS	selector = 0000 base = 0000H limit = FFFFH AR = Present, R/W, Accessed	selector = 0000 base =0000H limit = 0FFFFH AR = Present, R/W, Accessed
EDX	000006xxH	000006xxH
EAX	0[3]	0
EBX, ECX, ESI, EDI, EBP, ESP	00000000H	00000000H
LDTR, Task Register	selector = 0000H base = 00000000H limit = FFFFH AR = Present, R/W	selector = 0000H base = 00000000H limit = FFFFH AR = Present, R/W
GDTR,IDTR	base = 00000000H limit = FFFFH AR = Present, R/W	base = 00000000H limit = FFFFH AR = Present, R/W
DR0, DR1, DR2, DR3	00000000H	00000000H
DR6	FFFF0FF0H	FFFF0FF0H
DR7	00000400H	00000400H
Time Stamp Counter	0	Unchanged
Perf. Counters and Event Select	0	Unchanged
All Other MSRs	Undefined	Unchanged
Data and Code Cache, TLBs	Invalid	Invalid
Fixed MTRRs	Disabled	Unchanged
Variable MTRRs	Disabled	Unchanged
Machine Check Architecture	Undefined	Unchanged
APIC	Enabled	Unchanged

NOTES:

1. The 10 most-significant bits of the EFLAGS register are undefined following a reset. Software should not depend on the states of any of these bits.

2. The CD and NW flags are unchanged, bit 4 is set to 1, all other bits are cleared.

3. If Built-In Self Test (BIST) is invoked, EAX is 0 only if all tests passed.

8.1.3.   Model and Stepping Information

Following a hardware reset, the EDX register contains component identification and revision information (see Figure 8-2). The device ID field is set to the value 6H, 5H, 4H, or 3H to indicate a Pentium Pro, Pentium, Intel486, or Intel386 processor, respectively. Different values may be returned for the various members of these Intel Architecture families. For example the Intel386 SX processor returns 23H in the device ID field. Binary object code can be made compatible with other Intel processors by using this number to select the correct initialization software.

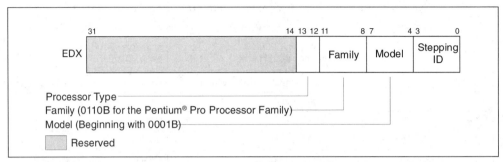

Figure 8-2. Processor Type and Signature in the EDX Register after Reset

The stepping ID field contains a unique identifier for the processor's stepping ID or revision level. The upper word of EDX is reserved following reset.

8.1.4.   First Instruction Executed

The first instruction that is fetched and executed following a hardware reset is located at physical address FFFFFFF0H. This address is 16 bytes below the uppermost physical address of the Pentium Pro processor. The EPROM containing the software-initialization code must be located at this address.

The address FFFFFFF0H is beyond the 1-MByte addressable range of the processor while in real-address mode. The processor is initialized to this starting address as follows. The CS register has two parts: the visible segment selector part and the hidden base address part. In real-address mode, the base address is normally formed by shifting the 16-bit segment selector value 4 bits to the left to produce a 20-bit base address. However, during a hardware reset, the segment selector in the CS register is loaded with F000H and the base address is loaded with FFFF0000H. The starting address is thus formed by adding the base address to the value in the EIP register (that is, FFFF0000 + FFF0H = FFFFFFF0H).

The first time the CS register is loaded with a new value after a hardware reset, the processor will follow the normal rule for address translation in real-address mode (that is, [CS base address = CS segment selector * 16]). To insure that the base address in the CS register remains unchanged until the EPROM based software-initialization code is completed, the code must not contain a far jump or far call (which would cause the CS selector value to be changed).

8.2.   FPU INITIALIZATION

Software-initialization code can determine the whether the processor contains or is attached to an FPU by using the CPUID instruction. The code must then initialize the FPU and set flags in control register CR0 to reflect the state of the FPU environment.

A hardware reset places the Pentium processor FPU in the state shown in Table 8-2. This state is different from the state the processor is placed in when executing an FINIT or FNINIT instruction (also shown in Table 8-2). If the FPU is to be used, the software-initialization code should execute an FINIT/FNINIT instruction following a hardware reset. These instructions, tag all data registers as empty, clear all the exception masks, set the TOP-of-stack value to 0, and select the default rounding and precision controls setting (round to nearest and 64-bit precision).

Table 8-2. FPU State Following Power-Up or Reset and the FINIT/FNINIT Instructions

FPU Register	Power-Up or Reset	FINIT/FNINIT Instruction
ST0 through ST7	+0.0	Unchanged
FPU Control Word	0040H	037FH
FPU Status Word	0000H	0000H
Tag Word	5555H	FFFFH
Data Operand Segment Selector	0000H	0000H
Data Operand Pointer	00000000H	00000000H
CS Segment Selector	0000H	0000H
Instruction Pointer	00000000H	00000000H

If the processor is reset by asserting the INIT# pin, the FPU state is not changed.

8.2.1. Configuring the FPU Environment

Initialization code must load the appropriate values into the MP, EM, and NE flags of control register CR0. These bits are cleared on hardware reset of the processor. Figure 8-3 shows the suggested settings for these flags, depending on the Intel Architecture processor being initialized. Initialization code can test for the type of processor present before setting or clearing these flags.

Table 8-3. Recommended Settings of EM and MP Flags on Intel Architecture Processors

EM	MP	NE	Intel Architecture Processor
1	0	1	Intel486™ SX, Intel386™ DX, and Intel386 SX processors only, without the presence of a math coprocessor.
0	1	1	Pentium® Pro, Pentium, Intel486 DX, and Intel386 DX processors, and Intel487™ SX, Intel387™ DX, and Intel387 SX math coprocessors.

The EM flag determines whether floating-point instructions are executed by the FPU (EM is cleared) or generate a device-not-available exception (#NM) so that an exception handler can emulate the floating-point operation (EM = 1). Ordinarily, the EM flag is cleared when an FPU or math coprocessor is present and set if they are not present. If the EM flag is set and no FPU, math coprocessor, or floating-point emulator is present, the system will hang when a floating-point instruction is executed.

The MP flag determines whether WAIT/FWAIT instructions react to the setting of the TS flag. If the MP flag is clear, WAIT/FWAIT instructions ignore the setting of the TS flag; if the MP flag is set, they will generate a device-not-available exception (#NM) if the TS flag is set. Generally, the MP flag should be set for processors with an integrated FPU and clear for processors without an integrated FPU and without a math coprocessor present. However, an operating system can choose to save the floating-point context at every context switch, in which case there would be no need to set the MP bit.

Table 2-1 shows the actions taken for floating-point and WAIT/FWAIT instructions based on the settings of the EM, MP, and TS flags.

The NE flag determines whether unmasked floating-point exceptions are handled by generating a floating-point error exception (NE is set) or through an external interrupt (NE is cleared). Normally, this flag is set. In systems where an external interrupt controller is used to invoke numeric exception handlers (such as DOS-based systems), the NE bit should be cleared.

8.2.2.   Setting the Processor for FPU Software Emulation

Setting the EM flag causes the processor to generate a device-not-available exception (#NM) and trap to a software exception handler whenever it encounters a floating-point instruction. Setting this flag has two functions:

- It allows floating-point code to run on an Intel processor that neither has an integrated FPU or is connected to an external math coprocessor.

- It allows floating-point code to be executed using a special floating-point emulator, regardless of whether an FPU or math coprocessor is present.

To emulate floating-point instructions, the EM, MP, and NE flag in control register CR0 should be set as shown in Table 8-4.

Table 8-4. Software Emulation Settings of EM, MP, and NE Flags

CR0 Bit	Value
EM	1
MP	0
NE	1

Regardless of the value of the NE bit, the Intel486 SX processor generates a device-not-available exception (#NM) upon encountering any floating point instruction.

8.3.   CACHE ENABLING

The Pentium Pro processor contains two internal caches: level 1 (L1) and level 2 (L2). These caches are enabled by clearing the CD flag in control register CR0. (It is set during a hardware reset.) Because all cache lines are invalid following reset initialization, it is not necessary to invalidate the cache before enabling caching.

Depending on the hardware and operating system or executive requirements, additional configuration of the processor's caching facilities will probably be required. The NW flag in control register CR0 controls whether write-through or write-back caching is used. Page-level caching can be controlled with the PCD and PWT flags in page-directory and page-table entries. The memory type range registers (MTRRs) control the caching characteristics of the regions of physical memory. See Chapter 11, *Memory Cache Control*, for detailed information on configuration of the caching facilities in the Pentium Pro processor and system memory.

8.4. MODEL SPECIFIC REGISTERS (MSRS)

The Pentium Pro processor contains a large number of model-specific registers (MSRs). These registers are by definition implementation specific; that is, they are not guaranteed to be supported on future Intel Architecture processors and/or to have the same functions. The MSRs are provided to control a variety of hardware- and software-related features, including:

- Debug extensions (see Section 10.4., "Last Branch, Interrupt, and Exception Recording").

- The performance-monitoring counters (see Section 10.6., "Performance Monitoring Counters").

- The machine-check exception capability and its accompanying machine-check architecture (see Chapter 16, *Machine Check Architecture*).

- The MTRRs (see Section 11.11., "Memory Type Range Registers (MTRRs)").

The MSRs can be read and written to using the RDMSR and WRMSR instructions, respectively.

When performing software initialization of the Pentium Pro processor, many of the MSRs will need to be initialized to set up things like performance monitoring events, run-time machine checks, and memory types for physical memory.

The list of available MSRs is given in Appendix C, *Model-Specific Registers (MSRs)*. The references earlier in this section show where the functions of the various groups of MSRs are described in this manual.

8.5. MEMORY TYPE RANGE REGISTERS (MTRRS)

Memory type range registers allow a particular type of caching mechanism (or no caching) to be specified in system memory for selected physical address ranges. They allow memory accesses to be optimized for various types of memory such as RAM, ROM, frame buffer memory, and memory-mapped I/O devices.

In general, initializing the MTRRs is normally handled by the software initialization code or BIOS and is not an operating system or executive function. At the very least, all the MTRRs must be cleared to 0, which selects the uncached (UC) memory type. See Section 11.11., "Memory Type Range Registers (MTRRs)" for detailed information on the MTRRs.

8.6. SOFTWARE INITIALIZATION FOR REAL-ADDRESS MODE OPERATION

Following a hardware reset (either through a power-up or the assertion of the RESET# pin) the processor is placed in real-address mode and begins executing software initialization code from physical address FFFFFFF0H. Software initialization code must first set up the necessary data structures for handling basic system functions, such as a real-mode IDT for handling interrupts and exceptions. If the processor is to remain in real-address mode, software must then load additional operating-system or executive code modules and data structures to allow reliable execution of application programs in real-address mode.

If the processor is going to operate in protected mode, software must load the necessary data structures to operate in protected mode and then switch to protected mode. The protected mode data structures that must be loaded are described in Section 8.7., "Software Initialization for Protected Mode Operation".

8.6.1. Real-Address Mode IDT

In real-address mode, the only system data structure that must be loaded into memory is the IDT (also called the "interrupt vector table"). By default, the address of the base of the IDT is physical address 0H. This address can be changed by using the LIDT instruction to change the base address value in the IDTR. Software initialization code needs to load interrupt- and exception-handler pointers into the IDT before interrupts can be enabled.

The actual interrupt- and exception-handler code can be contained either in EPROM or RAM; however, the code must be located within the 1-MByte addressable range of the processor in real-address mode. If the handler code is to be stored in RAM, it must be loaded along with the IDT.

8.6.2. NMI Interrupt Handling

The NMI interrupt is always enabled (except when multiple NMIs are nested). If the IDT and the NMI interrupt handler need to be loaded into RAM, there will be a period of time following hardware reset when an NMI interrupt cannot be handled. During this time, hardware must provide a mechanism to prevent an NMI interrupt from halting code execution until the IDT and the necessary NMI handler software is loaded. Here are two examples of how NMIs can be handled during the initial states of processor initialization:

* A simple 'IDT and NMI interrupt handler can be provided in EPROM. This allows an NMI interrupt to be handled immediately after reset initialization.

* The system hardware can provide a mechanism to enable and disable NMIs by passing the NMI# signal through an AND gate controlled by a flag in an I/O port. Hardware can clear the flag when the processor is reset, and software can set the flag when it is ready to handle NMI interrupts.

8.7. SOFTWARE INITIALIZATION FOR PROTECTED MODE OPERATION

The Pentium Pro processor is placed in real-address mode following a hardware reset. At this point in the initialization process, some basic data structures and code modules must be loaded into physical memory to support further initialization of the processor, as described in Section 8.6., "Software Initialization for Real-Address Mode Operation". Before the processor can be switched to protected mode, the software initialization code must load a minimum number of 'protected mode data structures and code modules into memory to support reliable operation of the processor in protected mode. These data structures include the following:

- A protected-mode IDT.
- A GDT.
- An optional TSS.
- An optional LDT.
- If paging is to be used, at least one page directory and one page table.
- A code segment that contains the code to be executed when the processor switches to protected mode.
- One or more code modules that contain the necessary interrupt and exception handlers.

Software initialization code must also initialize the following system registers before the processor can be switched to protected mode:

- The memory type range registers (MTRRs).
- The GDTR.
- (Optional.) The IDTR. This register can also be initialized immediately after switching to protected mode, prior to enabling interrupts.
- Control registers CR1 through CR4.

With these data structures, code modules, and system registers initialized, the processor can be switched to protected mode by loading control register CR0 with a value that sets the PE flag (bit 0).

8.7.1. Protected-Mode System Data Structures

The contents of the protected-mode system data structures loaded into memory during software initialization, depend largely on the type of memory management the protected-mode operating-system or executive is going to support: flat, flat with paging, segmented, or segmented with paging.

To implement a flat memory model without paging, software initialization code must at a minimum load a GDT with one code and one data segment descriptor. A null descriptor in the first GDT entry is also required. The stack can be placed in a normal read/write data segment, so no descriptor for the stack is required. A flat memory model with paging also requires a page directory and at least one page table (see Section 8.7.3., "Initializing Paging").

Before the GDT can be used, the base address and limit for the GDT must be loaded into the GDTR register using an LGDT instruction.

A multi-segmented model may require additional segments for the operating system, as well as segments and LDTs for each application program. LDTs require segment descriptors in the GDT. Some operating systems allocate new segments and LDTs as they are needed. This provides maximum flexibility for handling a dynamic programming environment. However, many operating systems use a single LDT for all tasks, allocating GDT entries in advance. An embedded system, such as a process controller, might pre-allocate a fixed number of segments and LDTs for a fixed number of application programs. This would be a simple and efficient way to structure the software environment of a real-time system.

8.7.2. Initializing Protected-Mode Exceptions and Interrupts

Software initialization code must at a minimum load a protected-mode IDT with gate descriptor for each exception vector that the processor can generate. If interrupt or trap gates are used, the gate descriptors can all point to the same code segment, which contains the necessary exception handlers. If task gates are used, one TSS and accompanying code, data, and task segments are required for each exception handler called with a task gate.

If hardware allows interrupts to be generated, gate descriptors must be provided in the IDT for one or more for the interrupt handlers.

Before the IDT can be used, the base address and limit for the IDT must be loaded into the IDTR register using an LIDT instruction. This operation is typically carried out immediately after switching to protected mode.

8.7.3. Initializing Paging

Paging is controlled by a mode flag. If the PG flag in control register CR0 controls paging. When this flag is clear (its state following a hardware reset), the paging mechanism is turned off; when it is set, paging is enabled. Before setting the PG flag, the following data structures and registers must be initialized:

- Software must load at least one page directory and one page table into physical memory. The page table can be eliminated if the page directory contains a directory entry pointing to itself. Here, the page directory and page table reside in the same page.

- Control register CR3 (also called the PDBR register) is loaded with the physical base address of the page directory.

- (Optional) Software may provide one set of code and data descriptors in the GDT or in an LDT for supervisor mode and another set for user mode.

With this paging initialization complete, paging can be enabled and the processor can be switched to protected mode at the same time by loading of control register CR0 with the PG and PE flags set.

8.7.4.   Initializing Multitasking

If the multitasking mechanism is not going to be used and changes to more privileged (numerically lower privilege levels) segments are not allowed, it is not necessary load a TSS into memory or to initialize the task register.

If the multitasking mechanism is used or changes to more privileged segments are allowed, software initialization code must load at least one TSS and an accompanying TSS descriptor. (A TSS is required to change privilege levels because pointers to the privileged-level 0, 1, and 2 stack segments and the stack pointers for these stacks are obtained from the TSS.) TSS descriptors must not be marked as busy when they are created; they should be marked busy by the processor only as a side-effect of performing a task switch. As with descriptors for LDTs, TSS descriptors reside in the GDT.

After the processor has switched to protected mode, the LTR instruction can be used to load a segment selector for a TSS descriptor into the task register. This instruction marks the TSS descriptor as busy, but does not perform a task switch. The processor can, however, use the TSS to locate pointers to privilege-level 0, 1, and 2 stacks. The segment selector for the TSS must be loaded before software performs its first task switch in protected mode, because a task switch copies the current task state into the TSS.

After the LTR instruction has been executed, further operations on the task register are performed by task switching. As with other segments and LDTs, TSSs and TSS descriptors can be either pre-allocated or allocated as needed.

8.8.   MODE SWITCHING

To use the processor in protected mode, a mode switch must be performed from real-address mode. Once in protected mode, software generally does not need to return to real-address mode. To run software written to run in real-address mode (8086 mode), it is generally more convenient to run the software in virtual-8086 mode, than to switch back to real-address mode.

8.8.1.   Switching to Protected Mode

Before switching to protected mode, a minimum set of system data structures and code modules must be loaded into memory, as described in Section 8.7., "Software Initialization for Protected Mode Operation". Once these tables are created, software initialization code can switch into protected mode.

Protected mode is entered by executing a MOV CR0 instruction that sets the PE flag in the CR0 register. (In the same instruction, the PG flag in register CR0 can be set to enable paging.) Execution in protected mode begins with a CPL of 0.

The 32-bit Intel Architecture processors have slightly different requirements for switching to protected mode. To insure upwards and downwards code compatibility with all 32-bit Intel Architecture processors, it is recommended that the following steps be performed:

1. Disable interrupts. A CLI instruction disables maskable (INTR) interrupts. NMI interrupts can be disabled with external circuitry. (Software must guarantee that no exceptions or interrupts are generated during the mode switching operation.)

2. Execute the LGDT instruction to load the GDTR register with the base address of the GDT.

3. Execute a MOV CR0 instruction that sets the PE flag (and optionally the PG flag) in control register CR0.

4. Immediately following the MOV CR0 instruction, execute a far JMP or far CALL instruction. (This operation is typically a far jump or call to the next instruction in the instruction stream.)

   The JMP or CALL instruction immediately after the MOV CR0 instruction changes the flow of execution and in effect empties the processor of instructions prefetched in real-address mode.

   The code for the MOV CR0 instruction and the JMP or CALL instruction must come from a page that is identity mapped (that is, the linear address before the jump is the same as the physical address after paging and protected mode is enabled). The target instruction for the JMP or CALL instruction does not need to be identity mapped.

5. If a local descriptor table is going to be used, execute the LLDT instruction to load the segment selector for the LDT in the LDTR register.

6. After entering protected mode, the segment registers continue to hold the contents they had in real-address mode. The JMP or CALL instruction in step 4 resets the CS register. Perform one of the following operations to update the contents of the remaining segment registers.

   — Reload segment registers DS, SS, ES, FS, and GS. If the ES, FS, and/or GS registers are not going to be used, load them with a null selector.

   — Perform a JMP or CALL instruction to a new task, which automatically resets the values of the segment registers and branches to a new code segment.

7. If a jump or call to a task was not performed in step 6, execute the LTR instruction to load the task register with a segment selector to the initial protected-mode task.

8. Execute the LIDT instruction to load the IDTR register with the address and limit of the protected-mode IDT.

9. Execute the STI instruction to enable maskable interrupts and perform the necessary hardware operation to enable NMI interrupts.

8.8.2. Switching Back to Real-Address Mode

The processor switches back to real-address mode if software clears the PE bit in the CR0 register with a MOV CR0 instruction. A procedure that re-enters real-address mode should perform the following steps:

1. Disable interrupts. A CLI instruction disables maskable (INTR) interrupts. NMI interrupts can be disabled with external circuitry.

2. If paging is enabled, perform the following operations:

   — Transfer program control to linear addresses that are identity mapped to physical addresses (that is, linear addresses equal physical addresses).

   — Insure that the GDT and IDT are in identity mapped pages.

   — Clear the PG bit in the CR0 register.

   — Move 0H into the CR3 register to flush the TLB.

3. Transfer program control to a readable segment that has a limit of 64 KBytes (FFFFH). This operation loads the CS register with the segment limit required in real-address mode.

4. Load segment registers SS, DS, ES, FS, and GS with a selector for a descriptor containing the following values, which are appropriate for real-address mode:

   — Limit = 64 KBytes (0FFFFH)

   — Byte granular (G = 0)

   — Expand up (E = 0)

   — Writable (W = 1)

   — Present (P = 1)

   — Base = any value

   The segment registers must be loaded with non-null segment selectors or the segment registers will be unusable in real-address mode. Note that if the segment registers are not reloaded, execution continues using the descriptor attributes loaded during protected mode.

5. Execute an LIDT instruction to point to a real-address mode interrupt table that is within the 1-MByte real-address mode address range.

6. Clear the PE flag in the CR0 register to switch to real-address mode.

7. Execute a far JMP instruction to jump to a real-address mode program. This operation flushes the instruction queue and loads the appropriate base and access rights values in the CS register.

8. Load the SS, DS, ES, FS, and GS registers as needed by the real-address mode code. If any of the registers are not going to be used in real-address mode, write 0s to them.

9. Execute the STI instruction to enable maskable interrupts and perform the necessary hardware operation to enable NMI interrupts.

NOTE

All the code that is executed in steps 1 through 9 must be in a single page and the linear addresses in that page must be identity mapped to physical addresses.

8.9. INITIALIZATION AND MODE SWITCHING EXAMPLE

This section provides an initialization and mode switching example that can be incorporated into an application. This code was originally written to initialize the Intel386 processor, but it will execute successfully on the Pentium Pro, Pentium, and Intel486 processors. The code in this example is intended to reside in EPROM and to run following a hardware reset of the processor. The function of the code is to do the following:

- Establish a basic real-address mode operating environment.

- Load the necessary protected-mode system data structures into RAM.

- Load the system registers with the necessary pointers to the data structures and the appropriate flag settings for protected-mode operation.

- Switch the processor to protected mode.

Figure 8-3 shows the physical memory layout for the processor following a hardware reset and the starting point of this example. The EPROM that contains the initialization code resides at the upper end of the processor's physical memory address range, starting at address FFFFFFFFH and going down from there. The address of the first instruction to be executed is at FFFFFFF0H, the default starting address for the processor following a hardware reset.

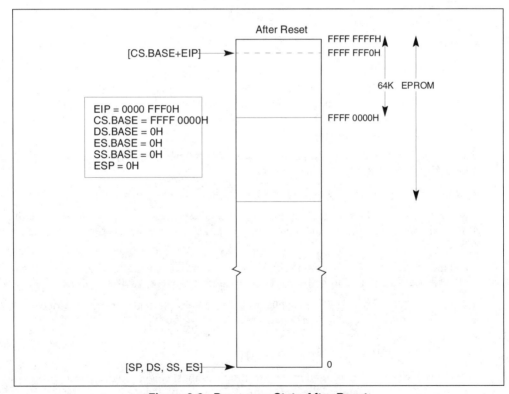

Figure 8-3. Processor State After Reset

The main steps carried out in this example are summarized in Table 8-5. The source listing for the example (with the filename STARTUP.ASM) is given in Example 8-1. The line numbers given in Table 8-5 refer to the source listing.

The following are some additional notes concerning this example:

* When the processor is switched into protected mode, the original code segment base-address value of FFFF0000H (located in the hidden part of the CS register) is retained and execution continues from the current offset in the EIP register. The processor will thus continue to execute code in the EPROM until a far jump or call is made to a new code segment, at which time, the base address in the CS register will be changed.

Table 8-5. Main Initialization Steps in STARTUP.ASM Source Listing

STARTUP.ASM Line Numbers		Description
From	To	
157	157	Jump (short) to the entry code in the EPROM
162	169	Construct a temporary GDT in RAM with one entry: 0 - null 1 - R/W data segment, base = 0, limit = 4 GBytes
171	172	Load the GDTR to point to the temporary GDT
174	177	Load CR0 with PE flag set to switch to protected mode
179	181	Jump near to clear real mode instruction queue
184	186	Load DS, ES registers with GDT[1] descriptor, so both point to the entire physical memory space.
188	195	Perform specific board initialization that is imposed by the new protected mode
196	218	Copy the application's GDT from ROM into RAM
220	238	Copy the application's IDT from ROM into RAM
241	243	Load application's GDTR
244	245	Load application's IDTR
247	261	Copy the application's TSS from ROM into RAM
263	267	Update TSS descriptor and other aliases in GDT (GDT alias or IDT alias)
277	277	Load the task register (without task switch) using LTR instruction
282	286	Load SS, ESP with the value found in the application's TSS
287	287	Push EFLAGS value found in the application's TSS
288	288	Push CS value found in the application's TSS
289	289	Push EIP value found in the application's TSS
290	293	Load DS, ES with the value found in the application's TSS
296	296	Perform IRET; pop the above values and enter the application code

- Maskable interrupts are disabled after a hardware reset and should remain disabled until the necessary interrupt handlers have been installed. The NMI interrupt is not disabled following a reset. The NMI# pin must thus be inhibited from being asserted until an NMI handler has been loaded and made available to the processor.

- The use of a temporary GDT allows simple transfer of tables from the EPROM to anywhere in the RAM area. A GDT entry is constructed with its base pointing to address 0 and a limit of 4 GBytes. When the DS and ES registers are loaded with this descriptor, the temporary GDT is no longer needed and can be replaced by the application GDT.

- This code loads one TSS and no LDTs. If more TSSs exist in the application, they must be loaded into RAM. If there are LDTs they may be loaded as well.

8.9.1. Assembler Usage

In this example, the Intel assembler ASM386 and build tools BLD386 are used to assemble and build the initialization code module. The following assumptions are used when using the Intel ASM386 and BLD386 tools.

- The ASM386 will generate the right operand size opcodes according to the code segment attribute. The attribute is assigned either by the ASM386 invocation controls or in the code segment definition.

- If a code segment that is going to run in real-address mode is defined, it must be set to a USE 16 attribute. If a 32-bit operand is used in an instruction in this code segment (for example, MOV EAX, EBX), the assembler automatically generates an operand prefix for the instruction that forces the processor to execute a 32-bit operation, even though its default code segment attribute is 16-bit.

- Intel's ASM386 assembler allows specific use of the 16- or 32-bit instructions, for example, LGDTW, LGDTD, IRETD. If the generic instruction LGDT is used, the default segment attribute will be used to generate the right opcode.

8.9.2. STARTUP.ASM Listing

The source code listing to move the processor into protected mode is provided in Example 8-1. This listing does not include any opcode and offset information.

Example 8-1. STARTUP.ASM

```
DOS 5.0(045-N) 386(TM) MACRO ASSEMBLER STARTUP  09:44:51  08/19/92
PAGE 1


DOS 5.0(045-N) 386(TM) MACRO ASSEMBLER V4.0, ASSEMBLY OF MODULE
STARTUP
OBJECT MODULE PLACED IN startup.obj
ASSEMBLER INVOKED BY: f:\386tools\ASM386.EXE startup.a58 pw (132 )
```

```
LINE      SOURCE

  1       NAME     STARTUP
  2
  3              ;;;;;;;;;;;;;;;;;;;;;;;;;;;;;;;;;;;;;;;;;;
                   ;;;;;;;;;;;;;;;;;;;;;;;;;;;;;;;;;;;
  4       ;
  5       ;   ASSUMPTIONS:
  6       ;
  7       ;     1.   The bottom 64K of memory is ram, and can be used for
  8       ;          scratch space by this module.
  9       ;
 10       ;     2.   The system has sufficient free usable ram to copy the
 11       ;          initial GDT, IDT, and TSS
 12       ;
 13       ;;;;;;;;;;;;;;;;;;;;;;;;;;;;;;;;;;;;;;;;;;;;;;;;;;;;;;;;;;;;;;;
 14
 15       ; configuration data - must match with build definition
 16
 17       CS_BASE        EQU     0FFFF0000H
 18
 19        ; CS_BASE is the linear address of the segment STARTUP_CODE
 20        ; - this is specified in the build language file
 21
 22       RAM_START      EQU     400H
 23
 24       ; RAM_START  is the start of free, usable ram in the linear
 25       ; memory  space.   The GDT,  IDT, and  initial TSS  will be
 26       ; copied above this space, and a small data segment will be
 27       ; discarded at  this linear  address.   The 32-bit  word at
 28       ; RAM_START will contain  the linear  address of  the first
 29       ; free byte above the copied tables - this may be useful if
 30       ; a memory manager is used.
 31
 32       TSS_INDEX      EQU      10
 33
 34       ; TSS_INDEX is the  index of the  TSS of the  first task to
 35       ; run after startup
 36
 37
 38        ;;;;;;;;;;;;;;;;;;;;;;;;;;;;;;;;;;;;;;;;;;;;;;;;;;;;;;;;;;;;;;;
 39
 40       ; ------------------------ STRUCTURES and EQU ---------------
 41       ; structures for system data
 42
 43       ; TSS structure
 44       TASK_STATE  STRUC
```

```
45      link              DW  ?
46      link_h            DW  ?
47      ESP0              DD  ?
48      SS0               DW  ?
49      SS0_h             DW  ?
50      ESP1              DD  ?
51      SS1               DW  ?
52      SS1_h             DW  ?
53      ESP2              DD  ?
54      SS2               DW  ?
55      SS2_h             DW  ?
56      CR3_reg           DD  ?
57      EIP_reg           DD  ?
58      EFLAGS_reg        DD  ?
59      EAX_reg           DD  ?
60      ECX_reg           DD  ?
61      EDX_reg           DD  ?
62      EBX_reg           DD  ?
63      ESP_reg           DD  ?
64      EBP_reg           DD  ?
65      ESI_reg           DD  ?
66      EDI_reg           DD  ?
67      ES_reg            DW  ?
68      ES_h              DW  ?
69      CS_reg            DW  ?
70      CS_h              DW  ?
71      SS_reg            DW  ?
72      SS_h              DW  ?
73      DS_reg            DW  ?
74      DS_h              DW  ?
75      FS_reg            DW  ?
76      FS_h              DW  ?
77      GS_reg            DW  ?
78      GS_h              DW  ?
79      LDT_reg           DW  ?
80      LDT_h             DW  ?
81      TRAP_reg          DW  ?
82      IO_map_base       DW  ?
83   TASK_STATE  ENDS
84
85   ; basic structure of a descriptor
86   DESC     STRUC
87      lim_0_15          DW  ?
88      bas_0_15          DW  ?
89      bas_16_23         DB  ?
90      access            DB  ?
91      gran              DB  ?
```

```
 92        bas_24_31              DB ?
 93  DESC      ENDS
 94
 95  ; structure for use with LGDT and LIDT instructions
 96  TABLE_REG   STRUC
 97        table_lim              DW ?
 98        table_linear           DD ?
 99  TABLE_REG   ENDS
100
101  ; offset of GDT and IDT descriptors in builder generated GDT
102  GDT_DESC_OFF     EQU 1*SIZE(DESC)
103  IDT_DESC_OFF     EQU 2*SIZE(DESC)
104
105  ; equates for building temporary GDT in RAM
106  LINEAR_SEL            EQU    1*SIZE (DESC)
107  LINEAR_PROTO_LO      EQU    00000FFFFH  ; LINEAR_ALIAS
108  LINEAR_PROTO_HI      EQU    000CF9200H
109
110  ; Protection Enable Bit in CR0
111  PE_BIT  EQU 1B
112
113  ; ------------------------------------------------------------
114
115  ; ----------------------- DATA SEGMENT----------------------
116
117  ; Initially, this  data segment starts at linear 0, according
118  ; to the processor's power-up state.
119
120  STARTUP_DATA     SEGMENT RW
121
122  free_mem_linear_base    LABEL    DWORD
123  TEMP_GDT                LABEL    BYTE  ; must be first in segment
124  TEMP_GDT_NULL_DESC   DESC    <>
125  TEMP_GDT_LINEAR_DESC DESC    <>
126
127  ; scratch areas for LGDT and LIDT instructions
128  TEMP_GDT_SCRATCH TABLE_REG   <>
129  APP_GDT_RAM      TABLE_REG   <>
130  APP_IDT_RAM      TABLE_REG   <>
131          ; align end_data
132  fill    DW        ?
133
134  ; last thing in this segment - should be on a dword boundary
135  end_data    LABEL    BYTE
136
137  STARTUP_DATA     ENDS
138  ; ------------------------------------------------------------
```

```
139
140
141   ; ----------------------- CODE SEGMENT---------------------
142   STARTUP_CODE SEGMENT ER PUBLIC USE16
143
144   ; filled in by builder
145       PUBLIC  GDT_EPROM
146   GDT_EPROM   TABLE_REG   <>
147
148   ; filled in by builder
149       PUBLIC  IDT_EPROM
150   IDT_EPROM   TABLE_REG   <>
151
152   ; entry point into startup code - the bootstrap will vector
153   ; here  with a  near JMP  generated by  the builder.   This
154   ; label must be in the top 64K of linear memory.
155
156       PUBLIC  STARTUP
157   STARTUP:
158
159   ; DS,ES address the bottom 64K of flat linear memory
160       ASSUME  DS:STARTUP_DATA, ES:STARTUP_DATA
161   ; See Figure 8-4
162   ; load GDTR with temporary GDT
163           LEA     EBX,TEMP_GDT  ; build the TEMP_GDT in low ram,
164           MOV     DWORD PTR [EBX],0   ; where we can address
165           MOV     DWORD PTR [EBX]+4,0
166           MOV     DWORD PTR [EBX]+8, LINEAR_PROTO_LO
167           MOV     DWORD PTR [EBX]+12, LINEAR_PROTO_HI
168           MOV     TEMP_GDT_scratch.table_linear,EBX
169           MOV     TEMP_GDT_scratch.table_lim,15
170
171                   DB      66H         ; execute a 32 bit LGDT
172           LGDT    TEMP_GDT_scratch
173
174   ; enter protected mode
175           MOV     EBX,CR0
176           OR      EBX,PE_BIT
177           MOV     CR0,EBX
178
179    ; clear prefetch queue
180           JMP     CLEAR_LABEL
181   CLEAR_LABEL:
182
183    ; make DS and ES address 4G of linear memory
184           MOV     CX,LINEAR_SEL
185           MOV     DS,CX
```

```
186          MOV     ES,CX
187
188     ; do board specific initialization
189     ;
190                       ;
191                       ; ......
192                       ;
193
194
195          ; See Figure 8-5
196          ; copy EPROM GDT to ram at:
197          ;              RAM_START + size (STARTUP_DATA)
198          MOV     EAX,RAM_START
199          ADD     EAX,OFFSET (end_data)
200          MOV     EBX,RAM_START
201          MOV     ECX, CS_BASE
202          ADD     ECX, OFFSET (GDT_EPROM)
203          MOV     ESI, [ECX].table_linear
204          MOV     EDI,EAX
205          MOVZX   ECX, [ECX].table_lim
206          MOV     APP_GDT_ram[EBX].table_lim,CX
207          INC     ECX
208          MOV     EDX,EAX
209          MOV     APP_GDT_ram[EBX].table_linear,EAX
210          ADD     EAX,ECX
211     REP MOVS     BYTE PTR ES:[EDI],BYTE PTR DS:[ESI]
212
213          ; fixup GDT base in descriptor
214          MOV     ECX,EDX
215          MOV     [EDX].bas_0_15+GDT_DESC_OFF,CX
216          ROR     ECX,16
217          MOV     [EDX].bas_16_23+GDT_DESC_OFF,CL
218          MOV     [EDX].bas_24_31+GDT_DESC_OFF,CH
219
220          ; copy EPROM IDT to ram at:
221          ; RAM_START+size(STARTUP_DATA)+SIZE (EPROM GDT)
222          MOV     ECX, CS_BASE
223          ADD     ECX, OFFSET (IDT_EPROM)
224          MOV     ESI, [ECX].table_linear
225          MOV     EDI,EAX
226          MOVZX   ECX, [ECX].table_lim
227          MOV     APP_IDT_ram[EBX].table_lim,CX
228          INC     ECX
229          MOV     APP_IDT_ram[EBX].table_linear,EAX
230          MOV     EBX,EAX
231          ADD     EAX,ECX
232     REP MOVS     BYTE PTR ES:[EDI],BYTE PTR DS:[ESI]
```

```
233
234                          ; fixup IDT pointer in GDT
235          MOV            [EDX].bas_0_15+IDT_DESC_OFF,BX
236          ROR            EBX,16
237          MOV            [EDX].bas_16_23+IDT_DESC_OFF,BL
238          MOV            [EDX].bas_24_31+IDT_DESC_OFF,BH
239
240                          ; load GDTR and IDTR
241          MOV            EBX,RAM_START
242          DB      66H            ; execute a 32 bit LGDT
243          LGDT           APP_GDT_ram[EBX]
244          DB      66H            ; execute a 32 bit LIDT
245          LIDT           APP_IDT_ram[EBX]
246
247                          ; move the TSS
248          MOV            EDI,EAX
249          MOV            EBX,TSS_INDEX*SIZE(DESC)
250          MOV            ECX,GDT_DESC_OFF ;build linear address for TSS
251          MOV            GS,CX
252          MOV            DH,GS:[EBX].bas_24_31
253          MOV            DL,GS:[EBX].bas_16_23
254          ROL            EDX,16
255          MOV            DX,GS:[EBX].bas_0_15
256          MOV            ESI,EDX
257          LSL            ECX,EBX
258          INC            ECX
259          MOV            EDX,EAX
260          ADD            EAX,ECX
261      REP MOVS           BYTE PTR ES:[EDI],BYTE PTR DS:[ESI]
262
263                          ; fixup TSS pointer
264          MOV            GS:[EBX].bas_0_15,DX
265          ROL            EDX,16
266          MOV            GS:[EBX].bas_24_31,DH
267          MOV            GS:[EBX].bas_16_23,DL
268          ROL            EDX,16
269      ;save start of free ram at linear location RAMSTART
270          MOV            free_mem_linear_base+RAM_START,EAX
271
272      ;assume no  LDT used in  the initial task  - if necessary,
273      ;code  to move the LDT could be added, and should resemble
274      ;that used to move the TSS
275
276      ; load task register
277          LTR     BX   ; No task switch, only descriptor loading
278      ; See Figure 8-6
279      ; load minimal set of registers necessary to simulate task
```

```
280      ; switch
281
282
283          MOV     AX,[EDX].SS_reg      ; start loading registers
284          MOV     EDI,[EDX].ESP_reg
285          MOV     SS,AX
286          MOV     ESP,EDI              ; stack now valid
287          PUSH    DWORD PTR [EDX].EFLAGS_reg
288          PUSH    DWORD PTR [EDX].CS_reg
289          PUSH    DWORD PTR [EDX].EIP_reg
290          MOV     AX,[EDX].DS_reg
291          MOV     BX,[EDX].ES_reg
292          MOV     DS,AX       ; DS and ES no longer linear memory
293          MOV     ES,BX

294
295          ; simulate far jump to initial task
296          IRETD
297
298   STARTUP_CODE   ENDS
*** WARNING #377 IN 298, (PASS 2) SEGMENT CONTAINS PRIVILEGED
INSTRUCTION(S)
299
300   END STARTUP, DS:STARTUP_DATA, SS:STARTUP_DATA
301
302


ASSEMBLY COMPLETE,   1 WARNING,   NO ERRORS.
```

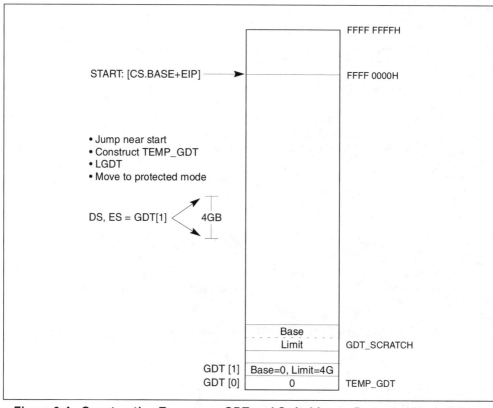

Figure 8-4. Constructing Temporary GDT and Switching to Protected Mode (Lines 162-172 of List File)

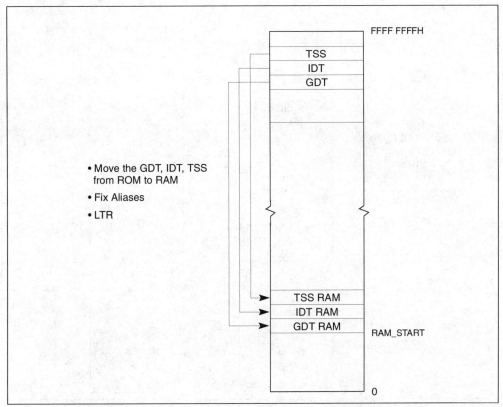

Figure 8-5. Moving the GDT, IDT and TSS from ROM to RAM (Lines 196-261 of List File)

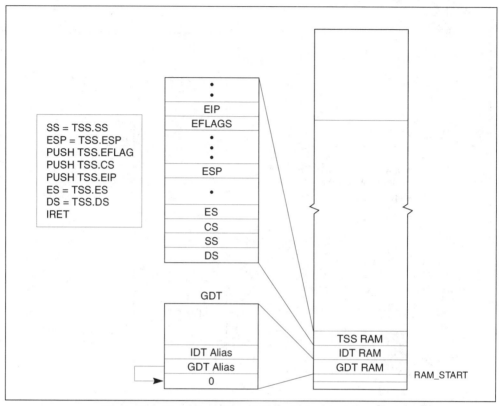

Figure 8-6. Task Switching (Lines 282-296 of List File)

8.9.3.   MAIN.ASM Source Code

The file MAIN.ASM shown in Example 8-2 defines the data and stack segments for this application and can be substituted with the main module task written in a high-level language that is invoked by the IRET instruction executed by STARTUP.ASM.

Example 8-2. MAIN.ASM

```
NAME     main_module
data     SEGMENT RW
     dw 1000 dup(?)
DATA     ENDS
stack stackseg 800
CODE SEGMENT ER   use32 PUBLIC
main_start:
     nop
     nop
     nop
CODE   ENDS
END main_start, ds:data, ss:stack
```

8.9.4.　Supporting Files

The batch file shown in Example 8-3 can be used to assemble the source code files STARTUP.ASM and MAIN.ASM and build the final application.

Example 8-3.　Batch File to Assemble and Build the Application

```
ASM386 STARTUP.ASM
ASM386 MAIN.ASM
BLD386 STARTUP.OBJ, MAIN.OBJ buildfile(EPROM.BLD) bootstrap(STARTUP)
Bootload
```

BLD386 performs several operations in this example:

- It allocates physical memory location to segments and tables.

- It generates tables using the build file and the input files.

- It links object files and resolves references.

- It generates a boot-loadable file to be programmed into the EPROM.

Example 8-4 shows the build file used as an input to BLD386 to perform the above functions.

Example 8-4.　Build File

```
INIT_BLD_EXAMPLE;

SEGMENT
        *SEGMENTS(DPL = 0)
    ,   startup.startup_code(BASE = 0FFFF0000H)
    ;

TASK
        BOOT_TASK(OBJECT = startup, INITIAL,DPL = 0,
                            NOT INTENABLED)
    ,   PROTECTED_MODE_TASK(OBJECT = main_module,DPL = 0,
                            NOT INTENABLED)
    ;

TABLE
    GDT (
        LOCATION = GDT_EPROM
    ,   ENTRY = (
            10:   PROTECTED_MODE_TASK
    ,                 startup.startup_code
    ,         startup.startup_data
    ,         main_module.data
    ,         main_module.code
    ,         main_module.stack
```

```
                    )
               ),

        IDT (
            LOCATION = IDT_EPROM
            );

MEMORY
    (
        RESERVE = (0..3FFFH
                        -- Area for the GDT, IDT, TSS copied from
ROM
        ,                   60000H..0FFFEFFFFH)
        ,   RANGE = (ROM_AREA = ROM (0FFFF0000H..0FFFFFFFFH))
                                -- Eprom size 64K
        ,   RANGE = (RAM_AREA = RAM (4000H..05FFFFH))
        );

END
```

Table 8-6 shows the relationship of each build item with an ASM source file.

Table 8-6. Relationship Between BLD Item and ASM Source File

Item	ASM386 and Startup.A58	BLD386 Controls and BLD file	Effect
Bootstrap	public startup startup:	bootstrap start(startup)	Near jump at 0FFFFFFF0H to start
GDT location	public GDT_EPROM GDT_EPROM TABLE_REG <>	TABLE GDT(location = GDT_EPROM)	The location of the GDT will be programmed into the GDT_EPROM location
IDT location	public IDT_EPROM IDT_EPROM TABLE_REG <>	TABLE IDT(location = IDT_EPROM	The location of the IDT will be programmed into the IDT_EPROM location
RAM start	RAM_START equ 400H	memory(reserve = (0..3FFFH))	RAM_START is used as the ram destination for moving the tables. It must be excluded from the application's segment area.
Location of the application TSS in the GDT	TSS_INDEX EQU 10	TABLE GDT(ENTRY=(10: PROTECTED_MODE_TASK))	Put the descriptor of the application TSS in GDT entry 10
EPROM size and location	size and location of the initialization code	SEGMENT startup.code (base= 0FFFF0000H) ...memory (RANGE(ROM_AREA = ROM(x..y))	Initialization code size must be less than 64K and resides at upper most 64K of the 4GB memory space.

intel®

9

System Management Mode (SMM)

CHAPTER 9
SYSTEM MANAGEMENT MODE (SMM)

The Pentium Pro processor implements Intel's System Management Mode (SMM) architecture. This chapter describes the architectural features of SMM. For a detailed hardware description, refer to the *Pentium® Pro Family Developer's Manual, Volume 1*.

9.1. SYSTEM MANAGEMENT MODE OVERVIEW

SMM is a special-purpose operating mode provided for handling system-wide functions like power management, system hardware control, or proprietary OEM-designed code. It is intended for use only by system firmware, not by applications software or general-purpose systems software. The main benefit of SMM is that it offers a distinct processor environment that operates transparently to the operating system or executive and software applications.

When SMM is invoked through a system management interrupt (SMI), the processor saves the current state of the processor (the processor's context), then switches to a separate operating environment contained in system management RAM (SMRAM). (A multiplexed status signal, EXF4, allows system hardware to decode accesses to SMRAM.) While in SMM, the processor executes SMI handler code to perform tasks such as powering down unused disk drives or monitors, executing proprietary code, or placing the whole system in a suspended state. When the SMI handler has completed its task (or the system receives a resume signal), the handler executes a resume (RSM) instruction. This instruction causes the processor to reload the saved context of the processor, switch back to protected or real mode, and resume executing the interrupted application or operating-system program or task.

The following SMM mechanisms make it transparent to applications programs and operating systems:

- The only way to enter SMM is by means of an SMI.

- The processor executes SMM code in a separate address space (SMRAM) that can be made inaccessible from the other operating modes.

- Upon entering SMM, the processor saves the context of the interrupted program or task.

- All interrupts normally handled by the operating system are disabled upon entry into SMM.

- The RSM can be executed only in SMM.

SMM is similar to real-address mode in that there are no privilege levels or address mapping. An SMM program can address up to 4 GBytes of memory and can execute all I/O and applicable system instructions. See Section 9.5., "SMI Handler Execution Environment" for more information about the SMM execution environment.

9.2. SYSTEM MANAGEMENT INTERRUPT (SMI)

The only way to enter SMM is by signaling an SMI through the SMI# pin on the processor or through an SMI message received through the APIC bus. The SMI is a non-maskable external interrupt that operates independently from the processor's interrupt- and exception-handling mechanism and the local APIC. The SMI takes precedence over an NMI and a maskable interrupt. SMM is non-reentrant; that is, the SMI is disabled while the processor is in SMM.

9.3. SWITCHING BETWEEN SMM AND THE OTHER PROCESSOR OPERATING MODES

Figure 2-2 shows how the processor moves between SMM and the other processor operating modes (protected, real-address, and virtual-8086). Signaling an SMI while the processor is in real-address, protected, or virtual-8086 modes always causes the processor to switch to SMM. Upon execution of the RSM instruction, the processor always returns to the mode it was in when the SMI occurred.

9.3.1. Entering SMM

The processor always handles an SMI on an architecturally defined "interruptible" point in program execution (which is commonly at an Intel Architecture instruction boundary). When the processor receives an SMI, it waits for all instructions to retire and for all stores to complete. The processor then issues an SMIACK transaction on the system bus, saves its current context in SMRAM (see Section 9.4., "SMRAM"), and begins to execute the SMI handler.

A SMI has a greater priority than debug exceptions and external interrupts. Thus, if an NMI, maskable interrupt, or a debug exception occurs at an instruction boundary, only the SMI is handled. Subsequent SMI requests are not acknowledged while the processor is in SMM. The first SMI interrupt request that occurs while the processor is in SMM is latched and serviced when the processor exits SMM with the RSM instruction. The processor will latch only one SMI while in SMM.

See Section 9.5., "SMI Handler Execution Environment" for a detailed description of the execution environment when in SMM.

9.3.1.1. EXITING FROM SMM

The only way to exit SMM is to execute the RSM instruction. The RSM instruction is only available to the SMI handler; if the processor is not in SMM, attempts to execute the RSM instruction result in an invalid-opcode exception (#UD) being generated.

The RSM instruction restores the processor's context by loading the state save image from SMRAM back into the processor's registers. It then returns program control back to the interrupted program.

If the processor detects invalid state information saved in the SMRAM, it enters the shutdown state and generates a special bus cycle to indicate it has entered shutdown state. Shutdown happens only in the following situations:

- A reserved bit in control register CR4 is set to 1 on a write to CR4. This error should not happen unless SMI handler code modifies reserved areas of the SMRAM saved state map (see Section 9.4.1., "SMRAM State Save Map").

- An illegal combination of bits is written to control register CR0, in particular PG set to 1 and PE set to 0, or NW set to 1 and CD set to 0.

In shutdown mode, the processor stops executing instructions until a RESET#, INIT# or NMI# is asserted. The FLUSH# signal is also recognized by the Pentium Pro processor in the shutdown state, but the SMI# signal is not.

If the processor is in the HALT state when the SMI is received, the processor handles the return from SMM slightly differently (see Section 9.10., "Auto HALT Restart"). Also, the SMBASE address can be changed on a return from SMM (see Section 9.11., "SMBASE Relocation").

9.4. SMRAM

While in SMM, the processor executes code and stores data in the SMRAM space. The SMRAM space is mapped to the physical address space of the processor and can be up to 4 GBytes in size. The processor uses this space to save the context of the processor and to store the SMI handler code, data and stack. It can also be used to store system management information (such as the system configuration) and OEM-specific information.

The default SMRAM size is 64 KBytes beginning at a base physical address in physical memory called the SMBASE (see Figure 9-1). The SMBASE default value following a hardware reset is 30000H. The processor looks for the first instruction of the SMI handler at the address [SMBASE + 8000H]. It stores the processors state in the area from [SMBASE + FE00H] to [SMBASE + FFFFH]. See Section 9.4.1., "SMRAM State Save Map" for a description of the mapping of the state save area.

The system logic is minimally required to decode the physical address range for the SMRAM from [SMBASE + 8000H] to [SMBASE + FFFFH]. A larger area can be decoded if need. The size of this SMRAM can be between 32 KBytes and 4 GBytes.

The location of the SMRAM can be changed by changing the SMBASE value (see Section 9.11., "SMBASE Relocation"). It should be noted that all P6 processors in a multiple-processor system are initialized with the same SMBASE value (30000H). Initialization software must sequentially place each processor in SMM and change its SMBASE so that it does not overlap those of other processors.

The actual physical location of the SMRAM can be in system memory or in a separate RAM memory. An SMIACT transaction is issued on the system bus when the processor receives an SMI. System logic can use this transaction to decode accesses to the SMRAM and redirect them to specific SMRAM memory. If a separate RAM memory is used for SMRAM, system logic should provide a programmable method of mapping the SMRAM into system memory space when the processor is not in SMM. This mechanism will enable start-up procedures to initialization of the SMRAM space (that is, load SMI handler) before executing the SMI handler during SMM.

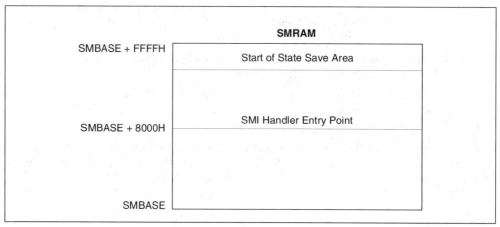

Figure 9-1. SMRAM Usage

9.4.1. SMRAM State Save Map

When the processor initially enters SMM, it writes its state to the state save area of the SMRAM. The state save area begins at [SMBASE + FFFFH], with state information being added to [SMBASE + FE00H]. Table 9-1 shows the state save map. The offset in column 1 is relative to the SMBASE value. Reserved spaces should not be used by software.

Some of the registers in the SMRAM state save area (marked YES in column 3) may be read and changed by the SMI handler, with the changed values restored to the processor registers by the RSM instruction. Some register images are read-only, and must not be modified (modifying these registers will result in unpredictable behavior). An SMI handler should not rely on any values stored in an area that is marked as reserved.

Table 9-1. SMRAM State Save Map

SMBASE + Offset	Register	Writable?
7FFCH	CR0	No
7FF8H	CR3	No
7FF4H	EFLAGS	Yes
7FF0H	EIP	Yes
7FECH	EDI	Yes
7FE8H	ESI	Yes
7FE4H	EBP	Yes
7FE0H	ESP	Yes
7FDCH	EBX	Yes
7FD8H	EDX	Yes
7FD4H	ECX	Yes

Table 9-1. SMRAM State Save Map (Contd.)

SMBASE + Offset	Register	Writable?
7FD0H	EAX	Yes
7FCCH	DR6	No
7FC8H	DR7	No
7FC4H	TR*	No
7FC0H	LDT Base*	No
7FBCH	GS*	No
7FB8H	FS*	No
7FB4H	DS*	No
7FB0H	SS*	No
7FACH	CS*	No
7FA8H	ES*	No
7FA7H - 7F98H	Reserved	No
7F94H	IDT Base	No
7F93H - 7F8CH	Reserved	No
7F88H	GDT Base	No
7F87H - 7F04H	Reserved	No
7F02H	Auto HALT Restart Field (Word)	Yes
7F00H	I/O Instruction Restart Field (Word)	Yes
7EFCH	SMM Revision Identifier Field (Doubleword)	No
7EF8H	SMBASE Field (Doubleword)	Yes
7EF7H - 7E00H	Reserved	No

NOTE:
* Upper two bytes are reserved.

The following registers are saved (but not readable) and restored upon exiting SMM:

- Control register CR4.

- The hidden segment descriptor information stored in segment registers CS, DS, ES, FS, GS, and SS.

If an SMI request is issued for the purpose of powering down the processor, the values of all reserved locations in the SMM state save must be saved to non-volatile memory.

The following registers are not automatically saved and restored following an SMI and the RSM instruction, respectively:

- Debug registers DR0 through DR3.

- The FPU registers.

- The MTRRs.

- Control register CR2.

These registers usually do not have to be saved during an SMI handler's execution, as their contents will not change unless an FPU instruction is executed in SMM. However, if an SMI is used to power down the processor, a power-on reset will be required before returning to SMM, which will reset these registers back to their default values. So an SMI handler that is going to trigger power down should first read these registers directly, and save them (along with the rest of RAM) to nonvolatile storage. After the power-on reset, the continuation of the SMI handler should restore these values, along with the rest of the system's state. Anytime the SMI handler changes these registers in the processor it must also save and restore them.

9.4.2. SMRAM Caching

SMRAM can be cached. If it is cached, it is good practice to flush the processor's caches upon entering SMM (execute an INVD instruction) and prior to executing the RSM instruction to exit SMM. Flushing the caches is not necessary if SMRAM resides in a dedicated section of system memory and is never paged out. SMRAM should not be paged.

If the SMRAM is located in its own physical RAM (not part of system memory), the processor's caches must be flushed upon entering SMM. If the SMRAM is cached, the caches must be flushed prior to executing the RSM instruction.

9.5. SMI HANDLER EXECUTION ENVIRONMENT

After saving the current context of the processor, the processor initializes its core registers to the values shown in Table 9-2. Upon entering SMM, the PE and PG flags in control register CR0 are cleared, which places the processor is in an environment similar to real-address mode. The differences between the SMM execution environment and the real-address mode execution environment are as follows:

- The addressable SMRAM address space ranges from 0 to FFFFFFFFH (4 GBytes). (The physical address extension (enabled with the PAE flag in control register CR4) is not supported in SMM.)

- The normal 64-KByte segment limit for real-address mode is increased to 4 GBytes.

- The default operand and address sizes are set to 16 bits, which restricts the addressable SMRAM address space to the 1-MByte real-address mode limit. However, operand-size and address-size override prefixes can be used to access the address space beyond the 1-MByte.

Table 9-2. Processor Register Initialization in SMM

Register	Contents
Genera-purpose registers	Undefined
EFLAGS	00000002H
EIP	00008000H
CS selector	SMM Base shifted right 4 bits (default 3000H)
CS base	SMM Base (default 30000H)
DS, ES, FS, GS, SS Selectors	0000H
DS, ES, FS, GS, SS Bases	000000000H
DS, ES, FS, GS, SS Limits	0FFFFFFFFH
CR0	PE, EM, TS and PG flags set to 0; others unmodified
DR6	Undefined
DR7	00000400H

- Near jumps and calls can be made to anywhere in the 4-GByte address space if a 32-bit operand-size override prefix is used. Due to the real-address-mode style of base-address formation, a far call or jump cannot transfer control to a segment with a base address of more than 20 bits (1 MByte). However, since the segment limit in SMM is 4 GBytes, offsets into a segment that go beyond the 1-MByte limit are allowed when using 32-bit operand-size override prefixes. Any program control transfer that does not have a 32-bit operand-size override prefix truncates the EIP value to the 16 low-order bits.

- Data and the stack can be located anywhere in the 4-GByte address space, but can be accessed only with a 32-bit address-size override if they are located above 1 MByte. As with the code segment, the base address for a data or stack segment cannot be more than 20 bits.

The value in segment register CS is automatically set to the default of 30000H for the SMBASE shifted 4 bits to the right; that is, 3000H. The EIP register is set to 8000H. When the EIP value is added to shifted CS value (the SMBASE), the resulting linear address points to the first instruction of the SMI handler.

The other segment registers (DS, SS, ES, FS, and GS) are cleared to 0 and their segment limits are set to 4 GBytes. In this state, the SMRAM address space may be treated as a single flat 4-Gbyte linear address space. If a segment register is loaded with a 16-bit value, that value is then shifted left by 4 bits and loaded into the segment base (hidden part of the segment register). The limits and attributes are not modified.

Maskable interrupts and exceptions, NMI interrupts, SMI interrupts, A20M interrupts, single-step traps, breakpoint traps, and INIT operations are inhibited when the processor enters SMM. Maskable interrupts and exceptions, single-step traps, and breakpoint traps can be enabled in SMM if the SMM execution environment provides and initializes an interrupt table and the necessary interrupt and exception handlers (see Section 9.6., "Exceptions and Interrupts Within SMM").

9.6. EXCEPTIONS AND INTERRUPTS WITHIN SMM

When the processor enters SMM, all hardware interrupts are disabled in the following manner:

- The IF flag in the EFLAGS register is cleared, which inhibits maskable interrupts from being generated.

- The TF flag in the EFLAGS register is cleared, which disables single-step traps

- Debug register DR7 is cleared, which disables breakpoint traps.

- NMI, SMI, and A20M interrupts are blocked by internal SMM logic. (See Section 9.7., "NMI Handling While in SMM" for further information about how NMIs are handled in SMM.)

Software-invoked interrupts and exceptions can still occur, and maskable interrupts can be enabled by setting the IF flag. Intel recommends that SMM code be written in so that it does not invoke software interrupts (with the INTn , INTO, INT3, or BOUND instructions) or generate exceptions.

If the SSM handler requires interrupt and exception handling, an SMM interrupt table and the necessary exception and interrupt handles must be created and initialized from within SMM. Until the interrupt table is correctly initialized, exceptions and software interrupts will result in unpredictable processor behavior.

The following restrictions apply when designing SMM interrupt and exception handling facilities:

- The interrupt table must be located at linear address 0.

- Due to the real-address mode style of base address formation, an interrupt or exception cannot transfer control to a segment with a base address of more that 20 bits.

- An interrupt or exception cannot transfer control to a segment offset of more than 16 bits (64 KBytes).

- When an exception or interrupt occurs, only the 16 least-significant bits of the return address (EIP) are pushed onto the stack. If the offset of the interrupted procedure is greater than 64 KBytes, it is not possible for the interrupt/exception handler to return control to that procedure. (One solution to this problem for a handler to adjust the return address on the stack).

- The SMBASE relocation feature affects the way the processor will return from an interrupt or exception generated while the SMI handler is executing. For example, if the SMBASE is relocated to above 1 MByte, but the exception handlers are below 1 MByte, a normal return to the SMI handler is not possible. One solution to this problem is to provide the exception handler with a mechanism for calculating a return address above 1 MByte from the 16-bit return address on the stack, then use a 32-bit far call to return to the interrupted procedure.

- If an SMI handler needs access to the debug trap facilities, it must insure that an SMM accessible debug handler is available and save the current contents of debug registers DR0 through DR3 (for later restoration). Debug registers DR0 through DR3 and DR7 must then be initialized with the appropriate values.

- If an SMI handler needs access to the single-step mechanism, it must insure that an SMM accessible single-step handler is available, and then set the TF flag in the EFLAGS register.

- If the SMI design requires the processor to respond to maskable interrupts (hardware or software) while in SMM, it must ensure that an SMM accessible interrupt handlers are available and then set the IF flag in the EFLAGS register (using the STI instruction). Software interrupts are not blocked upon entry to SMM, so they do not need to be enabled.

9.7. NMI HANDLING WHILE IN SMM

NMI interrupts are blocked upon entry to the SMI handler. If an NMI request occurs during the SMI handler, it is latched and serviced after the processor exits SMM. Only one NMI request will be latched during the SMI handler. If an NMI request is pending when the processor executes the RSM instruction, the NMI is serviced before the next instruction of the interrupted code sequence.

9.8. USING THE FPU IN SMM

The SMI handler can execute floating-point instructions while in SMM; however, it is the responsibility of the handler to save the context of the FPU prior to using it and restore that context prior to exiting SMM. The SMI handler should perform the following steps before executing floating-point instructions:

1. Use the CPUID instruction to insure that the processor contains an FPU.

2. Use the FSAVE instruction to save the current context of the FPU.

3. If floating-point exception handlers are not present and accessible in SMM, set all the floating-point mask bits in the FPU control word, to mask floating-point exceptions. When the FPU detects and exception condition, it will then always produce a masked result that is suitable for most applications.

If the SMI handler has executed floating-point instructions, it should restore the context of the FPU to the values saved in step 3 (using the FRSTOR instruction) prior to exiting SMM.

9.9. SMM REVISION IDENTIFIER

The SMM revision identifier field is used to indicate the version of SMM and the SMM extensions that are supported by the processor (see Figure 9-2). The SMM revision identifier is written during SMM entry and can be examined in SMRAM space at offset 7EFCH. The lower word of the SMM revision identifier refers to the version of the base SMM architecture.

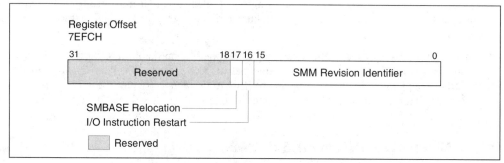

Figure 9-2. SMM Revision Identifier

The upper word of the SMM revision identifier refers to the extensions available. If the I/O instruction restart flag (bit 16) is set, the processor supports the I/O instruction restart (see Section 9.12., "I/O Instruction Restart"); if the SMBASE relocation flag (bit 17) is set, SMRAM base address relocation is supported (see Section 9.11., "SMBASE Relocation").

9.10. AUTO HALT RESTART

If the processor is in a HALT state (due to the prior execution of a HLT instruction) when it receives an SMI, the processor records the fact in the auto HALT restart flag in the saved processor state (see Figure 9-3). (This flag is located at offset 7F02H and bit 0 in the state save area of the SMRAM.)

If the processor sets the auto HALT restart flag upon entering SMM (indicating that the SMI occurred when the processor was in the HALT state), the SMI handler has two options:

- It can leave the auto HALT restart flag set, which instructs the RSM instruction to return program control to the HLT instruction, which in effect causes the processor to re-enter the HALT state after handling the SMI. (This is the default operation.)

- It can clear the auto HALT restart flag, with instructs the RSM instruction to return program control to the instruction following the HLT instruction. The default operation is to restart the HLT instruction.

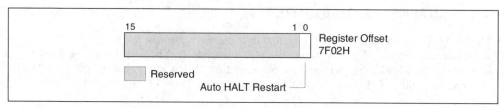

Figure 9-3. Auto HALT Restart Field

These options are summarized in Table 9-3. Note that if the processor was not in a HALT state when the SMI was received (the auto HALT restart flag is cleared), setting the flag to 1 will cause unpredictable behavior when the RSM instruction is executed.

Table 9-3. Auto HALT Restart Flag Values

Value of Flag After Entry to SMM	Value of Flag When Exiting SMM	Action of Processor When Exiting SMM
0	0	Returns to next instruction in interrupted program or task
0	1	Unpredictable
1	0	Returns to next instruction after HLT instruction
1	1	Returns to HALT state

If the HLT instruction is restarted, the processor will generate a memory access to fetch the HLT instruction (if it is not in the internal cache), and execute a HLT bus transaction. This behavior results in multiple HLT bus transactions for the same HLT instruction.

9.10.1. Executing the HLT Instruction in SMM

The HLT instruction should not be executed during SMM, unless interrupts have been enabled by setting the IF flag in the EFLAGS register. If the processor is halted in SMM, the only event that can remove the processor from this state is a maskable hardware interrupt or a hardware reset.

9.11. SMBASE RELOCATION

The default base address for the SMRAM is 30000H. This value is contained in an internal processor register called the SMBASE register. The operating system or executive can relocate the SMRAM by setting the SMBASE field in the saved state map (at offset 7EF8H) to a new value (see Figure 9-4). The RSM instruction reloads the internal SMBASE register with the value in the SMBASE field each time it exits SMM. All subsequent SMI requests will use the new SMBASE value. (The processor reset the value in its internal SMBASE register to 30000H on a RESET, but does not change it on an INIT.) In multiple-processor systems, initialization software must adjust the SMBASE value for each processor so that the SMRAM state save areas for each processor do not overlap.

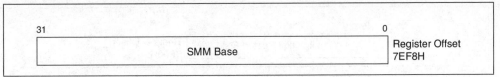

Figure 9-4. SMBASE Relocation Field

If the SMBASE relocation flag in the SMM revision identifier field indicates the ability to relocate the SMBASE (see Section 9.9., "SMM Revision Identifier").

9.11.1. Relocating SMRAM to an Address Above 1 MByte

In SMM, the segment base-registers can only be updated by changing the value in the segment registers. The segment registers contain only 16 bits, which allows only 20 bits to be used for a segment base address (the segment register is shifted left 4 bits to determine the segment base-address). If SMRAM is relocated to an address above 1 MByte, software operating in real-address mode can no longer initialize the segment registers to point to the SMRAM base address (SMBASE).

The SMRAM can still be accessed by using 32-bit address-size override prefixes to generate an offset to the correct address. For example, if the SMBASE has been relocated to FFFFFFH (immediately below the 16-MByte boundary) and the DS, ES, FS, and GS registers are still initialized to 0H, data in SMRAM can be accessed by using 32-bit displacement registers, as in the following example:

```
mov    esi,00FFxxxxH; 64K segment immediately below 16M
mov    ax,ds:[esi]
```

A stack located above the 1-MByte boundary can be accessed in the same manner.

9.12. I/O INSTRUCTION RESTART

If the I/O instruction restart flag in the SMM revision identifier field is set (see Section 9.9., "SMM Revision Identifier"), the I/O instruction restart mechanism is present on the processor. This mechanism allows an interrupted I/O instruction to be re-executed upon returning from SMM mode. For example, if an I/O instruction is used to access a powered-down I/O device, the device can respond by asserting SMI#. The resulting SMI then invokes the SMI handler to power-up the device. Upon returning from the SMI handler, the I/O instruction restart mechanism can be used to re-execute the I/O instruction that caused the SMI.

The I/O instruction restart field (at offset 7F00H in the SMM state-save area, see Figure 9-5) controls I/O instruction restart. When an RSM instruction is executed, if this field contains the value FFH, then the EIP register is modified to point to the I/O instruction that received the SMI request. The processor will then automatically re-execute the I/O instruction that the SMI trapped. (The processor saves the necessary machine state to insure that re-execution of the instruction is handled coherently.)

Figure 9-5. I/O Instruction Restart Field

If the I/O instruction restart field contains the value 00H when the RSM instruction is executed, then the processor begins program execution with the instruction following the I/O instruction. (When a repeat prefix is being used, the next instruction may be the next I/O instruction in the repeat loop.) Not re-executing the interrupted I/O instruction is the default behavior; the processor automatically initializes the I/O instruction restart field to 00H upon entering SMM. Table 9-4 summarizes the states of the I/O instruction restart field.

Table 9-4. I/O Instruction Restart Field Values

Value of Flag After Entry to SMM	Value of Flag When Exiting SMM	Action of Processor When Exiting SMM
00H	00H	Does not re-execute trapped I/O instruction.
00H	FFH	Re-executes trapped I/O instruction.

It is the responsibility of the SMI handler to examine the state of the processor to determine the cause of the SMI and to determine if an I/O instruction was interrupted and should be restarted upon exiting SMM. The I/O instruction restart mechanism does not indicate the cause of the SMI.

9.12.1. SMM Multiple Processor Considerations

The following should be noted when designing multiple processor systems:

* Any processor in a multiprocessor system can respond to an SMM.

* Each processor needs its own SMRAM space. This space can be in system memory or in a separate RAM.

* The SMRAMs for different processors can be overlapped in the same memory space. The only stipulation is that each processor needs its own state save area and its own dynamic data storage area. Code and static data can be shared among processors. Because there is no requirement to align the SMBASE on a 32-KByte boundary, this can be handled by overlapping SMRAM spaces.

* The SMI handler will need to initialize the SMBASE for each processor.

* Processors can respond to local SMIs through their SMI# pins or to SMIs received through the APIC interface. The APIC interface can distribute SMIs to different processors.

* Two or more processors can be executing in SMM at the same time.

SMM is not re-entrant, because the SMRAM State Save Map is fixed relative to the SMBASE. If there is a need to support two or more processors in SMM mode at the same time then each processor should have dedicated, non-overlapping SMRAM spaces. This can be done by using the SMBASE Relocation feature (see Section 9.11., "SMBASE Relocation").

intel ®

10

Debugging and Performance Monitoring

CHAPTER 10
DEBUGGING AND PERFORMANCE MONITORING

The Pentium Pro processor provides extensive debugging facilities for use in debugging code and monitoring code execution and processor performance. These facilities are valuable for debugging applications software, system software, and multitasking operating systems.

The debugging support is accessed through the debug registers (DB0 through DB7) and two model-specific registers (MSRs). The debug registers of the Pentium Pro processor hold the addresses of memory and I/O locations, called breakpoints. Breakpoints are user-selected locations in a program, a data-storage area in memory, or specific I/O ports where a programmer or system designer wishes to halt execution of a program and examine the state of the processor by invoking debugger software. A debug exception (#DB) is generated when a memory or I/O access is made to one of these breakpoint addresses. A breakpoint is specified for a particular form of memory or I/O access, such as a memory read and/or write operation or an I/O read and/or write operation. The debug registers support both instruction breakpoints and data breakpoints. The MSRs (which are new in the Pentium Pro processor) monitor branches, interrupts, and exceptions and record the addresses of the last branch, interrupt or exception taken and the last branch taken before an interrupt or exception.

10.1. OVERVIEW OF THE DEBUGGING SUPPORT FACILITIES

The following processor facilities support debugging and performance monitoring:

- **Debug exception (#DB)**—Transfers program control to the debugger procedure or task when a debug event occurs.

- **Breakpoint exception (#BP)**—Transfers program control to the debugger procedure or task when an INT3 instruction is executed.

- **Breakpoint-address registers (DB0 through DB3)**—Specifies the addresses of up to 4 breakpoints.

- **Debug status register (DB6)**—Reports the conditions that were in effect when a debug or breakpoint exception was generated.

- **Debug control register (DB7)**—Specifies the forms of memory or I/O access that cause breakpoints to be generated.

- **DebugCtlMSR register**—Enables last branch, interrupt, and exception recording; taken branch traps; the breakpoint reporting pins; and trace messages.

- **LastBranchToIP and LastBranchFromIP MSRs**—Specifies the source and destination addresses of the last branch, interrupt, or exception taken. The address saved is the offset in the code segment of the branch (source) or target (destination) instruction.

- **LastExceptionToIP and LastExceptionFromIP MSRs**—Specifies the source and destination addresses of the last branch that was taken prior to an exception or interrupt being generated. The address saved is the offset in the code segment of the branch (source) or target (destination) instruction.

- **T (trap) flag, TSS**—Generates a debug exception (#DB) when an attempt is made to switch to a task with the T flag set in its TSS.

- **RF (resume) flag, EFLAGS register**— Suppresses multiple exceptions to the same instruction.

- **TF (trap) flag, EFLAGS register**—Generates a debug exception (#DB) after every execution of an instruction.

- **Breakpoint instruction (INT3)**—Generates a breakpoint exception (#BP), which transfers program control to the debugger procedure or task. This instruction is an alternative way to set code breakpoints. It is especially useful when more than four breakpoints are desired, or when breakpoints are being placed in the source code.

These facilities allow a debugger to be called either as a separate task or as a procedure in the context of the current program or task. The following conditions can be used to invoke the debugger:

- Task switch to a specific task.

- Execution of the breakpoint instruction.

- Execution of any instruction.

- Execution of an instruction at a specified address.

- Read or write of a byte, word, or doubleword at a specified memory address.

- Write to a byte, word, or doubleword at a specified memory address.

- Input of a byte, word, or doubleword at a specified I/O address.

- Output of a byte, word, or doubleword at a specified I/O address.

- Attempt to change the contents of a debug register.

10.2. DEBUG REGISTERS

The eight debug registers (see Figure 10-1) control the debug operation of the processor. These registers can be written to and read using the move to or from debug register form of the MOV instruction. A debug register may be the source or destination operand for one of these instructions. The debug registers are privileged resources; a MOV instruction that accesses these registers can only be executed in real-address mode, in SMM, or in protected mode at a CPL of 0. An attempt to read or write the debug registers from any other privilege level generates a general-protection exception (#GP).

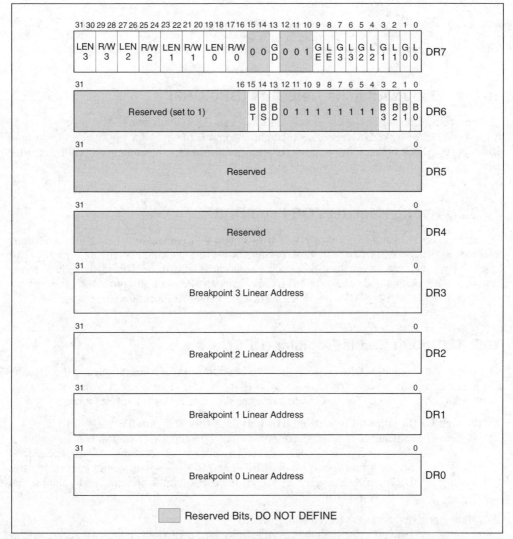

Figure 10-1. Debug Registers

The primary function of the debug registers is to set up and monitor from 1 to 4 breakpoints, numbered 0 though 3. For each breakpoint, the following information can be specified and detected with the debug registers:

- The linear address where the breakpoint is to occur.

- The length of the breakpoint location (1, 2, or 4 bytes).

- The operation that must be performed at the address for a debug exception to be generated.

- Whether the breakpoint is enabled.

- Whether the breakpoint condition was present when the debug exception was generated.

The following paragraphs describe the functions of flags and fields in the debug registers.

10.2.1. Debug Address Registers (DR0-DR3)

Each of the four debug-address registers (DR0 through DR3) holds the 32-bit linear address of a breakpoint (see Figure 10-1). Breakpoint comparisons are made before physical address translation occurs. Each breakpoint condition is specified further by the contents of debug register DR7.

10.2.2. Debug Registers DR4 and DR5

Debug registers DR4 and DR5 are reserved in the Pentium Pro processor when debug extensions are enabled (when the DE flag in control register CR4 is set), and attempts to reference the DR4 and DR5 registers cause an invalid-opcode exception (#UD) to be generated. When debug extensions are not enabled (when the DE flag is clear), the Pentium Pro processor aliases these registers to debug registers DR6 and DR7, as in earlier Intel Architecture processors.

10.2.3. Debug Status Register (DR6)

The debug status register (DR6) reports the debug conditions that were sampled at the time the last debug exception was generated (see Figure 10-1). Updates to this register only occur when an exception is generated. The flags in this register show the following information:

B0 through B3 (breakpoint condition detected) flags (bits 0 through 3)
> Indicates (when set) that its associated breakpoint condition was met when a debug exception was generated. These flags are set if the condition described for each breakpoint by the LENn, and R/Wn flags in debug control register DR7 is true. They are set even if the breakpoint is not enabled by the Ln and Gn flags in register DR7.

BD (debug register access detected) flag (bit 13)
> Indicates that the next instruction in the instruction stream will access one of the debug registers (DR0 through DR7). This flag is enabled when the GD (general detect) flag in debug control register DR7 is set. See Section 10.2.4., "Debug Control Register (DR7)" for further explanation of the purpose of this flag.

BS (single step) flag (bit 14)
> Indicates (when set) that the debug exception was triggered by the single-step execution mode (enabled with the TF flag in the EFLAGS register). The single-step mode is the highest-priority debug exception. When the BS flag is set, any of the other debug status bits also may be set.

BT (task switch) flag (bit 15)

> Indicates (when set) that the debug exception resulted from a task switch where the T flag (debug trap flag) in the TSS of the target task was set (see Section 6.2.1., "Task State Segment (TSS)" for the format of a TSS). There is no flag in debug control register DR7 to enable or disable this exception; the T flag of the TSS is the only enabling flag.

Note that the contents of the DR6 register are never cleared by the processor. To avoid any confusion in identifying debug exceptions, the debug handler should clear the register before returning to the interrupted program or task.

10.2.4. Debug Control Register (DR7)

The debug control register (DR7) enables or disables breakpoints and sets breakpoint conditions (see Figure 10-1). The flags and fields in this register control the following things:

L0 through L3 (local breakpoint enable) flags (bits 0, 2, 4, and 6)

> Enable (when set) the breakpoint condition for the associated breakpoint for the current task. When a breakpoint condition is detected and its associated Ln flag is set, a debug exception is generated. The processor automatically clears these flags on every task switch to avoid unwanted breakpoint conditions in the new task.

G0 through G3 (global breakpoint enable) flags (bits 1, 3, 5, and 7)

> Enable (when set) the breakpoint condition for the associated breakpoint for all tasks. When a breakpoint condition is detected and its associated Gn flag is set, a debug exception is generated. The processor does not clear these flags on a task switch, allowing a breakpoint to be enabled for all tasks.

LE and GE (local and global exact breakpoint enable) flags (bits 8 and 9)

> (Not supported in the Pentium Pro processor.) When set, these flags cause the processor to detect the exact instruction that caused a data breakpoint condition. For backward and forward compatibility with other Intel Architecture processors, Intel recommends that the LE and GE flags be set to 1 if exact breakpoints are required.

GD (general detect enable) flag (bit 13)

> Enables (when set) debug-register protection, which causes a debug exception to be generated prior to any MOV instruction that accesses a debug register. When such a condition is detected, the BD flag in debug status register DR6 is set prior to generating the exception. This condition is provided to support in-circuit emulators. (When the emulator needs to access the debug registers, emulator software can set the GD flag to prevent interference from the program currently executing on the processor.) The processor clears the GD flag upon entering to the debug exception handler, to allow the handler access to the debug registers.

R/W0 through R/W3 (read/write) fields (bits 16, 17, 20, 21, 24, 25, 28, and 29)

Specifies the breakpoint condition for the corresponding breakpoint. The DE (debug extensions) flag in control register CR4 determines how the bits in the R/W*n* fields are interpreted. When the DE flag is set, the processor interprets these bits as follows:

00—Break on instruction execution only.
01—Break on data writes only.
10—Break on I/O reads or writes.
11—Break on data reads or writes but not instruction fetches.

When the DE flag is clear, the processor interprets the R/W*n* bits the same as the Intel486 and Intel386 processors, which is as follows:

00—Break on instruction execution only.
01—Break on data writes only.
10—Undefined.
11—Break on data reads or writes but not instruction fetches.

LEN0 through LEN3 (Length) fields (bits 19, 19, 22, 23, 26, 27, 30, and 31)

Specify the size of the memory location at the address specified in the corresponding breakpoint address register (DR0 through DR3). These fields are interpreted as follows:

00—1-byte length
01—2-byte length
10—Undefined
11—4-byte length

If the corresponding RW*n* field in register DR7 is 00 (instruction execution), then the LEN*n* field should also be 00. The effect of using any other length is undefined.

10.2.5. Breakpoint Field Recognition

The breakpoint address registers (debug registers DR0 through DR3) and the LEN*n* fields for each breakpoint define a range of sequential byte addresses for a data or I/O breakpoint. The LEN*n* fields permit specification of a 1-, 2-, or 4-byte range beginning at the linear address specified in the corresponding debug register (DR*n*). Two-byte ranges must be aligned on word boundaries and 4-byte ranges must be aligned on doubleword boundaries. I/O breakpoint addresses are zero extended from 16 to 32 bits for purposes of comparison with the breakpoint address in the selected debug register. These requirements are enforced by the processor; it uses the LEN*n* field bits to mask the lower address bits in the debug registers. Unaligned data or I/O breakpoint addresses do not yield the expected results.

A data breakpoint for reading or writing data is triggered if any of the bytes participating in an access is within the range defined by a breakpoint address register and its LEN*n* field. Table 10-1 gives an example setup of the debug registers and the data accesses that would subsequently trap or not trap on the breakpoints.

Table 10-1. Breakpointing Examples

Debug Register Setup			
Debug Register	**R/Wn**	**Breakpoint Address**	**LENn**
DR0	R/W0 = 11 (Read/Write)	A0001H	LEN0 = 00 (1 byte)
DR1	R/W1 = 01 (Write)	A0002H	LEN1 = 00 (1 byte)
DR2	R/W2 = 11 (Read/Write)	B0002H	LEN2 = 01) (2 bytes)
DR3	R/W3 = 01 (Write)	C0000H	LEN3 = 11 (4 bytes)
Data Accesses			
Operation		**Address**	**Access Length (In Bytes)**
Data operations that trap			
Read or write		A0001H	1
Read or write		A0001H	2
Write		A0002H	1
Write		A0002H	2
Read or write		B0001H	4
Read or write		B0002H	1
Read or write		B0002H	2
Write		C0000H	4
Write		C0001H	2
Write		C0003H	1
Data operations that do not trap			
Read or write		A0000H	1
Read		A0002H	1
Read or write		A0003H	4
Read or write		B0000H	2
Read		C0000H	2
Read or write		C0004H	4

A data breakpoint for an unaligned operand can be constructed using two breakpoints, where each breakpoint is byte-aligned, and the two breakpoints together cover the operand. These breakpoints generate exceptions only for the operand, not for any neighboring bytes.

Instruction breakpoint addresses must have a length specification of 1 byte (the LENn field is set to 00). The behavior of code breakpoints for other operand sizes is undefined. The processor recognizes an instruction breakpoint address only when it points to the first byte of an instruction. If the instruction has any prefixes, the breakpoint address must point to the first prefix.

10.3. DEBUG EXCEPTIONS

The Pentium Pro processor dedicates two interrupt vectors to handling debug exceptions: vector 1 (debug exception) and vector 3 (breakpoint exception). The following sections describe how these exceptions are generated and typical exception handler operations for handling these exceptions.

10.3.1. Debug Exception (#DB)—Interrupt Vector 1

The debug-exception handler is usually a debugger program or is part of a larger software system. The processor generates a debug exception for any of several conditions. The debugger can check flags in the DR6 and DR7 registers to determine which condition caused the exception and which other conditions might also apply. Table 10-2 shows the states of these flags following the generation of each kind of breakpoint condition.

Table 10-2. Debug Exception Conditions

DR6 Flags Tested	DR7 Flags Tested	Description
BS = 1		Single-step trap
Bn = 1 and (GEn or LEn = 1)	R/Wn = 0	Instruction breakpoint, at addresses defined by DRn and LENn
Bn = 1 and (GEn or LEn = 1)	R/Wn = 1	Data write breakpoint, at addresses defined by DRn and LENn
Bn = 1 and (GEn or LEn = 1)	R/Wn = 2	I/O read or write breakpoint, at addresses defined by DRn and LENn
Bn = 1 and (GEn or LEn = 1)	R/Wn = 3	Data read or write (but not instruction fetches), at addresses defined by DRn and LENn
BD = 1		General detect fault, resulting from an attempt to modify debug registers (usually in conjunction with in-circuit emulation)
BT = 1		Task switch

Instruction-breakpoint and general-detect conditions (see Section 10.3.1.3., "General-Detect Exception Condition") result in faults; other debug-exception conditions result in traps. The debug exception may report either or both at one time. The following sections describe each class of debug exception. See Chapter 5, "Interrupt 1—Debug Exception (#DB)" for additional information about this exception.

10.3.1.1. INSTRUCTION-BREAKPOINT EXCEPTION CONDITION

The processor reports an instruction breakpoint when it attempts to execute an instruction at an address specified in a breakpoint-address register (DB0 through DR3) that has been set up to detect instruction execution (R/W flag is set to 0). The processor generates the exception before it executes the target instruction for the breakpoint. As a result, an instruction breakpoint condition causes a fault-class exception to be generated. Instruction breakpoints are the highest priority breakpoint exceptions and are guaranteed to be serviced before any other exceptions that may be detected during the decoding or execution of an instruction.

Prior to returning to the interrupted program following a debug exception caused by an instruction-breakpoint, the debugger software should set the RF flag in the EFLAGS image saved on the stack. Setting this flag causes the processor to ignore instruction-breakpoint conditions until the interrupted instruction is executed, and thus prevents an instruction-breakpoint loop from being created. Setting the RF flag does not prevent other types of debug-exception conditions (such as, I/O or data breakpoints) from being detected, nor does it prevent non-debug exceptions from being generated. (The processor automatically clears the RF flag following the successful execution of the instruction that originally caused the instruction-breakpoint debug exception to be generated.) See Section 2.3., "System Flags and Fields in the EFLAGS Register" for more information about the RF flag.

10.3.1.2.   DATA MEMORY AND I/O BREAKPOINT EXCEPTION CONDITIONS

Data memory and I/O breakpoints are reported when the processor attempts to access a memory or I/O address specified in a breakpoint-address register (DB0 through DR3) that has been set up to detect data or I/O accesses (R/W flag is set to 1, 2, or 3). The processor generates the exception after it executes the instruction that made the access, so these breakpoint condition causes a trap-class exception to be generated.

Because data breakpoints are traps, the original data is overwritten before the trap exception is generated. If a debugger needs to save the contents of a write breakpoint location, it should save the original contents before setting the breakpoint. The handler can report the saved value after the breakpoint is triggered. The address in the debug registers can be used to locate the new value stored by the instruction that triggered the breakpoint.

The Pentium Pro, Pentium, and Intel486 processors ignore the GE and LE flags in DR7. In the Intel386 processor, exact data breakpoint matching does not occur unless it is enabled by setting the LE and/or the GE flags.

The Pentium Pro processor, however, is unable to report data breakpoints exactly for the REP MOVS and REP STOS instructions until the completion of the iteration after the iteration in which the breakpoint occurred.

For repeated INS and OUTS instructions that generate an I/O-breakpoint debug exception, the processor generates the exception after the completion of the first iteration. Repeated INS and OUTS instructions generate an I/O-breakpoint debug exception after the iteration in which the memory address breakpoint location is accessed.

10.3.1.3.   GENERAL-DETECT EXCEPTION CONDITION

When the GD flag in DR7 is set, the general-detect debug exception occurs when a program attempts to access any of the debug registers (DR0 through DR7) at the same time they are being used by another application, such as an emulator or debugger. This additional protection feature guarantees full control over the debug registers when required. The debug exception handler can detect this condition by checking the state of the BD flag of the DR6 register. The processor generates the exception before it executes the MOV instruction that accesses a debug register, which causes a fault-class exception to be generated.

10.3.1.4.   SINGLE-STEP EXCEPTION CONDITION

The processor generates a single-step debug exception if it detects that the TF flag in the EFLAGS register is set. The exception is a trap-class exception, because the exception is generated after the instruction is generated. (Note that the processor does not generate this exception after an instruction that sets the TF flag. For example, if the POPF instruction is used to set the TF flag, a single-step trap does not occur until after the instruction that follows the POPF instruction.)

The processor clears the TF flag before calling the exception handler. If the TF flag was set in a TSS at the time of a task switch, the exception occurs after the first instruction is executed in the new task.

The TF flag normally is not cleared by privilege changes inside a task. The INT*n* and INTO instructions, however, do clear this flag. Therefore, software debuggers that single-step code must recognize and emulate INT*n* or INTO instructions rather than executing them directly. To maintain protection, the operating system should check the CPL after any single-step trap to see if single stepping should continue at the current privilege level.

The interrupt priorities guarantee that, if an external interrupt occurs, single stepping stops. When both an external interrupt and a single-step interrupt occur together, the single-step interrupt is processed first. This operation clears the TF flag. After saving the return address or switching tasks, the external interrupt input is examined before the first instruction of the single-step handler executes. If the external interrupt is still pending, then it is serviced. The external interrupt handler does not run in single-step mode. To single step an interrupt handler, single step an INT*n* instruction that calls the interrupt handler.

10.3.1.5. TASK-SWITCH EXCEPTION CONDITION

The processor generates a debug exception after a task switch if the T flag of the new task's TSS is set. This exception is generated after program control has passed to the new task, and after the first instruction of that task is executed. The exception handler can detect this condition by examining the BT flag of the DR6 register.

Note that, if the debug exception handler is a task, the T bit of its TSS should not be set. Failure to observe this rule will put the processor in a loop.

10.3.2. Breakpoint Exception (#BP)—Interrupt Vector 3

The breakpoint exception (interrupt 3) is caused by execution of an INT 3 instruction (see Chapter 5, "Interrupt 3—Breakpoint Exception (#BP)"). Debuggers use break exceptions in the same way that they use the breakpoint registers; that is, as a mechanism for suspending program execution to examine registers and memory locations. With earlier Intel Architecture processors, breakpoint exceptions are used extensively for setting instruction breakpoints. With the Pentium Pro, Pentium, Intel486, and Intel386 processors, it is more convenient to set breakpoints with the breakpoint-address registers (DR0 through DR3). However, the breakpoint exception still is useful for breakpointing debuggers, because the breakpoint exception can call a separate exception handler. The breakpoint exception is also useful when it is necessary to set more breakpoints than there are debug registers or when breakpoints are being placed in the source code of a program under development.

10.4. LAST BRANCH, INTERRUPT, AND EXCEPTION RECORDING

The Pentium Pro processor provides five MSRs for recording the last branch, interrupt, or exception taken by the processor: DebugCtlMSR, LastBranchToIP, LastBranchFromIP, LastExceptionToIP, and LastExceptionFromIP. These registers can be used to set breakpoints on branches, interrupts, and exceptions and to single-step from one branch to the next.

10.4.1. DebugCtlMSR Register

The DebugCtlMSR register enables last branch, interrupt, and exception recording; taken branch breakpoints; the breakpoint reporting pins; and trace messages. This register can be written to using the WRMSR instruction, when operating at privilege level 0 or when in real-address mode. A protected-mode operating system procedure is required to provide user access to this register. Figure 10-2 shows the flags in the DebugCtlMSR register. The functions of these flags are as follows:

LBR (last branch/interrupt/exception) flag (bit 0)
> When set, the processor records the source and target addresses for the last branch and the last exception or interrupt taken by the processor prior to a debug exception being generated. The processor clears this flag whenever a debug exception, such as an instruction or data breakpoint or single-step trap occurs.

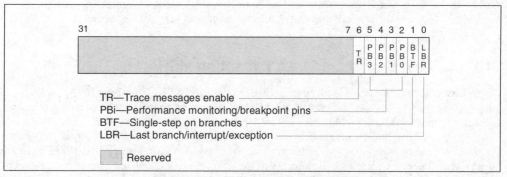

Figure 10-2. DebugCtlMSR Register

BTF (single-step on branches) flag (bit 1)
> When set, the processor treats the TF flag in the EFLAGS register as a "single-step on branches" flag rather than a "single-step on instructions" flag. This mechanism allows single-stepping the processor on taken branches. Software must set both the BTF and TF flag to enable debug breakpoints on branches; the processor clears both flags whenever a debug exception occurs.

PBi (performance monitoring/breakpoint pins) flags (bits 2 through 5)
> When these flags are set, the performance monitoring/breakpoint pins on the processor (BP0#, BP1#, BP2#, and BP3#) report breakpoint matches in the

corresponding breakpoint-address registers (DR0 through DR3). The processor asserts then deasserts the corresponding BP*i*# pin when a breakpoint match occurs. When a PB*i* flag is clear, the performance monitoring/breakpoint pins report performance events. Processor execution is not affected by reporting performance events.

TR (trace message enable) flag (bit 6)

When set, trace messages are enabled. Thereafter, when the processor detects a branch, exception, or interrupt, it sends the "to" and "from" addresses out on the system bus as part of a branch trace message. A debugging device that is monitoring the system bus can read these messages and synchronize operations with branch, exception, and interrupt events. Setting this flag greatly reduces the performance of the processor. When trace messages are enabled, the values stored in the LastBranchToIP, LastBranchFromIP, LastExceptionToIP, and LastExceptionFromIP MSRs are undefined.

Note that the "from" addresses sent out on the system bus may differ from those stored in the LastBranchFromIP MSRs or LastExceptionFromIP MSRs. The from address sent out on the bus is always the next instruction in the instruction stream following a successfully completed instruction. For example, if a branch completes successfully, the address stored in the Last-BranchFromIP MSR is the address of the branch instruction, but the address sent out on the bus in the trace message is the address of the instruction following the branch instruction. If the processor faults on the branch, the address stored in the LastBranchFromIP MSR is again the address of the branch instruction and that same address is sent out on the bus.

10.4.2. Last Branch and Last Exception MSRs

The LastBranchToIP and LastBranchFromIP MSRs are 32-bit registers for recording the instruction pointers for the last branch, interrupt, or exception that the processor took prior to a debug exception being generated (see Figure 10-2). When a branch occurs, the processor loads the address of the branch instruction into the LastBranchFromIP MSR and loads the target address for the branch into the LastBranchToIP MSR. When an interrupt or exception occurs (other than a debug exception), the address of the instruction that was interrupted by the exception or interrupt is loaded into the LastBranchFromIP MSR and the address of the exception or interrupt handler that is called is loaded into the LastBranchToIP MSR.

The LastExceptionToIP and LastExceptionFromIP MSRs (also 32-bit registers) record the instruction pointers for the last branch that the processor took to prior to an exception or interrupt being generated. When an exception or interrupt occurs, the contents of the LastBranchToIP and LastBranchFromIP MSRs are copied into these registers before the to and from addresses of the exception or interrupt are recorded in the LastBranchToIP and LastBranchFromIP MSRs.

These registers can be read using the RDMSR instruction.

10.4.3. Monitoring Branches, Exceptions, and Interrupts

When the LBR flag in the DebugCtlMSR register is set, the processor automatically begins recording branches that it takes, exceptions that are generated (except for debug exceptions), and interrupts that are serviced. Each time a branch, interrupt, or exception occurs, the processor records the to and from instruction pointers in the LastBranchToIP and LastBranchFromIP MSRs. In addition, for interrupts and exceptions, the processor copies the contents of the LastBranchToIP and LastBranchFromIP MSRs into the LastExceptionToIP and LastException-FromIP MSRs prior to recording the to and from addresses of the interrupt or exception.

When the processor generates a debug exception (#DB), it automatically clears the LBR flag before executing the exception handler, but does not touch the last branch and last exception MSRs. The addresses for the last branch, interrupt, or exception taken are thus retained in the LastBranchToIP and LastBranchFromIP MSRs and the addresses of the last branch prior to an interrupt or exception are retained in the LastExceptionToIP, and LastExceptionFromIP MSRs.

The debugger can use the last branch, interrupt, and/or exception addresses in combination with code segment selectors retrieved from the stack to reset breakpoints in the breakpoint-address registers (DR0 through DR3), allowing a backward trace from the manifestation of a particular bug toward its source. Because the instruction pointers recorded in the LastBranchToIP, LastBranchFromIP, LastExceptionToIP, and LastExceptionFromIP MSRs are offsets into a code segment, software must determine the segment base address of the code segment associated with the control transfer to calculate the linear address to be placed in the breakpoint-address registers. The segment base address can be determined by reading the segment selector for the code segment from the stack and using it to locate the segment descriptor for the segment in the GDT or LDT. The segment base address can then be read from the segment descriptor.

Before resuming program execution from a debug-exception handler, the handler should set the LBR flag again to re-enable last branch and last exception/interrupt recording.

10.4.4. Single-Stepping on Branches, Exceptions, and Interrupts

When the BTF flag in the DebugCtlMSR register and the TF flag in the EFLAGS register are both set, the processor generates a single-step debug exception the next time it takes a branch, generates an exception, or services an interrupt. This mechanism allows the debugger to single-step on control transfers caused by branches, exceptions, or interrupts. This "control-flow single stepping" helps isolate a bug to a particular block of code before instruction single-stepping further narrows the search. If the BTF flag is set when the processor generates a debug exception, the processor clears the flag along with the TF flag. The debugger must then reset both the BTF and the TF flags before resuming program execution to continue control-flow single stepping.

10.4.5. Initializing Last Branch or Last Exception/Interrupt Recording

The LastBranchToIP, LastBranchFromIP, LastExceptionToIP, and LastException-FromIP MSRs are enabled by setting the LBR flag in the DebugCtlMSR register. Control-flow single stepping is enabled by setting the BTF flag in the DebugCtlMSR register. The processor clears both the LBR and the BTF flags whenever a debug exception is generated. The debug-exception handler must thus explicitly set these flags before returning to the interrupted program to re-enable these mechanisms.

10.5. TIME-STAMP COUNTER

The Pentium Pro processor provides a 64-bit time-stamp counter that is incremented every processor clock cycle. The counter is incremented even when the processor is halted by the HLT instruction or the external STPCLK# pin.

The time-stamp counter is model specific. Following execution of the CPUID instruction, the TSC flag in register EDX (bit 4) indicates (when set) that the time-stamp counter is present. (See the description of the CPUID instruction in Chapter 11, *Instruction Set Reference*, in the *Pentium® Pro Family Developer's Manual, Volume 2*.)

The time-stamp counter is set to 0 following a hardware reset of the processor. The RDTSC instruction reads the time stamp counter and is guaranteed to return a monotonically increasing unique value whenever executed, except for 64-bit counter wraparound. Intel guarantees, architecturally, that the time-stamp counter frequency and configuration will be such that it will not wraparound within 10 years after being reset to 0. The period for counter wrap is several thousands of years in the Pentium Pro and Pentium processors.

Normally, the RDTSC instruction can be executed by programs and procedures running at any privilege level and in virtual-8086 mode. The TSD flag in control register CR4 (bit 2) allows use of this instruction to be restricted to only programs and procedures running at privilege level 0. A secure operating system would set the TSD flag during system initialization to disable user access to the time-stamp counter. An operating system that disables user access to the time-stamp counter should emulate of the instruction through a user-accessible programming interface.

The RDTSC instruction is not serializing or ordered with other instructions. Thus, it does not necessarily wait until all previous instructions have been executed before reading the counter. Similarly, subsequent instructions may begin execution before the RDTSC instruction operation is performed.

The RDMSR and WRMSR instructions can read and write the time stamp counter, respectively, as a model specific register (TSC). The ability to read and write the time stamp counter with the RDMSR and WRMSR instructions is not an architectural feature, and may not be supported by future Intel Architecture processors. Writing to the time-stamp counter with the WRMSR instruction resets the count. Only the low order 32-bits of the time-stamp counter can be written to; the high-order 32 bits are 0 extended (cleared to all 0s).

10.6. PERFORMANCE MONITORING COUNTERS

The Pentium Pro processor provides two 40-bit performance counters, allowing two types of events to be monitored simultaneously. These counters can either count events or measure duration. When counting events, a counter is incremented each time a specified event takes place or a specified number of events takes place. When measuring duration, a counter counts the number of processor clocks that occur while a specified condition is true. The counters can count events or measure durations that occur at any privilege level. Appendix B, *Performance Monitoring Counters*, lists the events that can be counted with the performance monitoring counters.

The performance monitoring counters are supported by four MSRs: the performance event select MSRs (PerfEvtSel0 and PerfEvtSel1) and the performance counter MSRs (PerfCtr0 and PerfCtr1). These registers can be read from and written to using the RDMSR and WRMSR instructions, respectively. They can be accessed using these instructions only when operating at privilege level 0. The PerfCtr0 and PerfCtr1 MSRs can be read from any privilege level using the RDPMC (read performance-monitoring counters) instruction.

10.6.1. PerfEvtSel0 and PerfEvtSel1 MSRs

The PerfEvtSel0 and PerfEvtSel1 MSRs control the operation of the performance-monitoring counters, with one register used to set up each counter. They specify the events to be counted, how they should be counted, and the privilege levels at which counting should take place. Figure 10-3 shows the flags and fields in these MSRs.

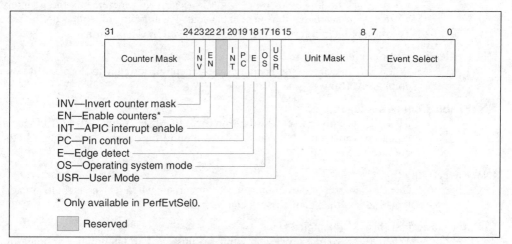

Figure 10-3. PerfEvtSel0 and PerfEvtSel1 Registers.

The functions of the flags and fields in the PerfEvtSel0 and PerfEvtSel1 MSRs are as follows:

Event select field (bits 0 through 7)
> Select the event to be monitored (see Appendix B, *Performance Monitoring Counters*, for a list of events and their 8-bit codes).

Unit mask field (bits 8 through 15)
> Further qualifies the event selected in the event select field. For example, for some cache events, the mask is used as a MESI-protocol qualifier of cache states (see Table B-1).

USR (user mode) flag (bit 16)

Events are counted only when the processor is operating at privilege levels 1, 2 or 3. This flag can be used in conjunction with the OS flag.

OS (operating system mode) flag (bit 17)

Events are counted only when the processor is operating at privilege level 0. This flag can be used in conjunction with the USR flag.

E (edge detect) flag (bit 18)

Enables (when set) edge detection of events. The processor counts the number of deasserted to asserted transitions of any condition that can be expressed by the other fields. The mechanism is limited in that it does not permit back-to-back assertions to be distinguished. This mechanism allows software to measure not only the fraction of time spent in a particular state, but also the average length of time spent in such a state (for example, the time spent waiting for an interrupt to be serviced).

PC (pin control) flag (bit 19)

When set, the processor toggles the PM*i* pins when the counter overflows; when clear, the processor toggles the PM*i* pins and increments the counter when performance monitoring events occur. The toggling of a pin is defined as assertion of the pin for two bus clocks followed by deassertion.

INT (APIC interrupt enable) flag (bit 20)

When set, the processor generates an exception through its local APIC on counter overflow.

EN (Enable Counters) Flag (bit 22)

This flag is only present in the PerfEvtSel0 MSR. When set, performance counting is enabled in both performance-monitoring counters; when clear, both counters are disabled.

INV (invert) flag (bit 23)

Inverts the result of the counter-mask comparison when set, so that both greater than and less than comparisons can be made.

Counter mask field (bits 24 through 31)

When non-zero, the processor compares this mask to the number of count of events during a single cycle. If the event count is greater than or equal to this mask, the counter is incremented by one. Otherwise the counter is not incremented. This mask can be used to count events only if multiple occurrences happen per clock (for example, two or more instructions retired per clock). If the counter-mask field is 0, then the counter is incremented each cycle by the number of events that occurred that cycle.

10.6.2. PerfCtr0 and PerfCtr1 MSRs

The performance-counter MSRs (PerfCtr0 and PerfCtr1) contain the event or duration counts for the selected events being counted. The RDPMC instruction can be used by programs or procedures running at any privilege level and in virtual-8086 mode to read these counters. The PCE flag in control register CR4 (bit 8) allows the use of this instruction to be restricted to only programs and procedures running at privilege level 0.

The RDPMC instruction is not serializing or ordered with other instructions. Thus, it does not necessarily wait until all previous instructions have been executed before reading the counter. Similarly, subsequent instructions may begin execution before the RDPMC instruction operation is performed.

Only the operating system, executing at privilege level 0, can directly manipulate the performance counters, using the RDMSR and WRMSR instructions. A secure operating system would set the TSD flag during system initialization to disable direct user access to the performance-monitoring counters, but provide a user-accessible programming interface that emulates the RDPMC instruction.

The WRMSR instruction cannot arbitrarily write to the performance-monitoring counter MSRs (PerfCtr0 and PerfCtr1). Instead, the lower-order 32 bits of each MSR may be written with any value, and the high-order 8 bits are sign-extended according to the value of bit 31. This operation allows writing both positive and negative values to the performance counters.

10.6.3. Starting and Stopping the Performance-Monitoring Counters

The performance-monitoring counters are started by writing valid setup information in the PerfEvtSel0 and/or PerfEvtSel1 MSRs and setting the enable counters flag in the PerfEvtSel0 MSR. If the setup is valid, the counters begin counting following the execution of a WRMSR instruction that sets the enable counter flag. The counters can be stopped by clearing the enable counters flag or by clearing all the bits in the PerfEvtSel0 and PerfEvtSel1 MSRs. Counter 1 alone can be stopped by clearing the PerfEvtSel1 MSR.

10.6.4. Event and Time-Stamp Monitoring Software

To use the performance-monitoring counters and time-stamp counter, the operating system needs to provide an event-monitoring device driver. This driver should include procedures for handling the following operations:

- Feature checking.
- Initialize and start counters.
- Stop counters.
- Read the event counters.
- Read the time stamp counter.

The event monitor feature determination procedure must determine whether the current processor supports the performance-monitoring counters and time-stamp counter. This procedure compares the family and model of the processor returned by the CPUID instruction with those of processors known to support performance monitoring. The current processors supporting performance counters are the Pentium Pro and Pentium processors. The procedure also checks the MSR and TSC flags returned to register EDX by the CPUID instruction to determine if the MSRs and the RDTSC instruction are supported.

The initialize and start counters procedure sets the PerfEvtSel0 and/or PerfEvtSel1 MSRs for the events to be counted and the method used to count them and initializes the counter MSRs (PerfCtr0 and PerfCtr1) to starting counts. The stop counters procedure stops the performance counters. (See Section 10.6.3., "Starting and Stopping the Performance-Monitoring Counters" for more information about starting and stopping the counters.)

The read counters procedure reads the values in the PerfCtr0 and PerfCtr1 MSRs, and a read time-stamp counter procedure reads the time-stamp counter. These procedures would be provided in lieu of enabling the RDTSC and RDPMC instructions that allow application code to read the counters.

10.6.5. Monitoring Counter Overflow

The Pentium Pro processor provides the option of generating a local APIC interrupt when a performance-monitoring counter overflows. This mechanism is enabled by setting the interrupt enable flag in either the PerfEvtSel0 or the PerfEvtSel1 MSR. The primary use of this option is for statistical performance sampling.

To use this option, the operating system do the following things:

- Provide an interrupt vector for handling the counter-overflow interrupt.

- Initialize the APIC PERF local vector entry to direct the interrupt to the appropriate processor.

- Provide an entry to the IDT that points to a stub exception handler that returns without executing any instructions.

- Provide an event monitor driver that provides the actual interrupt handler and modifies the reserved IDT entry to point to its interrupt routine.

When interrupted by a counter overflow, the interrupt handler needs to perform the following actions:

- Save the instruction pointer (EIP register), code segment selector, TSS segment selector, counter values and other relevant information at the time of the interrupt.

- Reset the counter to its initial setting and return from the interrupt.

An event monitor application utility or another application program can read the information collected for analysis of the performance of the profiled application.

intel.

11

Memory Cache Control

CHAPTER 11
MEMORY CACHE CONTROL

This chapter describes the processors memory cache and cache control mechanisms, the TLBs and the write buffer. It also describes the memory type range registers (MTRRs) and how the are used to control caching of physical memory locations.

11.1. INTERNAL CACHES, TLBS, AND BUFFERS

The Pentium Pro processor provides on-chip caches, translation look aside buffers (TLBs), and a write buffer for temporary on-chip storage of instructions and data (see Figure 11-1). Table 11-1 shows the characteristics of these caches and buffers for the first version of the Pentium Pro processor. **The sizes and characteristics of these units are machine specific and may change in future versions of the processor.** The CPUID instruction returns the sizes and characteristics of the caches and buffers for the processor the instruction is executed on (see "CPUID—CPU Identification" in Chapter 11, *Instruction Set Reference*, of the *Pentium® Pro Family Developer's Manual, Volume 2*).

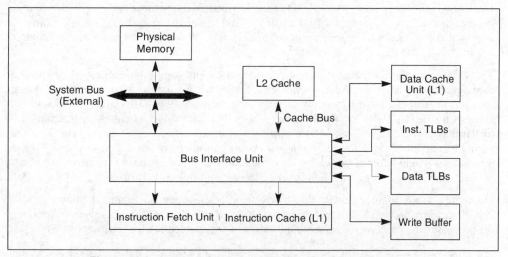

Figure 11-1. Internal Caches in the Pentium® Pro Processor

The processor provides two separate on-chip caches: the level 1 (L1) cache and the level 2 (L2) cache (see Figure 11-1). The L1 cache is closely coupled to the instruction fetch unit and execution units of the processor. It is divided into two 8-KByte sections: one dedicated to caching instructions and one to caching data. The 256-KByte L2 cache is closely coupled to the L1 cache through the processor's cache bus and the bus interface unit. The L2 cache is a unified cache for storage of both instructions and data.

Table 11-1. Characteristics of the Caches, TLBs, and Write Buffer in the First Version of the Pentium® Pro Processor

Cache or Buffer	Characteristics
L1 Instruction Cache	8 KBytes, 4-way set associative, 32-byte cache line size
L1 Data Cache	8 KBytes, 2-way set associative, 32-byte cache line size
L2 Unified Cache	256 KBytes, 4-way set associative, 32-byte cache line size
Instruction TLB (4-KByte Pages)	64 entries, 4-way set associative
Data TLB (4-KByte Pages)	64 entries, 4-way set associative
Instruction TLB (Large Pages)	4 entries, 4-way set associative
Data TLB (Large Pages)	8 entries, 4-way set associative
Write Buffer	8 entries

The cache lines in the Pentium Pro processor's L1 and L2 caches are 32 bytes wide. The processor always reads a cache line from system memory beginning on a 32-byte boundary. (A 32-byte aligned cache line begins at an address with its 5 least-significant bits clear.) A cache line can be filled from memory with a 4-transfer burst transaction. The caches do not support partially-filled cache lines, so caching even a single doubleword requires caching an entire line.

The L1 and L2 caches are available in all execution modes. Using these caches greatly improves the performance of the processor both in single- and multiple-processor systems. Caching can also be used in system management mode (SMM); however, it must be handled carefully (see Section 9.4.2., "SMRAM Caching").

The TLBs store the most recently used page-directory and page-table entries. They speed up memory accesses when paging is enabled by reducing the number of memory accesses that are required to read the page tables stored in system memory. The TLBs are divided into four groups: instruction TLBs for 4-KByte pages, data TLBs for 4-KByte pages; instruction TLBs for large pages (2-MByte or 4-MByte pages), and data TLBs for large pages. The TLBs are normally active only in protected mode with paging enabled. When paging is disabled or the processor is in real-address mode, the TLBs maintain their contents until explicitly or implicitly flushed (see Section 11.9., "Invalidating the Translation Lookaside Buffers (TLBs)").

The write buffer is associated with the processors instruction execution units. It allows writes to system memory and/or the internal caches to be saved and in some cases combined to optimize the processors bus accesses. The write buffer is always enabled in all execution modes.

The processor's caches are for the most part transparent to software. When enabled, instructions and data flow through these caches without the need for explicit software control. However, knowledge of the behavior of these caches may be useful in optimizing software performance. For example, knowledge of cache dimensions and replacement algorithms are an indication of how large of a data structure can be operated on at once without causing cache thrashing.

In multiprocessor systems, maintenance of cache consistency may, in rare circumstances, require intervention by system software. For these rare cases, the processor provides privileged cache control instructions for use in flushing caches.

11.2. CACHING TERMINOLOGY

The Pentium Pro processor uses the MESI (modified, exclusive, shared, invalid) cache protocol to maintain consistency with internal caches and caches in other processors (see Section 11.4., "Cache Control Protocol").

When the processor recognizes that an operand being read from memory is cacheable, the processor reads an entire 32-byte line into the appropriate cache (L1, L2, or both). This operation is called a *cache line fill*. If the memory location containing that operand is still cached the next time the processor attempts the operand, the processor can read the operand from the cache instead of going back to memory. This operation is called a *cache hit*.

When the processor attempts to write an operand to a cacheable area of memory, it first checks if a cache line for that memory location exists in the cache. If a valid cache line does exist, the processor (depending on the write policy currently in force) can write the operand into the cache instead of writing it out to system memory. This operation is called a *write hit*. If a write misses the cache (that is, a valid cache line is not present for area of memory being written to), the processor performs a cache line fill, write allocation. Then it writes the operand into the cache line and (depending on the write policy currently in force) can also writes it out to memory. If the operand is to be written out to memory, it is written first into the write buffer, and then written from the write buffer to memory when the system bus is available.

When operating in multiple-processor system, the Pentium Pro processors have the ability to *snoop* other processors accesses to system memory and to their internal caches. They use this snooping ability to keep their internal caches consistent both with system memory and with the caches in other processors on the bus. For example, if through snooping one processor detects that another processor intends to write to a memory location that it currently has cached in *shared state*, the snooping processor will invalidate its cache line forcing it to perform a cache line fill the next time it accesses the same memory location.

Likewise, if a processor detects (through snooping) that another processor is trying to access a memory location that it has modified in its cache, but has not yet written back to system memory, the snooping processor will signal the other processor (by means of the HITM# signal) that the cache line is held in modified state and will preform an implicit write-back of the modified data. The implicit write-back is transferred directly to the initial requesting processor and snooped by the memory controller to assure that system memory has been updated. Here, the processor with the valid data may pass the data to the other processors without actually writing it to system memory; however, it is the responsibility of the memory controller to snoop this operation and update memory.

11.3. METHODS OF CACHING AVAILABLE

The processor allows any area of system memory to be cached in the L1 and L2 caches. Within individual pages or regions of system memory, it also allows the type of caching (also called *memory type*) to be specified, using a variety of system flags and registers (see Section 11.5., "Cache Control"). The caching methods available are as follows:

- Uncacheable (UC)—System memory locations are not cached. All reads and writes appear on the system bus and are executed in program order, without reordering. No speculative memory accesses, page table walks, or prefetches of speculated branch targets are made. This type of cache-control is useful for memory-mapped I/O devices. When used with normal RAM, it greatly reduces processor performance.

- Write Combining (WC)—System memory locations are not cached and coherency is not enforced by the processor's bus coherency protocol. Speculative reads are allowed. Writes may be delayed and combined in the write buffer to reduce memory accesses. This type of cache-control is appropriate for frame buffers, where the order of writes is unimportant as long as the writes update memory so they can be seen on the graphics display.

- Write-through (WT)—Writes and reads to and from system memory are cached. Reads come from cache lines on cache hits; read misses cause cache fills. Speculative reads are allowed. All writes are written to a cache line (when possible) and through to system memory. When writing through to memory, invalid cache lines are never filled, and valid cache lines are either filled or invalidated. Write combining is allowed. This type of cache-control is appropriate for frame buffers or when there are devices on the system bus that access system memory, but do not perform snooping of memory accesses. It enforces coherency between caches in the processors and system memory.

- Write-back (WB)—Writes and reads to and from system memory are cached. Reads come from cache lines on cache hits; read misses cause cache fills. Speculative reads are allowed. Write misses cause cache line fills, and writes are performed entirely in the cache, when possible. Write combining is allowed. The write-back memory type reduces bus traffic by eliminating many unnecessary writes to system memory. Writes to a cache line are not immediately forwarded to system memory; instead, they are accumulated in the cache. The modified cache lines are written to system memory later, when a write-back operation is performed. Write-back operations are triggered when cache lines need to be deallocated, such as when new cache lines are being allocated in a cache that is already full. They also are triggered by the mechanisms used to maintain cache consistency. This type of cache-control provides the best performance, but it requires that all devices that access system memory on the system bus be able to snoop memory accesses to insure system memory and cache coherency.

- Write protected (WP)—Reads come from cache lines when possible, and read misses cause cache fills. Writes are propagated to the system bus and cause corresponding cache lines on all processors on the bus to be invalidated. Speculative reads are allowed.

11.3.1. Choosing A Memory Type

The simplest system memory model does not use memory-mapped I/O with read or write side effects, does not include a frame buffer, and uses the write-back memory type for all memory. An I/O agent can perform direct memory access (DMA) to write-back memory and the cache protocol maintains cache coherency.

A system can use uncacheable memory for other memory-mapped I/O, and should always use uncacheable memory for memory-mapped I/O with read side effects.

Dual-ported memory can be considered a write side effect, making relatively prompt writes desirable, because those writes cannot be observed at the other port until they reach the memory agent. A system can use uncacheable, write-through, or write-combining memory for frame buffers or dual-ported memory that contains pixel values displayed on a screen. Frame buffer memory is typically large (a few megabytes) and is usually written more than it is read by the processor. Using uncacheable memory for a frame buffer generates very large amounts of bus traffic, because operations on the entire buffer are implemented using partial writes rather than line writes. Using write-through memory for a frame buffer can displace almost all other useful cached lines in the processor's L2 cache and L1 data cache. Therefore, systems should use write-combining memory for frame buffers whenever possible.

Software can use page-level cache control, to assign appropriate effective memory types when software will not access data structures in ways that benefit from write-back caching. For example, software may read a large data structure once and not access the structure again until the structure is rewritten by another agent. Such a large data structure should be marked as uncacheable, or reading it will evict cached lines that the processor will be referencing again. A similar example would be a write-only data structure that is written to (to export the data to another agent), but never read by software. Such a structure can be marked as uncacheable, because software never reads the values that it writes (though as uncacheable memory, it will be written using partial writes, while as write-back memory, it will be written using line writes, which may not occur until the other agent reads the structure and triggers implicit write-backs).

11.4. CACHE CONTROL PROTOCOL

In the L1 data cache and the L2 cache, the MESI (modified, exclusive, shared, invalid) cache protocol maintains consistency with caches of other processors. The L1 data cache and the L2 cache has two MESI status flags per cache line. Each line can thus be marked as being in one of the states defined in Table 11-2. In general, the operation of the MESI protocol is transparent to programs.

In the L1 instruction cache implements only the "SI" part of the MESI protocol, because the instruction cache is not writable. The instruction cache monitors changes in the data cache to maintain consistency between the caches when instructions are modified. See Section 11.7., "Self-Modifying Code" for more information on the implications of caching instructions.

Table 11-2. MESI Cache Line States

Cache Line State	M (Modified)	E (Exclusive)	S (Shared)	I (Invalid)
This cache line is valid?	Yes	Yes	Yes	No
The memory copy is...	...out of date	...valid	...valid	—
Copies exist in caches of other processors?	No	No	Maybe	Maybe
A write to this line ...	...does not go to bus	...does not go to bus	...goes to bus and updates cache	...goes directly to bus

11.5. CACHE CONTROL

The processor provides the following cache-control mechanisms for use in enabling caching and/or restricting caching to various pages or regions in memory (see Figure 11-2):

- CD flag, bit 30 of control register CR0—Controls caching of system memory locations (see Section 2.5., "Control Registers"). If the CD flag is clear, caching is enabled for the whole of system memory, but may be restricted for individual pages or regions of memory by other cache-control mechanisms. When the CD flag is set, caching is prevented in the L1 and L2 caches (that is, cache fills and updates are prevented), but they will still respond to snoop traffic. They should be explicitly flushed to insure memory coherency. For highest processor performance, both the CD and the NW flags in control register CR0 should be cleared. Table 11-3 shows the interaction of the CD and NW flags.

NOTE

The effect of setting the CD flag is different for the Pentium Pro processor than for earlier Intel Architecture processors. Setting the CD flag for the Pentium Pro processor does not disable the caches as it does on earlier processors. Instead, it merely prevents cache line fills and updates. The processor will still read data from the caches on cache hits and invalidate cache lines on writes. To insure memory coherency after the CD flag is set, the caches should be explicitly flushed (see Section 11.5.2., "Preventing Caching"). Also, setting the CD flag does not force strict ordering of memory accesses unless the MTRRs are disabled and/or all memory is referenced as uncached (see Section 7.2.1., "Strengthening or Weakening the Processor-Order Model").

- NW flags in control register CR0—Controls the write policy for system memory locations (see Section 2.5., "Control Registers"). If the NW and CD flags are clear, write-back is enabled for the whole of system memory, but may be restricted for individual pages or regions of memory by other cache-control mechanisms. Table 11-3 shows how the other combinations of CD and NW flags affects caching.

- PCD flag in the page-directory and page-table entries—Controls caching for individual page tables and pages, respectively, (see Section 3.6.4., "Page-Directory and Page-Table Entries"). This flag only has effect when paging is enabled and the CD flag in control register CR0 is clear. The PCD flag enables caching of the page table or page when clear and prevents caching when set.

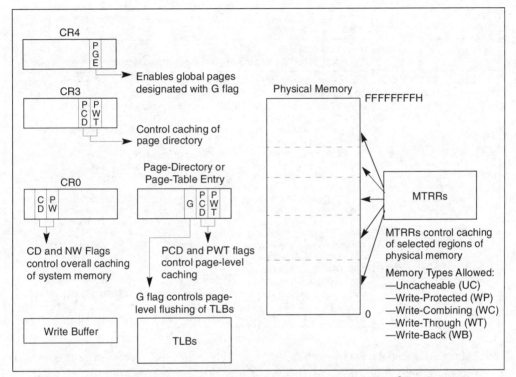

Figure 11-2. Cache-Control Mechanisms Available in the Pentium® Pro Processor

- PWT flag in the page-directory and page-table entries—Controls the write policy for individual page tables and pages, respectively, (see Section 3.6.4., "Page-Directory and Page-Table Entries"). This flag only has effect when paging is enabled and the NW flag in control register CR0 is clear. The PWT flag enables write-back caching of the page table or page when clear and write-through caching when set.

- PCD and PWT flags in control register CR3. Control the global caching and write policy for the page directory (see Section 2.5., "Control Registers"). The PCD flag enables caching of the page directory when clear and prevents caching when set. The PWT flag enables write-back caching of the page directory when clear and write-through caching when set. These flags do not affect the caching and write policy for individual page tables. These flags only have effect when paging is enabled and the CD flag in control register CR0 is clear.

Table 11-3. Cache Operating Modes

CD	NW	Caching and Read/Write Policy
0	0	Normal highest performance cache operation. - Read hits access the cache; read misses may cause replacement. - Write hits update the cache. - Only writes to shared lines and write misses update system memory. - Write hits can change shared lines to exclusive under control of the MTRRs. - Invalidation is allowed.
0	1	Invalid setting. A general-protection exception (#GP) with an error code of 0 is generated.
1	0	Cache updates prevented. Memory coherency is maintained; existing contents locked in cache. - Read hits access the cache; read misses do not cause replacement. - Write hits update cache. - Only write hits to shared lines and write misses update memory. - Invalidation is allowed. - Strict memory ordering is not enforced unless the MTRRs are disabled and/or all memory is referenced as uncached (see Section 7.2.1., "Strengthening or Weakening the Processor-Order Model").
1	1	Cache updated prevented. Memory coherency is not maintained. - Read hits access the cache; read misses do not cause replacement. - Write hits update cache but not memory. - Write hits change exclusive lines to modified. - Shared lines remain shared after write hit. - Write misses access memory. - Invalidation is inhibited. - Invalidation is allowed. - Strict memory ordering is not enforced unless the MTRRs are disabled and/or all memory is referenced as uncached (see Section 7.2.1., "Strengthening or Weakening the Processor-Order Model").

- G (global) flag in the page-directory and page-table entries—Controls the flushing of TLB entries for individual pages. See Section 3.7., "Translation Lookaside Buffers (TLBs)" for more information about this flag.

- PGE (page global enable) flag in control register CR4—Enables the establishment of global pages with the G flag. See Section 3.7., "Translation Lookaside Buffers (TLBs)" for more information about this flag.

- Memory type range registers (MTRRs)—Control the type of caching used in specific regions of physical memory. Any of the caching types described in Section 11.3., "Methods of Caching Available" can be selected. See Section 11.11., "Memory Type Range Registers (MTRRs)" for a detailed description of the MTRRs.

11.5.1. Precedence of Cache Controls

The cache control flags and MTRRs operate hierarchically for restricting caching. That is, if the CD flag is set, caching is prevented globally (see Table 11-3). If the CD flag is clear, either the PCD flags and/or the MTRRs can be used to restrict caching. If there is an overlap of page-level caching control and MTRR caching control, the mechanism that prevents caching has precedence. For example, if an MTRR makes a region of system memory uncachable, a PCD flag cannot be used to enable caching for a page in that region. The converse is also true; that is, if the PCD flag is set, an MTRR cannot be used to make a region of system memory cacheable.

In cases where there is a overlap in the assignment of the write-back and write-through caching policies to a page and a region of memory, the write-through policy takes precedence. The write-combining policy (which can only be assigned through an MTRR) takes precedence over either write-through or write-back.

Table 11-4 describes the mapping from MTRR memory types and page-level caching attributes to effective memory types, when normal caching is in effect (the CD and NW flags in control register CR0 are clear). Combinations that appear in gray are implementation-defined and may be implemented differently on future Intel Architecture processors. System designers are encouraged to avoid these implementation-defined combinations.

Table 11-4. Effective Memory Type Depending on MTRR, PCD, and PWT Settings

MTRR Memory Type	PCD Value	PWT Value	Effective Memory Type
UC	X	X	UC
WC	0	0	WC
	0	1	WC
	1	0	WC
	1	1	UC
WT	0	X	WT
	1	X	UC
WP	0	0	WP
	0	1	WP
	1	0	UC
	1	1	UC
WB	0	0	WB
	0	1	WT
	1	X	UC

NOTE:

This table assumes that the CD and NW flags in register CR0 are set to 0. The effective memory types in the grey areas are implementation defined and may be different in future Intel Architecture processors.

When normal caching is in effect, the effective memory type is determined using the following rules:

1. If the PCD and PWT attributes for the page are both 0, then the effective memory type is identical to the MTRR-defined memory type.

2. If the PCD flag is set, then the effective memory type is UC.

3. If the PCD flag is clear and the PWT flag is set, the effective memory type is WT for the WB memory type and the MTRR-defined memory type for all other memory types.

4. Setting the PCD and PWT flags to opposite values is considered model-specific for the WP and WC memory types and architecturally-defined for the WB, WT, and UC memory types.

11.5.2. Preventing Caching

The L1 and L2 caches are enabled by default following a hardware reset (resulting from a power-up or the asserting of the RESET# pin); however, all memory types are set for uncached (UC) in the MTRRs. To prevent the L1 and L2 caches from performing all caching operations after they have been enabled and have received cache fills, perform the following steps:

1. Execute a WBINVD instruction to invalidate the caches or to flush them to memory and invalidate them, respectively.

2. Set the CD and NW flags in control register CR0 to 1.

3. Disable the MTRRs and set the default memory type to uncached or set all MTRRs for the uncached memory type (see the discussion of the discussion of the TYPE field and the E flag in Section 11.11.2.1., "MTRRdefType Register").

The caches must be flushed when the CD flag is cleared to insure system memory coherency. If the caches are not flushed in step 1, cache hits on reads will still occur and data will be read from valid cache lines.

11.6. CACHE MANAGEMENT INSTRUCTIONS

The INVD and WBINVD instructions are used to invalidate the contents of the L1 and L2 caches. The INVD instruction invalidates all internal (data and instruction) cache entries, then generates a special bus cycle (called a SYNC cycle) that indicates that external caches (level 3 caches) also should be invalidated. The INVD instruction should be used with care. It does not force a write-back of modified cache lines; therefore, it can cause the caches to become inconsistent with system memory. Unless there is a specific requirement or benefit to invalidating the caches without writing back the modified lines (such as, during testing or fault recovery where cache coherency with main memory is not a concern), software should use the WBINVD instruction.

The WBINVD instruction first writes back any modified lines in the caches, then invalidates the contents of both the L1 and L2 caches. It ensures that cache coherency with main memory is maintained regardless of the write policy in effect (that is, write-through or write-back). Following this operation, the WBINVD instruction generates a FLUSH cycle to indicate to external cache controllers that write-back of modified data and invalidation of external caches should occur.

11.7. SELF-MODIFYING CODE

A write to a memory location in a code segment that is currently cached in the processor causes the associated cache line (or lines) to be invalidated. This check is based on the physical address of the instruction. In addition, the Pentium Pro processor checks whether a write to a code segment may modify an instruction that has been prefetched for execution. If the write affects a prefetched instruction, the prefetch queue is invalidated. This latter check is based on the linear address of the instruction.

In practice, the check on linear addresses should not create compatibility problems among Intel Architecture processors. Applications that include self-modifying code use the same linear address for modifying and fetching the instruction. Systems software, such as a debugger, that might possibly modify an instruction using a different linear address than that used to fetch the instruction, will execute a serializing operation, such as an IRET instruction, before the modified instruction is executed, which will automatically resynchronize the instruction cache and prefetch queue.

11.8. IMPLICIT CACHING

Implicit caching occurs when a memory element is made potentially cacheable, although the element may never have been accessed in normal the von Neumann sequence. Implicit caching occurs on the Pentium Pro processor due to its aggressive prefetching and TLB miss handling. Implicit caching is an extension of the behavior of existing Intel386, Intel486, and Pentium processor systems, since software has never been able to deterministically predict the behavior of instruction prefetch.

To avoid problems related to implicit caching, the operating system must explicitly invalidate the cache when changes are made to cacheable data that the cache coherency mechanism does not automatically handle. This includes writes to dual-ported or physically aliased memory boards that are not detected by the snooping mechanisms of the processor, and changes to page table entries in memory.

The code in Example 11-1 shows the effect of implicit caching on page table entries. The linear address F000H points to physical location B000H (the page table entry for F000H contains the value B000H), and the page table entry for linear address F000 is PTE_F000.

Example 11-1. Effect of Implicit Caching on Page Table Entries

```
mov EAX, CR3       ; Invalidate the TLB
mov CR3, EAX       ; by copying CR3 to itself
mov PTE_F000, A000H; Change F000H to point to A000H
mov EBX, [F000H];
```

Because of speculative execution in the Pentium Pro processor, the last MOV instruction performed would place the value at physical location B000H into EBX, rather than the value at the new physical address A000H. This situation is remedied by placing a TLB invalidation between the load and the store.

11.9. INVALIDATING THE TRANSLATION LOOKASIDE BUFFERS (TLBS)

The processor updates its address translation caches (TLBs) transparently to software. Several mechanisms are available, however, that allow software and hardware to invalidate the TLBs either explicitly or as a side effect of another operation. The following operations invalidate all TLB entries except global entries. (A global entry is one for which the G (global) flag is set in its corresponding page-directory and page-table entry.)

*   Writing to control register CR3.

*   A task switch that changes control register CR3.

The following operations invalidate all TLB entries, irrespective of the setting of the G flag:

*   Asserting or de-asserting the FLUSH# pin.

*   Writing to an MTRR (with a WRMSR instruction).

*   Writing to control register CR0 to modify the PG or PE flag.

*   Writing to control register CR4 to modify the PSE, PGE, or PAE flag.

*   Executing an INVD or WBINVD instruction. (The INVLPG instruction invalidates the TLB for a specific page.)

See Section 3.7., "Translation Lookaside Buffers (TLBs)" for additional information about the TLBs.

11.10. WRITE BUFFER

The Pentium Pro processor temporarily stores each write (store) to memory in a write buffer. The write buffer improves processor performance by allowing the processor to continue executing instructions without having to wait until a write to memory and/or to a cache is complete. It also allows writes to be delayed for more efficient use of memory-access bus cycles.

In general, the existence of the write buffer is transparent to software, even in systems that use multiple processors. The Pentium Pro processor ensures that write operations are always carried out in program order. It also insures that the contents of the write buffer are always drained to memory in the following situations:

*   When an exception or interrupt is generated.

*   When a serializing instruction is executed.

*   When an I/O instruction is executed.

*   When a locking operation is performed.

*   When a BINIT operation is performed.

The discussion of write ordering in Section 7.2., "Memory Ordering" gives a detailed description of the operation of the write buffer.

11.11. MEMORY TYPE RANGE REGISTERS (MTRRS)

The memory type range registers (MTRRs) provide a mechanism for associating the memory types (see Section 11.3., "Methods of Caching Available") with physical-address ranges in system memory. They allow the processor to optimize operations for different types of memory such as RAM, ROM, frame-buffer memory, and memory-mapped I/O devices. They also simplify system hardware design by eliminating the memory control pins used for this function on earlier Intel Architecture processors and the external logic needed to drive them.

The MTRR mechanism allows up to 96 memory ranges to be defined in physical memory (see Figure 11-3), and it defines a set of model-specific registers (MSRs) for specifying the type of memory that is contained in each range. Table 11-5 shows the memory types that can be specified and their properties; see Section 11.3., "Methods of Caching Available" for a more detailed description of each memory type.

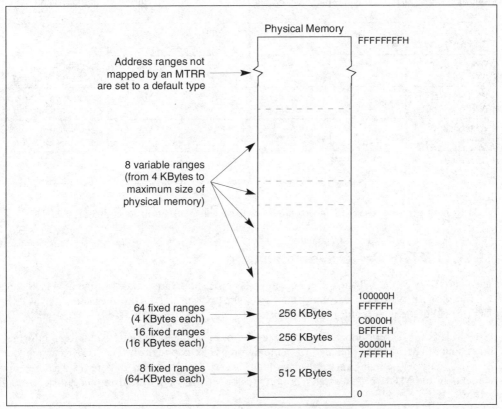

Figure 11-3. Mapping Physical Memory With MTRRs

Following a hardware reset, the Pentium Pro processor disables all the fixed and variable MTRRs, which in effect makes all of physical memory uncachable. Initialization software should then set the MTRRs to a specific, system-defined memory map. Typically, the BIOS (basic input/output system) software configures the MTRRs. The operating system or executive is then free to modify the memory map using the normal page-level cacheability attributes.

In a multiprocessor system, different Pentium Pro processors should use the identical MTRR memory map so that software has a consistent view of memory, independent of the processor executing a program.

Table 11-5. MTRR Memory Types and Their Properties

Mnemonic	Encoding in MTRR	Cacheable in L1 and L2 Caches	Writeback Cacheable	Allows Speculative Reads	Memory Ordering Model
Uncacheable (UC)	0	No	No	No	Strong Ordering
Write Combining (WC)	1	No	No	Yes	Weak Ordering
Write-through (WT)	4	Yes	No	Yes	Speculative Processor Ordering
Write-protected (WP)	5	Yes for reads, no for writes	No	Yes	Speculative Processor Ordering
Writeback (WB)	6	Yes	Yes	Yes	Speculative Processor Ordering
Reserved Encodings*	2, 3, 7 through 255				

NOTE:

* Using these encoding result in a general-protection exception (#GP) being generated.

11.11.1. MTRR Feature Identification

The availability of the MTRR feature is model-specific. Software can determine if MTRRs are supported on a processor by executing the CPUID instruction and reading the state of the MTRR flag (bit 12) in the feature information register (EDX).

If the MTRR flag is set (indicating that the processor implements MTRRs), additional information about MTRRs can be obtained from the 64-bit MTRRcap register. The MTRRcap register is a read-only MSR that can be read with the RDMSR instruction. Figure 11-4 shows the contents of the MTRRcap register. The functions of the flags and field in this register are as follows:

VCNT (variable range registers count) field, bits 0 through 7

Indicates the number of variable ranges implemented on the processor. The Pentium Pro processor has eight pairs of MTRRs for setting up eight variable ranges.

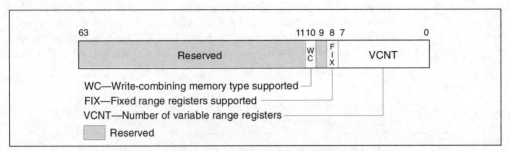

Figure 11-4. MTRRcap Register

FIX (fixed range registers supported) flag, bit 8
> Fixed range MTRRs (MTRRfix64K_00000 through MTRRfix4K_0F8000) are supported when set; no fixed range registers are supported when clear.

WC (write combining) flag, bit 10
> The write-combining (WC) memory type is supported when set; the WC type is not supported when clear.

Bit 9 and bits 11 through 63 in the MTRRcap register are reserved. If software attempts to write to the MTRRcap registers, a general-protection exception (#GP) is generated.

For the Pentium Pro processor, the MTRRcap register always contains the value 508H.

11.11.2. Setting Memory Ranges with MTRRs

The memory ranges and the types of memory specified in each range are set by three groups of registers: the MTRRdefType register, the fixed-range MTRRs, and the variable range MTRRs. These registers can be read and written to using the RDMSR and WRMSR instructions, respectively. The MTRRcap register indicates the availability of these registers on the processor (see Section 11.11.1., "MTRR Feature Identification").

11.11.2.1. MTRRDEFTYPE REGISTER

The MTRRdefType register sets the default properties of the regions of physical memory that are not encompassed by MTRRs (see Figure 11-4). The functions of the flags and field in this register are as follows:

Type field, bits 0 through 7
> Indicates the default memory type used for those physical memory address ranges that do not have a memory type specified for them by an MTRR. (See Table 11-5 for the encoding of this field.) If the MTRRs are disabled, this field defines the memory type for all of physical memory. The legal values for this field are 0, 1, 4, 5, and 6. All other values result in a general-protection exception (#GP) being generated.

Intel recommends the use of the UC (uncached) memory type for all physical memory addresses where memory does not exist. To assign the MC type to non-existent memory locations, it can either be specified as the default type in the Type field or be explicitly assigned with the fixed and variable MTRRs.

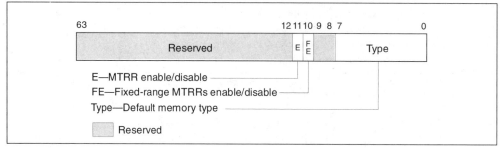

Figure 11-5. MTRRdefType Register

FE (fixed MTRRs enabled) flag, bit 10

Fixed-range MTRRs are enabled when set; fixed-range MTRRs are disabled when clear. When the fixed-range MTRRs are enabled, they take priority over the variable-range MTRRs when overlaps in ranges occur. If the fixed-range MTRRs are disabled, the variable-range MTRRs can still be used and can map the range ordinarily covered by the fixed-range MTRRs.

E (MTRRs enabled) flag, bit 11

MTRRs are enabled when set; all MTRRs are disabled when clear, and the default memory type (specified with the TYPE field) is mapped to all of physical memory. When this flag is set, the FE flag can disable the fixed-range MTRRs; when the flag is clear, the FE flag has no affect.

Bits 8 and 9, and bits 12 through 63, in the MTRRdefType register are reserved; the processor generates a general-protection exception (#GP) if software attempts to write non-zero values to them.

11.11.2.2. FIXED RANGE MTRRS

The fixed memory ranges are mapped with 8 fixed-range registers of 64 bits each. Each of these registers is divided into 8-bit fields that are used to specify the memory type for each of the sub-ranges the register controls. Table 11-6 shows the relationship between the fixed physical-address ranges and the corresponding fields of the fixed-range MTRRs; Table 11-5 shows the encoding of these field:

- **Register MTRRfix64K_00000.** Maps the 512-KByte address range from 0H to 7FFFFH. This range is divided into eight 64-KByte sub-ranges.

- **Registers MTRRfix16K_80000 and MTRRfix16K_A0000.** Maps the two 128-KByte address ranges from 80000H to BFFFFH. This range is divided into sixteen 16-KByte sub-ranges, 8 ranges per register.

Table 11-6. Address Mapping for Fixed-Range MTRRs

Address Range (hexadecimal)								Register
63 56	55 48	47 40	39 32	31 24	23 16	15 8	7 0	
70000-7FFFF	60000-6FFFF	50000-5FFFF	40000-4FFFF	30000-3FFFF	20000-2FFFF	10000-1FFFF	00000-0FFFF	MTRRfix64K_00000
9C000 9FFFF	98000-98FFF	94000-97FFF	90000-93FFF	8C000-8FFFF	88000-8BFFF	84000-87FFF	80000-83FFF	MTRRfix16K_80000
BC000 BFFFF	B8000-BBFFF	B4000-B7FFF	B0000-B3FFF	AC000-AFFFF	A8000-ABFFF	A4000-A7FFF	A0000-A3FFF	MTRRfix16K_A0000
C7000 C7FFF	C6000-C6FFF	C5000-C5FFF	C4000-C4FFF	C3000-C3FFF	C2000-C2FFF	C1000-C1FFF	C0000-C0FFF	MTRRfix4K_C0000
CF000 CFFFF	CE000-CEFFF	CD000-CDFFF	CC000-CCFFF	CB000-CBFFF	CA000-CAFFF	C9000-C9FFF	C8000-C8FFF	MTRRfix4K_C8000
D7000 D7FFF	D6000-D6FFF	D5000-D5FFF	D4000-D4FFF	D3000-D3FFF	D2000-D2FFF	D1000-D1FFF	D0000-D0FFF	MTRRfix4K_D0000
DF000 DFFFF	DE000-DEFFF	DD000-DDFFF	DC000-DCFFF	DB000-DBFFF	DA000-DAFFF	D9000-D9FFF	D8000-D8FFF	MTRRfix4K_D8000
E7000 E7FFF	E6000-E6FFF	E5000-E5FFF	E4000-E4FFF	E3000-E3FFF	E2000-E2FFF	E1000-E1FFF	E0000-E0FFF	MTRRfix4K_E0000
EF000 EFFFF	EE000-EEFFF	ED000-EDFFF	EC000-ECFFF	EB000-EBFFF	EA000-EAFFF	E9000-E9FFF	E8000-E8FFF	MTRRfix4K_E8000
F7000 F7FFF	F6000-F6FFF	F5000-F5FFF	F4000-F4FFF	F3000-F3FFF	F2000-F2FFF	F1000-F1FFF	F0000-F0FFF	MTRRfix4K_F0000
FF000 FFFFF	FE000-FEFFF	FD000-FDFFF	FC000-FCFFF	FB000-FBFFF	FA000-FAFFF	F9000-F9FFF	F8000-F8FFF	MTRRfix4K_F8000

- **Registers MTRRfix4K_C0000. and MTRRfix4K_F8000.** Maps eight 32-KByte address ranges from C0000H to FFFFFH. This range is divided into sixty-four 4-KByte sub-ranges, 8 ranges per register.

See the *Pentium® Pro BIOS Writer's Guide* for examples of assigning memory types with fixed-range MTRRs.

11.11.2.3. VARIABLE RANGE MTRRS

The Pentium Pro processor permits software to specify the memory type for eight variable-size address ranges, using a pair of MTRRs for each range. The first of each pair (MTRRphysBase$n$) defines the base address and memory type for the range, and the second (MTRRphysMask$n$) contains a mask that is used to determine the address range. The "n" suffix indicates registers pairs 0 through 7. Figure 11-6 shows flags and fields in these registers. The functions of the flags and fields in these registers are as follows:

Type field, bits 0 through 7

Specifies the memory type for the range (see Table 11-5 for the encoding of this field.)

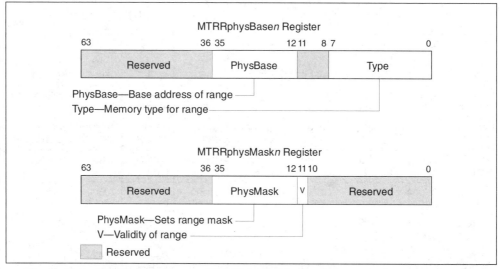

Figure 11-6. MTRRphysBase*n* and MTRRphysMaskn Variable-Range Register Pair

PhysBase field, bits 12 through 35

Specifies the base address of the address range. This 24-bit value is extended by 12 bits at the low end to form the base address, which automatically aligns the address on a 4-KByte boundary.

PhysMask field, bits 12 through 35

Specifies a 24-bit mask that determines the range of the region being mapped, according to the following relationship:

Address_Within_Range AND PhysMask = PhysBase AND PhysMask

This 24-bit value is extended by 12 bits at the low end to form the mask value. See Section 11.11.3., "Example Base and Mask Calculations" for more information and some examples of base address and mask computations.

V (valid) flag, bit 11

Enables the register pair when set; disables register pair when clear.

All other bits in the MTRRphysBase*n* and MTRRphysMask*n* registers are reserved; the processor generates a general-protection exception (#GP) if software attempts to write to them.

Overlapping variable MTRR ranges are not supported generically. However, two variable ranges are allowed to overlap, if the following conditions are present:

- If both of them are UC (uncached).

- If one range is of type UC and the other is of type WB (write back).

In both cases above, the effective type for the overlapping region is UC. The processor's behavior is undefined for all other cases of overlapping variable ranges.

A variable range can overlap a fixed range (provided the fixed range MTRR's are enabled). Here, the memory type specified in the fixed range register overrides the one specified in variable-range register pair.

NOTE

Some mask values can result in discontinuous ranges. In a discontinuous range, the area not mapped by the mask value is set to the default memory type. Intel does not encourage the use of discontinuous ranges, because they require could physical memory to be present throughout the entire 4-GByte physical memory map. If memory is not provided for the complete memory map, the behaviour of the processor is undefined.

11.11.3. Example Base and Mask Calculations

The base and mask values entered into the variable-range MTRR pairs are 24-bit values that the processor extends to 36-bits. For example, to enter a base address of 2 MBytes (200000H) to the MTRRphysBase3 register, the 12 least-significant bits are truncated and the value 200H is entered into the PhysBase field. The same operation must be performed on mask values. For instance, to map the address range from 200000H to 3FFFFFH (2 MBytes to 4 MBytes), a mask value of FFFFE00000H is required. Here again, the 12 least-significant bits of this mask value are truncated, so that the value entered in the PhysMask field of the MTRRphysMask3 register is FFFFE00H. This mask is chosen so that when any address in the 200000H to 3FFFFFH range is ANDed with the mask value it will return the same value as when the base address is ANDed with the mask value (which is 200000H).

To map the address range from 400000H 7FFFFFH (4 MBytes to 8 MBytes), a base value of 400H is entered in the PhysBase field and a mask value of FFFFC00H is entered in the PhysMask field.

Here is a real-life example of setting up the MTRRs for an entire system. Assume that the system has the following characteristics:

- 96 MBytes of system memory is mapped as write-back memory (WB) for highest system performance.

- A custom 4-MByte I/O card is mapped to uncached memory (UC) at a base address of 64 MBytes. This restriction forces the 96 MBytes of system memory to addressed from 0 to 64 MBytes and from 68 MBytes to 100 MBytes, leaving a 4-MByte hole for the I/O card.

- An 8-MByte graphics card is mapped to write-combining memory (WC) beginning at address A0000000H.

- The BIOS area from 15 MBytes to 16 MBytes si mapped to UC memory.

The following settings for the MTRRs will yield the proper mapping of the physical address space for this system configuration. The x0_0x notation is used below to add clarity to the large numbers represented.

MTRRPhysBase0 = 0000_0000_0000_0006h
MTRRPhysMask0 = 0000_000F_FC00_0800h Caches 0-64 MB as WB cache type.
MTRRPhysBase1 = 0000_0000_0400_0006h
MTRRPhysMask1 = 0000_000F_FE00_0800h Caches 64-96 MB as WB cache type.
MTRRPhysBase2 = 0000_0000_0600_0006h
MTRRPhysMask2 = 0000_000F_FFC0_0800h Caches 96-100 MB as WB cache type.
MTRRPhysBase3 = 0000_0000_0400_0000h
MTRRPhysMask3 = 0000_000F_FFC0_0800h Caches 64-68 MB as UC cache type.
MTRRPhysBase4 = 0000_0000_00F0_0000h
MTRRPhysMask4 = 0000_000F_FFF0_0800h Caches 15-16 MB as UC cache type
MTRRPhysBase5 = 0000_0000_A000_0001h
MTRRPhysMask5 = 0000_000F_FF80_0800h Cache A0000000h-A0800000 as WC type.

This MTRR setup uses the ability to overlap any two memory ranges (as long as the ranges are mapped to WB and UC memory types) to minimize the number of MTRR registers that are required to configure the memory environment. This setup also fulfills the requirement that two register pairs are left for operating system usage.

11.11.4. Range Size and Alignment Requirement

The range that is to be mapped to a variable-range MTRR must meet the following "power of 2" size and alignment rules:

1. The minimum range size is 4 KBytes, and the base address of this range must be on at least a 4-KByte boundary.

2. For ranges greater than 4 KBytes, each range must be of length 2^n and its base address must be aligned on a 2^n boundary, where n is a value equal to or greater than 12. The base-address alignment value cannot be less than its length. For example, an 8-KByte range cannot be aligned on a 4-KByte boundary. It must be aligned on at least an 8-KByte boundary.

11.11.4.1. MTRR PRECEDENCES

If the MTRRs are not enabled (by setting the E and FE flags in the MTRRdefType register), then all memory accesses are of the default memory type (specified in the Type field of the MTRRdefType register). If the MTRRs are enabled, then the memory type used for a memory access is determined as follows:

1. If the physical address falls within the first 1 MByte of physical memory and fixed MTRRs are enabled, the processor uses the memory type stored for the appropriate fixed-range MTRR.

2. Otherwise, the processor attempts to matches the physical address with a memory type range set with a pair of variable-range MTRRs:

   a. If one variable memory range matches, the processor uses the memory type stored in the MTRRphysBase*n* register for that range.

b. If two or more variable memory ranges match and the memory types are UC, the UC memory type used.

c. If two or more variable memory ranges match and the memory types are UC and WB, the UC memory type is used.

d. If two or more variable memory ranges match and the memory types are other than UC and WB, the behaviour of the processor is undefined.

3. If no fixed or variable memory range matches, the processor uses the default memory type.

11.11.5. MTRR Initialization

On a hardware reset, the Pentium Pro processor clears the valid flags in the variable-range MTRRs and clears the E flag in the MTRRdefType register to disable all MTRRs. All other bits in the MTRRs are undefined. Prior to initializing the MTRRs, software (normally the system BIOS) must initialize all fixed-range and variable-range MTRR registers fields to 0. Software can then initialize the MTRRs according to the types of memory known to it, including memory on devices that it auto-configures. This initialization is expected to occur prior to booting the operating system.

See Section 11.11.8., "Multiple-Processor Considerations" for information on initializing MTRRs in multiple-processor systems.

11.11.6. Remapping Memory Types

A system designer may re-map memory types to tune performance or because a future processor may not implement all memory types supported by the Pentium Pro processor. The following rules support coherent memory-type re-mappings:

1. A memory type should not be mapped into another memory type that has a weaker memory ordering model. For example, the uncacheable type cannot be mapped into any other type, and the write-back, write-through, and write-protected types cannot be mapped into the weakly ordered write-combining type.

2. A memory type that does not delay writes should not be mapped into a memory type that does delay writes, because applications of such a memory type may rely on its write-through behavior. Accordingly, the write-through type cannot be mapped into the write-back type.

3. A memory type that views write data as not necessarily stored and read back by a subsequent read, such as the write-protected type, can only be mapped to another type with the same behaviour (and there are no others for the Pentium Pro processor) or to the uncacheable type.

In many specific cases, a system designer can have additional information about how a memory type is used, allowing additional mappings. For example, write-through memory with no associated write side effects can be mapped into write-back memory.

11.11.7. MTRR Maintenance Programming Interface

The operating system maintains the MTRRs after booting and sets up or changes the memory types for memory-mapped devices. The operating system should provide a driver and application programming interface (API) to access and set the MTRRs. The function calls MemTypeGet() and MemTypeSet() define this interface.

11.11.7.1. MEMTYPEGET() FUNCTION

The MemTypeGet() function returns the memory type of the physical memory range specified by the parameters base and size. The base address is the starting physical address and the size is the number of bytes for the memory range. The function automatically aligns the base address and size to 4-KByte boundaries. Pseudocode for the MemTypeGet() function is given in Example 11-2.

Example 11-2. MemTypeGet() Pseudocode

```
#define MIXED_TYPES -1     /* 0 < MIXED_TYPES || MIXED_TYPES > 256 */

IF CPU_FEATURES.MTRR /* processor supports MTRRs */
    THEN
        Align BASE and SIZE to 4-KByte boundary;
        IF (BASE + SIZE) wrap 4-GByte address space
            THEN return INVALID;
        FI;
        IF MTRRdefType.E = 0
            THEN return UC;
        FI;
        FirstType ← Get4KMemType (BASE);
        /* Obtains memory type for first 4-KByte range */
        /* See Get4KMemType (4KByteRange) in Example 11-3 */
        FOR each additional 4-KByte range specified in SIZE
                NextType ← Get4KMemType (4KByteRange);
                IF NextType ≠ FirstType
                    THEN return MixedTypes;
                FI;
        ROF;
        return FirstType;
    ELSE return UNSUPPORTED;
FI;
```

If the processor does not support MTRRs, the function returns UNSUPPORTED. If the MTRRs are not enabled, then the UC memory type is returned. If more than one memory type corresponds to the specified range, a status of MIXED_TYPES is returned. Otherwise, the memory type defined for the range (UC, WC, WT, WB, or WP) is returned.

The pseudocode for the Get4KMemType() function in Example 11-3 obtains the memory type for a single 4-KByte range at a given physical address. The sample code determines whether an

PHY_ADDRESS falls within a fixed range by comparing the address with the known fixed ranges: 0 to 7FFFFH (64-KByte regions), 80000H to BFFFFH (16-KByte regions), and C0000H to FFFFFH (4-KByte regions). If an address falls within one of these ranges, the appropriate bits within one of its MTRRs determine the memory type.

Example 11-3. Get4KMemType() Pseudocode

```
IF MTRRcap.FIX AND MTRRdefType.FE /* fixed registers enabled */
    THEN IF PHY_ADDRESS is within a fixed range
        return MTRRfixed.Type;
FI;
FOR each variable-range MTRR in MTRRcap.VCNT
    IF MTRRphysMask.V = 0
        THEN continue;
    FI;
    IF (PHY_ADDRESS AND MTRRphysMask.Mask) = (MTRRphysBase.Base
            AND MTRRphysMask.Mask)
        THEN
            return MTRRphysBase.Type;
    FI;
ROF;
return MTRRdefType.Type;
```

11.11.7.2. MEMTYPESET() FUNCTION

The MemTypeSet() function in Example 11-4 sets a MTRR for the physical memory range specified by the parameters base and size to the type specified by type. The base address and size are multiples of 4 KBytes and the size is not 0.

Example 11-4. MemTypeSet Pseudocode

```
IF CPU_FEATURES.MTRR (* processor supports MTRRs *)
    THEN
        IF BASE and SIZE are not 4-KByte aligned or size is 0
            THEN return INVALID;
        FI;
        IF (BASE + SIZE) wrap 4-GByte address space
            THEN return INVALID;
        FI;
        IF TYPE is invalid for Pentium Pro processor
            THEN return UNSUPPORTED;
        FI;
        IF TYPE is WC and not supported
            THEN return UNSUPPORTED;
        FI;
        IF MTRRcap.FIX is set AND range can be mapped using a fixed-range MTRR
            THEN
```

```
                    pre_mtrr_change();
                    update affected MTRR;
                    post_mtrr_change();
            FI;

        ELSE (* try to map using a variable MTRR pair *)
            IF MTRRcap.VCNT = 0
                THEN return UNSUPPORTED;
            FI;
            IF conflicts with current variable ranges
                THEN return RANGE_OVERLAP;
            FI;
            IF no MTRRs available
                THEN return VAR_NOT_AVAILABLE;
            FI;
            IF BASE and SIZE do not meet the power of 2 requirements for variable MTRRs
                THEN return INVALID_VAR_REQUEST;
            FI;
            pre_mtrr_change();
            Update affected MTRRs;
            post_mtrr_change();
FI;

pre_mtrr_change()
    BEGIN
        disable interrupts;
        Save current value of CR4;
        disable and flush caches;
        flush TLBs;
        disable MTRRs;
        IF multiprocessing
            THEN maintain consistency through IPIs;
        FI;
    END
post_mtrr_change()
    BEGIN
        flush caches and TLBs;
        enable MTRRs;
        enable caches;
        restore value of CR4;
        enable interrupts;
    END
```

The physical address to variable range mapping algorithm in the MemTypeSet function detects conflicts with current variable range registers by cycling through them and determining whether the physical address in question matches any of the current ranges. During this scan, the algorithm can detect whether any current variable ranges overlap and can be concatenated into a single range.

The pre_mtrr_change() function disables interrupts prior to changing the MTRRs, to avoid executing code with a partially valid MTRR setup. The algorithm disables caching by setting the CD flag and clearing the NW flag in control register CR0. The caches are invalidated using the WBINVD instruction. The algorithm disables the page global flag (PGE) in control register CR4, if necessary, then flushes all TLB entries by updating control register CR3. Finally, it disables MTRRs by clearing the E flag in the MTRRdefType register.

After the memory type is updated, the post_mtrr_change() function re-enables the MTRRs and again invalidates the caches and TLBs. This second invalidation is required because of the processor's aggressive prefetch of both instructions and data. The algorithm restores interrupts and re-enables caching by setting the CD flag.

An operating system can batch multiple MTRR updates so that only a single pair of cache invalidations occur.

11.11.8. Multiple-Processor Considerations

In multiple-processor systems, the operating systems must maintain MTRR consistency between all the processors in the system. The Pentium Pro processor provides no hardware support to maintain this consistency. In general, all processors must have the same MTRR values.

This requirement implies that when the operating system initializes a multiple-processor system, it must load the MTRRs of the boot processor while the E flag in register MTRRdefType is 0. The operating system then directs other processors to load their MTRRs with the same memory map. After all the processors have loaded their MTRRs, the operating system signals them to enable their MTRRs. Barrier synchronization is used to prevent further memory accesses until all processors indicate that the MTRRs are enabled. This synchronization is likely to be a shoot-down style algorithm, with shared variables and interprocessor interrupts.

Any change to the value of the MTRRs in a multiple-processor system requires the operating system to repeat the loading and enabling process to maintain consistency, using the following procedure:

1. Broadcast to all processors to execute the following code sequence.

2. Disable interrupts.

3. Wait for all processors to reach this point.

4. Enter the no-fill cache mode. (Set the CD flag in control register CR0 to 1 and the NW flag to 0.)

5. Flush all caches using the WBINVD instruction.

6. Clear the PGE flag in control register CR4 (if set).

7. Flush all TLBs. (Execute a MOV from control register CR3 to another register and then a MOV from that register back to CR3).

8. Disable all range registers (by clearing the E flag in register MTRRdefType). If only variable ranges are being modified, software may clear the valid bits for the affected register pairs instead.

9. Update the MTRRs.

10. Enable all range registers (by setting the E flag in register MTRRdefType). If only variable-range registers were modified and their individual valid bits were cleared, then set the valid bits for the affected ranges instead.

11. Flush all caches and all TLBs a second time. (The TLB flush is required for Pentium Pro processors. Executing the WBINVD instruction is not needed using Pentium Pro processors, but it may be needed in future systems.)

12. Enter the normal cache mode to re-enable caching. (Set the CD and NW flags in control register CR0 to 0.)

13. Set PGE flag in control register CR4, if previously cleared.

14. Wait for all processors to reach this point.

15. Enable interrupts.

11.11.9. Large Page Size Considerations

The MTRRs provide memory typing for a limited number of regions that have a 4 KByte granularity (the same granularity as 4-KByte pages). The memory type for a given page is cached in the processor's TLBs. When using large pages (2 or 4 MBytes), a single page-table entry covers multiple 4-KByte granules, each with a single memory type. Because the memory type for a large page is cached in the TLB, the processor can behave in an undefined manner if a large page is mapped to a region of memory that MTRRs have mapped with multiple memory types.

Undefined behavior can be avoided by insuring that all MTRR memory-type ranges within a large page are of the same type. If a large page maps to region of memory containing different MTRR-defined memory types, the PCD and PWT flags in the page-table entry should be set for the most conservative memory type for that range. For example, a large page used for memory mapped I/O and regular memory is mapped as UC memory. Alternatively, the operating system can map the region using multiple 4-KByte pages each with its own memory type. The requirement that all 4-KByte ranges in a large page are of the same memory type implies that large pages with different memory types may suffer a performance penalty, since they must be marked with the lowest common denominator memory type.

The Pentium Pro processor provides special support for the physical memory range from 0 to 4 MBytes, which is potentially mapped by both the fixed and variable MTRRs. This support is invoked when the Pentium Pro processor detects a large page overlapping the first 1 MByte of this memory range with a memory type that conflicts with the fixed MTRRs. Here, the processor maps the memory range as multiple 4-KByte pages within the TLB. This operation insures correct behavior at the cost of performance. To avoid this performance penalty, operating-system software should reserve the large page option for regions of memory at addresses greater than or equal to 4 MBytes.

intel®

12

8086 Emulation

The Pentium Pro processor provides two ways to execute new or legacy programs that are assembled and/or compiled to run on an Intel 8086 processor:

- Real-address mode.
- Virtual-8086 mode.

Figure 2-2 shows the relationship of these operating modes to protected mode and system management mode (SMM).

When the processor is powered up or reset, it is placed in the real-address mode. This operating mode almost exactly duplicates the execution environment of the Intel 8086 processor, with some extensions. Virtually any program assembled and/or compiled to run on an Intel 8086 processor will run on the Pentium Pro processor in this mode.

When running in protected mode, the processor can be switched to virtual-8086 mode to run 8086 programs. This mode also duplicates the execution environment of the Intel 8086 processor, with extensions. In virtual-8086 mode, an 8086 program runs as a separate protected-mode task. Legacy 8086 programs are thus able to run under an operating system (such as Microsoft* Windows) that takes advantage of protected mode and to use protected mode facilities, such as the protected-mode interrupt- and exception-handling facilities. Protected-mode multitasking permits multiple virtual-8086-mode tasks be run (with each one running an separate 8086 program) to be run on the processor along with other non-virtual-8086-mode tasks.

This section describes both the basic real-address mode execution environment and the virtual-8086-mode execution environment.

12.1. REAL-ADDRESS MODE

The real-address mode of the Pentium Pro processor runs programs written for the Intel 8086, Intel 8088, Intel 80186, and Intel 80188 processors, or for the real-address mode of the Intel 286, Intel386, Intel486, Pentium, and Pentium Pro processors.

The execution environment of the processor in real-address mode is designed to duplicate the execution environment of the Intel 8086 processor. To an 8086 program, a Pentium Pro processor operating in real-address mode behaves like a high-speed 8086 processor. The principal features of this architecture are defined in Chapter 3, *Basic Execution Environment*, of the *Pentium® Pro Family Developer's Manual, Volume 2*. The following is a summary of the core features of the real-address mode execution environment:

- The 1-MByte physical address space ranges from 0 to FFFFFH. To access operands in this address space, it is divided into 64-KByte segments. The base of a segment is specified with a 16-bit segment selector, which is zero extended to form a 20-bit offset from address

0 in the address space. An operand within a segment is addressed with a 16-bit offset from the base of the segment. A physical address is thus formed by adding the offset to the 20-bit segment base (see Section 12.1.1., "Address Translation in Real-Address Mode").

- All operands are 8-bit or 16-bit values.

- Six 16-bit general-purpose registers are provided: AX, BX, CX, DX, SP, BP, SI, and DI.

- Four segment registers are provided: CS, DS, SS, and ES. The CS register contains the segment selector for the code segment; the DS and ES registers contain segment selectors for data segments; and the SS register contains the segment selector for the stack segment.

- The instruction pointer is contained in the 16-bit IP register (referred to in the Pentium Pro processor as the EIP register).

- The 16-bit FLAGS register contains status and control flags. (This register is known in the Pentium Pro processor as the EFLAGS register.)

- All of the Intel 8086 instructions are supported (see Section 12.1.3., "Instructions Supported in Real-Address Mode").

- A single, 16-bit-wide procedure stack is provided for handling procedure calls and calls to interrupt and exception handlers. This stack is contained in the stack segment identified with the SS register. The SP (stack pointer) register contains an offset into the stack segment. The stack grows down (toward lower segment offsets) from the stack pointer. The BP (base pointer) register also contains an offset into the stack segment that can be used as a pointer to a parameter list. When a CALL instruction is executed, the processor pushes the current instruction pointer (the 16 least-significant bits of the EIP register and, on far calls, the current value of the CS register) onto the stack. On a return, initiated with a RET instruction, the processor pops the saved instruction pointer from the stack into the EIP register (and CS register on far returns). When an implicit call to an interrupt or exception handler is executed, the processor pushes the EIP, CS, and EFLAGS (low-order 16-bits only) registers onto the stack. On a return from an interrupt or exception handler, initiated with an IRET instruction, the processor pops the saved instruction pointer and EFLAGS image from the stack into the EIP, CS, and EFLAGS registers.

- A single interrupt table called the interrupt descriptor table (IDT) is provided for handling interrupts and exceptions. Interrupt and exception vectors provide an index into entries in this table. Each entry provides a pointer to an interrupt- or exception-handling procedure. See Handling Interrupts and Exceptions for more details.

- The floating-point unit (FPU) in the Pentium Pro processor is active and available to execute FPU instructions in real-address mode. Programs written to run on the Intel 8087 and Intel287 math coprocessors can be run in real-address mode without modification.

The following extensions to the Intel 8086 execution environment are available in the Pentium Pro processor in real-address mode. If backwards compatibility to Intel 286 and Intel 8086 processors is required, these features should not be used in new programs written to run in real-address mode.

- Two additional segment registers (FS and GS) are available.

- Many of the integer and system instructions that have been added to later Intel Architecture processors can be executed in real-address mode (see Section 12.1.3., "Instructions Supported in Real-Address Mode").

- The 32-bit operand prefix can be used in real-address mode programs to execute the 32-bit forms of instructions. This prefix also allows real-address mode programs to use the 32-bit general-purpose registers in the Pentium Pro processor.

- The 32-bit address prefix can be used in real-address mode programs, allowing 32-bit offsets.

The following sections describe address formation, registers, available instructions, and interrupt and exception handling in real-address mode. For information on I/O in real-address mode, see Chapter 8, *Input/Output*, in the *Pentium® Pro Family Developer's Manual, Volume 2*.

12.1.1. Address Translation in Real-Address Mode

In real-address mode, the processor does not interpret segment selectors as indexes into a descriptor table; instead, it uses them directly to form linear addresses as the 8086 processor does. It shifts the segment selector left by 4 bits to form a 20-bit base address (see Figure 12-1). The offset into a segment is added to the base address to create a linear address that maps directly to the physical address space.

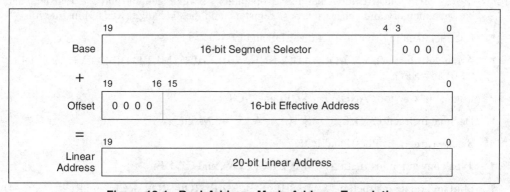

Figure 12-1. Real-Address Mode Address Translation

When using 8086-style address translation, it is possible to specify addresses larger than 1 MByte. For example, with a segment selector value of FFFFH and an offset of FFFFH, the effective address would be 10FFEFH (1 megabyte plus 64 KBytes). The 8086 processor, which can form addresses only up to 20 bits long, truncates the high-order bit, thereby "wrapping" this address to FFEFH. When operating in real-address mode, however, the Pentium Pro processor does not truncate such an address and uses it as a physical address. (Note, however, that on the Pentium Pro, Pentium, and Intel486 processors, the A20M# signal can be used in real-address mode to mask address line A20, thereby mimicking the 20-bit wrap-around behavior of the 8086 processor.)

The Pentium Pro processor can generate 32-bit offsets using an address override prefix; however, in real-address mode, the value of a 32-bit address may not exceed FFFFH without causing an exception. For full compatibility with Intel 286 real-address mode, pseudo-protection faults (interrupt 12 or 13) occur if an effective address is generated outside the range 0 through FFFFH.

12.1.2. Registers Supported in Real-Address Mode

The register set available in real-address mode includes all the registers defined for the 8086 processor plus the new registers introduced in later Intel Architecture processors, such as the FS and GS segment registers, the debug registers, the control registers, and the floating-point unit registers. The 32-bit operand prefix allows a real-address mode program to use the 32-bit general-purpose registers (EAX, EBX, ECX, EDX, ESP, EBP, ESI, and EDI).

12.1.3. Instructions Supported in Real-Address Mode

The following instructions make up the core instruction set for the 8086 processor. If backwards compatibility to the Intel 286 and Intel 8086 processors is required, only these instructions should be used in a new program written to run in real-address mode.

- Move (MOV) instructions that move operands between general-purpose registers and between memory and general-purpose registers, and the exchange (XCHG) instruction.

- Load segment register instructions LDS and LES.

- Arithmetic instructions ADD, ADC, SUB, SBB, MUL, MULI, DIV, DIVI, INC, DEC, CMP, and NEG.

- Logical instructions AND, OR, XOR, and NOT.

- Decimal instructions DAA, DAS, AAA, AAS, AAM, and AAD.

- Stack instructions PUSH and POP.

- Type conversion instructions CWD, CDQ, CBW, and CWDE.

- Shift and rotate instructions SAL, SHL, SHR, SAR, ROL, ROR, RCL, and RCR.

- TEST instruction.

- Control instructions JMP, Jcc, CALL, RET, LOOP, LOOPE, and LOOPNE.

- Interrupt instructions INTn, INTO, and IRET.

- EFLAGS control instructions STC, CLC, CMC, CLD, STD, LAHF, SAHF, PUSHF, and POPF.

- I/O instructions IN, INS, OUT, and OUTS.

- Load effective address (LEA) instruction, and translate (XLATB) instruction.

- LOCK prefix.

- Repeat prefixes REP, REPE, REPZ, REPNE, and REPNZ.

- Processor halt (HLT) instruction.

- No operation (NOP) instruction.

The following instructions added to later Intel Architecture processors can be executed in real-address mode, if backwards compatibility to the Intel 286 and Intel 8086 processors is not required.

- Move (MOV) instructions that operate on the control and debug registers.

- Load segment register instructions LSS, LFS, and LGS.

- Generalized multiply instructions and multiply immediate data.

- Shift and rotate by immediate counts.

- Stack instructions PUSHA, PUSHAD, POPA and POPAD, and PUSH immediate data.

- Move with sign extension instructions MOVSX and MOVZX.

- Long-displacement J*cc* instructions.

- Exchange instructions CMPXCHG, CMPXCHG8B, and XADD.

- String instructions MOVS, CMPS, SCAS, LODS, and STOS.

- Bit test and bit scan instructions BT, BTS, BTR, BTC, BSF, and BSR; the byte-set-on condition instruction SET*cc*; and the byte swap (BSWAP) instruction.

- Double shift instructions SHLD and SHRD.

- EFLAGS control instructions PUSHFH and POPFH.

- ENTER and LEAVE control instructions.

- BOUND instruction.

- CPU identification (CPUID) instruction.

- System instructions CLTS, INVD, WINVD, INVLPG, LGDT, SGDT, LIDT, SIDT, LMSW, SMSW, RDMSR, WRMSR, RDTSC, RDPMC, and RSM.

Execution of any of the other Pentium Pro processor instructions (not given in the previous two lists) in real-address mode result in an invalid-opcode exception (#UD) being generated.

12.1.4. Interrupt and Exception Handling

When operating in real-address mode, software must provide interrupt and exception handling facilities that are separate from those provided in protected mode. Even during the early stages of processor initialization when the processor is still in real-address mode, elementary real-address mode interrupt and exception handling facilities must be provided to insure reliable operation of the processor.

The Pentium Pro processor handles interrupts and exceptions in real-address mode similar to the way it handles them in protected mode. When the processor receives an interrupt or generates an exception, it uses the vector number of interrupt or exception as an index into the interrupt table. (In the Pentium Pro processor, the interrupt table is called the interrupt descriptor table (IDT). The entry in the IDT provides a pointer to an interrupt- or exception-handler procedure. The processor performs the following actions to make an implicit call to the selected handler:

1. Pushes the current values of the CS and EIP registers onto the stack. (Only the 16 least-significant bits of the EIP register are pushed.)

2. Pushes the low-order 16 bits of the EFLAGS register onto the stack.

3. Clears the IF flag in the EFLAGS register to disable interrupts.

4. Clears the TF flag, in the EFLAGS register.

5. Transfers program control to the location specified in the IDT.

An IRET instruction at the end of the handler procedure reverses these steps to return program control to the interrupted program. Exceptions do not return error codes in real-address mode.

The IDT is an array of 4-byte entries (see Figure 12-2). Each entry consists of a far pointer to a handler procedure, made up of a segment selector and an offset. The processor scales the interrupt or exception vector by 4 to obtain an index into the interrupt table. Following reset, the base of the IDT is located at physical address 0 and its limit is set to 3FFH. In the Intel 8086 processor, the base address and limit of the IDT cannot be changed. In the Pentium Pro processor, the base address and limit of the IDT are contained in the IDTR register and can be changed using the LIDT instruction. (For backward compatibility to Intel 286 and Intel 8086 processors, the default base address and limit of the IDT should not be changed.)

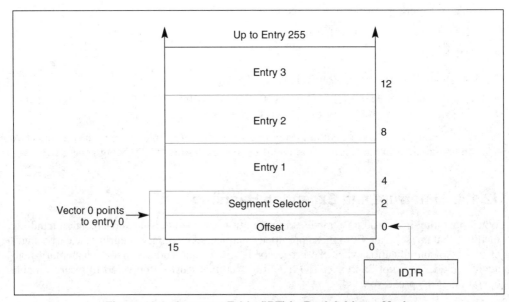

Figure 12-2. Interrupt Table (IDT) in Real-Address Mode

Table 12-1 shows the exception and interrupt vectors that can be generated in real-address mode and virtual-8086 mode, and in the Intel 8086 processor. See Chapter 5, *Interrupt and Exception Handling*, for a description of the exception conditions. Note that the name of the segment overrun exception (vector 13) is different in the Pentium Pro processor. For the 32-bit Intel Architecture processors, the function of this exception has been expanded to cover all general-protection exceptions (#GP).

Table 12-1. Real-Address Mode Exceptions and Interrupts

Vector No.	Description	Real-Address Mode	Virtual-8086 Mode	Intel 8086 Processor
0	Divide Error (#DE)	Yes	Yes	Yes
1	Debug Exception (#DB)	Yes	Yes	Yes
2	NMI Interrupt	Yes	Yes	Yes
3	Breakpoint (#BP)	Yes	Yes	Yes
4	Overflow (#OF)	Yes	Yes	Yes
5	BOUND Range Exceeded (#BR)	Yes	Yes	Reserved
6	Invalid Opcode (#UD)	Yes	Yes	Yes
7	Device Not Available (#NM)	Yes	Yes	Yes
8	Double Fault (#DF)	Yes	Yes	Yes
9	(Intel reserved. Do not use.)	Reserved	Reserved	Reserved
10	Invalid TSS (#TS)	Reserved	Yes	Reserved
11	Segment Not Present (#NP)	Reserved	Yes	Reserved
12	Stack Fault (#SS)	Yes	Yes	Yes
13	General Protection (#GP)*	Yes	Yes	Yes
14	Page Fault (#PF)	Reserved	Yes	Reserved
15	(Intel reserved. Do not use.)	Reserved	Reserved	Reserved
16	Floating-Point Error (#MF)	Yes	Yes	Yes
17	Alignment Check (#AC)	Reserved	Yes	Reserved
18	Machine Check (#MC)	Yes	Yes	Reserved
19-31	(Intel reserved. Do not use.)	Reserved	Reserved	Reserved
32-255	Maskable Interrupts	Yes	Yes	Yes

NOTE:

* In the Intel 8086 processor, vector 13 is the segment overrun exception. For the 32-bit Intel Architecture processors, the function of this exception has been expanded to cover all general-protection error conditions.

12.2. VIRTUAL-8086 MODE

Virtual-8086 mode is actually a special type of a task that runs in the Pentium Pro processor's protected mode. When the operating-system or executive switches to a virtual-8086-mode task, the processor emulates an Intel 8086 processor. The execution environment of the processor while in the 8086-emulation state is the same as is described in Section 12.1., "Real-Address Mode" for real-address mode, including the extensions. The major difference between the two modes is that in virtual-8086 mode the 8086 emulator uses some protected-mode services (such as the protected-mode interrupt and exception handling facilities).

As in real-address mode, any new or legacy program that has been assembled and/or compiled to run on an Intel 8086 processor will run in a virtual-8086-mode task. And several 8086 programs can be run as virtual-8086-mode tasks concurrently using the processor's multitasking facilities.

12.2.1. Enabling Virtual-8086 Mode

The processor runs in virtual-8086 mode when the VM (virtual machine) flag in the EFLAGS register is set. This flag can only be set when the processor switches to a new task, or returns to a task that was suspended to handle an interrupt or exception.

System software cannot change the state of the VM flag directly in the EFLAGS register (for example, by using the POPFH instruction). Instead it changes the flag in the image of the EFLAGS register stored in the TSS or on the stack following a call to an interrupt- or exception-handler procedure. Software sets the VM flag in the EFLAGS image in the TSS when first creating a virtual-8086 task.

The processor tests this flag under two general conditions:

- When loading segment registers, to determine whether to use 8086-style address translation.

- When decoding instructions, to determine which instructions are not supported in virtual-8086 mode and which instructions are sensitive to IOPL.

12.2.2. Structure of a Virtual-8086 Task

A virtual-8086-mode task consists of the following items:

- A 32-bit TSS for the task.

- The 8086 program.

- A virtual-8086 monitor.

- Operating-system services.

The TSS of the new task must be a 32-bit TSS, not a 16-bit TSS, because the 16-bit TSS does not load the most-significant word of the EFLAGS register, which contains the VM flag.

The processor enters virtual-8086 mode to run the 8086 program and returns to protected mode to run the monitor.

The virtual-8086 monitor is 32-bit protected-mode code module that runs at a CPL of 0. The monitor consists of initialization, interrupt- and exception-handling, and I/O emulation procedures that emulate a personal computer or other 8086-based platform. As with any Pentium Pro processor code module, code-segment descriptors for the virtual-8086 monitor must exist in the GDT or in the task's LDT. The linear addresses above 10FFEFH are available for the virtual-8086 monitor, the operating system, and other system software. The monitor also may need data-segment descriptors so it can examine the IDT or other parts of the 8086 program in the first 1 MByte of the address space.

The 8086 operating-system services consists of a kernel and/or operating-system procedures that the 8086 program makes calls to. These services can be implemented in either of the following two ways:

- They can be included in the 8086 program. This approach is desirable for either of the following reasons:

  — The 8086 program code modifies the 8086 operating-system services.

  — There is not sufficient development time to merge the 8086 operating-system services into main operating system or executive.

- They can be implemented or emulated in the virtual-8086 monitor. This approach is desirable for any of the following reasons:

  — The 8086 operating-system procedures can be more easily coordinated among several virtual-8086 tasks.

  — The 8086 operating-system procedures can be easily emulated by calls to the main operating system or executive.

The approach chosen for implementing the 8086 operating-system services may result different virtual-8086-mode tasks using different 8086 operating-system services.

12.2.3. Paging of Virtual-8086 Tasks

Even though a program running in virtual-8086 mode can use only 20-bit linear addresses, the processor converts these addresses into 32-bit linear addresses before mapping them to the physical address space. If paging is being used, the 8086 address space for a program running in virtual-8086 mode can be paged and located in set of pages in physical address space. If paging is use, it is transparent to the program running in virtual-8086 mode just as it is for any task running on the processor.

Paging is not necessary for a single virtual-8086-mode task, but paging is useful or necessary in the following situations:

- When running multiple virtual-8086-mode tasks. Each task must map the lower 1 MByte of linear addresses to different physical address locations.

- When emulating the 8086 address-wraparound that occurs at 1 MByte. When using 8086-style address translation, it is possible to specify addresses larger than 1 MByte. These addresses automatically wraparound in the Intel 8086 processor (see Section 12.1.1., "Address Translation in Real-Address Mode"). If any 8086 programs depend on address wraparound, the same effect can be achieved in a virtual-8086-mode task by mapping the linear addresses between 100000H and 110000H and linear addresses between 0 and 10000H to the same physical addresses.

- When creating a virtual address space larger than the physical address space.

- When sharing the 8086 operating-system services or ROM code that is common to several 8086 programs running as different 8086-mode tasks.

- When redirecting or trapping references to memory-mapped I/O devices.

12.2.4. Protection within a Virtual-8086 Task

Protection is not enforced between the segments of an 8086 program. The following techniques can be used to protect the system software running in a virtual-8086-mode task from the 8086 program:

- Reserve the first 1 MByte plus 64 KBytes of each task's linear address space for the 8086 program. An 8086 processor task cannot generate addresses outside this range.

- Use the U/S flag of page-table entries to protect the virtual-8086 monitor and other system software in the virtual-8086 mode task space. When the processor is in virtual-8086 mode, the CPL is 3. Therefore, an 8086 processor program has only user privileges. If the pages of the virtual-8086 monitor have supervisor privilege, they cannot be accessed by the 8086 program.

12.2.5. Entering Virtual-8086 Mode

Figure 12-3 summarizes the methods of entering and leaving virtual-8086 mode. The processor switches to virtual-8086 mode in either of the following situations:

- When dispatching or switching to a task in which the EFLAGS register image stored in the TSS has the VM flag set.

- When executing an IRET instruction and the VM flag in the EFLAGS image on the stack is set.

- When executing an IRET instruction and the NT flag in the EFLAGS register is set and task being returned to is a virtual-8086-mode task.

When a task switch is used to enter virtual-8086 mode, the TSS for the virtual-8086-mode task must be a 32-bit TSS. (If the new TSS is a 16-bit TSS, the upper word of the EFLAGS register is not in the TSS, causing the processor to clear the VM flag when it loads the EFLAGS register.) The processor updates the VM flag prior to loading the segment registers from their images in the new TSS. The new setting of the VM flag determines whether the processor interprets the contents of the segment registers as 8086-style segment selectors or protected-mode segment selectors. When the VM flag is set, the segment registers are loaded from the TSS, using 8086-style address translation to form base addresses.

See Section 12.3., "Interrupt and Exception Handling in Virtual-8086 Mode" for information on entering virtual-8086 mode on a return from an interrupt or exception handler.

12.2.6. Leaving Virtual-8086 Mode

The processor leaves virtual-8086 mode in any of the following situations (see Figure 12-3):

- When the operating system suspends the virtual-8086-mode task.

- When the processor switches to a protected-mode task.

- When the processor services an interrupt or exception that was generated while in virtual-8086 mode.

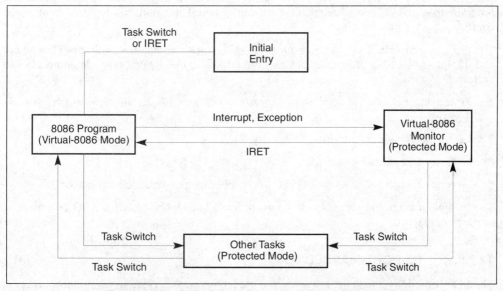

Figure 12-3. Entering and Leaving Virtual-8086 Mode

A task switch from a virtual-8086 task to any other task loads the EFLAGS register from the TSS of the new task. If the new TSS is a 32-bit TSS and the VM flag in the EFLAGS image is clear or if the new TSS is a 16-bit TSS, the processor clears the VM flag of the EFLAGS register, loads the segment registers from the new TSS using protected-mode address formation, and begins executing the new task in 32-bit protected mode.

See Section 12.3., "Interrupt and Exception Handling in Virtual-8086 Mode" for information on leaving virtual-8086 mode to handle an interrupt or exception generated in virtual-8086 mode.

12.2.7. Sensitive Instructions

When the Pentium processor is running in virtual-8086 mode, the CLI, STI, PUSHF, POPF, INT*n*, and IRET instructions are sensitive to IOPL. The IN, INS, OUT, and OUTS instructions, which are sensitive to IOPL in protected mode, are not sensitive in virtual-8086 mode. Following is a complete list of instructions which are sensitive in virtual-8086 mode:

The CPL is always 3 while running in virtual-8086 mode; if the IOPL is less than 3, an attempt to use the instructions listed above triggers a general-protection exception (#GP). These instructions are sensitive to IOPL to give the virtual-8086 monitor a chance to emulate the facilities they affect.

12.2.8. Virtual-8086 Mode I/O

Many 8086 programs written for non-multitasking systems directly access I/O ports. This practice may cause problems in a multitasking environment. If more than one program accesses the same port, they may interfere with each other. Most multitasking systems require application programs to access I/O ports through the operating system. This results in simplified, centralized control.

The processor provides I/O protection for creating I/O that is compatible with the environment and transparent to 8086 programs. Designers may take any of several possible approaches to protecting I/O ports:

- Protect the I/O address space and generate exceptions for all attempts to perform I/O directly.

- Let the 8086 program perform I/O directly.

- Generate exceptions on attempts to access specific I/O ports.

- Generate exceptions on attempts to access specific memory-mapped I/O ports.

The method of controlling access to I/O ports depends upon whether they are I/O-port mapped or memory mapped.

12.2.8.1. I/O-PORT-MAPPED I/O

The I/O permission bit map in the TSS can be used to generate exceptions on attempts to access specific I/O port addresses. The I/O permission bit map of each virtual-8086-mode task determines which I/O addresses generate exceptions for that task. Because each task may have a different I/O permission bit map, the addresses that generate exceptions for one task may be different from the addresses for another task. This differs from protected mode because the IOPL is not checked. See Chapter 8, *Input/Output*, in the *Pentium® Pro Family Developer's Manual, Volume 2* for more information about the I/O permission bit map.

12.2.8.2. MEMORY-MAPPED I/O

In systems which use memory-mapped I/O, the paging facilities of the processor can be used to generate exceptions for attempts to access I/O ports. The virtual-8086 monitor may use paging to control memory-mapped I/O in these ways:

- Map part of the linear address space of each task that needs to perform I/O to the physical address space where I/O ports are placed. By putting the I/O ports at different addresses (in different pages), the paging mechanism can enforce isolation between tasks.

- Map part of the linear address space to pages that are not-present. This generates an exception whenever a task attempts to perform I/O to those pages. System software then can interpret the I/O operation being attempted.

Software emulation of the I/O space may require too much operating system intervention under some conditions. In these cases, it may be possible to generate an exception for only the first attempt to access I/O. The system software then may determine whether a program can be given exclusive control of I/O temporarily, the protection of the I/O space may be lifted, and the program allowed to run at full speed.

12.2.8.3. SPECIAL I/O BUFFERS

Buffers of intelligent controllers (for example, a bit-mapped frame buffer) also can be emulated using page mapping. The linear space for the buffer can be mapped to a different physical space for each virtual-8086-mode task. The virtual-8086 monitor then can control which virtual buffer to copy onto the real buffer in the physical address space.

12.3. INTERRUPT AND EXCEPTION HANDLING IN VIRTUAL-8086 MODE

When the Pentium Pro processor receives an interrupt or detects an exception condition while in virtual-8086 mode, it executes an implicit call to an interrupt or exception handler, just as it does in protected or real-address mode. The interrupt or exception handler that is called and the mechanism used to call it depends on the state of various system flags and fields, which include the following:

- VME flag (bit 0 in control register CR4)—Enables the virtual mode extension for the processor when set (see Section 2.5., "Control Registers").

- IOPL field (bits 12 and 13 in the EFLAGS register)—Controls how interrupts are handled when the processor is in virtual-8086 mode (see Section 2.3., "System Flags and Fields in the EFLAGS Register").

- Interrupt redirection bit map (32 bytes in the TSS, see Figure 12-4)—Contains 256 flags that indicates how software interrupts (interrupts generated by the INTn instruction) should be handled when they occur in virtual-8086 mode. A software interrupt can be directed either to the interrupt and exception handlers in the currently running 8086 program or to the protected-mode interrupt and exception handlers. Hardware interrupts and exceptions are always directed back to the protected-mode interrupt and exception handlers.

These flags and fields allow the interrupt or exception to be handled by a protected-mode interrupt or exception handler or be redirected back to the interrupt and exception handlers that are part of the 8086 program. Table 12-2 shows the various actions the processor takes when it detects a interrupt or exception condition in virtual-8086 mode, depending on the settings of the VME flag, IOPL field, and the bits in the interrupt redirection bit map. This table also introduces six different methods of handling interrupts or exceptions in virtual-8086 mode.

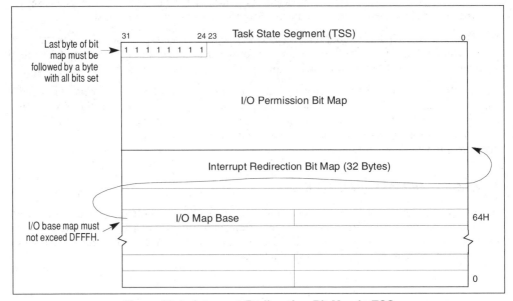

Figure 12-4. Interrupt Redirection Bit Map in TSS

The VME flag enables the processor's virtual mode extension. When this flag is clear, the processor responds to interrupts and exceptions in virtual-8086 mode in the same manner as an Intel486 processor does. When this flag is set, the virtual mode extension provides the following enhancements to virtual-8086 mode:

- Speeds up interrupt handling in virtual-8086 mode by allowing interrupts to be redirected back to the interrupt and exception handlers that are part of the currently running 8086 program.

- Supports virtual interrupts for software written to run on the 8086 processor.

The IOPL flag interacts with the VME flag and the bits in the interrupt redirection bit map to determine how specific interrupts and exceptions should be handled.

Table 12-2. Interrupt and Exception Handling Methods While in Virtual-8086 Mode

Method	VME	IOPL	Bit in Redir. Bitmap*	Processor Action
1	0	3	X	**Interrupt from Virtual-8086 Mode to Protected Mode:** - Clears VM and TF flags - If service through interrupt gate, clears IF flag - Switches to privilege-level 0 (PL0) stack - Pushes GS, FS, DS and ES onto PL0 stack - Clears GS, FS, DS and ES to 0 - Pushes SS, ESP, EFLAGS, CS and EIP of interrupted task onto PL0 stack - Sets CS and EIP from interrupt gate
2	0	< 3	X	**General-protection exception (#GP)**
3	1	< 3	1	**General-protection exception (#GP)**
4	1	3	1	**Interrupt from Virtual-8086 Mode to Protected Mode:** - Clears VM and TF flags - If service through interrupt gate, clears IF flag - Switches to PL0 stack - Pushes GS, FS, DS and ES onto PL0 stack - Clears GS, FS, DS and ES to 0 - Pushes SS, ESP, EFLAGS, CS and EIP of the interrupted task onto PL0 stack - Sets CS and EIP from interrupt gate
5	1	3	0	**Redirect to 8086 Interrupt:** - Clears TF flag - Pushes FLAGS after clearing NT and IOPL - Pushes CS and IP - Loads CS and IP from interrupt vector table at linear address 0 - Clears IF flag
6	1	< 3	0	**Redirect to Virtual 8086 Interrupt with VIF and VIP flag support:** VIF flag clear or VIF set and NMI or exception occurs - Interrupts and exceptions handled in same manner as method 5 VIF flag set and maskable hardware interrupt occurs - Performs a method 4 style call to the #GP exception handler - Handler sets VIP flag in EFLAGS image and returns to 8086 program VIP flag set when VIF flag is cleared with CLI instruction - Performs a method 4 style call to the #GP exception handler - Handler clears VIF and VIP flag in EFLAGS image and returns to 8086 program

NOTE:

* When set to 0, interrupt is redirected back to the 8086 program; when set to 1, interrupt is directed to protected-mode handler.

The interrupt redirection bit map is a 32-byte field in the TSS. This map is located directly below the I/O permission bit map in the TSS. Each bit in the interrupt redirection bit map is mapped to an interrupt or exception vector. Bit 0 in the interrupt redirection bit map (which maps to vector zero in the interrupt table) is located at the I/O base map address in the TSS minus 32. When a bit in this bit map is set, it indicates that the associated software interrupt should be handled in through the protected mode IDT and interrupt and exception handlers. When a bit in this bit map is clear, the associated software interrupt should be redirected back to the interrupt table in the 8086 program (located at linear address one in the programs address space). Redirecting software interrupts back to the 8086 program potentially speeds up interrupt handling because a switch back and forth between virtual-8086 mode and protected mode is not required. This latter interrupt handling technique is particularly useful for 8086 operating systems that use the INT*n* instruction to call operating system procedures.

When the virtual mode extension is enabled (the VME flag is set), two additional flags are activated in the EFLAGS register:

- VIF (virtual interrupt) flag, bit 19 of the EFLAGS register.

- VIP (virtual interrupt pending) flag, bit 20 of the EFLAGS register.

(See Section 2.3., "System Flags and Fields in the EFLAGS Register" for a description of these flags.)

These flags allow interrupt and exception handlers to use a virtual IF flag (a virtual version of the IF flag in the EFLAGS register) to inhibit external interrupts from interrupting a program running in virtual-8086 mode. These flags provide software a means of implementing a virtual IF flag that is compatible with multitasking and multiple processor implementations. The use of the VIF and VIP flags is described in Section 12.3.5., "Method 6 Interrupt and Exception Handling".

The CPUID instruction can be used to verify that the virtual mode extension is implemented on the processor. Bit 1 of the feature flags register (EDX) indicates the availability of the virtual mode extension (see "CPUID—CPU Identification" in Chapter 11, *Instruction Set Reference*, of the *Pentium® Pro Family Developer's Manual, Volume 2*).

Table 12-2 describes six methods (or mechanisms) for handling interrupts and exceptions in virtual-8086 mode, depending on the setting of the VME flag, the IOPL field, and the bits in the interrupt redirection bit map. The following sections describe the actions that processor takes and the possible actions of interrupt and exception handlers for each of these methods. These sections describe three different possible interrupt and exception handlers:

- Protected-mode interrupt and exceptions handlers—These are the standard handlers that the processor calls through the protected-mode IDT.

- Virtual-8086 mode monitor interrupt and exception handlers—These handlers are resident in the virtual-8086 mode monitor. They are typically called by the protected-mode interrupt and exception handlers.

- 8086 program interrupt and exception handlers—These handlers are part of the 8086 program that is running in virtual-8086 mode.

The following sections describe how these handlers are used, depending on the selected method of interrupt and exception handling.

12.3.1. Method 1 Interrupt and Exception Handling

When the VME flag in control register CR4 is clear and the IOPL field is 3, the processor handles virtual-8086 mode interrupts and exceptions in the same manner as they are handled by the Intel486 processor. It executes an implicit call to the interrupt or exception handler in the protected-mode IDT pointed to by the interrupt or exception vector. The IDT entry for an interrupt or exception generated in a virtual-8086-mode task must contain either:

- A 32-bit trap gate or 32-bit interrupt gate, which must point to a nonconforming, privilege-level 0, code segment.

- A task gate.

The following sections describe various ways a virtual-8086 mode interrupt or exception can be handled after the implicit call has been made to a protected-mode handler.

12.3.1.1. HANDLING A VIRTUAL-8086 MODE INTERRUPT OR EXCEPTION THROUGH A PROTECTED-MODE TRAP OR INTERRUPT GATE

When an interrupt or exception vector points to a 32-bit trap or interrupt gate in the IDT, the processor performs the following steps.

1. Switches to 32-bit protected mode and privilege level 0.

2. Saves the state of the processor on the privilege-level 0 stack. The states of the EIP, CS, EFLAGS, ESP, SS, ES, DS, FS, and GS registers are saved (see Figure 12-5).

3. Clears the segment registers. Saving the DS, ES, FS, and GS registers on the stack and then clearing the registers lets the interrupt or exception handler safely save and restore these registers regardless of the type segment selectors they contain (protected-mode or 8086-style). Interrupt and exception handlers, which may be called in the context of either a protected-mode task or a virtual-8086-mode task, can use the same code sequences for saving and restoring the registers for any task. Clearing these registers before execution of the IRET instruction does not cause a trap in the interrupt handler. Interrupt procedures that expect values in the segment registers or that return values in the segment registers must use the register images saved on the stack for privilege level 0.

4. Clears the VM flag in the EFLAGS register.

5. Begins executing selected the interrupt or exception handler.

If the trap or interrupt gate references a procedure in a conforming segment or in a segment at a privilege level other than 0, the processor generates a general-protection exception (#GP). Here, the error code is the segment selector of the code segment to which a call was attempted.

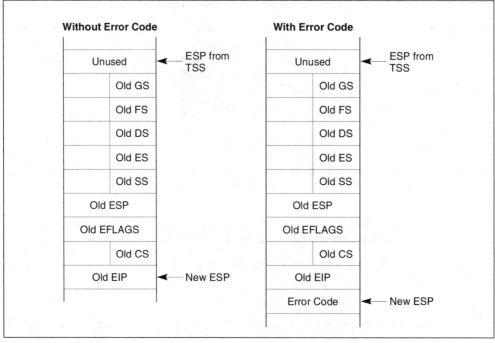

Figure 12-5. Privilege Level 0 Stack After Interrupt or Exception in Virtual-8086 Mode

Interrupt and exception handlers can examine the VM flag on the stack to determine if the interrupted procedure was running in virtual-8086 mode. If so, the interrupt or exception can be handled in one of three ways:

- The protected-mode interrupt or exception handler that was called can handle the interrupt or exception.

- The protected-mode interrupt or exception handler can call the virtual-8086 monitor to handler the interrupt or exception.

- The virtual-8086 monitor can in turn pass control back to the 8086 program's interrupt and exception handler.

If the interrupt or exception is one that the virtual-8086 monitor needs to handle and the VM flag is set in the EFLAGS image stored on the stack, the interrupt handler can call to the virtual-8086 monitor. The virtual-8086 monitor also runs at privilege level 0. It can then either handle the interrupt or exception itself or call a virtual-8086-mode handler.

If the interrupt or exception is handled with a protected-mode handler, the handler can return to the interrupted program in virtual-8086 mode by executing an IRET instruction. This instruction loads the EFLAGS and segment registers from the images saved in the privilege level 0 stack (see Figure 12-5). A set VM flag in the EFLAGS image causes the processor to switch back to virtual-8086 mode. The CPL at the time the IRET instruction is executed must be 0, otherwise the processor does not change the state of the VM flag.

If the interrupt or execution is handled by the virtual-8086-monitor handler, the handler must first return to the protected-mode handler by executing an IRET instruction. An IRET instruction in the protected-mode handler executes the return to the interrupted program in virtual-8086 mode.

12.3.1.2. HANDLING A VIRTUAL-8086 MODE INTERRUPT OR EXCEPTION WITH THE 8086 PROGRAM INTERRUPT OR EXCEPTION HANDLER

Because it was designed to run on an 8086 processor, an 8086 program running in a virtual-8086-mode task contains an 8086-style interrupt table (IDT), which starts at linear address 0. If the virtual-8086 monitor directs an interrupt or exception vector back to the virtual-8086-mode task it came from, the handlers in the 8086 program can handle the interrupt or exception. Sending an interrupt or exception back to the 8086 program involves the following steps:

1. Use the 8086 interrupt vector to locate the appropriate handler procedure in the 8086 program interrupt table.

2. Store the EFLAGS (low-order 16 bits only), CS and EIP values of the 8086 program on the privilege-level 3 stack. This is the stack that the virtual-8086-mode task is using.

3. Change the return link on the privilege-level 0 stack to point to the privilege-level 3 handler procedure.

4. Execute an IRET instruction to pass control to the 8086 program handler.

5. When the IRET instruction from the privilege-level 3 handler again calls the virtual-8086 monitor, restore the return link on the privilege-level 0 stack to point to the original, interrupted, privilege-level 3 procedure.

6. Execute an IRET instruction to pass control back to the interrupted 8086 program.

12.3.1.3. HANDLING A VIRTUAL-8086 MODE INTERRUPT OR EXCEPTION THROUGH A TASK GATE

When an interrupt or exception vector points to a task gate in the IDT, the processor performs a task switch to the selected interrupt- or exception-handling task. The following actions are carried out as part of this task switch:

1. The EFLAGS register with the VM flag set is saved in the current TSS.

2. The link field in the TSS of the called task is loaded with the segment selector of the TSS for the interrupted virtual-8086-mode task.

3. The EFLAGS register is loaded from the image in the new TSS, which clears the VM flag and causes the processor to switch to protected mode.

4. The NT flag in the EFLAGS register is set.

5. Clears the VM flag in the EFLAGS register.

6. Begins executing selected the interrupt- or exception-handler task.

When an IRET instruction is executed in the handler task and the NT flag in the EFLAGS register is set, the processors switches from a protected-mode interrupt- or exception-handler task back to a virtual-8086-mode task. Here, the EFLAGS and segment registers are loaded from images saved in the TSS for the virtual-8086-mode task. If, the VM flag is set in the EFLAGS image, the processor to switches to virtual-8086 mode on the task switch. The CPL at the time the IRET instruction is executed must be 0, otherwise the processor does not change the state of the VM flag.

12.3.2. Methods 2 or 3 Interrupt and Exception Handling

When an interrupt and exception occurs in virtual-8086 mode and the method 2 or 3 conditions are present, the processor generates a general-protection exception (#GP). Method 2 is enabled when the VME flag is set to 0 and the IOPL value is less than 3. Here the IOPL value is used to bypass the protected-mode interrupt and exception handlers and cause all interrupts and exceptions that occur in virtual-8086 mode to be treated as a protected-mode general-protection exception. The general-protection exception handler can then emulate an 8086 interrupt and exception handler.

Method 3 performs the same operation as method 2, except that is allows bits in the interrupt redirection bit map to determine which interrupts and exceptions are directed to the general-protection exception handler. Those interrupts or exception vectors with the a redirection bit set to 1 are handled by the general-protection exception handler and those with a bit set to 0 are handled as method 6 interrupts and exceptions (that is, they are redirected back to the 8086 program with virtual interrupt support).

12.3.3. Method 4 Interrupt and Exception Handling

Method 4 interrupt and exception handling allows method 1 style handling when the virtual mode extension is enabled; that is, the interrupt or exception is directed to a protected mode handler (see Section 12.3.1., "Method 1 Interrupt and Exception Handling"). Method 4 handling is enabled when the VME flag is set to 1, the IOPL value is 3, and the bit for the interrupt or exception vector in the redirection bit map is set to 1.

12.3.4. Method 5 Interrupt and Exception Handling

Method 5 interrupt and exception handling provides a streamlined method of redirecting software interrupts (invoked with the INT*n* instruction) that occurs in virtual 8086 mode back to the 8086 program's interrupt vector table and its interrupt and exception handlers. Method 5 handling is enabled when the VME flag is set to 1, the IOPL value is 3, and the bit for the interrupt vector in the redirection bit map is set to 0. The processor performs the following actions to make an implicit call to the selected 8086 program interrupt or exception handler:

1. Pushes the current values of the CS and EIP registers onto the current stack. (Only the 16 least-significant bits of the EIP register are pushed and no stack switch occurs.)

2. Pushes the low-order 16 bits of the EFLAGS register onto the stack with the NT and IOPL bits cleared.

3. Clears the IF flag in the EFLAGS register to disable interrupts.

4. Clears the TF flag, in the EFLAGS register.

5. Locates the 8086 program interrupt vector table at linear address 0 for the 8086-mode task.

6. Loads the CS and EIP registers with values from the vector table entry pointed to by the interrupt or exception vector. Only the 16 low-order bits of the EIP are loaded and the 16 high-order bits are set to 0.

7. Begins execution the selected interrupt or exception handler.

Exceptions do not return error codes when using this method of handling exceptions.

An IRET instruction at the end of the handler procedure reverses these steps to return program control to the interrupted 8086 program.

The method 5 handling actions are virtually identical to the actions the processor takes when handling interrupts and exception in real-address mode. The benefit of using method 5 handling to access the 8086 program handlers is that it avoids the overhead of method 1 handling, which requires first going to the virtual-8086 mode monitor as described in Section 12.3.1.1., "Handling a Virtual-8086 Mode Interrupt or Exception Through a Protected-Mode Trap or Interrupt Gate" and Section 12.3.1.2., "Handling a Virtual-8086 Mode Interrupt or Exception With the 8086 Program Interrupt or Exception Handler".

12.3.5. Method 6 Interrupt and Exception Handling

With method 6 interrupt and exception handling, the processor performs the same operation as with method 5, except that it adds to ability to use the virtual interrupt flag (VIF) and interrupt pending flag (VIP) in the EFLAGS interrupt to control maskable hardware interrupts. Method 6 handling is enabled when the VME flag is set to 1, the IOPL value is less than 3, and the bit for the interrupt or exception vector in the redirection bit map is set to 0.

Existing 8086 programs commonly set and clear the IF flag in the EFLAGS register to disable and enable maskable interrupts, respectively, (for example, to disable interrupts while handling another interrupt or an exception). This practice works well in single task environments, but can cause problems in multitasking and multiple processor environments. When using earlier Intel Architecture processors, this problem was often solved by creating a virtual IF flag in software. The Pentium Pro and Pentium processors provide hardware support for this virtual IF flag through the VIF and VIP flags. The virtual interrupt flag mechanism operates as follows.

When the processor is set up for method 6 handling of interrupts and exceptions, the CLI and STI instructions operate on the VIF flag instead of the IF flag. When an 8086 program executes the CLI instruction, the processor sets the VIF flag to inhibit maskable hardware interrupts from interrupting program execution; when it executes the STI instruction, the processor clears the VIF flag. The VIP flag is read by the processor but never explicitly written by the processor. It can only be written by software. The processor uses the setting of the VIF and VIP flags to determine how to handle interrupts or exceptions as follows.

If the processor receives an interrupt or exception and the VIF flag is clear (maskable hardware interrupts enabled), the processor performs the same operation as it does for method 5 interrupt and exception handling (that is, it redirects handling to the 8080 program's interrupt and exception handlers). The processor also handles interrupts and exceptions in this manner if the VIF flag is set, and the processor receives either an NMI interrupt or an exception (interrupt vectors 0 through 18).

If the processor receives a maskable hardware interrupt (interrupt vector 32 through 255) when the VIF flag is set, processor performs and the interrupt handler software must perform the following operations:

1. The processor makes a call to a protected mode interrupt handler as described in the following steps. These steps are almost identical to those described for method 1 interrupt and exception handling in Section 12.3.1.1., "Handling a Virtual-8086 Mode Interrupt or Exception Through a Protected-Mode Trap or Interrupt Gate":

   a. Switches to 32-bit protected mode and privilege level 0.

   b. Saves the state of the processor on the privilege-level 0 stack. The states of the EIP, CS, EFLAGS, ESP, SS, ES, DS, FS, and GS registers are saved (see Figure 12-5). In the EFLAGS image on the stack, the IOPL field is set to 3 and the VIF flag is copied to the IF flag.

   c. Clears the segment registers.

   d. Clears the VM flag in the EFLAGS register.

   e. Begins executing selected the protected-mode interrupt handler.

2. The recommended action of the protected-mode interrupt handler is to read the VM flag from the EFLAGS image on the stack. If this flag is set, the handler makes a call to the virtual-8086 monitor.

3. The virtual-8086 monitor reads the VIF flag in the EFLAGS register. If the flag is set, the virtual-8086 monitor sets the VIP flag in the EFLAGS register to indicate that there is an interrupt pending and returns to the protected mode handler.

4. The protected mode handler executes a return to virtual-8086 mode.

5. Upon returning to virtual-8086 mode, the processor continues execution of the 8086 program without handling the interrupt.

When the 8086 program executes the STI instruction to clear the VIF flag, the processor does the following:

1. Checks the VIP flag.

   a. If the VIP flag is clear, the processor clears the VIF flag.

   b. If the VIP flag is set, the processor generates a general-protection exception (#GP).

2. The recommended action of the protected-mode general-protection exception handler is to then call the virtual-8086 monitor and let it handle the pending interrupt.

A typical action of the virtual-8086 monitor is to clear the VIF and VIP flags in the EFLAGS image on the stack and execute a return to the virtual-8086 mode (through the protected-mode exception handler). The next time the processor receives a maskable hardware interrupt, (providing the VIF flag is still clear) it will handle it in the same manner as with method 5 interrupt and exception handling.

Note that the states of the VIF and VIP flags are not modified in real-address mode or during transitions between real-address and protected modes.

12.4. PROTECTED MODE VIRTUAL INTERRUPTS

The Pentium Pro and Pentium processors also support the VIF and VIP flags in the EFLAGS register in protected mode by setting the PVI (protected-mode virtual interrupt) flag in the CR4 register. Setting the PVI flag allows applications running at privilege level 3 to execute the CLI and STI instructions without causing a general-protection exception (#GP) or affecting hardware interrupts.

When the PVI flag is set to 1, the CPL is 3, and the IOPL is less than 3, the CLI and STI instructions set and clear the VIF flag in the EFLAGS register, leaving IF unaffected. In this mode of operation, an application running in protected mode and at a CPL of 3 can inhibit interrupts in the same manner as is described in Section 12.3.5., "Method 6 Interrupt and Exception Handling" for a virtual-8086 mode task. When the application executes the CLI instruction, the processor sets the VIF flag. If the processor receives a maskable hardware interrupt when the VIF flag is set, the processor makes an implicit call the general-protection exception handler. This handler can then set the VIP flag in the EFLAGS register and return to the privilege-level 3 application, which continues program execution. When the application executes a STI instruction to clear the VIF flag, the processor automatically executes an implicit call to the general-protection exception handler, which can then handle the pending interrupt. The typical method of handling the pending interrupt is to clear the VIF and VIP flags in the EFLAGS image on the stack and execute a return to the application program. The next time the processor receives a maskable hardware interrupt, the processor will handle it in the normal manner for interrupts received while the processor is operating at a CPL of 3.

As with the virtual mode extension (enabled with the VME flag in the CR4 register), the protected mode virtual interrupt extension only affects maskable hardware interrupts (interrupt vectors 32 through 255). NMI interrupts and exceptions are handled in the normal manner.

When protected mode virtual interrupts are disabled (CR4.PVI=0) or CPL<3 or IOPL=3, then the CLI and STI instructions execute in a manner compatible with the Intel486 processor. That is, if the CPL is greater (less privileged) than the I/O privilege level (IOPL), a general exception occurs. If the IOPL=3, CLI and STI clear or set the IF flag, respectively.

PUSHF, POPF, and IRET are executed like the Intel486 processor, regardless of whether protected mode virtual interrupts are enabled.

It is only possible to enter virtual-8086 mode through a task switch or the execution of an IRET instruction, and it is only possible to leave virtual-8086 mode by faulting to the virtual-8086 mode handler. In both cases, the EFLAGS register is saved and restored. This is not true, however, in protected mode when the PVI flag is set and the processor is not in virtual-8086 mode. It is possible to call a procedure at a different privilege level, in which case the EFLAGS register is not saved or modified. However, the state of VIF and VIP is never examined by the processor when the privilege level is not 3.

intel®

13

Mixing 16-Bit and 32-Bit Code

CHAPTER 13
MIXING 16-BIT AND 32-BIT CODE

Intel Architecture code modules can be either 16-bit modules or 32-bit modules. Table 13-1 shows the characteristic of 16-bit and 32-bit code modules.

Table 13-1. Characteristics of 16-Bit and 32-Bit Code Modules

Characteristic	16-Bit Code Modules	32-Bit Code Modules
Segment Size	0 to 64 KBytes	0 to 4 GBytes
Operand Sizes	8 bits and 16 bits	8 bits and 32 bits
Pointer Offset Size (Address Size)	16 bits	32 bits
Stack Pointer Size	16 Bits	32 Bits
Control Transfers Allowed to Code Segments of This Size	16 Bits	32 Bits

The Pentium Pro processor functions most efficiently when executing 32-bit code modules. It can, however, also execute 16-bit code modules, in any of the following ways:

- In real-address mode.

- In virtual-8086 mode.

- System management mode (SMM).

- As a protected mode task, when the code segment for the task is configured as a 16-bit code module.

- By integrating 16-bit operations into a 32-bit code module.

Real-address mode, virtual-8086 mode, and SMM are native 16-bit modes. A legacy program assembled and/or compiled to run on an Intel 8086 or Intel 286 processor should run in real-address mode or virtual-8086 mode without modification. Sixteen-bit code modules can also be written to run in real-address mode for handling system initialization or to run in SMM for handling system management functions. See Chapter 12, *8086 Emulation*, for detailed information on real-address mode and virtual-8086 mode; see Chapter 9, *System Management Mode (SMM)*, for information on SMM.

This chapter describes how to integrate 16-bit code modules with 32-bit code modules when operating in protected mode and how to mix 16-bit and 32-bit code within a 32-bit code module.

13.1. DEFINING 16-BIT AND 32-BIT CODE MODULES

The following features of the Pentium Pro processor are used to distinguish between and support 16-bit and 32-bit code modules:

*   The D (default operand size) flag in code-segment descriptors.

*   The B (default stack size) flag in stack-segment descriptors.

*   16-bit and 32-bit call gates, interrupt gates, and trap gates.

*   Operand-size and address-size instruction prefixes.

*   16-bit and 32-bit general-purpose registers.

The D flag in a code-segment descriptor determines the default operand-size and address-size for the instructions of a code segment. (In real-address mode and virtual-8086 mode, which do not use segment descriptors, the default is 16 bits.) A code segment with its D flag set is a 32-bit segment; a code segment with its D flag clear is a 16-bit segment.

The B flag in the stack segment descriptor specifies the size of stack pointer (the 32-bit ESP register or the 16-bit SP register) used by the processor for implicit stack references. The B flag for all data descriptors also controls upper address range for expand down segments.

When transferring program control to another code segment through a call gate, interrupt gate, or trap gate, the operand size and stack pointer size used during the transfer is determined by the type of gate used (16-bit or 32-bit). The gate type determines how return information is saved on the stack (or stacks).

For most efficient and trouble-free operation of the processor, 32-bit programs or tasks should have the D flag in the code-segment descriptor and the B flag in the stack-segment descriptor set, and 16-bit programs or tasks should have these flags clear. Program control transfers from 16-bit code modules to 32-bit modules (and vice versa) are handled most efficiently through call, interrupt, or trap gates.

Instruction prefixes can be used to override the default operand size and address size of a code module. These prefixes can be used in protected mode as well as in real-address mode and virtual-8086 mode. An operand-size or address-size prefix only changes the size for the duration of the instruction.

Operand prefixes or register names (established by the assembler) can be used to select the register size to be used (16-bit and 32-bit). The register size affects the size of operands and the results of arithmetic and effective-address calculations.

13.2. MIXING 16-BIT AND 32-BIT OPERATIONS WITHIN A CODE MODULE

The following two instruction prefixes allow mixing of 32-bit and 16-bit operations within one segment:

- The operand-size prefix (66H)
- The address-size prefix (67H)

These prefixes reverse the default size selected by the D flag in the code-segment descriptor. For example, the processor can interpret the (MOV *mem*, *reg*) instruction in any of four ways:

- In a 32-bit code segment:

  — Moves 32 bits from a 32-bit register to memory using a 32-bit effective address.

  — If preceded by an operand-size prefix, moves 16 bits from a 16-bit register to memory using a 32-bit effective address.

  — If preceded by an address-size prefix, moves 32 bits from a 32-bit register to memory using a 16-bit effective address.

  — If preceded by both an address-size prefix and an operand-size prefix, moves 16 bits from a 16-bit register to memory using a 16-bit effective address.

- In a 16-bit code segment:

  — Moves 16 bits from a 16-bit register to memory using a 16-bit effective address.

  — If preceded by an operand-size prefix, moves 32 bits from a 32-bit register to memory using a 16-bit effective address.

  — If preceded by an address-size prefix, moves 16 bits from a 16-bit register to memory using a 32-bit effective address.

  — If preceded by both an address-size prefix and an operand-size prefix, moves 32 bits from a 32-bit register to memory using a 32-bit effective address.

The previous examples show that any instruction can generate any combination of operand size and address size regardless of whether the instruction is in a 16- or 32-bit segment. The choice of the 16- or 32-bit default for a code segment is normally based on the following criteria:

- Performance. Always used 32-bit code modules when possible. They run much faster than 16-bit code modules on the Pentium Pro processor.

- The operating system the code module will be running on. If the operating system is a 16-bit operating system, it may not support 32-bit code modules.

- Mode of operation. If the code module is being designed to run in real-address mode, virtual-8086 mode, or SMM, it must be a 16-bit code module.

- Backward compatibility to earlier Intel Architecture processors. If a code module must be able to run on an Intel 8086 or Intel 286 processor, it must be a 16-bit code module.

13.3. SHARING DATA AMONG MIXED-SIZE CODE SEGMENTS

Data segments can be accessed from both 16-bit and 32-bit code segments. When a data segment that is larger than 64 KBytes is to be shared among 16- and 32-bit code segments, the data that is to be accessed from the 16-bit code segments must be located within the first 64 KBytes of the data segment. The reason for this is that 16-bit pointers by definition can only point to the first 64 KBytes of a segment.

A stack that spans less than 64 KBytes can be shared by both 16- and 32-bit code segments. This class of stacks includes:

- Stacks in expand-up segments with the G (granularity) and B (big) flags in the stack-segment descriptor clear.

- Stacks in expand-down segments with the G and B flags clear.

- Stacks in expand-up segments with the G flag set and the B flag clear and where the stack is contained completely within the lower 64 KBytes. (Offsets greater than FFFFH can be used for data, other than the stack, which is not shared.)

See Section 3.4.3., "Segment Descriptors" for a description of the G and B flags and the expand-down stack type.

The B flag cannot, in general, be used to change the size of stack used by a 16-bit code segment. This flag controls the size of the stack pointer only for implicit stack references such as those caused by interrupts, exceptions, and the PUSH, POP, CALL, and RET instructions. It does not control explicit stack references, such as accesses to parameters or local variables. A 16-bit code segment can use a 32-bit stack only if the code is modified so that all explicit references to the stack are preceded by the 32-bit address-size prefix, causing those references to use 32-bit addressing and explicit writes to the stack pointer are preceded by a 32-bit operand-size prefix.

In 32-bit, expand-down segments, all offsets may be greater than 64 KBytes; therefore, 16-bit code cannot use this kind of stack segment unless the code segment is modified to use 32-bit addressing.

13.4. TRANSFERRING CONTROL AMONG MIXED-SIZE CODE SEGMENTS

There are three ways for a procedure in a 16-bit code segment to safely make a call to a 32-bit code segment:

- Make the call through a 32-bit call gate.

- Make a 16-bit call to a 32-bit interface procedure. The interface procedure then makes a 32-bit call to the intended destination.

- Modify the 16-bit procedure, inserting an operand-size prefix before the call, to change it to a 32-bit call.

Likewise, there are three ways for procedure in a 32-bit code segment to safely make a call to a 16-bit code segment:

- Make the call through a 16-bit call gate. Here, the offset cannot exceed FFFFH.

- Make a 32-bit call to a 16-bit interface procedure. The interface procedure then makes a 16-bit call to the intended destination.

- Modify the 32-bit procedure, inserting an operand-size prefix before the call, changing it to a 16-bit call. Be certain that the return offset does not exceed FFFFH.

These methods of transferring program control overcome the following architectural limitations imposed on calls between 16-bit and 32-bit code segments:

- Pointers from 16-bit code segments (which by default can only be 16-bits) cannot be used to address data or code located beyond FFFFH in a 32-bit segment.

- The operand-size attributes for a CALL and its companion RETURN instruction must be the same to maintain stack coherency. This is also true for implicit calls to interrupt and exception handlers and their companion IRET instructions.

- A 32-bit parameters (particularly a pointer parameter) greater than FFFFH cannot be squeezed into a 16-bit parameter location on a stack.

- The size of the stack pointer (SP or ESP) changes when switching between 16-bit and 32-bit code segments.

These limitations are discussed in greater detail in the following sections.

13.4.1.   Code-Segment Pointer Size

For control-transfer instructions that use a pointer to identify the next instruction (that is, those that do not use gates), the operand-size attribute determines the size of the offset portion of the pointer. The implications of this rule are as follows:

- A JMP, CALL, or RET instruction from a 32-bit segment to a 16-bit segment is always possible using a 32-bit operand size, providing the 32-bit pointer does not exceed FFFFH.

- A JMP, CALL, or RET instruction from a 16-bit segment to a 32-bit segment cannot address a destination greater than FFFFH.

See Section 13.4.5., "Writing Interface Procedures" for an interface procedure that can transfers program control from 16-bit segments to destinations in 32-bit segments beyond FFFFH.

13.4.2.   Stack Management for Control Transfer

Because the procedure stack is managed differently for 16-bit procedure calls than for 32-bit calls, the operand-size attribute of the RET instruction must match that of the CALL instruction (see Figure 13-1). On a 16-bit call, the processor pushes the contents of the 16-bit IP register and (for calls between privilege levels) the 16-bit SP register. The matching RET instruction must also use a 16-bit operand size to pop these 16-bit values from the stack into the 16-bit registers.

A 32-bit CALL instruction pushes the contents of the 32-bit EIP register and (for inter-privilege-level calls) the 32-bit ESP register. Here, the matching RET instruction must use a 32-bit operand size to pop these 32-bit values from the stack into the 32-bit registers. If the two parts of a CALL/RET instruction pair do not have matching operand sizes, the stack will not be managed correctly and the values of the instruction pointer and stack pointer will not be restored to correct values.

While executing 32-bit code, if a call is made to a 16-bit code segment at a lower or equal privilege level (that is, the DPL of the called code segment is less than or equal to the CPL of the called code segment) through a 16-bit call gate, then the upper 16-bits of the ESP register may be unreliable upon returning to the 32-bit code segment (that is, after executing a RET in the 16-bit code segment).

When the CALL instruction and its matching RET instruction are in code segments that have D flags with the same values (that is, both are 32-bit code segments or both are 16-bit code segments), the default settings may be used. When the CALL instruction and its matching RET instruction are in segments which have different D-flag settings, an operand-size prefix must be used.

13.4.2.1. CONTROLLING THE OPERAND-SIZE ATTRIBUTE FOR A CALL

Three things can determine the operand-size of a call:

* The D flag in the segment descriptor for the calling code segment.
* Any operand-size instruction prefix.
* The type of call gate (16-bit or 32-bit), if a call is made through a call gate.

When a call is made with a pointer (rather than a call gate), the D flag for the calling code segment determines the operand-size operand for the CALL instruction. This operand-size attribute can be overridden by prepending an operand-size prefix to the CALL instruction. So, for example, if the D flag for a code segment is set for 16 bits and a 32-bit operand-size prefix is used with a CALL instruction, the processor will cause the information stored on the stack to be stored in 32-bit format. If the call is to a 32-bit code segment, the instructions in that code segment will be able to read the stack coherently. Also, a RET instruction from the 32-bit code segment without an operand-size prefix will maintain stack coherency with the 16-bit code segment being returned to.

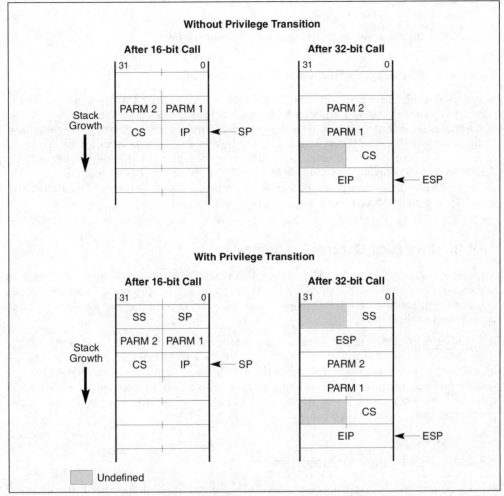

Figure 13-1. Stack after Far 16- and 32-Bit Calls

When a CALL instruction references a call gate descriptor, the type of call is determined by the type of call gate (16-bit or 32-bit). The offset to the destination in the code segment being called is taken from the gate descriptor; therefore, if a 32-bit call gate is used, a procedure in a 16-bit code segment can call a procedure located more than 64 Kbytes from the base of a 32-bit code segment, because a 32-bit call gate uses a 32-bit offset.

An unmodified 16-bit code segment that has run successfully on an 8086 processor or in real-mode on a later Intel Architecture processor will have its D flag clear and will not use operand-size override prefixes. As a result, all CALL instructions in this code segment will use the 16-bit operand-size attribute. Procedures in these code segments can be modified to safely call procedures to 32-bit code segments in either of two ways:

- Relink the CALL instruction to point to 32-bit call gates (see Section 13.4.2.2., "Passing Parameters With a Gates").

- Add a 32-bit operand-size prefix to each CALL instruction.

13.4.2.2.   PASSING PARAMETERS WITH A GATES

When referencing 32-bit gates with 16-bit procedures, it is important to consider the number of parameters passed in each procedure call. The count field of the gate descriptor specifies the size of the parameter string to copy from the current stack to the stack of a more privileged (numerically lower privilege level) procedure. The count field of a 16-bit gate specifies the number of 16-bit words to be copied, whereas the count field of a 32-bit gate specifies the number of 32-bit doublewords to be copied. The count field for a 32-bit gate must thus be half the size of the number of words being placed on the stack by a 16-bit procedure. Also, the 16-bit procedure must use an even number of words as parameters.

13.4.3.   Interrupt Control Transfers

A program-control transfer caused by an exception or interrupt is always carried out through an interrupt or trap gate (located in the IDT). Here, the type of the gate (16-bit or 32-bit) determines the operand-size attribute used in the implicit call to the exception or interrupt handler procedure in another code segment.

A 32-bit interrupt or trap gate provides a safe interface to a 32-bit exception or interrupt handler when the exception or interrupt occurs in either a 32-bit or a 16-bit code segment. It is sometimes impractical, however, to place exception or interrupt handlers in 16-bit code segments, because only 16-bit return addresses are saved on the stack. If an exception or interrupt occurs in a 32-bit code segment when the EIP was greater than FFFFH, the 16-bit handler procedure cannot provide the correct return address.

13.4.4.   Parameter Translation

When segment offsets or pointers (which contain segment offsets) are passed as parameters between 16-bit and 32-bit procedures, some translation is required. If a 32-bit procedure passes a pointer to data located beyond 64 KBytes to a 16-bit procedure, the 16-bit procedure cannot use it. Except for this limitation, interface code can perform any format conversion between 32-bit and 16-bit pointers that may be needed.

Parameters passed by value between 32-bit and 16-bit code also may require translation between 32-bit and 16-bit formats. The form of the translation is application-dependent.

13.4.5. Writing Interface Procedures

Placing interface code between 32-bit and 16-bit procedures can be the solution to the following interface problems:

- Allowing procedures in 16-bit code segments to call procedures with offsets greater than FFFFH in 32-bit code segments.

- Matching operand-size attributes between companion CALL and RET instructions.

- Translating parameters (data).

- The possible invalidation of the upper bits of the ESP register.

The interface procedure is simplified where these rules are followed.

1. The interface procedure must reside in a 32-bit code segment (the D flag for the code-segment descriptor is set).

2. All procedures that may be called by 16-bit procedures must have offsets not greater than FFFFH.

3. All return addresses saved by 16-bit procedures must have offsets not greater than FFFFH.

The interface procedure becomes more complex if any of these rules are violated. For example, if a 16-bit procedure calls a 32-bit procedure with an entry point beyond FFFFH, the interface procedure will need to provide the offset to the entry point. The mapping between 16- and 32-bit addresses is only performed automatically when a call gate is used, because the gate descriptor for a call gate contains a 32-bit address. When a call gate is not used, the gate descriptor must provide the 32-bit address.

The structure of the interface procedure depends on the types of calls it is going to support, as follows:

- **Calls from 16-bit procedures to 32-bit procedures.** Calls to the interface procedure from a 16-bit code segment are made with 16-bit CALL instructions (by default, because the D flag for the calling code-segment descriptor is clear), and 16-bit operand-size prefixes are used with RET instructions to return from the interface procedure to the calling procedure. Calls from the interface procedure to 32-bit procedures are performed with 32-bit CALL instructions (by default, because the D flag for the interface procedure's code segment is set), and returns from the called procedures to the interface procedure are performed with 32-bit RET instructions (also by default).

- **Calls from 32-bit procedures to 16-bit procedures.** Calls to the interface procedure from a 32-bit code segment are made with 32-bit CALL instructions (by default), and returns to the calling procedure from the interface procedure are made with 32-bit RET instructions (also by default). Calls from the interface procedure to 16-bit procedures require the CALL instructions to have a 16-bit operand-size prefixes, and returns from the called procedures to the interface procedure are performed with 16-bit RET instructions (by default).

intel®

14

Code Optimization

CHAPTER 14
CODE OPTIMIZATION

This chapter provides some general guidelines for programming Intel Architecture processors. For additional information refer to AP-500, *Optimizations for Intel's 32-Bit Processors*, order number 241799.

14.1. ADDRESSING MODES AND REGISTER USAGE

This section gives examples of code sequences that result on delays based on addressing modes and register usage.

An address generation interlock (AGI) occurs when a register being used as the base or index component of an effective address calculation was the destination register of a previous instruction. An AGI causes a 1-clock delay.

In the following sequence, the MOV instruction has a one clock stall on the Pentium Pro, Pentium, Intel486 and processors.

```
add edx, 4
mov esi, [edx]
```

On the Intel486 processor, only adjacent instructions can cause AGI's. On the Pentium Pro and Pentium processors, with their higher degree of concurrent execution, instructions that are up to three instructions away can interact to cause an AGI. Consider the following fabricated worst case sequence:

```
add esi, 4
pop ebx
inc ebx
mov edx, [esi]
```

This sequence executes on the Intel486 processor in four clocks. Due to the pairing of instructions on the Pentium Pro and Pentium processors, the MOV instruction needs the value of ESI, which is not available until the ADD completes the execute (EX) stage. This delay results in a one clock stall for the MOV instruction. Therefore, the above instruction sequence executes in three clocks on the Pentium Pro and Pentium processors.

Instructions that generate implicit writes/reads to registers (such as the PUSH, POPO, RET, and CALL instructions, which implicitly address the ESP register) also suffer from the AGI penalty (an explicit write followed by an explicit or implicit read). The following examples show stalls resulting from the dependence on the ESP register by the PUSH and POP instructions:

```
sub esp, 24        / 1 clock stall
  (sub)
push ebx

mov esp, ebp       / 1 clock stall
  (mov)
pop ebp
```

The PUSH and POP instructions also implicitly write to the ESP register. These writes, however, does not cause an AGI when the next instruction addresses through the ESP register (implicit write followed by explicit or implicit read through ESP). The following example demonstrates that an implicit write followed by an explicit or implicit read of the ESP register does not generate an AGI.

```
push edi           / no stall
mov  ebx, [esp]
```

On the Intel486 CPU, there is a one clock penalty for decoding an instruction with either an index or an immediate-displacement combination. On the Pentium Pro and Pentium processors, there is no one clock penalty. There also is no penalty for an indexed instruction on the Pentium Pro and Pentium processors, as shown in the following example.

```
mov result, 555    / 555 is immediate, result is displacement
mov dword ptr [esp+4], 1 / 1 is immediate, 4 is displacement
```

Unlike the Intel486 CPU, there is no one clock penalty with the Pentium Pro and Pentium processors when using a register immediately after its sub-register was written, as demonstrated in the following examples.

```
mov al, 0          /1
mov [ebp], eax     /2 no delay on Pentium Pro and Pentium processors

mov al, 0          /1
  (mov)            /2 one clock delay on Intel486 CPU
mov [ebp], eax     /3
```

14.2. ALIGNMENT

The effect of data misalignment on the Pentium Pro and Pentium processors is similar to its effect on the Intel486 CPU. However, code alignment requirements are not as strict as on the Intel486 CPU.

14.2.1. Code Alignment

Unlike the Intel486 CPU, alignment of code on a cache line boundary (32-byte on Pentium Pro and Pentium processors, 16-byte on Intel486 CPU) does not have a substantial effect on Pentium Pro and Pentium processors performance. However, labels may be aligned as recommended for the Intel486 CPU because the incremental cost on the Pentium Pro and Pentium processors is negligible and it improves the efficiency of the Intel486 CPU.

14.2.2. Data Alignment

A misaligned access in the data cache costs an extra 3 clock cycles on the Pentium Pro, Pentium, and Intel486 processors.

- **4-byte Data**. The alignment of 4-byte objects should be on a 4-byte boundary.

- **2-byte Data**. A 2-byte object should be fully contained within an aligned 4-byte word (i.e., its binary address should be xxxx00, xxxx01, xxxx10, but not xxxx11). (A 2-byte data object has to be aligned on a 2-byte boundary to avoid a penalty.)

- **8-byte Data**. The penalty for a misaligned 8-byte data object (64-bit, for example, double-precision reals) access is 3 clock cycles (as in Intel486 CPU). An 8-byte datum should be aligned on an 8-byte boundary.

14.3. PREFIXED OPCODES

The prefixes lock, segment override, address size, 2-byte opcode map (0F), and operand size are decoded in 1 clock for each prefix. Note that this includes all the 16-bit instructions when executing in 32-bit mode because an operand size prefix is required (for example, MOV WORD PTR [..], ADD WORD PTR [..], ...). Use 32-bit operands for 32-bit segments and 16-bit operands for 16-bit segments as much as possible to avoid the additional byte for prefixes.

The near conditional jump instructions that have a 0FH prefix are decoded differently. In this case, the processor does not take an extra clock. Other 0F opcodes behave as normal prefixed instructions.

14.4. OPERAND AND REGISTER USAGE

The guidelines for operand and register usage should be followed to improve processor performance:

- Use the EAX register when possible. Many instructions are 1 byte shorter when the EAX register is used, for example, loads and stores to memory when absolute addresses are used, transfers to other registers using the XCHG instruction, and operations using immediate operands.

- Use the DS register to access the data segment when possible. Instructions that deal with the DS register are one byte shorter than instructions that use the other data segments, because of the lack of a segment-override prefix.

- Use the ESP register to reference the stack in the deepest level of procedure calls.

- When several references are made to a variable addressed with a displacement, load the displacement into a register.

14.5. INTEGER INSTRUCTION SELECTION

This section gives some instruction sequences to avoid and some sequences to use when generating Intel Architecture assembly code.

- The LEA instruction is useful in the following circumstances:

  — The LEA instruction may be used sometimes as a three- or four-operand addition instruction. LEA ECX,[EAX+EBX*4+ARRAY_NAME]).

  — In many cases, an LEA instruction (or a sequence of LEA instructions, add and shift instructions) may be used to replace constant multiply instructions.

  — The LEA instruction can also be used to avoid copying a register when both operands to an ADD instruction are being used after the add, since the LEA instruction need not overwrite its operands.

  The disadvantage of the LEA instruction is that it increases the possibility of an AGI stall with previous instructions.

- Complex Instructions. Avoid using complex instructions (ENTER, LEAVE, LOOP, string instructions, etc.) when short sequences of simple instructions will handle the coding requirements just as well.

- Zero-Extension of Short Integers. The MOVZX instruction has a prefix and takes 3 cycles to execute (a total of 4 cycles). As with the Intel486 CPU, the following code sequence is recommended instead of using the MOVZX instruction with a prefix:

```
xor eax, eax
mov al, mem
```

  If sequence occurs within a loop, it may be possible to pull the XOR out of the loop if the only assignment to the EAX register is the MOV AL, MEM. This has greater importance for the Pentium Pro and Pentium processors due to their concurrency of instruction execution.

  Access 16-bit data with the MOVSX and MOVZX instructions. These instructions sign-extend and zero-extend word operands to doubleword length. This eliminates the need for an extra instruction to initialize the high word.

- 8/16-Bit Operands. With 8-bit operands, try to use the byte opcodes, rather than using 32-bit operations on sign and zero extended bytes. The prefixes for operand size overrides apply to 16-bit operands, not to 8-bit operands.

  Sign Extension is usually quite expensive. Often, the semantics can be maintained by zero extending 16-bit operands. Specifically, the C code in the following example does not need sign extension nor does it need prefixes for operand size overrides.

```
static short int a,b;
if (a==b) {
}
```

- Compares. Use the TEST instruction when comparing a value in a register with 0. This instruction essentially AND's the operands together without writing to a destination register. If you AND a value with itself and the result sets the 0 condition flag, the value was 0.

  Use the TEST instruction when comparing the result of a boolean AND with an immediate constant for equality or inequality if the register is EAX. (IF (AVAR & 8) { }).

- Address Calculations. Pull address calculations into load and store instructions. Internally, memory reference instructions can have four operands: a relocatable load time segment base, a base register, a displacement, and a scaled index register. In many cases, several integer instructions can be eliminated by fully using the operands of memory references.

  When there is a choice to use either a base or index register, always choose the base because there is a one clock penalty on an Intel486 CPU for using an index.

- Clearing a Register. The preferred sequence to move 0 to a register is XOR REG, REG. This saves code space but sets the condition codes. In contexts where the condition codes must be preserved, use: MOV REG, 0.

- Integer Divide. Typically, an integer divide is preceded by a CDQ instruction. (Divide instructions use EDX:EAX as the dividend and CDQ sets up EDX.) It is better to copy EAX into EDX, then right shift EDX 31 places to sign extend. The copy/shift takes the same number of clocks as CDQ on the Pentium Pro, Pentium, and Intel486 CPU processors, but the copy/shift scheme allows two other instructions to execute at the same time on the Pentium Pro and Pentium processors. If you know the value is positive, use XOR EDX, EDX.

- Avoid Compares with Immediate 0. Often when a value is compared with 0, the operation producing the value sets condition codes that can be tested directly by a JCC instruction. (The most notable exceptions are the MOV and LEA instructions. In these cases, use the TEST instruction.)

- Integer Multiply by Constant. The integer multiply by an immediate can usually be replaced by a faster series of shift's, add's, sub's, and LEA's.

  In general, if there are 8 or fewer bits set in the binary representation of the constant, it is better not to do the integer multiply. On an Intel486 CPU, the break even point is lower: it is profitable if 6 bits or less are in the constant. Basically, shift and add for each bit set.

- In place of using an ENTER instruction at lexical level 0, use a code sequence like:

```
PUSH EBP
MOV EBP, ESP
SUB ESP, BYTE_COUNT
```

- Jump Instructions. The jump instructions come in two forms: one form has an 8-bit immediate for relative jumps in the range from 128 bytes back to 127 bytes forward, the other form has a full 32-bit displacement. Many assemblers use the long form in situations where the short form can be used. When it is clear that the short form may be used, explicitly specify the destination operand as being byte length. This tells the assembler to use the short form. Note that some assemblers perform this optimization automatically.

- Task Switching. For fastest task switching, perform task switching in software. This allows a smaller processor state to be saved and restored. See Chapter 6, *Task Management*, for a discussion of multitasking.

- Segment Register Loads. Minimize segment register loads and use of far pointers as much as possible. Increased protection between segments costs performance as a substantial number of clocks are required to load the segment registers.

intel

15

Intel Architecture Compatibility

CHAPTER 15
INTEL ARCHITECTURE COMPATIBILITY

The Pentium Pro processor is fully binary compatible with all Intel Architecture processors, including the Pentium, Intel486 DX and SX, Intel386 DX and SX, Intel 286, and the 8086/8088 processors. Compatibility means that, within certain limited constraints, programs that execute on previous generations of Intel Architecture processors will produce identical results when executed on the Pentium Pro processor. The compatibility constraints and any implementation differences between the Intel Architecture processors are described in this chapter and in Chapter 10, *Intel Architecture Compatibility*, in the *Pentium® Pro Family Developer's Manual, Volume 2*. The compatibility issues described in this chapter deal with the system architecture. Compatibility issues regarding new instructions, the basic execution environment, and the floating-point unit (FPU) and math coprocessors are covered in the *Pentium® Pro Family Developer's Manual, Volume 2*.

The Pentium Pro processor also includes extensions to the registers, instruction set, and control functions found in earlier Intel Architecture processors. Those extensions have been defined with consideration for compatibility with previous and future processors. This chapter also summarizes the compatibility considerations for those extensions.

15.1. RESERVED BITS

Throughout this manual, certain bits are marked as reserved in many register and memory layout descriptions. When bits are marked as undefined or reserved, it is essential for compatibility with future processors that software treat these bits as having a future, though unknown effect. Software should follow these guidelines in dealing with reserved bits:

- Do not depend on the states of any reserved bits when testing the values of registers or memory locations that contain such bits. Mask out the reserved bits before testing.

- Do not depend on the states of any reserved bits when storing them to memory or to a register.

- Do not depend on the ability to retain information written into any reserved bits.

- When loading a register, always load the reserved bits with the values indicated in the documentation, if any, or reload them with values previously read from the same register.

Avoid any software dependence upon the state of reserved Pentium Pro processor bits. Depending on the values of reserved bits will make software dependent upon the unspecified manner in which the Pentium Pro processor handles these bits. Depending upon reserved values risks incompatibility with future processors.

Software written for an Pentium, Intel486, or Intel386 processor that handles reserved bits correctly will port to the Pentium Pro processor without generating exceptions.

15.2. SERIALIZING INSTRUCTIONS

Certain instructions have been defined to serialize instruction execution to ensure that modifications to flags, registers and memory are completed before the next instruction is executed (or in Pentium Pro processor terminology "committed to machine state"). Because the Pentium Pro processor uses branch-prediction and out-of-order execution techniques to improve performance, instruction execution is not generally serialized until the results of an executed instruction are committed to machine state (see Chapter 2, *Introduction to the Intel Pentium® Pro Processor* of the *Pentium® Pro Family Developer's Manual, Volume 2*). As a result, at places in a program or task where it is critical to have execution completed for all previous instructions before executing the next instruction (for example, at a branch, at the end of a procedure, or in multiprocessor dependent code), it is useful to add a serializing instruction. See Section 7.3., "Serializing Instructions" for more information on serializing instructions.

15.3. INITIALIZATION AND RESET

This section identifies the state of the integer and floating-point units for the various processors and floating-point processor (FPU) extensions.

15.3.1. Integer Unit Initialization on Power-Up or Reset

Table 15-1 identifies the values of the integer unit registers for the 32-bit Intel Architecture processors following a power-up or hardware reset from the RESET# pin. These values are the same regardless of whether the built-in self test (BIST) is executed.

Table 15-1. Processor State Following Power-Up or Reset

Register	Pentium® Pro Processor	Pentium Processor	Intel486™ Processor	Intel386™ Processor
EFLAGS[1]	00000002H	00000002H	00000002H	FFFC802AH
EIP	0000FFF0H	0000FFF0H	0000FFF0H	0000FFF0H
CR0	60000010H	60000010H	60000010H	7FFFFFE0H
CR2	00000000H	00000000H	00000000H	00000000H
CR3	00000000H	00000000H	00000000H	00000000H
CR4	00000000H	00000000H	00000000H	00000000H
CS	0F000H base=0FFFF000H limit=0FFFFH AR=00000093H	0F000H base=0FFFF000H limit=0FFFFH AR=00000093H	0F000H base=0FFFF000H limit=0FFFFH AR=0FF3F93FFH	0F000F000H base=0FFFF000H limit=0FFFFH AR=0FF3F93FFH
SS, DS, ES, FS, GS	0000 base=00000000H limit=0FFFFH AR=00000093H	0000 base=00000000H limit=0FFFFH AR=00000093H	0000 base=00000000H limit=0FFFFH AR=0FF3F93FFH	0000 base=00000000H limit=0FFFFH AR=0FF3F93FFH

Table 15-1. Processor State Following Power-Up or Reset (Contd.)

Register	Pentium® Pro Processor	Pentium Processor	Intel486™ Processor	Intel386™ Processor
EDX	0000x6xxH	0000x5xxH	0000x4xxH	00000308H
EAX	0[2]	0[2]	0[2]	0[2]
EBX, ECX, ESI, EDI, EBP, ESP	00000000H	00000000H	00000000H	00000000H
GDTR,LDTR	00000000 base=00000000H limit=0FFFFH AR=00000082H	00000000 base=00000000H limit=0FFFFH AR=00000082H	xxxx0000 base=00000000H limit=0FFFFH AR=0FFFFFFFFH	00000000 base=00000000H limit=0FFFFH AR=0FFFFFFFFH
IDTR	00000000 base=00000000H limit=0FFFFH AR=00000082H	00000000 base=00000000H limit=0FFFFH AR=00000082H	xxxx0000 base=00000000H limit=0FFFFH AR=0FFFFFFFFH	00000000 base=00000000H limit=0FFFFH AR=0FFFFFFFFH
Task Register	0	0	NA	NA
DR0, DR1, DR2, DR3	00000000H	00000000H	00000000H	00000000H
DR6	FFFF0FF0H	FFFF0FF0H	FFFF1FF0H	FFFF1FF0H
DR7	00000400H	00000400H	00000000H	00000000H
Time Stamp Counter	0	0	NA[3]	NA
Control and Event Select	0	0	NA	NA
All Other MSR's	Undefined	Undefined	NA	NA
Data and Code Cache	Invalid	Invalid	Invalid	NA
TLB(s)	Invalid	Invalid	Invalid	NA
Fixed MTRRs	Disabled	Not Implemented	Not Implemented	Not Implemented
Variable MTRRs	Disabled	Not Implemented	Not Implemented	Not Implemented
Machine Check Architecture	Undefined	Undefined	Not Implemented	Not Implemented
APIC	Enabled	Enabled	Not Implemented	Not Implemented

NOTES:

1. The 10 most-significant bits (14 for the Intel486™ and Intel386™ processor's) of the EFLAGS register are undefined following power-up. Undefined bits are reserved. Software should not depend on the states of any of these bits.

2. If BIST is invoked, EAX is 0 only if all tests passed.

3. Not Applicable.

15.3.2. FPU Initialization on Power-Up or Reset

Table 15-2 shows the state of the FPU registers for 32-bit Intel Architecture FPUs and math coprocessors following a power-up or hardware reset.

Table 15-2. FPU State Following Power-Up or Reset

Register	Pentium® Pro Processor FPU[1]	Pentium Processor FPU[1]	Intel486™ Processor FPU[2]	Intel387™ Math CoProcessor[3]
ST0-ST7	+0.0	+0.0	+0.0	+0.0
Control Word	0040H	0040H	037FHH	037FH
Status Word	0000H	0000H	0000H	0000H
Tag Word	5555H	5555H	0FFFFH	0FFFFH
IP Offset	00000000H	00000000H	00000000H	00000000H
Data Operand Offset	00000000H	00000000H	00000000H	00000000H
CS Selector	0000H	0000H	0000H	0000H
Operand Selector	0000H	0000H	0000H	0000H

NOTES:

1. The state of the FPU is left unchanged on the Pentium® Pro and Pentium processor FPUs following and INIT.
2. The BIST must be requested during a reset to initialize the Intel486™ FPU to the values shown; otherwise, the state of the FPU is left unchanged.
3. The BIST must be requested during a reset to initialize the Intel387™ math coprocessor to the values shown; otherwise, the state of the FPU is left unchanged.

Following an Intel386 processor reset, the processor identifies its coprocessor type (Intel287 or Intel387 DX math coprocessor) by sampling its ERROR# input some time after the falling edge of RESET# signal and before execution of the first floating-point instruction. The Intel287 coprocessor keeps its ERROR# output in inactive state after hardware reset; the Intel387 coprocessor keeps its ERROR# output in active state after hardware reset.

Upon hardware reset or execution of the FINIT instruction, the Intel387 math coprocessor signals an error condition. The Pentium Pro, Pentium, and Intel486 processors, like the Intel287 coprocessor, do not.

15.3.3. Intel486™ SX Processor and Intel487™ SX Math Coprocessor Initialization

When initializing an Intel486 SX processor and an Intel487 SX math coprocessor, the initialization routine should check the presence of the math coprocessor and should set the FPU related flags (EM, MP, and NE) in control register CR0 accordingly (see Section 2.5., "Control Registers" for a complete description of these flags). Table 15-3 gives the recommended settings for these flags when the math coprocessor is present. The FSTCW instruction will give a value of FFFFH for the Intel486 SX microprocessor and 037FH for the Intel487 SX math coprocessor.

Table 15-3. Recommended Values of the FP Related Bits for Intel486™ SX Microprocessor/Intel487™ SX Math Coprocessor System

CR0 Flags	Intel486™ SX Processor Only	Intel487™ SX Math Coprocessor Present
EM	1	0
MP	0	1
NE	1	0, for DOS systems 1, for user-defined exception handler

The EM and MP flags in register CR0 are interpreted as shown in Table 15-4.

Table 15-4. EM and MP Flag Interpretation

EM	MP	Interpretation
0	0	Floating-point instructions are passed to FPU; WAIT/FWAIT and other waiting-type instructions ignore TS.
0	1	Floating-point instructions are passed to FPU; WAIT/FWAIT and other waiting-type instructions test TS.
1	0	Floating-point instructions trap to emulator; WAIT/FWAIT and other waiting-type instructions ignore TS.
1	1	Floating-point instructions trap to emulator; WAIT/FWAIT and other waiting-type instructions test TS.

Following is an example code sequence to initialize the system and check for the presence of Intel486 SX processor/Intel487 SX math coprocessor.

```
fninit
fstcw mem_loc
mov ax, mem_loc
cmp ax, 037fh
jz Intel487_SX_Math_CoProcessor_present;ax=037fh
jmp Intel486_SX_microprocessor_present;ax=ffffh
```

If the Intel487 SX math coprocessor is not present, the following code can be run to set the CR0 register for the Intel486 SX processor.

```
mov eax, cr0
and eax, fffffffdh  ;make MP=0
or eax, 0024h       ;make EM=1, NE=1
mov cr0, eax
```

This initialization will cause any floating-point instruction to generate a device not available exception (#NH), interrupt 7. The software emulation will then take control to execute these instructions. This code is not required if an Intel487 SX math coprocessor is present in the system. In that case, the typical initialization routine for the Intel486 SX microprocessor will be adequate.

Also, when designing an Intel486 SX processor based system with an Intel487 SX math coprocessor, timing loops should be independent of clock speed and clocks per instruction. One way to attain this is to implement these loops in hardware and not in software (for example, BIOS).

15.4. CONTROL REGISTERS

The following sections identify the new control registers and control register flags and fields that have been added to the various versions of the 32-bit Intel Architecture. See Figure 2-5 for the location of these flags and fields in the control registers.

15.4.1. New Pentium® Pro Processor Control Flags

Control register CR4 contains three new control flags in the Pentium Pro processor:

- PAE (bit 5)—Physical address extension. Enables paging mechanism to reference 36-bit physical addresses when set; restricts physical addresses to 32 bits when clear (see Section 15.5.1.1., "Physical Memory Addressing Extension").

- PGE (bit 7)—Page global enable. Inhibits flushing of frequently-used or shared pages on task switches (see Section 15.5.1.2., "Global Pages".

- PCE (bit 8)—Performance-monitoring counter enable. Enables execution of the RDPMC instruction at any protection level.

The content of CR4 is 0H following a hardware reset.

15.4.2. New Pentium® Processor Control Register and Flags

One new control register (CR4) was defined for the Pentium processor. Register CR4 contains flags that enable certain new extensions provided in the Pentium processor:

- VME—Virtual-8086 mode extensions. Enables support for a virtual interrupt flag in virtual-8086 mode (see Section 12.3., "Interrupt and Exception Handling in Virtual-8086 Mode").

- PVI—Protected-mode virtual interrupts. Enables support for a virtual interrupt flag in protected mode (see Section 12.4., "Protected Mode Virtual Interrupts").

- TSD—Time stamp disable. Restricts the execution of the RDTSC instruction to procedures running at privileged level 0.

- DE—Debugging extensions. Causes an undefined opcode (#UD) exception to be generated when debug registers DR4 and DR5 are references for improved performance (see Section 10.2.2., "Debug Registers DR4 and DR5").

- PSE—Page size extensions. Enables 4-MByte pages when set (see Section 3.6.1., "Paging Options").

- MCE—Machine check enable. Enables the machine check exception, allowing exception handling for certain hardware error conditions (see Chapter 16, *Machine Check Architecture*).

15.4.3. New Intel486™ Processor Control Register Flags

Five new flags are defined in the CR0 register for the Intel486 processor:

- NE—Numeric error. Enables the standard mechanism for reporting floating-point numeric errors.

- WP—Write protect. Write-protects user-level pages against supervisor-mode accesses.

- AM—Alignment mask. Controls whether alignment checking is performed. Operates in conjunction with the AC (Alignment Check) flag.

- NW—Not write-through. Enables write-throughs and cache invalidation cycles when clear and disables invalidation cycles and write-throughs that hit in the cache when set.

- CD—Cache disable. Enables the internal cache when clear and disables the cache when set.

Two new flags have been defined in the CR3 register:

- PCD—Page-level cache disable. The state of this flag is driven on the PCD# pin during bus cycles that are not paged, such as interrupt acknowledge cycles, when paging is enabled. The PCD# pin is used to control caching in an external cache on a cycle-by-cycle basis.

- PWT—Page-level write through. The state of this flag is driven on the PWT# pin during bus cycles that are not paged, such as interrupt acknowledge cycles, when paging is enabled. The PWT# pin is used to control write through in an external cache on a cycle-by-cycle basis.

15.5. MEMORY MANAGEMENT FACILITIES

The following sections describe the new memory management facilities available in the various Intel Architecture processors and some compatibility differences.

15.5.1. New Memory Management Control Flags

The Pentium Pro processor provides three new memory management features: physical memory addressing extension, the global bit in page table entries, and general support for larger page sizes. These features are only available when operating in protected mode.

15.5.1.1. PHYSICAL MEMORY ADDRESSING EXTENSION

The new PAE (physical address extension) flag in control register CR4, bit 5, enables 4 additional address lines on the processor, allowing 36-bit physical addresses. This option can only be used when paging is enabled, using a new page table mechanism provided to support the larger physical address range (see Section 3.8., "Physical Address Extension").

15.5.1.2. GLOBAL PAGES

The new PGE (page global enable) flag in control register CR4, bit 7, provides a mechanism for preventing frequently used pages from being flushed from the translation lookaside buffer (TLB). When this flag is set, frequently used pages (such as pages containing kernel procedures or common data tables) can be marked global by setting the global flag in a page-directory or page-table entry. On a task switch or a write to control register CR3 (which normally causes the TLBs to be flushed), the entries in the TLB marked global are not flushed. Marking pages global in this manner prevents unnecessary reloading of the TLB due to TLB misses on frequently used pages. See Section 3.7., "Translation Lookaside Buffers (TLBs)" for a detailed description of this mechanism.

15.5.1.3. LARGER PAGE SIZES

The Pentium Pro processor supports large page sizes. This facility is enabled with the PSE (page size extension) flag in control register CR4, bit 4. When this flag is set, the processor supports either 4-KByte or 4-MByte page sizes when normal paging is used and 4-KByte and 2-MByte page sizes when the physical address extension is used. See Section 3.6.1., "Paging Options" for more information about large page sizes.

15.5.2. Cache Control Flags on the Pentium® Pro, Pentium®, and Intel486™ Processors

The CD and NW flags in control register CR0 implement a writeback strategy for the data cache of the Pentium Pro and Pentium processor. On the Intel486 processor, these values implement a write-through strategy. See Table 15-5 for a comparison of these bits on the Pentium Pro, Pentium, and Intel486 processors. For complete information on caching, see Chapter 11, *Memory Cache Control*.

15.5.3. Descriptor Types and Contents

Operating-system code that manages space in descriptor tables often contains an invalid value in the access-rights field of descriptor-table entries to identify unused entries. Access rights values of 80H and 00H remain invalid for the Pentium Pro, Pentium, Intel486, Intel386, and Intel 286 processors. Other values that were invalid on the Intel 286 processor may be valid on the 32-bit processors because uses for these bits have been defined.

Table 15-5. Cache Mode Differences Between the Pentium® Pro Processor, Pentium®, and Intel486™ Processors

CD	NW	Pentium® Pro Processor and Pentium Processor	Intel486™ Processor
0	0	Normal highest performance cache operation. Read hits access the cache.	Normal highest performance cache operation. Read hits access the cache.
		Read misses may cause replacements.	Read misses may cause replacements.
		These lines will enter the Exclusive or Shared state under the control of the WB/WT# pin.	
		Write hits update the cache.	Write hits update the cache.
		Only writes to shared lines and write misses appear externally	All writes appear externally.
		Writes to Shared lines can be changed to the Exclusive State under the control of the WB/WT# pin.	
		Invalidations are allowed.	Invalidations are allowed.
0	1	Invalid Operation (#GP)	Invalid Operation (#GP)
1	0	Cache disabled. Memory consistency maintained. Contents locked in cache. Read hits access the cache.	Cache disabled. Memory consistency maintained. Contents locked in cache. Read hits access the cache.
		Read misses do not cause replacement.	Read misses do not cause replacement.
		Write hits update the cache.	Write hits update the cache.
		Only writes to Shared lines and write misses update external memory	All writes update external memory
		Writes to Shared lines can be changed to the Exclusive State under the control of the WB/WT# pin.	
		Invalidations are allowed.	Invalidations are allowed.
1	1	Cache disabled. Memory consistency not maintained. Read hits access the cache.	Cache disabled. Memory consistency not maintained. Read hits access the cache.
1	1	Cache disabled. Memory consistency not maintained. Read hits access the cache.	Cache disabled. Memory consistency not maintained. Read hits access the cache.

Table 15-5. Cache Mode Differences Between the Pentium® Pro Processor, Pentium®, and Intel486™ Processors (Contd.)

CD	NW	Pentium® Pro Processor and Pentium Processor	Intel486™ Processor
		Read misses do not cause replacement.	Read misses do not cause replacement.
		Write hits update the cache, but do not access memory.	Write hits update the cache, but do not access memory.
		Write hits will cause Exclusive State lines to change to Modified State	
		Shared lines will remain in the Shared state after write hits.	
		Write misses access memory.	Write misses access memory.
		Inquire and Invalidation Cycles do not effect the cache state or contents.	Inquire and Invalidation Cycles do not effect the cache state or contents.
		This is the state after reset.	This is the state after reset.

15.5.4. Changes in Segment Descriptor Loads

On the Intel386 processor, loading a segment descriptor always causes a locked read and write to set the accessed bit of the descriptor. On the Pentium Pro, Pentium, and Intel486 processors, the locked read and write occur only if the bit is not already set.

15.6. DEBUG FACILITIES

The Pentium Pro and Pentium processors includes extensions to the Intel486 processor debugging support for breakpoints. To use the new breakpoint features, it is necessary to set the DE flag in control register CR4.

15.6.1. Differences in Debug Register DR6

It is not possible to write a 1 to reserved bit 12 in debug status register DR6 on the Pentium Pro and Pentium processors; however, it is possible to write a 1 in this bit on the Intel486 processor. See Section 15.3.1., "Integer Unit Initialization on Power-Up or Reset" for the different setting of this register following a power-up or hardware reset.

15.6.2. Differences in Debug Register DR7

The Pentium Pro and Pentium processors determines the type of breakpoint access by the R/W0 through R/W3 fields in debug control register DR7 as follows:

00   Break on instruction execution only.

01   Break on data writes only.

10   Undefined if the DE flag in control register CR4 is cleared; break on I/O reads or writes but not instruction fetches if the DE flag in control register CR4 is set.

11   Break on data reads or writes but not instruction fetches.

On the Pentium Pro and Pentium processors, reserved bits 11, 12, 14 and 15 are hard-wired to 0. On the Intel486 processor, however, bit 12 can be set. See Section 15.3.1., "Integer Unit Initialization on Power-Up or Reset" for the different setting of this register following a power-up or hardware reset.

15.6.3.   Debug Registers DR4 and DR5

Although the DR4 and DR5 registers are documented as reserved, previous generations of processors aliased references to these registers to debug registers DR6 and DR7, respectively. When debug extensions are not enabled (the DE flag in control register CR4 is cleared), the Pentium Pro and Pentium processors remain compatible with existing software by allowing these aliased references. When debug extensions are enabled (the DE flag is set), attempts to reference registers DR4 or DR5 will result in an invalid-opcode exception (#UD).

15.6.4.   Test Registers

The implementation of test registers on the Intel486 processor used for testing the cache and TLB has been redesigned using MSRs on the Pentium Pro and Pentium processors. (Note that MSRs used for this function are different on the Pentium Pro and Pentium processors.) The MOV to and from test register instructions generate invalid-opcode exceptions (#UD) on the Pentium Pro processor.

15.6.5.   Recognition of Breakpoints

For the Pentium processor, it is recommended that debuggers execute the LGDT instruction before returning to the program being debugged to ensure that breakpoints are detected. This operation does not need to be performed on the Pentium Pro, Intel486, or Intel386 processors.

15.7.   EXCEPTIONS

This section describes the new exceptions added to the 32-bit Intel Architecture processors and implementation differences in existing exception handling. See Chapter 5, *Interrupt and Exception Handling*, for a detailed description of the Pentium Pro processor exceptions.

15.7.1. New Pentium® Pro Processor Exception Conditions

No new exceptions were added to the Pentium Pro processor. The set of available exceptions is the same as for the Pentium processor. The following exception conditions were added to the Pentium Pro processor:

- Machine-check exception (#MC, interrupt 18)—New exception conditions. Many exception conditions have been added to the machine-check exception and a new architecture has been added for handling and reporting on hardware errors. See Chapter 16, *Machine Check Architecture*, for a detailed description of the new conditions.

15.7.2. New Pentium® Processor Exceptions and/or Exception Conditions

The following exceptions and/or exception conditions were added to the Pentium processor:

- General-protection exception (#GP, interrupt 13)—

  — New exception condition added. An attempt to write a 1 to a reserved bit position of a special register causes a general-protection exception to be generated.

  — Change in writes using the CS register prefix. Following a switch from protected mode to real-address mode, the Intel486 processor requires a far jump control-flow instruction to be executed prior to performing a write using the CS segment register prefix (for example, MOV CS:[0], EAX). The far jump in protected mode on the Intel486 processor reloads the CS access rights to be writable. If this requirement is not met, a general-protection exception (#GP) occurs. This requirement has been eliminated on the Pentium processor, which leaves the access rights unchanged and ignores code segment access right protection checks in real-address mode. As a result, the code segment register can be used as a prefix in a write operation in real-address mode without generating an exception. For upwards and downwards compatibility, however, programmers may wish to include the far jump instruction prior to any writes to the code segment in real-address mode. The code segment can not be written to in protected mode on either the Pentium, and Intel486 processors.

- Page-fault exception (#PF, interrupt 14)—New exception condition added. When a 1 is detected in any of the reserved bit positions of a page-table entry, page-directory entry, or page directory pointer during address translation, a page fault exception is generated.

- Machine-check exception (#MC, interrupt 18)—New exception. This exception reports parity and other hardware errors. It is a model-specific exception and may not be implemented or implemented differently in future processors. The MCE flag in control register CR4 enables the machine-check exception. When this bit is clear (which it is at reset), the processor inhibits generation of the machine-check exception.

15.7.3. New Intel486™ Processor Exception

The following exception was added to the Intel486 processor:

- Alignment-check exception (#AC, interrupt 17)—New exception. Reports unaligned memory references when alignment checking is being performed.

15.7.4. New Intel386™ Processor Exceptions and/or Exception Conditions

The following exceptions and/or exception conditions were added to the Intel386 processor:

- Divide-error exception (#DE, interrupt 0)—

  — Change in exception handling. Divide-error exceptions on the Intel386 processors always leave the saved CS:IP value pointing to the instruction that failed. On the 8086 processor, the CS:IP value points to the next instruction.

  — Change in exception handling. The Intel386 processors can generate the largest negative number as a quotient for the IDIV instruction (80H and 8000H). The 8086 processor generates a divide-error exception instead.

- Invalid-opcode exception (#UD, interrupt 6)—New exception condition added. Improper use of the LOCK instruction prefix can generate an invalid-opcode exception.

- Page-fault exception (#PF, interrupt 14)—New exception condition added. If paging is enabled in a 16-bit program, a page-fault exception can be generated as follows. Paging can be used in a system with 16-bit tasks if all tasks use the same page directory. Because there is no place in a 16-bit TSS to store the PDBR register, switching to a 16-bit task does not change the value of the PDBR register. Tasks ported from the Intel 286 processor should be given 32-bit TSSs so they can make full use of paging.

- General-protection exception (#GP, interrupt 13)—New exception condition added. The Intel386 processor sets a limit of 15 bytes on instruction length. The only way to violate this limit is by putting redundant prefixes before an instruction. A general-protection exception is generated if the limit on instruction length is violated. The 8086 processor has no instruction length limit.

15.7.5. Machine-Check Architecture

The Pentium Pro processor has added a new architecture for handling and reporting on machine-check exceptions. This architecture (described in detail in Chapter 16, *Machine Check Architecture*) greatly expands the ability of the processor to report on internal hardware errors.

15.7.6. Priority OF Exceptions

The priority of exceptions are broken down into several major categories:

1. Traps on the previous instruction

2. External interrupts

3. Faults on fetching the next instruction

4. Faults in decoding the next instruction

5. Faults on executing an instruction

There are no changes in the priority of these major categories between the different processors, however, exceptions within these categories are implementation dependent and may change from processor to processor.

15.8. INTERRUPTS

The following differences in handling interrupts are found among the Intel Architecture processors.

15.8.1. Interrupt Propagation Delay

External hardware interrupts on the Pentium Pro processor may be recognized on different instruction boundaries than on the Pentium, Intel486, and Intel386 processors due to the super-scaler designs of the Pentium Pro and Pentium processors. Therefore, the EIP pushed onto the stack when servicing the interrupt on the Pentium Pro may be different then that for the Pentium, Intel486, and Intel386 processors.

15.8.2. NMI Interrupts

After an NMI interrupt is recognized by the Pentium Pro, Pentium, Intel486, Intel386, and Intel 286 processors, the NMI interrupt is masked until the first IRET instruction is executed, unlike the 8086 processor.

15.8.3. IDT Limit

The LIDT instruction can be used to set a limit on the size of the IDT. A double-fault exception (#DF) is generated if an interrupt or exception attempts to read a vector beyond the limit. Shutdown then occurs on the 32-bit Intel Architecture processors if the double-fault handler vector is beyond the limit. (The 8086 processor does not have a shutdown mode nor a limit.)

15.9. TASK SWITCHING AND TSS

This section identifies the implementation differences of task switching, additions to the TSS and the handling of TSSs and TSS segment selectors.

15.9.1. Pentium® Pro and Pentium® Processor TSS

When the virtual mode extensions are enabled (by setting the VME flag in control register CR4), the TSS in the Pentium Pro and Pentium processors contain an interrupt redirection bit map, which is used in virtual-8086 mode to redirect interrupts back to an 8086 program.

15.9.2. TSS Selector Writes

During task state saves, the Intel486 processor writes 2-byte segment selectors into a 32-bit TSS, leaving the upper 16 bits undefined. For performance reasons, the Pentium Pro and Pentium processors writes 4-byte segment selectors into the TSS with the upper 2 bytes being 0. For compatibility reasons, code should not depend on the value of the upper 16 bits of the selector in the TSS.

15.9.3. Order of Reads/Writes to The TSS

The order of reads and writes into the TSS is processor dependent. The Pentium Pro and Pentium processor may generate different page-fault addresses in control register CR2 in the same TSS area than the Intel486 and Intel386 processors, if a TSS crosses a page boundary (which is not recommended).

15.9.4. Using A 16-Bit TSS with 32-Bit Constructs

Task switches using 16-bit TSSs should be used only for pure 16-bit code. Any new code written using 32-bit constructs (operands, addressing, or the upper word of the EFLAGS register) should use only 32-bit TSSs. This is due to the fact that the 32-bit processors do not save the upper 16 bits of EFLAGS to a 16-bit TSS. A task switch back to a 16-bit task that was executing in virtual mode will never re-enable the virtual mode, as this flag was not saved in the upper half of the EFLAGS value in the TSS. Therefore, it is strongly recommended that any code using 32-bit constructs use a 32-bit TSS to ensure correct behavior in a multitasking environment.

15.9.5. Differences in I/O Map Base Addresses

The Intel486 processor considers the TSS segment to be a 16-bit segment and wraps around the 64K boundary. Any I/O accesses check for permission to access this I/O address at the I/O base address plus the I/O offset. If the I/O map base address exceeds the specified limit of 0DFFFH, an I/O access will wrap around and obtain the permission for the I/O address at an incorrect location within the TSS. A TSS limit violation does not occur in this situation on the Intel486 processor. However, the Pentium Pro and Pentium processors consider the TSS to be a 32-bit segment and a limit violation occurs when the I/O base address plus the I/O offset is greater than the TSS limit. By following the recommended specification for the I/O base address to be less than 0DFFFH, the Intel486 processor will not wrap around and access incorrect locations within the TSS for I/O port validation and the Pentium Pro and Pentium processors will not experience general-protection exceptions (#GP). Figure 15-1 demonstrates the different areas accessed by the Intel486 and the Pentium Pro and Pentium processors.

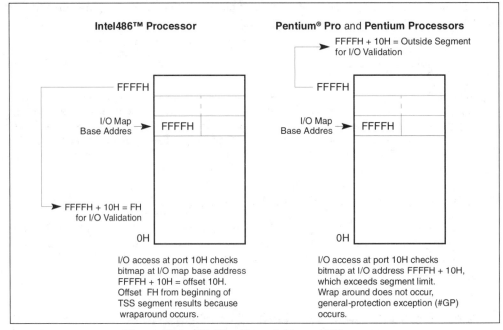

Figure 15-1. I/O Map Base Address Differences

15.10. CACHE MANAGEMENT

The Pentium Pro processor includes two levels of internal caches: L1 (level 1) and L2 (level 2). The L1 cache is divided into a instruction cache and a data cache; the L2 cache is a general-purpose cache. See Section 11.1., "Internal Caches, TLBs, and Buffers" for a description of these caches.

The Pentium processor includes separate level 1 instruction and data caches. The data cache supports a writeback (or alternatively write-through, on a line by line basis) policy for memory updates. Refer to Chapter 18 and the *Pentium® Processor Data Book* for more information about the organization and operation of the Pentium processor caches.

The Intel486 processor includes a single level 1 cache for both instructions and data.

The meaning of the CD and NW flags in control register CR0 have been redefined for the Pentium Pro and Pentium processors. For these processors, the recommended value (00B) enables writeback for the data cache of the Pentium processor and for the L1 data cache and L2 cache of the Pentium Pro processor. In the Intel486 processor, setting these flags to (00B) enables write-through for the cache.

External system hardware can force the Pentium processor to disable caching or to use the write-through cache policy should that be required. Refer to Chapter 18 and the *Pentium® Processor Data Book* for more information about hardware control of the Pentium processor caches. In the Pentium Pro processor, the MTRRs can be used to override the CD and NW flags (see Table 11-4).

The Pentium Pro and Pentium processors support page-level cache management in the same manner as the Intel486 processor by using the PCD and PWT flags in control register CR3, the page-directory entries, and the page-table entries. The Intel486 processor, however, is not affected by the state of the PWT flag since the internal cache of the Intel486 processor is a write-through cache.

15.10.1. Self Modifying Code with Cache Enabled

On the Intel486 processor, a write to an instruction in the cache will modify it in both the cache and memory. If the instruction was prefetched before the write, however, the old version of the instruction could be the one executed. To prevent this problem, it is necessary to flush the instruction prefetch unit of the Intel486 processor by coding a jump instruction immediately after any write that modifies an instruction. The Pentium Pro and Pentium processors, however, check whether a write may modify an instruction that has been prefetched for execution. This check is based on the linear address of the instruction. If the linear address of an instruction is found to be present in the prefetch queue, the Pentium Pro and Pentium processors flush the prefetch queue, eliminating the need to code a jump instruction after any writes that modify an instruction.

Because the linear address of the write is checked against the linear address of the instructions that have been prefetched, special care must be taken for self-modifying code to work correctly when the physical addresses of the instruction and the written data are the same, but the linear addresses differ. In such cases, it is necessary to execute a serializing operation to flush the prefetch queue after the write and before executing the modified instruction. See Section 7.3., "Serializing Instructions" for more information on serializing instructions.

NOTE

The check on linear addresses described above is not in practice a concern for compatibility. Applications that include self-modifying code use the same linear address for modifying and fetching the instruction. System software, such as a debugger, that might possibly modify an instruction using a different linear address than that used to fetch the instruction must execute a serializing operation, such as IRET, before the modified instruction is executed.

15.11. PAGING

This section identifies enhancements made to the paging mechanism and implementation differences in the paging mechanism for various Intel Architecture processors.

15.11.1. Pentium® Pro and Pentium® Processor Paging

The Pentium Pro and Pentium processors provide an extension to the memory management/paging functions of the Intel486 processor to support larger page sizes (see Section 3.6.1., "Paging Options").

15.11.2. Intel486™ Processor Paging

Two flags were introduced in the Intel486 processor to control the caching of pages:

- PCD (page-level cache disable) flag—Controls caching on a page-by-page basis.
- PWT (page-level write-through) flag—Controls the write-through/writeback caching policy on a page-by-page basis. Since the internal cache of the Intel486 processor is a write-through cache, it is not affected by the state of the PWT flag.

15.11.3. Enabling and Disabling Paging

Paging is enabled and disabled by loading a value into control register CR0 that modifies the PG flag. For backward and forward compatibility with all Intel Architecture processors, Intel recommends that the following operations be performed when enabling or disabling paging:

1. Execute a MOV CR0, REG instruction to either set (enable paging) or clear (disable paging) the PG flag.

2. Execute a near JMP instruction.

The sequence bounded by the MOV and JMP instructions should be identity mapped (that is, the instructions should reside on a page whose linear and physical addresses are identical).

For the Pentium Pro processor, the MOV CR0, REG instruction is serializing, so the jump operation is not required.

15.12. STACK OPERATIONS

This section identifies the differences in the stack mechanism for the various Intel Architecture processors.

15.12.1. Selector Pushes and Pops

When pushing a segment selector on to the stack, the Intel486 processor writes 2 bytes onto 4-byte stacks and decrements ESP by 4. The Pentium Pro and Pentium processors write 4 bytes with the upper 2 bytes being zeros.

When popping a segment selector from the stack, the Intel486 processor reads only 2 bytes. The Pentium Pro and Pentium processors read 4 bytes and discard the upper 2 bytes. This operation may have an effect if the ESP is close to the stack segment limit. On the Pentium Pro and Pentium processors, stack location at ESP plus 4 may be above the stack limit, in which case a stack fault exception (#SS) will be generated. On the Intel486 processor, stack location at ESP plus 2 may be less than the stack limit and no exception is generated.

15.12.2. Error Code Pushes

The Intel486 processor implements the error code pushed on the stack as a 16-bit value. When pushed onto a 32-bit stack, the Intel486 processor only pushes 2 bytes and updates ESP by 4. The Pentium Pro and Pentium processors' error code is a full 32 bits with the upper 16 bits set to zero. The Pentium Pro and Pentium processors, therefore, push 4 bytes and update ESP by 4. Any code that relies on the state of the upper 16 bits may produce inconsistent results.

15.12.3. Fault Handling Effects on the Stack

During the handling of certain instructions, such as CALL and PUSHA, faults may occur in different sequences for the different processors. For example, during far calls, the Intel486 processor pushes the old CS and EIP before a possible branch fault is resolved. A branch fault is a fault from a branch instruction occurring from a segment limit or access rights violation. If a branch fault is taken, the Intel486 processor will have corrupted memory below the stack pointer. However, the ESP register is backed up to make the instruction restartable. The Pentium Pro and Pentium processors issue the branch before the pushes. Therefore, if a branch fault does occur, these processors do not corrupt memory below the stack pointer. This implementation difference, however, does not constitute a compatibility problem, as only values at or above the stack pointer are considered to be valid.

15.12.4. Interlevel RET/IRET From a 16-Bit Interrupt or Call Gate

If a call or interrupt is made from a 32-bit stack environment through a 16-bit gate, only 16 bits of the old ESP can be pushed onto the stack. On the subsequent RET/IRET, the 16-bit ESP is popped but the full 32-bit ESP is updated since control is being resumed in a 32-bit stack environment. The Intel486 processor writes the SS selector into the upper 16 bits of ESP. The Pentium Pro and Pentium processors write zeros into the upper 16 bits.

15.13. MIXING 16- AND 32-BIT SEGMENTS

The features of the 16-bit Intel 286 processor are an object-code compatible subset of those of the Pentium Pro processor. The D (default operation size) flag in segment descriptors indicates whether the processor treats a code or data segment as a 16-bit or 32-bit segment; the B(default stack size) flag in segment descriptors indicates whether the processor treats a stack segment as a 16-bit or 32-bit segment.

The segment descriptors used by the Intel 286 processor are supported by the 32-bit Intel Architecture processors if the Intel-reserved word (highest word) of the descriptor is clear. On the 32-bit Intel Architecture processors, this word includes the upper bits of the base address and the segment limit.

The segment descriptors for data segments, code segments, local descriptor tables (there are no descriptors for global descriptor tables), and task gates are the same for the 16- and 32-bit processors. Other 16-bit descriptors (TSS segment, call gate, interrupt gate, and trap gate) are supported by the 32-bit processors. The 32-bit processors also have descriptors for TSS segments, call gates, interrupt gates, and trap gates that support the 32-bit architecture. Both kinds of descriptors can be used in the same system.

For those segment descriptors common to both 16- and 32-bit processors, clear bits in the reserved word cause the 32-bit processors to interpret these descriptors exactly as an Intel 286 processor does, that is:

- Base Address—The upper 8 bits of the 32-bit base address are clear, which limits base addresses to 24 bits.

- Limit—The upper 4 bits of the limit field are clear, restricting the value of the limit field to 64 Kbytes.

- Granularity bit—The G (granularity) flag is clear, indicating the value of the 16-bit limit is interpreted in units of 1 byte.

- Big bit—In a data-segment descriptor, the B flag is clear in the segment descriptor used by the 32-bit processors, indicating the segment is no larger than 64 Kbytes.

- Default bit—In a code-segment descriptor, the D flag is clear, indicating 16-bit addressing and operands are the default. In a stack-segment descriptor, the D flag is clear, indicating use of the SP register (instead of the ESP register) and a 64-Kbyte maximum segment limit.

For information on mixing 16- and 32-bit code in applications, see Chapter 13, *Mixing 16-Bit and 32-Bit Code*.

15.14. SEGMENT AND ADDRESS WRAPAROUND

This section discusses differences in segment and address wraparound between the Pentium Pro, Pentium, Intel486, Intel386, Intel 286, and 8086 processors.

15.14.1. Segment Wraparound

On the 8086 processor, an attempt to access a memory operand that crosses offset 65,535 or 0FFFFH or offset 0 (for example, moving a word to offset 65,535 or pushing a word when the stack pointer is set to 1) causes the offset to wrap around modulo 65,536 or 010000H. With the Intel 286 processor, any base and offset combination that addresses beyond 16 MBytes wraps around to the 1 MByte of the address space. The Pentium Pro, Pentium, Intel486, and Intel386 processors in real-address mode generate an exception in these cases:

- A general-protection exception (#GP) if the segment is a data segment (that is, if the CS, DS, ES, FS, or GS register is being used to address the segment).

- A stack-fault exception (#SS) if the segment is a stack segment (that is, if the SS register is being used).

An exception to this behavior occurs when a stack access is data aligned, and the stack pointer is pointing to the last aligned piece of data that size at the top of the stack (ESP is FFFFFFFCH). When this data is popped, no segment limit violation occurs and the stack pointer will wrap around to 0.

The address space of the Pentium Pro, Pentium, and Intel486 processors may wraparound at 1 MByte in real-address mode. An external A20M# pin forces wraparound if enabled. On Intel 8086 processors, it is possible to specify addresses greater than 1 MByte. For example, with a selector value FFFFH and an offset of FFFFH, the effective address would be 10FFEFH (1 MByte plus 65519 bytes). The 8086 processor, which can form addresses up to 20 bits long, truncates the uppermost bit, which "wraps" this address to FFEFH. However, the Pentium Pro, Pentium, and Intel486 processors do not truncate this bit if A20M# is not enabled.

If a stack operation wraps around the address limit, shutdown occurs. (The 8086 processor does not have a shutdown mode nor a limit.)

15.15. WRITE BUFFERS AND MEMORY ORDERING

The Pentium Pro processor provides a write buffer for temporary storage of writes (stores) to memory (see Section 11.10., "Write Buffer"). Writes stored in the write buffer are always written to memory in program order.

The Pentium processor has two write buffers, one corresponding to each of the pipelines. Writes in these buffers are always written to memory in the order they were generated by the processor core.

It should be noted that only memory writes are buffered and I/O writes are not. The Pentium Pro, Pentium, and Intel486 processors do not synchronize the completion of memory writes on the bus and instruction execution after a write. The OUT instruction or a serializing instruction needs to be executed to synchronize writes with the next instruction (see Section 7.3., "Serializing Instructions").

The Pentium Pro processor uses processor ordering to maintain consistency in the order that data is read (loaded) and written (stored) in a program and the order the processor actually carries out the reads and writes. With this type of ordering, reads can be carried out speculatively and in any order, reads can pass buffered writes, and writes to memory are always carried out in program order. (See Section 7.2., "Memory Ordering" for more information about processor ordering.)

No re-ordering of reads occurs on the Pentium processor. Specifically, the write buffers are flushed before the IN instruction is executed. No reads (as a result of cache miss) are reordered around previously generated writes sitting in the write buffers. The implication of this is that the write buffers will be flushed or emptied before a subsequent bus cycle is run on the external bus.

On the Intel486 processor, under certain conditions, a memory read will go onto the external bus before the memory writes pending in the buffer even though the writes occurred earlier in the program execution. A memory read will only be reordered in front of all writes pending in the buffers if all writes pending in the buffers are cache hits and the read is a cache miss. Under these conditions, the Intel486 processor will not read from an external memory location that needs to be updated by one of the pending writes.

Locked bus cycles are used for read-modify-write accesses to memory. During a locked bus cycle, the Intel486 processor will always access external memory, it will never look for the location in the on-chip cache. All data pending in the Intel486 processor's write buffers will be written to memory before a locked cycle is allowed to proceed to the external bus. Thus, the locked bus cycle can be used for eliminating the possibility of reordering read cycles on the Intel486 processor. The Pentium processor does check its cache on a read-modify-write access and, if the cache line has been modified, writes the contents back to memory before locking the bus. The Pentium Pro processor writes to its cache on a read-modify-write operation (if the access does not split across a cache line) and does not write back to system memory. If the access does split across a cache line, it locks the bus and accesses system memory.

I/O reads are never reordered in front of buffered memory writes on the Intel486 processor. This ensures an update of all memory locations before reading the status from an I/O device.

15.16. BUS LOCKING

The Intel 286 processor performs the bus locking differently than the Intel Pentium Pro, Pentium, Intel486, and Intel386 processors. Programs which use forms of memory locking specific to the Intel 286 processor may not run properly when run on later processors.

A locked instruction is guaranteed to lock only the area of memory defined by the destination operand, but may lock a larger memory area. For example, typical 8086 and Intel 286 configurations lock the entire physical memory space. Programmers should not depend on this.

On the Intel 286 processor, the LOCK prefix is sensitive to IOPL. If the CPL is greater than the IOPL, a general-protection exception (#GP) is generated. On the Intel386 DX, Intel486, and Pentium, and Pentium Pro processors, no check against IOPL is performed.

The Pentium processor automatically asserts the LOCK# signal when acknowledging external interrupts. After signaling an interrupt request, an external interrupt controller may use the data bus to send the interrupt vector to the processor. After receiving the interrupt request signal, the processor asserts LOCK# to insure that no other data appears on the data bus until the interrupt vector is received. This bus locking does not occur on the Pentium Pro processor.

15.17. BUS HOLD

Unlike the 8086 and Intel 286 processors, but like the Intel386 and Intel486 processors, the Pentium Pro and Pentium processors respond to requests for control of the bus from other potential bus masters, such as DMA controllers, between transfers of parts of an unaligned operand, such as two words which form a doubleword. Unlike the Intel386 processor, the Pentium Pro, Pentium and Intel486 processors respond to bus hold during reset initialization.

15.18. TWO WAYS TO RUN INTEL 286 PROCESSOR TASKS

When porting 16-bit programs to the Pentium Pro processor, there are two approaches to consider:

- Porting an entire 16 software system to a 32-bit processor, complete with the old operating system, loader, and system builder. Here, all tasks will have 16-bit TSSs. The 32-bit processor is being used as if it were a faster version of the 16-bit processor.

- Porting selected 16-bit applications to run in a 32-bit processor environment with a 32-bit operating system, loader, and system builder. Here, the TSSs used to represent 286 tasks should be changed to 32-bit TSSs. It is possible to mix 16 and 32-bit TSSs, but the benefits are small and the problems are great. All tasks in a 32-bit software system should have 32-bit TSSs. It is not necessary to change the 16-bit object modules themselves; TSSs are usually constructed by the operating system, by the loader, or by the system builder. See Chapter 13, *Mixing 16-Bit and 32-Bit Code*, for more detailed information about mixing 16-bit and 32-bit code.

Because the 32-bit processors use the contents of the reserved word of 16-bit segment descriptors, 16-bit programs that place values in this word may not run correctly on the 32-bit processors.

15.19. MODEL-SPECIFIC EXTENSIONS TO THE INTEL ARCHITECTURE

Certain extensions to the Intel Architecture are specific to a processor or family of Intel Architecture processors and may not be implemented or implemented in the same way in future processors. The following sections describe these model-specific extensions. The CPUID instruction indicates the availability of some of the model-specific features of the Pentium Pro processor.

15.19.1. Model-Specific Registers

The Pentium processor introduced a set of model-specific registers (MSRs) for use in controlling hardware functions and performance monitoring. To access these MSRs, two new instructions were added to the Intel Architecture: read MSR (RDMSR) and write MSR (WRMSR). The

MSRs in the Pentium processor are not guaranteed to be duplicated or provided in the next generation Intel Architecture processors.

The Pentium Pro processor greatly increased the number of MSRs available to software. See Appendix C, *Model-Specific Registers (MSRs)* for a complete list of the available MSRs. The new registers control the debug extensions, the performance counters, the machine-check exception capability, the machine check architecture, and the MTRRs. These registers are accessible using the RDMSR and WRMSR instructions. Specific information on some of these new MSRs is provided in the following sections. As with the Pentium processor MSR, the Pentium Pro processor MSRs are not guaranteed to be duplicated or provided in the next generation Intel Architecture processors.

15.19.2. RDMSR and WRMSR Instructions

The RDMSR (read model-specific register) and WRMSR (write model-specific register) instructions recognize a much larger number of model-specific registers in the Pentium Pro processor. (See "RDMSR—Read from Model Specific Register" and "WRMSR—Write to Model Specific Register" in Chapter 11, *Instruction Set Reference*, of the *Pentium® Pro Family Developer's Manual, Volume 2* for more information about these instructions.

15.19.3. Memory Type Range Registers

Memory type range registers (MTRRs) are a new feature introduced in the Pentium Pro processor that allow the processor to optimize memory operations for different types of memory, such as RAM, ROM, frame buffer memory, and memory-mapped I/O.

MTRRs are MSRs that contain an internal map of how physical address ranges are mapped to various types of memory. The processor uses this internal memory map to determine the cacheability of various physical memory locations and the optimal method of accessing memory locations. For example, if a memory location is specified in an MTRR as write-through memory, the processor handles accesses to this location as follows. It reads data from that location in lines and caches the read data or maps all writes to that location to the bus and updates the cache to maintain cache coherency. In mapping the physical address space with MTRRs, the processor recognizes five types of memory: uncacheable (UC), uncacheable, speculatable, write-combining (USWC), write-through (WT), write-protected (WP), and writeback (WB).

Earlier Intel Architecture processors (such as the Intel486 and Pentium processors) used the KEN# (cache enable) pin and external logic to maintain an external memory map and signal cacheable accesses to the processor. The MTRR mechanism simplifies hardware designs by eliminating the KEN# pin and the external logic required to drive it.

See Chapter 8, *Processor Management and Initialization*, and Appendix C, *Model-Specific Registers (MSRs)* for more information on the MTRRs.

15.19.4. Machine Check Exception and Architecture

The Pentium processor introduced a new exception called the machine-check exception (#MC, interrupt 18). This exception is used to detect hardware-related errors, such as a parity error on a read cycle.

The Pentium Pro processor extends the types of errors that can be detected and that generate a machine-check exception. It also provides a new machine-check architecture for recording information about a machine-check error and provides extended recovery capability.

The machine-check architecture provides several banks of reporting registers for recording machine-check errors. Each bank of registers is associated with a specific hardware unit in the processor. The primary focus of the machine checks is on bus and interconnect operations; however, checks are also made of translation lookaside buffer (TLB) and cache operations.

The machine-check architecture can correct some errors automatically and allow for reliable restart of instruction execution. It also collects sufficient information for software to use in correcting other machine errors not corrected by hardware.

See Chapter 16, *Machine Check Architecture* for more information on the machine-check exception and the machine-check architecture.

15.19.5. Performance Monitoring Counters

The Pentium Pro processor provides two performance-monitoring counters for use in monitoring internal hardware operations. These counters are event counters that can be programmed to count any of approximately 100 different types of events, such as the number of instructions decoded, number of interrupts received, or number of cache loads. Appendix B, *Performance Monitoring Counters* lists all the events that can be counted. The counters are set up, started, and stopped using two MSRs and the RDMSR and WRMSR instructions. The current count for a particular counter can be read using the new RDPMC instruction.

The performance-monitoring counters are useful for debugging programs, optimizing code, diagnosing system failures, or refining hardware designs. See Chapter 10, *Debugging and Performance Monitoring*, for more information on these counters.

intel®

16

Machine Check
Architecture

CHAPTER 16
MACHINE CHECK ARCHITECTURE

This chapter describes the Pentium Pro processor's machine check architecture and machine check exception mechanism. See Chapter 5, "Interrupt 18—Machine Check Exception (#MC)" for more information on the machine-check exception.

16.1. MACHINE CHECK EXCEPTIONS AND ARCHITECTURE

The Pentium Pro processor's machine check architecture provides a mechanism for detecting and reporting on hardware (machine) errors, such as system bus errors, ECC errors, parity errors, cache errors, and TLB errors. It consists of a set of model-specific registers (MSRs) that are used to set up machine checking and additional banks of MSRs for recording the errors that are detected. The processor signals the detection of a machine check error by generating a machine-check exception (#MC). A machine-check exception is generally an abort class exception. The implementation of the machine check architecture in the Pentium Pro processor does not ordinarily permit the processor to be restarted reliably after generating a machine-check exception; however, the machine-check-exception handler can collect information about the machine-check error from the machine-check MSRs.

16.2. COMPATIBILITY WITH PENTIUM® PROCESSOR

The Pentium Pro processor supports and extends the machine-check exception mechanism used in the Pentium processor. The Pentium processor reports the following machine-check errors:

* Data parity errors during a read cycles.
* Unsuccessful completions of a bus cycles.

The Pentium Pro processor uses the same mechanism as is used in the Pentium processor to report these errors.

16.3. MACHINE CHECK MSRS

The Pentium Pro processor's machine check MSRs consist of a set of global control and status registers and several error-reporting register banks (see Figure 16-1). Each error-reporting bank is associated with a specific hardware unit (or group of hardware units) within the processor. The RDMSR and WRMSR instructions are used to read and write these registers.

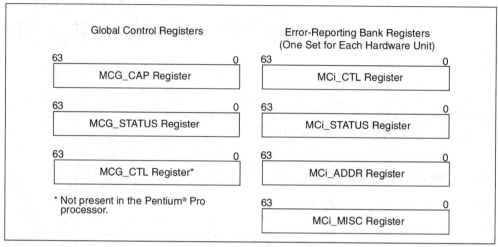

Figure 16-1. Machine Check MSRs

16.3.1. Machine Check Global Control MSRs

The machine-check global control registers include the MCG_CAP, MCG_STATUS, and MCG_CTL MSRs. See Appendix C, *Model-Specific Registers (MSRs)*, for the addresses of these registers.

16.3.1.1. MCG_CAP MSR

The MCG_CAP MSR is a read-only register that provides information about the machine-check architecture implementation in the processor (see Figure 16-2). It contains the following field and flag:

Count field, bits 0 through 7
> Indicates the number of hardware unit error-reporting banks available in a particular processor implementation.

MCG_CTL_P (register present) flag, bit 8
> Indicates that the MCG_CTL register is present when set, and absent when clear.

Bits 9 through 63 are reserved. The effect of writing to the MCG_CAP register is undefined. Figure 5-1 shows the bit fields of MCG_CAP.

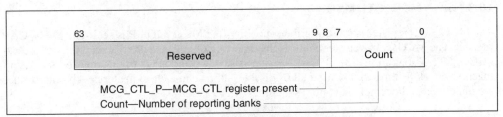

Figure 16-2. MCG_CAP Register

16.3.1.2. MCG_STATUS MSR

The MCG_STATUS MSR describes the current state of the processor after a machine check exception has occurred (see Figure 16-3). This register contains the following flags:

RIPV (restart IP valid) flag, bit 0

Indicates (when set) that program execution can be restarted reliably at the instruction pointed to by the instruction pointer pushed on the stack when the machine-check exception is generated. When clear, the program cannot be reliably restarted at the pushed instruction pointer.

EIPV (error IP valid) flag, bit 1

Indicates (when set) that the instruction pointed to by the instruction pointer pushed onto the stack when the machine check exception is generated is directly associated with the error. When this flag is cleared, the instruction pointed to may not be associated with the error.

MCIP (machine check in progress) flag, bit 2

Indicates (when set) that a machine check exception was generated. Software can set or clear this flag. The occurrence of a second Machine Check Event while MCIP is set will cause the processor to enter a shutdown state.

Bits 3 through 63 in the MCG_STATUS register are reserved.

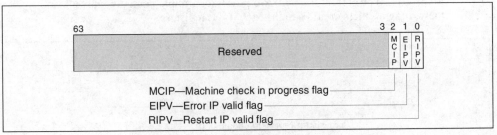

Figure 16-3. MCG_STATUS Register

16.3.1.3. MCG_CTL MSR

The MCG_CTL register is present if the capability flag MCG_CTL_P is set in the MCG_CAP register. The MCG_CTL register controls the reporting of machine check exceptions. If present (MCG_CTL_P flag in the MCG_CAP register is set), writing all 1s to this register enables all machine check features and writing all 0s disables all machine check features. All other values are undefined and/or implementation specific.

16.3.2. Error-Reporting Register Banks

Each error-reporting register bank can contains an MCi_CTL, MCi_STATUS, MCi_ADDR, and MCi_MISC MSR. The Pentium Pro processor provides five banks of error-reporting registers. The first error-reporting register (MC0_CTL) always starts at address 400H. See Table C-1 for the addresses of the other error-reporting registers.

16.3.2.1. MCI_CTL MSR

The MCi_CTL MSR controls error reporting for specific errors produced by a particular hardware unit (or group of hardware units). Each of the 64 flags (EEj) represents a potential error. Setting an EEj flag enables reporting of the associated error and clearing it disables reporting of the error. Writing the 64-bit value FFFFFFFFFFFFFFFFH to an MCi_CTL register enables logging of all errors. The processor does not write changes to bits that are not implemented. Figure 5-3 shows the bit fields of MCi_CTL

NOTE

Operating system or executive software must not modify the contents of the MC0_CTL register. The MC0_CTL register is internally aliased to the EBL_CR_POWERON register and as such controls system-specific error handling features. These features are platform specific. System specific firmware (the BIOS) is responsible for the appropriate initialization of MC0_CTL. The current Pentium Pro processor's implementation only allows the writing of all 1s or all 0s to the MCi_CTL registers.

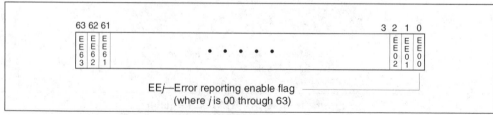

Figure 16-4. MCi_CTL Register

16.3.2.2.   MCI_STATUS MSR

The MCi_STATUS MSR contains information related to a machine check error if its VAL
(valid) flag is set (see Figure 16-5). Software is responsible for clearing the MCi_STATUS
register by writing it with all 0s; writing 1s to this register will cause a general-protection exception to be generated. The flags and fields in this register are as follows:

MCA (machine-check architecture) error code field, bits 0 through 15

Specifies the machine-check architecture-defined error code for the machine-check
error condition detected. The machine-check architecture-defined error codes are
guaranteed to be the same for all Intel Architecture processors that implement the
machine-check architecture. See Section 16.6., "Interpreting the MCA Error Codes"
for information on machine-check error codes.

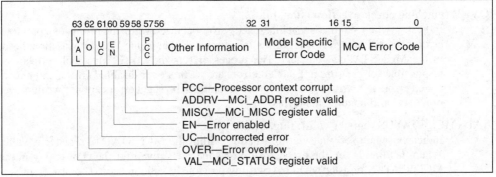

Figure 16-5. MCi_STATUS Register

Model-specific error code field, bits 16 through 31

Specifies the model-specific error code that uniquely identifies the machine-check
error condition detected. The model-specific error codes may differ among Intel Architecture processors for the same machine-check error condition.

Other information field, bits 32 through 56

The functions of the bits in this field are implementation specific and are not part of the
machine-check architecture. Software that is intended to be portable among Intel
Architecture processors should not rely on the values in this field.

PCC (processor context corrupt) flag, bit 57

Indicates (when set) that the state of the processor might have been corrupted by the
error condition detected and that reliable restarting of the processor may not be
possible. When clear, this flag indicates that the error did not affect the processor's
state.

ADDRV (MCi_ADDR register valid) flag, bit 58

Indicates (when set) that the MCi_ADDR register contains the address where the error
occurred (see Section 16.3.2.3., "MCi_ADDR MSR"). When clear, this flag indicates
that the MCi_ADDR register does not contain the address where the error occurred. Do
not read these registers if they are not implemented in the processor.

MISCV (MCi_MISC register valid) flag, bit 59

> Indicates (when set) that the MCi_MISC register contains additional information regarding the error. When clear, this flag indicates that the MCi_MISC register does not contain additional information regarding the error. Do not read these registers if they are not implemented in the processor

EN (error enabled) flag, bit 60

> Indicates (when set) that the error was enabled by the associated EEj bit of the MCi_CTL register.

UC (error uncorrected) flag, bit 61

> Indicates (when set) that the processor did not or was not able to correct the error condition. When clear, this flag indicates that the processor was able to correct the error condition.

OVER (machine check overflow) flag, bit 62

> Indicates (when set) that a machine-check error occurred while the results of a previous error were still in the error-reporting register bank (that is, the VAL bit was already set in the MCi_STATUS register). The processor sets the OVER flag and software is responsible for clearing it. Enabled errors are written over disabled errors, and uncorrected errors are written over corrected errors. Uncorrected errors are not written over previous valid uncorrected errors.

VAL (MCi_STATUS register valid) flag, bit 63

> Indicates (when set) that the information within the MCi_STATUS register is valid. When this flag is set, the processor follows the rules given for the OVER flag in the MCi_STATUS register when overwriting previously valid entries. The processor sets the VAL flag and software is responsible for clearing it.

16.3.2.3.   MCI_ADDR MSR

The MCi_ADDR MSR contains the address of the code or data memory location that produced the machine-check error if the ADDRV flag in the MCi_STATUS register is set (see Section 16.3.2.3., "MCi_ADDR MSR"). The address returned is either 32-bit virtual, 32-bit linear, or 36-bit physical address, depending upon the type of error encountered. Bits 36 through 63 of this register are reserved for future address expansion and are always read as zeros.

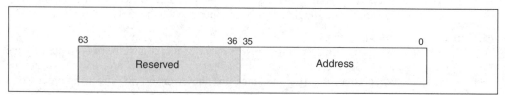

Figure 16-6. Machine Check Bank Address Register

16.3.2.4.   MCi_MISC MSR

The MCi_MISC MSR contains additional information describing the machine-check error if the MISCV flag in the MCi_STATUS register is set. This register is not implemented in any of the error-reporting register banks for the Pentium Pro processor.

16.3.3.   Mapping of the Pentium® Processor Machine-Check Errors to the Pentium® Processor Machine-Check Architecture

The Pentium processor reports machine-check errors using two registers: P5_MC_TYPE and P5_MC_ADDR. The Pentium Pro processor maps these registers into the MCi_STATUS and MCi_ADDR registers of the error-reporting register bank that reports on the type external bus errors reported in the P5_MC_TYPE and P5_MC_ADDR registers. The information in these registers can then be accessed in either of two ways:

- By reading the MCi_STATUS and MCi_ADDR registers as part of a generalized machine-check exception handler written for the Pentium Pro processor.

- By reading the P5_MC_TYPE and P5_MC_ADDR registers with the RDMSR instruction.

The second access capability permits a machine-check exception handler written to run on a Pentium processor to be run on a Pentium Pro processor. There is a limitation in that information returned by the Pentium Pro processor will be encoded differently than it is for the Pentium processor. To run the Pentium processor machine-check exception handler on a Pentium Pro processor, it must be rewritten to interpret the P5_MC_TYPE register encodings correctly.

16.4.   MACHINE CHECK AVAILABILITY

The machine-check architecture and machine-check exception (#MC) are model-specific features. Software can execute the CPUID instruction to determine whether a processor implements these features. Following the execution of the CPUID instruction, the settings of the MCA flag (bit 14) and MCE flag (bit 7) in the EDX register indicate whether the processor implements the machine-check architecture and machine-check exception, respectively.

16.5.   MACHINE CHECK INITIALIZATION

To use the processors machine check architecture, software must initialize the processor to activate the machine-check exception and the error-reporting mechanism. Example 16-1 gives pseudocode for performing this initialization. This pseudocode checks for the existence of the machine-check architecture and exception on the processor, then enables the machine-check exception and the error-reporting register banks. This initialization procedure is compatible with the Pentium Pro, Pentium, and future microprocessors.

Example 16-1. Machine Check Initialization Pseudocode

EXECUTE the CPUID instruction;
READ bits 7 (MCE) and 14 (MCA) of the EDX register;
IF CPU supports MCE
    THEN
        IF CPU supports MCA
            THEN
                IF MCG_CAP.MCG_CTL_P = 1 (* MCG_CTL register is present *)
                    Set MCG_CTL register to all 1s; (* enables all MCA features *)
                FI;
                COUNT ← MCG_CAP.Count;
                (* determine number of error-reporting banks supported *)
                FOR error-reporting banks (1 through COUNT) DO
                    Set MCi_CTL register to all 1s;
                    (* enables logging of all errors except for the MC0_CTL register *)
                OD
                FOR error-reporting banks (0 through COUNT) DO
                    Set MCi_STATUS register to all 0s; (* clears all errors *)
                OD
        FI;
    Set the MCE flag (bit 6) in CR4 register to enable machine check exceptions;
FI;

The MCi_STATUS registers can be written to while the processor is being powered up with valid information (such as an ECC error). As part of the initialization of the MCE exception handler, software might examine all the MCi_STATUS registers and log the contents of them, then rewrite them all to zeros. This procedure is not included in the initialization pseudocode in Example 16-1.

16.6. INTERPRETING THE MCA ERROR CODES

When the processor detects a machine-check error condition, it writes a 16-bit error code in the MCA Error Code field of one of the MCi_STATUS registers and sets the VAL (valid) flag in that register. The processor may also write a 16-bit Model-specific Error Code in the MCi_STATUS register depending on the implementation of the machine-check architecture of the processor.

The MCA error codes are architecturally defined for Intel Architecture processors; however, the specific MCi_STATUS register that a code is written into is model specific. To determine the cause of a machine-check exception, the machine-check exception handler must read the VAL flag for each MCi_STATUS register, and, if the flag is set, then read the MCA error code field of the register. It is the encoding of the MCACOD value that determines the type of error being reported and not the register bank reporting it.

There are two types of MCA error codes: simple error codes and compound error codes.

16.6.1. Simple Error Codes

Table 16-1 shows the simple error codes. These unique codes indicate global error information.

Table 16-1. Simple Error Codes

Error Code	Binary Encoding	Meaning
No Error	0000 0000 0000 0000	No error has been reported to this bank of error-reporting registers
Unclassified	0000 0000 0000 0001	This error has not been classified into the MCA error classes.
Microcode ROM Parity Error	0000 0000 0000 0010	Parity error in internal microcode ROM
External Error	0000 0000 0000 0011	The BINIT# from another processor caused this processor to enter machine check
FRC Error	0000 0000 0000 0100	FRC (functional redundancy check) master/slave error
Internal Unclassified	0000 01xx xxxx xxxx	Internal unclassified errors

16.6.2. Compound Error Codes

The compound error codes describe errors related to the TLBs, memory, caches, bus and interconnect logic. A set of sub-fields is common to all of the compound error encodings. These sub-fields describe the type of access, level in the memory hierarchy, and type of request. Table 16-2 shows the general form of the compound error codes. The interpretation column indicates the name of a compound error. The name is constructed by substituting mnemonics from Tables 16-2 through 16-6 for the sub-field names given within curly braces. For example, the error code ICACHEL1_RD_ERR is constructed from the form:

{TT}CACHE{LL}_{RRRR}_ERR

where {TT} is replaced by I, {LL} is replaced by L1, and {RRRR} is replaced by RD.

The 2-bit TT sub-field (see Table 16-2) indicates the type of transaction (data, instruction, or generic). It applies to the TLB, cache, and interconnect error conditions. The generic type is reported when the processor cannot determine the transaction type.

Table 16-2. General Forms of Compound Error Codes

Type	Form	Interpretation
TLB Errors	0000 0000 0001 TTLL	{TT}TLB{LL}_ERR
Memory Hierarchy Errors	0000 0001 RRRR TTLL	{TT}CACHE{LL}_{RRRR}_ERR
Bus and Interconnect Errors	0000 1PPT RRRR IILL	BUS{LL}_{PP}_{RRRR}_{II}_{TIMEOUT,}ERR

Table 16-3. Encoding for TT (Transaction Type) Sub-Field

Transaction Type	Mnemonic	Binary Encoding
Instruction	I	00
Data	D	01
Generic	G	10

The 2-bit LL sub-field (see Table 16-4) indicates the level in the memory hierarchy where the error occurred (level 0, level 1, level 2, or generic). The LL sub-field also applies to the TLB, cache, and interconnect error conditions. The Pentium Pro processor supports two levels in the cache hierarchy and one level in the TLBs. Again, the generic type is reported when the processor cannot determine the hierarchy level.

Table 16-4. Level Encoding for LL (Memory Hierarchy Level) Sub-Field

Hierarchy Level	Mnemonic	Binary Encoding
Level 0	L0	00
Level 1	L1	01
Level 2	L2	10
Generic	LG	11

The 4-bit RRRR sub-field (see Table 16-5) indicates the type of action associated with the error. Actions include read and write operations, prefetches, cache evictions, and snoops. Generic error is returned when the type of error cannot be determined. Generic read and generic write are returned when the processor cannot determine the type of instruction or data request that caused the error. Eviction and Snoop requests apply only to the caches. All of the other requests apply to TLBs, caches and interconnects.

Table 16-5. Encoding of Request (RRRR) Sub-Field

Request Type	Mnemonic	Binary Encoding
Generic Error	ERR	0000
Generic Read	RD	0001
Generic Write	WR	0010
Data Read	DRD	0011
Data Write	DWR	0100
Instruction Fetch	IRD	0101
Prefetch	PREFETCH	0110
Eviction	EVICT	0111
Snoop	SNOOP	1000

The bus and interconnect errors are defined with the 2-bit PP (participation), 1-bit T (time-out), and 2-bit II (memory or I/O) sub-fields, in addition to the LL and RRRR sub-fields (see Table 16-6). The bus error conditions are implementation dependent and related to the type of bus implemented by the processor. Likewise, the interconnect error conditions are predicated on a specific implementation-dependent interconnect model that describes the connections between the different levels of the storage hierarchy. The type of bus is implementation dependent, and as such is not specified in this document. A bus or interconnect transaction consists of a request involving an address and a response.

Table 16-6. Encodings of PP, T, and II Sub-Fields

Sub-Field	Transaction	Mnemonic	Binary Encoding
PP (Participation)	Local processor originated request	SRC	00
	Local processor responded to request	RES	01
	Local processor observed error as third party	OBS	10
	Generic		11
T (Time-out)	Request timed out	TIMOUT	1
	Request did not time out		0
II (Memory or I/O)	Memory Access	M	00
	Reserved		01
	I/O	IO	10
	Other transaction		11

16.6.3. Interpreting the Machine-Check Error Codes for External Bus Errors

Table 16-7 gives additional information for interpreting the MCA error code, model-specific error code, and other information error code fields for machine-check errors that occur on the external bus. This information can be used to design a machine-check exception handler for the Pentium Pro processor that offers greater granularity for the external bus errors.

Table 16-7. Encoding of MCi_STATUS Register for External Bus Errors

Bit No.	Bit Function	Bit Description
0-1	MCACOD	Undefined.
2-3	MCACOD	Bit 2 is set to 1 if the access was a special cycle. Bit 3 is set to 1 if the access was a special cycle OR a I/O cycle.
4-7	MCACOD	00WR; W = 1 for writes, R = 1 for reads
8-9	MCACOD	Undefined.

Table 16-7. Encoding of MCi_STATUS Register for External Bus Errors (Contd.)

10	MCACOD	Set to 0 for all EBL errors. Set to 1 for internal watch-dog timer time-out. For a watch-dog timer time-out, all the MCACOD bits except this bit 10 are set to 0. A watch-dog timer time-out only occurs if the BINIT driver is enabled.
11	MCACOD	Set to 1 for EBL errors. Set to 0 for internal watch-dog timer time-out.
12-15	MCACOD	Reserved.
16-18	Model Specific Error Cod	Reserved.
19-24	Model Specific Error Code	000000 for BQ_DCU_READ_TYPE error. 000010 for BQ_IFU_DEMAND_TYPE error. 000011 for BQ_IFU_DEMAND_NC_TYPE error. 000100 for BQ_DCU_RFO_TYPE error. 000101 for BQ_DCU_RFO_LOCK_TYPE error. 000110 for BQ_DCU_ITOM_TYPE error. 001000 for BQ_DCU_WB_TYPE error. 001010 for BQ_DCU_WCEVICT_TYPE error. 001011 for BQ_DCU_WCLINE_TYPE error. 001100 for BQ_DCU_BTM_TYPE error. 001101 for BQ_DCU_INTACK_TYPE error. 001110 for BQ_DCU_INVALL2_TYPE error. 001111 for BQ_DCU_FLUSHL2_TYPE error. 010000 for BQ_DCU_PART_RD_TYPE error. 010010 for BQ_DCU_PART_WR_TYPE error. 010100 for BQ_DCU_SPEC_CYC_TYPE error. 011000 for BQ_DCU_IO_RD_TYPE error. 011001 for BQ_DCU_IO_WR_TYPE error. 011100 for BQ_DCU_LOCK_RD_TYPE error. 011110 for BQ_DCU_SPLOCK_RD_TYPE error. 011101 for BQ_DCU_LOCK_WR_TYPE error.
27-25	Model Specific Error Cod	000 for BQ_ERR_HARD_TYPE error. 001 for BQ_ERR_DOUBLE_TYPE error. 010 for BQ_ERR_AERR2_TYPE error. 100 for BQ_ERR_SINGLE_TYPE error. 101 for BQ_ERR_AERR1_TYPE error.
28	Model Specific Error Cod	1 if FRC error is active.
29	Model Specific Error Cod	1 if BERR is driven.
30	Model Specific Error Code	1 if BINIT is driven for this processor.
31-34	Other Information	Reserved.

Table 16-7. Encoding of MCi_STATUS Register for External Bus Errors (Contd.)

35	Other Information BINIT	1 if BINIT is received from external bus.
36	Other Information RESPONSEP ARITY ERROR	This bit is asserted in the MCi_STATUS register if this component has received a parity error on the RS[2:0]# pins for a response transaction. The RS signals are checked by the RSP# external pin.
37	Other Information BUS BINIT	This bit is asserted in the MCi_STATUS register if this component has received a hard error response on a split transaction (one access that has needed to be split across the 64-bit external bus interface into two accesses).
38	Other Information TIMEOUT BINIT	This bit is asserted in the MCi_STATUS register if this component has experienced a ROB time-out, which indicates that no microinstruction has been retired for a predetermined period of time. A ROB time-out occurs when the 15-bit ROB time-out counter carries a 1 out of its high order bit. The timer is cleared when a microinstruction retires, an exception is detected by the core processor, RESET is asserted, or when a ROB BINIT occurs. The ROB time-out counter is prescaled by the 8-bit PIC timer which is a divide by 128 of the bus clock (the bus clock is 1:2, 1:3, 1:4 the core clock). When a carry out of the 8-bit PIC timer occurs, the ROB counter counts up by one. While this bit is asserted, it cannot be overwritten by another error.
42	Other Information HARD ERROR	This bit is asserted in the MCi_STATUS register if this component has initiated a bus transactions which has received a hard error response. While this bit is asserted, it cannot be overwritten.
39-41	Other Information	Reserved
42	Other Information HARD ERROR	This bit is asserted in the MCi_STATUS register if this component has initiated a bus transactions which has received a hard error response. While this bit is asserted, it cannot be overwritten.
43	Other Information IERR	This bit is asserted in the MCi_STATUS register if this component has experienced a failure that causes the IERR pin to be asserted. While this bit is asserted, it cannot be overwritten.
44	Other Information AERR	This bit is asserted in the MCi_STATUS register if this component has initiated 2 failing bus transactions which have failed due to Address Parity Errors (AERR asserted). While this bit is asserted, it cannot be overwritten.
45	Other Information UECC	Uncorrectable ECC error bit is asserted in the MCi_STATUS register for uncorrected ECC errors. While this bit is asserted, the ECC syndrome field will not be overwritten.
46	Other Information CECC	The correctable ECC error bit is asserted in the MCi_STATUS register for corrected ECC errors.

Table 16-7. Encoding of MCi_STATUS Register for External Bus Errors (Contd.)

47-54	Other Information SYNDROME	The ECC syndrome field in the MCi_STATUS register contains the 8-bit ECC syndrome only if the error was a correctable/uncorrectable ECC error, and there wasn't a previous valid ECC error syndrome logged in the MCi_STATUS register. A previous valid ECC error in MCi_STATUS is indicated by MCi_STATUS.bit45 (uncorrectable error occurred) being asserted. After processing an ECC error, machine check handling software should clear MCi_STATUS.bit45 so that future ECC error syndromes can be logged.
55-56	Other Information	Reserved

16.7. GUIDELINES FOR WRITING MACHINE CHECK SOFTWARE

The machine-check architecture and error logging can be used in two different ways:

- To detect machine errors during normal instruction execution, using the machine-check exception (#MC).

- To periodically check and log machine errors.

To use the machine-check exception, the operating system or executive software must provide a machine-check exception handler. This handler can be designed specifically for the Pentium Pro processor or be a portable handler that also handles Pentium machine-check errors.

A special program or utility is required to log machine errors.

Guidelines for writing a machine-check exception handler or a machine-error logging utility are given in the following sections.

16.7.1. Machine Check Exception Handler

The machine-check exception (#MC) corresponds to vector 18. To service machine-check exceptions, a trap gate must be added to the IDT, and the pointer in the trap gate must point to a machine-check exception handler. Two approaches can be taken to designing the exception handler:

- The handler can merely log all the machine status and error information, then call a debugger or shut down the system.

- The handler can analyze the reported error information and, in some cases, attempt to correct the error and restart the processor.

Virtually all the machine-check conditions detected with the Pentium Pro processor cannot be recovered from (they result in abort-type exceptions). The logging of status and error information is therefore a baseline implementation. See Section 16.7., "Guidelines for Writing Machine Check Software" for more information on logging errors.

For future implementations of the Pentium Pro processor, where recovery may be possible, the following things should be considered when writing a machine-check exception handler:

- To determine the nature of the error, the handler must read each of the error-reporting register banks. The count field in the MCG_CAP register gives number of register banks. The first register of register bank 0 is at address 400H.

- The VAL (valid) flag in each MCi_STATUS register indicates whether the error information in the register is valid. If this flag is clear, the registers in that bank do not contain valid error information and do not need to be checked.

- To write a portable exception handler, only the MCA error code field in the MCi_STATUS register should be checked. See Section 16.6., "Interpreting the MCA Error Codes" for information that can be used to write an algorithm to interpret this field.

- The RIPV, PCC, and OVER flags in each MCi_STATUS register indicate whether recovery from the error is possible. If either of these fields is set, recovery is not possible. The OVER field indicates that two or more machine-check error occurred. When recovery is not possible, the handler typically records the error information and signals an abort to the operating system.

- Corrected errors will have been corrected automatically by the processor. The UC flag in each MCi_STATUS register indicates whether the processor automatically corrected the error.

- The RIPV flag in the MCG_STATUS register indicates whether the program can be restarted at the instruction pointed to by the instruction pointer pushed on the stack when the exception was generated. If this flag is clear, the processor may still be able to be restarted (for debugging purposes), but not without loss of program continuity.

- For unrecoverable errors, the EIPV flag in the MCG_STATUS register indicates whether the instruction pointed to by the instruction pointer pushed on the stack when the exception was generated is related to the error. If this flag is clear, the pushed instruction may not be related to the error.

- The MCIP flag in the MCG_STATUS register indicates whether a machine-check exception was generated. Before returning from the machine-check exception handler, software should clear this flag so that it can be used reliably by an error logging utility. The MCIP flag also detects recursion. The machine check architecture does not support recursion. When the processor detects machine check recursion, it enters the shutdown state.

Example 16-2 gives typical steps carried out by a machine-check exception handler:

Example 16-2. Machine-Check Exception Handler Pseudocode

```
IF CPU supports MCE
    THEN
        IF CPU supports MCA
            THEN
                call errorlogging routine; (* returns restartability *)
        FI;
    ELSE (* Pentium processor compatible *)
        READ P5_MC_ADDR
        READ P5_MC_TYPE;
        report RESTARTABILITY to console;
FI;
IF error is not restartable
    THEN
        report RESTARTABILITY to console;
        abort system;
FI;
CLEAR MCIP flag in MCG_STATUS;
```

16.7.2. Pentium® Machine-Check Exception Handling

To make the machine-check exception handler portable to the Pentium processor and future, checks can be made (using the CPUID instruction) to determine the processor type. Then based on the processor type, machine-check exceptions can be handled specifically for Pentium Pro or future processors or for Pentium processors.

When machine-check exceptions are enabled for the Pentium processor (MCE flag is set in control register CR0), the machine-check exception handler uses the RDMSR instruction to read the error type from the P5_MC_TYPE register and the machine check address from the P5_MC_ADDR register. The handler then normally reports these register values to the system console before aborting execution (see Example 16-2).

16.7.3. Logging Correctable Machine Check Errors

If a machine-check error is correctable, the processor does not generate a machine-check exception for it. To detect correctable machine-check errors, a utility program must be written that reads each of the machine-check error-reporting register banks and logs the results in an accounting file or data structure. This utility can be implemented in either of the following ways:

- A system daemon that polls the register banks on an infrequent basis, such as hourly or daily.

- A user-initiated application that polls the register banks and records the exceptions. Here, the actual polling service is provided by an operating-system driver or through the system call interface.

Example 16-3 gives pseudocode for an error logging utility.

Example 16-3. Machine-Check Error Logging Pseudocode

```
Assume that execution is restartable;
IF the processor supports MCA
    THEN
    FOR each bank of machine-check registers
        DO
            READ MCi_STATUS;
            IF VAL flag in MCi_STATUS = 1
                THEN
                    IF ADDRV flag in MCi_STATUS = 1
                        THEN READ MCi_ADDR;
                    FI;
                    IF MISCV flag in MCi_STATUS = 1
                        THEN READ MCi_MISC;
                    FI;
                    IF MCIP flag in MCG_STATUS = 1
                        (* Machine check exception is in progress *)
                        AND PCC flag in MCi_STATUS = 1
                        AND RIPV flag in MCG_STATUS = 0
                        (* execution is not restartable *)
                            THEN
                                RESTARTABILITY = FALSE;
                                return RESTARTABILITY to calling procedure;
                    FI;
                    Save time stamp counter and processor ID;
                    Set MCi_STATUS to all 0s;
                    Execute serializing instruction (i.e. CPUID);
            FI;
        OD;
FI;
```

If the processor supports the machine-check architecture, the utility reads through the banks of error-reporting registers looking for valid register entries, and then saves the values of the MCi_STATUS, MCi_ADDR, MCi_MISC and MCG_STATUS registers for each bank that is valid. The routine minimizes processing time by recording the raw data into a system data structure or file, reducing the overhead associated with polling. User utilities analyze the collected data in an off-line environment.

When the MCIP flag is set in the MCG_STATUS register, a machine check exception is in progress and the machine-check exception handler has called the exception logging routine. Once the logging process has been completed the exception handling routine must determine whether execution can be restarted, which is usually possible when damage has not occurred (The PCC flag is clear, in the MCi_STATUS register) and when the Pentium Pro processor can guarantee that execution is restartable (the RIPV flag is set in the MCG_STATUS register). If execution cannot be restarted, the system is not recoverable and the exception handling routine should signal the console appropriately before returning the error status to the Operating System kernel for subsequent shutdown.

The machine-check architecture allows buffering of exceptions from a given error-reporting bank although the Pentium Pro processor does not implement this feature. The error logging routine should provide compatibility with future processors by reading each hardware error-reporting bank's MCi_STATUS register and then writing 0s to clear the OVER and VAL flags in this register. The error logging utility should re-read the MCi_STATUS register for the bank ensuring that the valid bit is clear. The processor will write the next error into the register bank and set the VAL flags.

Additional information that should be stored by the exception-logging routine includes the processor's time stamp counter value, which provides a mechanism to indicate the frequency of exceptions. A multiprocessing operating system stores the identity of the processor node incurring the exception using a unique identifier, such as the processors APIC ID (see Section 7.4.6., "Interrupt Destination and APIC ID").

The basic algorithm given in Example 16-3 can be modified to provide more robust recovery techniques. For example, software has the flexibility to attempt recovery using information unavailable to the hardware. Specifically, the machine-check exception handler can, after logging carefully analyze the error-reporting registers when the error-logging routine reports an error that does not allow execution to be restarted. These recovery techniques can use external bus related model-specific information provided with the error report to localize the source of the error within the system and determine the appropriate recovery strategy.

intel®

A

Opcode Map

The opcode tables in this section aid in interpreting Pentium processor object code. Use the 4 high-order bits of the opcode as an index to a row of the opcode table; use the 4 low-order bits as an index to a column of the table. If the opcode is 0FH, refer to the 2-byte opcode table and use the second byte of the opcode to index the rows and columns of that table.

The escape (ESC) opcode tables for floating-point instructions identify the 8 high-order bits of the opcode at the top of each page. If the accompanying modR/M byte is in the range 00H through BFH, bits 3 through 5 identified along the top row of the third table on each page, along with the REG bits of the modR/M, determine the opcode. ModR/M bytes outside the range 00H through BFH are mapped by the bottom two tables on each page.

A.1.   KEY TO ABBREVIATIONS

Operands are identified by a two-character code of the form Zz. The first character, an uppercase letter, specifies the addressing method; the second character, a lowercase letter, specifies the type of operand.

A.2.   CODES FOR ADDRESSING METHOD

The following abbreviations are used for addressing methods:

A   Direct address. The instruction has no modR/M byte; the address of the operand is encoded in the instruction; and no base register, index register, or scaling factor can be applied, for example, far JMP (EA).

C   The reg field of the modR/M byte selects a control register, for example, MOV (0F20, 0F22).

D   The reg field of the modR/M byte selects a debug register, for example, MOV (0F21,0F23).

E   A modR/M byte follows the opcode and specifies the operand. The operand is either a general-purpose register or a memory address. If it is a memory address, the address is computed from a segment register and any of the following values: a base register, an index register, a scaling factor, a displacement.

F   EFLAGS Register.

G   The reg field of the modR/M byte selects a general register, for example, AX (000).

I   Immediate data. The value of the operand is encoded in subsequent bytes of the instruction.

J   The instruction contains a relative offset to be added to the instruction pointer register, for example, JMP short, LOOP.

M   The modR/M byte may refer only to memory, for example, BOUND, LES, LDS, LSS, LFS, LGS, CMPXCHG8B.

O   The instruction has no modR/M byte; the offset of the operand is coded as a word or double word (depending on address size attribute) in the instruction. No base register, index register, or scaling factor can be applied, for example, MOV (A0–A3).

R   The mod field of the modR/M byte may refer only to a general register, for example, MOV (0F20-0F24, 0F26).

S   The reg field of the modR/M byte selects a segment register, for example, MOV (8C,8E).

T   The reg field of the modR/M byte selects a test register, for example, MOV (0F24,0F26).

X   Memory addressed by the DS:SI register pair, for example, MOVS, CMPS, OUTS, LODS.

Y   Memory addressed by the ES:DI register pair, for example, MOVS, CMPS, INS, STOS, SCAS.

A.3. CODES FOR OPERAND TYPE

The following abbreviations are used for operand types:

a   Two one-word operands in memory or two double-word operands in memory, depending on operand size attribute (used only by the BOUND instruction).

b   Byte, regardless of operand-size attribute.

c   Byte or word, depending on operand-size attribute.

d   Doubleword, regardless of operand-size attribute.

p   32-bit or 48-bit pointer, depending on operand size attribute.

q   Quadword, regardless of operand-size attribute.

s   6-byte pseudo-descriptor.

v   Word or doubleword, depending on operand-size attribute.

w   Word, regardless of operand-size attribute.

A.4.   REGISTER CODES

When an operand is a specific register encoded in the opcode, the register is identified by its name (for example, AX, CL, or ESI). The name of the register indicates whether the register is 32, 16, or 8 bits wide. A register identifier of the form eXX is used when the width of the register depends on the operand size attribute. For example, eAX indicates that the AX register is used when the operand size attribute is 16, and the EAX register is used when the operand size attribute is 32.

A.5.   OPCODE LOOK-UP EXAMPLES

This section provides several examples to demonstrate how the following opcode maps are used. See the introduction to Chapter 11, *Instruction Reference*, in the *Pentium® Pro Family Developer's Manual, Volume 2* for detailed information on the modR/M byte, register values, and the various addressing forms.

A.5.1.   One-Byte Opcode Integer Instructions

For 1-byte opcodes, the instruction and its operands can be determined from the hexadecimal opcode.

Opcode: 030500000000H

LSB address					MSB address
03	05	00	00	00	00

Looking at the 1-byte opcode map, the first digit (0) of the opcode indicates the row and the second digit (3) indicates the column. The instruction located at row 0, column 3 is an ADD instruction using the operand types Gv, Ev. The first operand of type Gv indicates a general register that is a word or doubleword depending on the operand-size attribute. The second operand (Ev) indicates that a modR/M byte follows that specifies whether the operand is a word or doubleword general-purpose register or a memory address. The modR/M byte for this instruction is 05H, which indicate that a 32-bit displacement follows (00000000H). The reg/opcode portion of the modR/M byte (bits 3 through 5) is 000 indicating the EAX register. Thus, it can be determined that the instruction for this opcode is ADD EAX, mem_op and the offset of mem_op is 00000000H.

A.5.2.   Two-Byte Opcode Integer Instructions

Instructions that begin with 0FH can be found in the two-byte opcode map. The second opcode byte is then used to reference a particular row and column. For example, the opcode 0FA4050000000003H, is located on the first page of the two-byte opcode map in row A, column 4. This indicates a SHLD instruction with the operands Ev, Gv, and Ib. These operands are defined as follows:

Ev   The modR/M byte follows the opcode to specify a word or doubleword operand

Gv   The reg field of the modR/M byte selects a general-purpose register

Ib   Immediate data is encoded in the subsequent byte of the instruction.

The third byte is the modR/M byte (05H). The mod and opcode/reg fields indicate that a 32-bit displacement follows, located in the EAX register is the source.

The next part of the opcode is the 32-bit displacement for the destination memory operand (00000000H) and finally the immediate byte representing the count of the shift (03H).

By this breakdown, it has been shown that this opcode represents the instruction:

```
SHLD DS:00000000H, EAX, 3
```

A.5.3.   Escape Opcodes

The escape (ESC) opcode maps are slightly different than the integer opcode maps. For instructions that have a modR/M byte in the range of 00H through BFH, bits 3 through 5 of the modR/M byte are used to determine the opcode. ModR/M bytes outside the range 00H through BFH are mapped by the tables at the bottom of each page.

A.5.3.1.   OPCODES WITH MODR/M BYTES IN THE 00H THROUGH BFH RANGE

The opcode DD0504000000 can be interpreted as follows. This instruction can be located on the page indicating DD as the first byte. Since the modR/M byte is in the 00H through BFH range (05H or 00000101B), bits 3 through 5 (000) of this byte indicate the opcode to be an FLD double-real instruction. The double-real value to be loaded is at 00000004H, which is the following 32-bit displacement in this opcode.

A.5.3.2.   OPCODES WITH MODR/M BYTES OUTSIDE THE 00H THROUGH BFH RANGE

Since the opcode of D8C1 has a modR/M byte outside the range 00H through BFH, the bottom two tables are used to determine this escape instruction on the page with D8 as the first byte. C1 indicates row C, column 1 which is an FADD instruction using ST, ST(1) as the operands.

One-Byte Opcode Map

	0	1	2	3	4	5	6	7
0	ADD						PUSH	POP
	Eb,Gb	Ev,Gv	Gb,Eb	Gv,Ev	AL,Ib	eAX,Iv	ES	ES
1	ADC						PUSH	POP
	Eb,Gb	Ev,Gv	Gb,Eb	Gv,Ev	AL,Ib	eAX,Iv	SS	SS
2	AND						SEG	DAA
	Eb,Gb	Ev,Gv	Gb,Eb	Gv,Ev	AL,Ib	eAX,Iv	=ES	
3	XOR						SEG	AAA
	Eb,Gb	Ev,Gv	Gb,Eb	Gb,Ev	AL,Ib	eAX,Iv	=SS	
4	INC general register							
	eAX	eCX	eDX	eBX	eSP	eBP	eSI	eDI
5	PUSH general register							
	eAX	eCX	eDX	eBX	eSP	eBP	eSI	eDI
	eAX	eCX	eDX	eBX	eSP	eBP	eSI	eDI
6	PUSHA	POPA	BOUND	ARPL	SEG	SEG	Operand	Address
	PUSHAD	POPAD	Gv,Ma	Ew,Gw	=FS	=GS	Size	Size
7	Short-displacement jump on condition (Jb)							
	JO	JNO	JB/JNAE/JC	JNB/JAE/JNC	JZ	JNZ	JBE	JNBE
8	Immediata Grpl		MOVB*	Grpl	TEST		XCHG	
	Eb,Ib	Ev,Iv	AL,immed 8	Eb,Ib	Eb,Gb	Ev,Gv	Eb,Gb	Ev,Gv
9	NOP	XCHG word or double-word register with eAX						
		eCX	eDX	eBX	eSP	eBP	eSI	eDI
A	MOV				MOVSB	MOVSW	CMPSB	CMPSW
	AL,Ob	eAX,Ov	Ob,AL	Ov,eAX	Xb,Yb	Xv,Yv	Xb,Yb	Xv,Yv
B	MOV immediate byte into byte register							
	AL	CL	DL	BL	AH	CH	DH	BH
C	Shift Grp2a		RET near		LES	LDS	MOV	
	Eb,Ib	Ev,Ib	Iw		Gv,Mp	Gv,Mp	Eb,Ib	Ev,Iv
D	Shift Grp2				AAM	AAD	*	XLAT
	Eb,1	Ev,1	Eb,CL	Ev,CL				
E	LOOPN	LOOPE	LOOP	JCXZ/JECXZ	IN		OUT	
	Jb	Jb	Jb	Jb	AL,Ib	eAX,Ib	Ib,AL	Ib,eAX
F	LOCK	*	REPNE	REP	HLT	CMC	Unary Grp3	
				REPE			Eb	Ev

* Reserved

One-Byte Opcode Map (Contd.)

	8	9	A	B	C	D	E	F
0	OR						PUSH	2-byte
	Eb,Gb	Ev,Gv	Gb,Eb	Gv,Ev	AL,Ib	eAX,Iv	CS	escape
1	SBB						PUSH	POP
	Eb,Gb	Ev,Gv	Gb,Eb	Gv,Ev	AL,Ib	eAX,Iv	DS	DS
2	SUB						SEG	DAS
	Eb,Gb	Ev,Gv	Gb,Eb	Gv,Ev	AL,Ib	eAX,Iv	=CS	
3	CMP	SEG	AAS					
	Eb,Gb	Ev,Gv	Gb,Eb	Gv,Ev	AL,Ib	eAX,Iv	=DS	
4	DEC general register							
	eAX	eCX	eDX	eBX	eSP	eBP	eSI	eDI
5	POP into general register							
	eAX	eCX	eDX	eBX	eSP	eBP	eSI	eDI
6	PUSH	IMUL	PUSH	IMUL	INSB	INSW/D	OUTSB	OUTSW/D
	Iv	Gv,Ev,Iv	Ib	Gv,Ev,Ib	Yb,DX	Yv,DX	Dx,Xb	DX,Xv
7	Short-displacement jump on condition (Jb)							
	JS	JNS	JP	JNP	JL	JNL	JLE	JNLE
8	MOV				MOV	LEA	MOV	POP
	Eb,Gb	Ev,Gv	Gb,Eb	Gv,Ev	Ew,Sw	Gv,M	Sw,Ew	Ev
9	CBW	CWD/CDQ	CALL	WAIT	PUSHF	POP	SAHF	LAHF
			aP		Fv	Fv		
A	TEST		STOSB	STOSW/D	LODSB	LODSW/D	SCASB	SCASW/D
	AL,Ib	eAX,Iv	Yb,AL	Yv,eAX	AL,Xb	eAX,Xv	AL,Yb	eAX,Yv
B	MOV immediate word or double into word or double register							
	eAX	eCX	eDX	eBX	eSP	eBP	eSI	eDI
C	ENTER	LEAVE	RET far	RET far	INT	INT	INTO	IRET
	Iw, Ib		Iw		3	Ib		
D	ESC (Escape to coprocessor instruction set)							
E	CALL	JMP			IN		OUT	
	Jv	Jv	Ap	Jb	AL,DX	eAX,DX	DX,AL	DX,eAX
F	CLC	STC	CLI	STI	CLD	STD	INC/DEC	INC/DEC
							Grp4	Grp5

Two Byte Opcode Map (First byte is 0FH)

	0	1	2	3	4	5	6	7
0	Grp6	*	LAR Gv,Ew	LSL Gv,Ew			CLTS	*
1	*	*	*	*				
2	MOV Rd,Cd	MOV Rd,Dd	MOV Cd,Rd	MOV Dd,Rd	MOV* Rd,Td		MOV* Td,Rd	
3	WRMSR	RDTSC	RDMSR					
4								
5								
6								
7								
8	Long-displacement jump on condition (Jv)							
	JO	JNO	JB	JNB	JZ	JNZ	JBE	JNBE
9	Byte Set on condition (Eb)							
	SETO	SETNO	SETB	SETNB	SETZ	SETNZ	SETBE	SETNBE
A	PUSH FS	POP FS	CPUID	BT Ev,Gv	SHLD Ev,Gv,Ib	SHLD Ev,Gv,CL	A step* CMPXCHG XBTS	A step* CMPXCHG IBTS
B	CMPXCHG Eb,Gb	CMPXCHG Ev,Gv	LSS Mp	BTR Ev,Gv	LFS Mp	LGS Mp	MOVZX Gv,Eb	MOVZX Gv,Ew
C	XADD Eb,Gb	XADD Ev,Gv						Group 9
D								
E								
F								

* Reserved

Two-Byte Opcode Map (First byte is 0FH) (Contd.)

	8	9	A	B	C	D	E	F
0	INVD	WBINVD						
1								
2								
3								
4								
5								
6								
7								
8	Long-displacement jump on condition (Jv)							
	JS	JNS	JP	JNP	JL	JNL	JLE	JNLE
	Byte set on condition (Eb)							
9	SETS	SETNS	SETP	SETNP	SETL	SETNL	SETLE	SETNLE
	Eb	Eb	Eb	Eb	Eb	Eb	Eb	Eb
A	PUSH GS	POP GS	RSM	BTS Ev,Gv	SHRD Ev,Gv,Ib	SHRD Ev,Gv,CL		IMUL Gv,Ev
B			Grp-8 Ev,Ib	BTC Ev,Gv	BSF Gv,Ev	BSR Gv,Ev	MOVSX Gv,Eb	Gv,Ew
C	BSWAP EAX	BSWAP ECX	BSWAP EDX	BSWAP EBX	BSWAP ESP	BSWAP EBP	BSWAP ESI	BSWAP EDI
D								
E								
F								

Opcodes Determined by Bits 5,4,3 of ModR/M Byte

	mod		nnn				R/M	
Group	000	001	010	011	100	101	110	111
1	ADD	OR	ADC	SBB	AND	SUB	XOR	CMP
2	ROL	ROR	RCL	RCR	SHL SAL	SHR		SAR
3	TEST Ib/Iv		NOT	NEG	MUL AL/eAX	IMUL AL/eAX	DIV AL/eAX	IDIV AL/eAX
4	INC Eb	DEC Eb						
5	INC Ev	DEC Ev	CALL Ev	CALL Ep	JMP Ev	JMP Ep	PUSH Ev	
6	SLDT Ew	STR Ew	LLDT Ew	LTR Ew	VERR Ew	VERW Ew		
7	SGDT Ms	SIDT Ms	LGDT Ms	LIDT Ms	SMSW Ew		LMSW Ew	INVLPG
8						BT	BTS	BTR	BTC
9		CMPXCH 8BMq						

Escape Opcodes with D8 as First Byte

mod		nnn		R/M	

ModR/M bytes in range of 00H through BFH, nnn are mapped according to the following table (opcode is determined by bits 3 through 5 of modR/M byte).

000	001	010	011	100	101	110	111
FADD single-real	FMUL single-real	FCOM single-real	FCOMP single-real	FSUB single-real	FSUBR single-real	FDIV single-real	FDIVR single-real

ModR/M bytes outside the range 00H through BFH are mapped by the tables below:

	0	1	2	3	4	5	6	7
C	FADD							
	ST,ST(0)	ST,ST(1)	ST,ST(2)	ST,ST(3)	ST,ST(4)	ST,ST(5)	ST,ST(6)	ST,ST(7)
D	FCOM							
	ST,ST(0)	ST,ST(1)	ST,T(2)	ST,ST(3)	ST,ST(4)	ST,ST(5)	ST,ST(6)	ST,ST(7)
E	FSUB							
	ST,ST(0)	ST,ST(1)	ST,ST(2)	ST,ST(3)	ST,ST(4)	ST,ST(5)	ST,ST(6)	ST,ST(7)
F	FDIV							
	ST,ST(0)	ST,ST(1)	ST,ST(2)	ST,ST(3)	ST,ST(4)	ST,ST(5)	ST,ST(6)	ST,ST(7)

	8	9	A	B	C	D	E	F
C	FMUL							
	ST,ST(0)	ST,ST(1)	ST,ST(2)	ST,ST(3)	ST,ST(4)	ST,ST(5)	ST,ST(6)	ST,ST(7)
D	FCOMP							
	ST,ST(0)	ST,ST(1)	ST,T(2)	ST,ST(3)	ST,ST(4)	ST,ST(5)	ST,ST(6)	ST,ST(7)
E	FSUBR							
	ST,ST(0)	ST,ST(1)	ST,ST(2)	ST,ST(3)	ST,ST(4)	ST,ST(5)	ST,ST(6)	ST,ST(7)
F	FDIVR							
	ST,ST(0)	ST,ST(1)	ST,ST(2)	ST,ST(3)	ST,ST(4)	ST,ST(5)	ST,ST(6)	ST,ST(7)

Escape Opcodes with D9 as First Byte

mod	nnn	R/M

ModR/M bytes in range of 00H through BFH, nnn are mapped according to the following table (opcode is determined by bits 3 through 5 of modR/M byte)

000	001	010	011	100	101	110	111
FLD single-real		FST single-real	FSTP single-real	FLDENV 14/28 bytes	FLDCW 2 bytes	FSTENV 14/28 bytes	FSTCW 2 bytes

ModR/M bytes outside the range 00H through BFH are mapped by the tables below

	0	1	2	3	4	5		7
C	FLD							
	ST,ST(0)	ST,ST(1)	ST,ST(2)	ST,ST(3)	ST,ST(4)	ST,ST(5)	ST,ST(6)	ST,ST(7)
D	FNOP							
E	FCHS	FABS			FTST	FXAM		
F	F2XM1	FYL2X	FPTAN	FPATAN	FXTRACT	FPREM1	FDECSTP	FINCSTP

	8	9	A	B	C	D	E	F
C	FXCH							
	ST,ST(0)	ST,ST(1)	ST,ST(2)	ST,ST(3)	ST,ST(4)	ST,ST(5)	ST,ST(6)	ST,ST(7)
D								
E	FLD1	FLDL2T	FLDL2E	FLDPI	FLDLG2	FLDLN2	FLDZ	
F	FPREM	FYL2XP1	FSQRT	FSINCOS	FRNDINT	FSCALE	FSIN	FCOS

Escape Opcodes with DA as First Byte

mod	nnn	R/M

ModR/M bytes in range of 00H through BFH, nnn are mapped according to the following table (opcode is determined by bits 3 through 5 of modR/M byte).

000	001	010	011	100	101	110	111
FIADD short-int*	FIMUL short-int*	FICOM short-int*	FICOMP short-int*	FISUB short-int*	FISUBR short-int*	FIDIV short-int*	FIDIVR short-int*

ModR/M bytes outside the range 00H through BFH are mapped by the tables below:

	0	1	2	3	4	5	6	7
C								
D								
E								
F								

	8	9	A	B	C	D	E	F
C								
D								
E		FUCOMPP						
F								

NOTE:

*   Short-int = 32 bit integer.

Escape Opcodes with DB as First Byt

mod	nnn	R/M

ModR/M bytes in range of 00H through BFH, nnn are mapped according to the following table (opcode is determined by bits 3 through 5 of modR/M byte).

ModR/M bytes outside the range 00H through BFH are mapped by the tables below:

000	001	010	011	100	101	110	111

	FILD short-int*		FIST short-int*	FISTP short-int*		FLD ext-real		FSTP ext-real

	0	1	2	3	4	5	6	7
C								
D								
E			FCLEX	FINIT				
F								

	8	9	A	B	C	D	E	F
C								
D								
E								
F								

NOTE:

* Short-int = 32 bit integer.

Escape Opcodes with DC as First Byte

mod	nnn	R/M

ModR/M bytes in range of 00H through BFH, nnn are mapped according to the following table (opcode is determined by bits 3 through 5 of modR/M byte).

000	001	010	011	100	101	110	111

FADD double-real	FMUL double-real	FCOM double-real	FCOMP double-real	FSUB double-real	FSUBR double-real	FDIV double-real	FDIVR double-real

ModR/M bytes outside the range 00H through BFH are mapped by the tables below:

	0	1	2	3	4	5	6	7
C	FADD							
	ST(0),ST	ST(1),ST	ST(2),ST	ST(3),ST	ST(4),ST	ST(5),ST	ST(6),ST	ST(7),ST
D								
E	FSUBR							
	ST(0),ST	ST(1),ST	ST(2),ST	ST(3),ST	ST(4),ST	ST(5),ST	ST(6),ST	ST(7),ST
F	FDIVR							
	ST(0),ST	ST(1),ST	ST(2),ST	ST(3),ST	ST(4),ST	ST(5),ST	ST(6),ST	ST(7),ST

	8	9	A	B	C	D	E	F
C	FMUL							
	ST(0),ST	ST(1),ST	ST(2),ST	ST(3),ST	ST(4),ST	ST(5),ST	ST(6),ST	ST(7),ST
D								
E	FSUB							
	ST(0),ST	ST(1),ST	ST(2),ST	ST(3),ST	ST(4),ST	ST(5),ST	ST(6),ST	ST(7),ST
F	FDIV							
	ST(0),ST	ST(1),ST	ST(2),ST	ST(3),ST	ST(4),ST	ST(5),ST	ST(6),ST	ST(7),ST

Escape Opcodes with DD as First Byte

mod	nnn	R/M

ModR/M bytes in range of 00H through BFH, nnn are mapped according to the following table (opcode is determined by bits 3 through 5 of modR/M byte).

000	001	010	011	100	101	110	111
FLD double-real		FST double-real	FSTP double-real	FRSTOR 98/108bytes		FSAVE 98/108bytes	FSTSW 2 bytes

ModR/M bytes outside the range 00H through BFH are mapped by the tables below:

	0	1	2	3	4	5	6	7
C	FFREE							
	ST(0)	ST(1)	ST(2)	ST(3)	ST(4)	ST(5)	ST(6)	ST(7)
D	FST							
	ST(0)	ST(1)	ST(2)	ST(3)	ST(4)	ST(5)	ST(6)	ST(7)
E	FUCOM							
	ST(0),ST	ST(1),ST	ST(2),ST	ST(3),ST	ST(4),ST	ST(5),ST	ST(6),ST	ST(7),ST
F								

	8	9	A	B	C	D	E	F
C								
D	FSTP							
	ST(0)	ST(1)	ST(2)	ST(3)	ST(4)	ST(5)	ST(6)	ST(7)
E	FUCOMP							
	ST(0)	ST(1)	ST(2)	ST(3)	ST(4)	ST(5)	ST(6)	ST(7)
F								

Escape Opcodes with DE as First Byte

mod	nnn	R/M

ModR/M bytes in range of 00H through BFH, nnn are mapped according to the following table (opcode is determined by bits 3 through 5 of modR/M byte).

000	001	010	011	100	101	110	111
FIADD word-int	FIMUL word-int	FICOM word-int	FICOMP word-int	FISUB word-int	FISUBR word-int	FIDIV word-int	FIDIVR word-int

ModR/M bytes outside the range 00H through BFH are mapped by the tables below:

	0	1	2	3	4	5	6	7
C	FADDP							
	ST(0),ST	ST(1),ST	ST(2),ST	ST(3),ST	ST(4),ST	ST(5),ST	ST(6),ST	ST(7),ST
D								
E	FSUBRP							
	ST(0),ST	ST(1),ST	ST(2),ST	ST(3),ST	ST(4),ST	ST(5),ST	ST(6),ST	ST(7),ST
F	FDIVRP							
	ST(0),ST	ST(1),ST	ST(2),ST	ST(3),ST	ST(4),ST	ST(5),ST	ST(6),ST	ST(7),ST

	8	9	A	B	C	D	E	F
C	FMULP							
	ST(0),ST	ST(1),ST	ST(2),ST	ST(3),ST	ST(4),ST	ST(5),ST	ST(6),ST	ST(7),ST
D		FCOMPP						
E	FSUBP							
	ST(0),ST	ST(1),ST	ST(2),ST	ST(3),ST	ST(4),ST	ST(5),ST	ST(6),ST	ST(7),ST
F	FDIVP							
	ST(0),ST	ST(1),ST	ST(2),ST.	ST(3),ST	ST(4),ST	ST(5),ST	ST(6),ST	ST(7),ST

Escape Opcodes with DF As First Byte

mod	nnn	R/M

ModR/M bytes in range of 00H through BFH, nnn are mapped according to the following table (opcode is determined by bits 3 through 5 of modR/M byte).

000	001	010	011	100	101	110	111
FILD word-int		FIST word-int	FISTP word-int	FBLD packed-BCD	FILD long-int	FBSTP packed-BCD	FISTP long-int

ModR/M bytes outside the range 00H through BFH are mapped by the tables below:

	0	1	2	3	4	5	6	7
C								
D								
E	FSTSW AX							
F								

	8	9	A	B	C	D	E	F
C								
D								
E								
F								

intel®

B

Performance
Monitoring Counters

Table B-1 lists the events that can be counted with the performance-monitoring counters and read with the RDPMC instruction. The unit column gives the microarchitecture or bus unit that produces the event; the event number column gives the hexadecimal number identifying the event; the mnemonic event name column gives the name of the event; the unit mask column gives the unit mask required (if any); the description column describes the event; and the comments column gives additional information about the event.

These performance monitoring events are intended to be used as guides for performance tuning. The counter values reported are not guaranteed to be absolutely accurate and should be used as a relative guide for tuning. Known discrepancies are documentation where applicable. All performance events are model specific to the Pentium Pro processor and are not architecturally guaranteed in future versions of the processor.   All performance event encodings not listed in Table B-1 are reserved and their use will result in undefined counter results.

See the end of the table for notes related to certain entries in the table.

Table B-1. Performance Monitoring Counters

Unit	Event Num.	Mnemonic Event Name	Unit Mask	Description	Comments
Data Cache Unit (DCU)	43H	DATA_MEM_REFS	00H	All memory references, both cacheable and non-cacheable	
	45H	DCU_LINES_IN	00H	Total lines allocated in the DCU.	
	46H	DCU_M_LINES_IN	00H	Number of M state lines allocated in the DCU.	
	47H	DCU_M_LINES_OUT	00H	Number of M state lines evicted from the DCU. This includes evictions via snoop HITM, intervention or replacement.	

Table B-1. Performance Monitoring Counters (Contd.)

Unit	Event Num.	Mnemonic Event Name	Unit Mask	Description	Comments
	48H	DCU_MISS_OUTSTANDING	00H	Weighted number of cycles while a DCU miss is outstanding.	An access that also misses the L2 is short-changed by 2 cycles. (i.e. if counts N cycles, should be N+2 cycles.) Subsequent loads to the same cache line will not result in any additional counts. Count value not precise, but still useful.
Instruction Fetch Unit (IFU)	80H	IFU_IFETCH	00H	Number of instruction fetches, both cacheable and non-cacheable.	
	81H	IFU_IFETCH_MISS	00H	Number of instruction fetch misses.	
	85H	ITLB_MISS	00H	Number of ITLB misses.	
	86H	IFU_MEM_STALL	00H	Number of cycles that the instruction fetch pipe stage is stalled, including cache misses, ITLB misses, ITLB faults, and victim cache evictions.	
	87H	ILD_STALL	00H	Number of cycles that the instruction length decoder is stalled.	
L2 Cache[1]	28H	L2_IFETCH	MESI 0FH	Number of L2 instruction fetches.	
	29H	L2_LD	MESI 0FH	Number of L2 data loads.	
	2AH	L2_ST	MESI 0FH	Number of L2 data stores.	
	24H	L2_LINES_IN	00H	Number of lines allocated in the L2.	
	26H	L2_LINES_OUT	00H	Number of lines removed from the L2 for any reason.	

Table B-1. Performance Monitoring Counters (Contd.)

Unit	Event Num.	Mnemonic Event Name	Unit Mask	Description	Comments
	25H	L2_M_LINES_INM	00H	Number of modified lines allocated in the L2.	
	27H	L2_M_LINES_OUTM	00H	Number of modified lines removed from the L2 for any reason.	
	2EH	L2_RQSTS	MESI 0FH	Number of L2 requests.	
	21H	L2_ADS	00H	Number of L2 address strobes.	
	22H	L2_DBUS_BUSY	00H	Number of cycles during which the data bus was busy.	
	23H	L2_DBUS_BUSY_RD	00H	Number of cycles during which the data bus was busy transferring data from L2 to the processor.	
External Bus Logic (EBL)[2]	62H	BUS_DRDY_CLOCKS	00H (Self) 20H (Any)	Number of clocks during which DRDY is asserted.	Unit Mask = 00H counts bus clocks when the processor is driving DRDY. Unit Mask = 20H counts in processor clocks when any agent is driving DRDY.
	63H	BUS_LOCK_CLOCKS	00H (Self) 20H (Any)	Number of clocks during which LOCK is asserted	Always counts in processor clocks
	60H	BUS_REQ_OUTSTANDING	00H (Self)	Number of bus requests outstanding.	Counts only DCU full-line cacheable reads, not RFOs, writes, instruction fetches, or anything else. Counts "waiting for bus to complete" (last data chunk received).
	65H	BUS_TRAN_BRD	00H (Self) 20H (Any)	Number of burst read transactions.	
	66H	BUS_TRAN_RFO	00H (Self) 20H (Any)	Number of read for ownership transactions.	
	67H	BUS_TRANS_WB	00H (Self) 20H (Any)	Number of write back transactions.	

Table B-1. Performance Monitoring Counters (Contd.)

Unit	Event Num.	Mnemonic Event Name	Unit Mask	Description	Comments
	68H	BUS_TRAN_ IFETCH	00H (Self) 20H (Any)	Number of instruction fetch transactions.	
	69H	BUS_TRAN_ INVAL	00H (Self) 20H (Any)	Number of invalidate transactions.	
	6AH	BUS_TRAN_ PWR	00H (Self) 20H (Any)	Number of partial write transactions.	
	6BH	BUS_TRANS_P	00H (Self) 20H (Any)	Number of partial transactions.	
	6CH	BUS_TRANS_IO	00H (Self) 20H (Any)	Number of I/O transactions.	
	6DH	BUS_TRAN_DEF	00H (Self) 20H (Any)	Number of deferred transactions.	
	6EH	BUS_TRAN_ BURST	00H (Self) 20H (Any)	Number of burst transactions.	
	70H	BUS_TRAN_ANY	00H (Self) 20H (Any)	Number of all transactions.	
	6FH	BUS_TRAN_MEM	00H (Self) 20H (Any)	Number of memory transactions	
	64H	BUS_DATA_RCV	00H (Self)	Number of bus clock cycles during which this processor is receiving data.	
	61H	BUS_BNR_DRV	00H (Self)	Number of bus clock cycles during which this processor is driving the BNR pin.	
	7AH	BUS_HIT_DRV	00H (Self)	Number of bus clock cycles during which this processor is driving the HIT pin.	Includes cycles due to snoop stalls.
	7BH	BUS_HITM_DRV	00H (Self)	Number of bus clock cycles during which this processor is driving the HITM pin.	Includes cycles due to snoop stalls.
	7EH	BUS_SNOOP_ STALL	00H (Self)	Number of clock cycles during which the bus is snoop stalled.	
Floating Point Unit	C1H	FLOPS	00H	Number of computational floating-point operations retired.	Counter 0 only

Table B-1. Performance Monitoring Counters (Contd.)

Unit	Event Num.	Mnemonic Event Name	Unit Mask	Description	Comments
	10H	FP_COMP_OPS_ EXE	00H	Number of computational floating-point operations executed.	Counter 0 only.
	11H	FP_ASSIST	00H	Number of floating-point exception cases handled by microcode.	Counter 1 only.
	12H	MUL	00H	Number of multiplies.	Counter 1 only.
	13H	DIV	00H	Number of divides.	Counter 1 only.
	14H	CYCLES_DIV_ BUSY	00H	Number of cycles during which the divider is busy.	Counter 0 only.
Memory Ordering	03H	LD_BLOCKS	00H	Number of store buffer blocks	
	04H	SB_DRAINS	00H	Number of store buffer drain cycles.	
	05H	MISALIGN_ MEM_REF	00H	Number of misaligned data memory references.	
Instruction Decoding and Retirement	C0H	INST_RETIRED	OOH	Number of instructions retired.	
	C2H	UOPS_RETIRED	00H	Number of UOPs retired.	
	D0H	INST_DECODER	00H	Number of instructions decoded.	
Interrupts	C8H	HW_INT_RX	00H	Number of hardware interrupts received.	
	C6H	CYCLES_INT_ MASKED	00H	Number of processor cycles for which interrupts are disabled.	
	C7H	CYCLES_INT_ PENDING_ AND_MASKED	00H	Number of processor cycles for which interrupts are disabled and interrupts are pending.	
Branches	C4H	BR_INST_ RETIRED	00H	Number of branch instructions retired.	

Table B-1. Performance Monitoring Counters (Contd.)

Unit	Event Num.	Mnemonic Event Name	Unit Mask	Description	Comments
	C5H	BR_MISS_PRED_ RETIRED	00H	Number of mispredicted branches retired.	
	C9H	BR_TAKEN_ RETIRED	00H	Number of taken branches retired.	
	CAH	BR_MISS_PRED_ TAKEN_RET	00H	Number of taken mispredictions branches retired.	
	E0H	BR_INST_ DECODED	00H	Number of branch instructions decoded.	
	E2H	BTB_MISSES	00H	Number of branches that miss the BTB.	
	E4H	BR_BOGUS	00H	Number of bogus branches.	
	E6H	BACLEARS	00H	Number of time BACLEAR is asserted	
Stalls	A2	RESOURCE_ STALLS	00H	Number of cycles during which there are resource related stalls.	
	D2H	PARTIAL_RAT_ STALLS	00H	Number of cycles or events for partial stalls	
Segment Register Loads	06H	SEGMENT_REG_ LOADS	00H	Number of segment register loads	
Clocks	79H	CPU_CLK_ UNHALTED	00H	Number of cycles during which the processor is not halted	

NOTES:

1. Several L2 cache events, where noted, can be further qualified using the Unit Mask (UMSK) field in the PerfEvtSel0 and PerfEvtSel1 registers. The lower 4 bits of the Unit Mask field are used in conjunction with L2 events to indicate the cache state or cache states involved. The Pentium®Pro processor identifies cache states using the "MESI" protocol and consequently each bit in the Unit Mask field represents one of the four states: UMSK[3] = M (8H) state, UMSK[2] = E (4H) state, UMSK[1] = S (2H) state, and UMSK[0] = I (1H) state. UMSK[3:0] = MES" (FH) should be used to collect data for all states; UMSK = 0H, for the applicable events, will result in nothing being counted.

2. All of the external bus logic (EBL) events, except where noted, can be further qualified using the Unit Mask (UMSK) field in the PerfEvtSel0 and PerfEvtSel1 registers. Bit 5 of the UMSK field is used in conjunction with the EBL events to indicate whether the processor should count transactions that are self generated (UMSK[5] = 0) or transactions that result from any processor on the bus (UMSK[5] = 1).

intel®

C

Model-Specific
Registers (MSRs)

Table C-1 lists the model-specific registers (MSRs) that can be read with the RDMSR and written with the WRMSR instructions. Register addresses are given in both hexadecimal and decimal; the register name is the mnemonic register name; the bit description describes individual bits in registers.

Table C-1. Model-Specific Registers (MSRs)

Register Address		Register Name	Bit Description
Hex	Dec		
0H	0	P5_MC_ADDR	
1H	1	P5_MC_TYPE	
10H	16	TSC	
1BH	27	APICBASE	
	8		Boot Strap Processor indicator Bit. BSP= 1
	10:9		Reserved
	11		APIC Global Enable Bit - Permanent til reset Enabled = 1, Disabled = 0
2AH	42	EBL_CR_POWERON	
	0		Data bus error code policy 1 = ECC 0 = Parity Read/Write
	1		Data Error Checking Enable 1 = Disabled 0 = Enabled Read/Write
	2		Response Error Checking Enable 1 = Disabled 0 = Enabled Read/Write
	3		AERR# Drive Enable 1 = Disabled 0 = Enabled Read/Write
	4		BERR# Enable for initiator bus requests 1 = Disabled 0 = Enabled Read/Write

Table C-1. Model-Specific Registers (MSRs) (Contd.)

Register Address		Register Name	Bit Description
Hex	Dec		
		6	BERR# Enable for initiator internal errors 1 = Disabled 0 = Enabled Read/Write
		7	BINIT# Driver Enable 1 = Disabled 0 = Enabled Read/Write
		8	Output Tri-state Enabled 1 = Enabled 0 = Disabled Read
		9	Execute BIST 1 = Enabled 0 = Disabled Read
		10	AERR# Observation Enabled 1 = Enabled 0 = Disabled Read
		12	BINIT# Observation Enabled 1 = Enabled 0 = Disabled Read
		13	IN Order Queue Depth 1 = 1 0 = 8 Read
		14	1M Power on Reset Vector 1 = 1M 0 = 4G Read
		15	FRC Mode Enable 1 = Enabled 0 = Disabled Read
		17:16	APIC Cluster ID Read
		21: 20	Symmetric Arbitration ID Read
		24:22	Clock Frequency Ratio Read
		25	Reserved

Table C-1. Model-Specific Registers (MSRs) (Contd.)

Register Address		Register Name	Bit Description
Hex	Dec		
		26	Low Power Enable Read
		31:27	Reserved
79H	121	BIOS_UPDT_TRIG	BIOS Update Trigger Register
8BH	139	BIOS_SIGN	BIOS Update Signature Register
C1H	193	PERFCTR0	
C2H	194	PERFCTR1	
FEH	254	MTRRcap	
179H	377	MCG_CAP	
17AH	378	MCG_STATUS	
17BH	379	MCG_CTL	
186H	390	EVNTSEL0	
		7:0	Event Select (See Performance Counter section for a list of event encodings)
		15:8	UMASK: Unit Mask Register Set to Zero to enable all count options
		16	USER: Controls the counting of events at Privilege levels of 1,2, and 3
		17	OS: Controls the counting of events at Privilege level of 0
		18	E: Occurrence/Duration Mode Select 1 = Occurrence 0 = Duration
		19	PC: Enabled the signalling of performance counter overflow via BP0 pin.
		20	INT: Enables the signalling of counter overflow via input to APIC 1 = Enable 0 = Disable
		22	ENABLE: Enables the counting of performance events in both counters 1 = Enable 0 = Disable

Table C-1. Model-Specific Registers (MSRs) (Contd.)

Register Address		Register Name	Bit Description
Hex	**Dec**		
		23	INV: Inverts the result of the CMASK condition 1 = Inverted 0 = Non-Inverted
		31:24	CMASK: Counter Mask
187H	391	EVNTSEL1	
		7:0	Event Select (See Performance Counter section for a list of event encodings)
		15:8	UMASK: Unit Mask Register Set to Zero to enable all count options
		16	USER: Controls the counting of events at Privilege levels of 1,2, and 3
		17	OS: Controls the counting of events at Privilege level of 0
		18	E: Occurrence/Duration Mode Select 1 = Occurrence 0 = Duration
		19	PC: Enabled the signalling of performance counter overflow via BP0 pin.
		20	INT: Enables the signalling of counter overflow via input to APIC 1 = Enable 0 = Disable
		23	INV: Inverts the result of the CMASK condition 1 = Inverted 0 = Non-Inverted
		31:24	CMASK: Counter Mask
1D9H	473	DEBUGCTLMSR	
		0	Enable/Disable Last Branch Records.
		1	Branch Trap Flag.
		2	Performance Monitoring/Break Point Pins
		3	Performance Monitoring/Break Point Pins

Table C-1. Model-Specific Registers (MSRs) (Contd.)

Register Address		Register Name	Bit Description
Hex	Dec		
		4	Performance Monitoring/Break Point Pins
		5	Performance Monitoring/Break Point Pins
		6	Enable/Disable Execution Trace Messages
		13:7	Reserved
		14	Enable/Disable Execution Trace Messages
		15	Enable/Disable Execution Trace Messages
1DBH	475	LASTBRANCHFROMIP	
1DCH	476	LASTBRANCHTOIP	
1DDH	477	LASTINTFROMIP	
1DEH	478	LASTINTTOIP	
1E0H	480	ROB_CR_BKUPTMPDR6	
		1:0	Reserved
		2	Fast String Enable bit. Default is enabled
200H	512	MTRRphysBase0	
201H	513	MTRRphysMask0	
202H	514	MTRRphysBase1	
203H	515	MTRRphysMask1	
204H	516	MTRRphysBase2	
205H	517	MTRRphysMask2	
206H	518	MTRRphysBase3	
207H	519	MTRRphysMask3	
208H	520	MTRRphysBase4	
209H	521	MTRRphysMask4	
20AH	522	MTRRphysBase5	
20BH	523	MTRRphysMask5	
20CH	524	MTRRphysBase6	
20DH	525	MTRRphysMask6	
20EH	526	MTRRphysBase7	
20FH	527	MTRRphysMask7	
250H	592	MTRRfix64K_00000	
258H	600	MTRRfix16K_80000	
259H	601	MTRRfix16K_A0000	

Table C-1. Model-Specific Registers (MSRs) (Contd.)

Register Address		Register Name	Bit Description
Hex	Dec		
268H	616	MTRRfix4K_C0000	
269H	617	MTRRfix4K_C8000	
26AH	618	MTRRfix4K_D0000	
26BH	619	MTRRfix4K_D8000	
26CH	620	MTRRfix4K_E0000	
26DH	621	MTRRfix4K_E8000	
26EH	622	MTRRfix4K_F0000	
26FH	623	MTRRfix4K_F8000	
2FFH	767	MTRRdefType	
		2:0	Default memory type
		10	Fixed MTRR enable
		11	MTRR Enable
400H	1024	MC0_CTL	
401H	1025	MC0_STATUS	
		63	MC_STATUS_V
		62	MC_STATUS_O
		61	MC_STATUS_UC
		60	MC_STATUS_EN
		59	MC_STATUS_MISCV
		58	MC_STATUS_ADDRV
		57	MC_STATUS_DAM
		31:16	MC_STATUS_MSCOD
		15:0	MC_STATUS_MACCOD
402H	1026	MC0_ADDR	
403H	1027	MC0_MISC	Defined in MCA architecture but not implemented in the Pentium® Pro processor
404H	1028	MC1_CTL	
405H	1029	MC1_STATUS	Bit definitions same as MC0_STATUS
406H	1030	MC1_ADDR	
407H	1031	MC1_MISC	Defined in MCA architecture but not implemented in the Pentium Pro processor
408H	1032	MC2_CTL	
409H	1033	MC2_STATUS	Bit definitions same as MC0_STATUS

Table C-1. Model-Specific Registers (MSRs) (Contd.)

| Register Address | | Register Name | Bit Description |
Hex	Dec		
40AH	1034	MC2_ADDR	
40BH	1035	MC2_MISC	Defined in MCA architecture but not implemented in the Pentium Pro processor
40CH	1036	MC4_CTL	
40DH	1037	MC4_STATUS	Bit definitions same as MC0_STATUS
40EH	1038	MC4_ADDR	Defined in MCA architecture but not implemented in the Pentium Pro processor
40FH	1039	MC4_MISC	Defined in MCA architecture but not implemented in the Pentium Pro processor
410H	1040	MC3_CTL	
411H	1041	MC3_STATUS	Bit definitions same as MC0_STATUS
412H	1042	MC3_ADDR	
413H	1043	MC3_MISC	Defined in MCA architecture but not implemented in the Pentium Pro processor

intel®

Index

INDEX

intel.

NORTH AMERICAN DISTRIBUTORS

ALABAMA

Anthem Electronics
600 Boulevard South
Suite 104F & H
Huntsville 35802
Tel: (205) 890-0302

Arrow/Schweber Electronics
1015 Henderson Road
Huntsville 35805
Tel: (205) 837-6955
FAX: (205) 721-1581

Hall-Mark Computer
4890 University Square
Huntsville 35816
Tel: (800) 409-1483

Hamilton Hallmark
4890 University Square
Suite 1
Huntsville 35816
Tel: (205) 837-8706
FAX: (205) 830-2565

MTI Systems Sales
4950 Corporate Drive
Suite 120
Huntsville 35805
Tel: (205) 830-9526
FAX: (205) 830-9557

Pioneer Technologies Group
4835 University Square
Suite 5
Huntsville 35805
Tel: (205) 837-9300
FAX: (205) 837-9358

Wyle Electronics
7800 Governers Dr., W.
Tower Building, 2nd Floor
Huntsville 35807
Tel: (205) 830-1119
FAX: (205) 830-1520

ARIZONA

Alliance Electronics
7550 East Redfield Rd
Scottsdale 85260
Tel: (602) 261-7988

Anthem Electronics
1555 West 10th Place
Suite 101
Tempe 85281
Tel: (602) 966-6600
FAX: (602) 966-4826

Arrow/Schweber Electronics
2415 West Erie Drive
Tempe 85282
Tel: (602) 431-0030
FAX: (602) 431-9555

Avnet Computer
1626 South Edwards Dr
Tempe 85281
Tel: (800) 426-7999

Hall-Mark Computer
4637 South 37th Place
Phoenix 85040
Tel: (800) 409-1483

Pioneer Standard
1438 West Broadway
Suite B-140
Tempe 85282
Tel: (602) 350-9335

Hamilton Hallmark
4637 South 36th Place
Phoenix 85040
Tel: (602) 437-1200
FAX: (602) 437-2348

Wyle Electronics
4141 East Raymond
Phoenix 85040
Tel: (602) 437-2088
FAX: (602) 437-2124

CALIFORNIA

Anthem Electronics
9131 Oakdale Avenue
Chatsworth 91311
Tel: (818) 775-1333
FAX: (818) 775-1302

Anthem Electronics
1 Oldfield Drive
Irvine 92718-2809
Tel: (714) 768-4444
FAX: (714) 768-6456

Anthem Electronics
580 Menlo Drive
Suite 8
Rocklin 95677
Tel: (916) 624-9744
FAX: (916) 624-9750

Anthem Electronics
9369 Carroll Park Drive
San Diego 92121
Tel: (619) 453-9005
FAX: (619) 546-7893

Anthem Electronics
1160 Ridder Park Drive
San Jose 95131
Tel: (408) 453-1200
FAX: (408) 441-4504

Arrow/Schweber Electronics
26707 West Agoura Road
Calabasas 91302
Tel: (818) 880-9686
FAX: (818) 772-8930

Arrow/Schweber Electronics
48834 Kato Road
Suite 103
Fremont 94538
Tel: (510) 490-9477
FAX: (510) 490-1084

Arrow/Schweber Electronics
6 Cromwell
Suite 100
Irvine 92718
Tel: (714) 581-4622
FAX: (714) 454-4206

Arrow/Schweber Electronics
9511 Ridgehaven Court
San Diego 92123
Tel: (619) 565-4800
FAX: (619) 279-8062

Arrow/Schweber Electronics
1180 Murphy Avenue
San Jose 95131
Tel: (408) 441-9700
FAX: (408) 453-4810

Avnet Computer
1 Mauchley
Irvine 92718
Tel: (800) 426-7999

Avnet Computer
371 Van Ness Way
Torrance 90501
Tel: (800) 426-7999

Avnet Computer
15950 Bernardo Ctr Dr
Suite 6
San Diego 92127
Tel: (800) 426-7999

Avnet Computer
1175 Bordeaux Drive
Suite A
Sunnyvale 94089
Tel: (800) 426-7999

Hall-Mark Computer
21150 Califa Street
Woodland Hills 91367
Tel: (800) 409-1483

Hall-Mark Computer
15950 Bernardo Ctr Dr
Suite C
San Diego 92127
Tel: (800) 409-1483

Hall-Mark Computer
1175 Bordeaux Drive
Sunnyvale 94089
Tel: (800) 409-1483

Hall-Mark Computer
1 Mauchly
Irvine 92718
Tel: (800) 409-1483

Hall-Mark Computer
580 Menlo Drive
Suite 2
Rocklin 95765
Tel: (800) 409-1483

Hamilton Hallmark
3170 Pullman Street
Costa Mesa 92626
Tel: (714) 641-4100
FAX: (714) 641-4122

Hamilton Hallmark
2105 Lundy Avenue
San Jose 95131
Tel: (408) 435-3500
FAX: (408) 435-3720

Hamilton Hallmark
4545 Viewridge Avenue
San Diego 92123
Tel: (619) 571-7540
FAX: (619) 277-6136

Hamilton Hallmark
21150 Califa Street
Woodland Hills 91367
Tel: (818) 594-0404
FAX: (818) 594-8234

Hamilton Hallmark
580 Menlo Drive
Suite 2
Rocklin 95762
Tel: (916) 624-9781
FAX: (916) 961-0922

Pioneer Standard
5126 Clareton Drive
Suite 106
Agoura Hills 91301
Tel: (818) 865-5800

Pioneer Standard
217 Technology Drive
Suite 110
Irvine 92718
Tel: (714) 753-5090

Pioneer Technologies Group
134 Rio Robles
San Jose 95134
Tel: (408) 954-9100
FAX: (408) 954-9113

Pioneer Standard
4370 La Jolla Village Drive
San Diego 92122
Tel: (619) 546-4906

Wyle Electronics
15370 Barranca Pkwy
Irvine 92713
Tel: (714) 753-9953
FAX: (714) 753-9877

Wyle Electronics
15360 Barranca Pkwy
Suite 200
Irvine 92713
Tel: (714) 753-9953
FAX: (714) 753-9877

Wyle Electronics
2951 Sunrise Blvd.
Suite 175
Rancho Cordova 95742
Tel: (916) 638-5282
FAX: (916) 638-1491

Hall-Mark Computer
15950 Bernardo Ctr Dr
Suite C
San Diego 92127
Tel: (800) 409-1483

Hall-Mark Computer
1175 Bordeaux Drive
Sunnyvale 94089
Tel: (800) 409-1483

Hall-Mark Computer
1 Mauchly
Irvine 92718
Tel: (800) 409-1483

Hall-Mark Computer
580 Menlo Drive
Suite 2
Rocklin 95765
Tel: (800) 409-1483

Hamilton Hallmark
3170 Pullman Street
Costa Mesa 92626
Tel: (714) 641-4100
FAX: (714) 641-4122

Hamilton Hallmark
2105 Lundy Avenue
San Jose 95131
Tel: (408) 435-3500
FAX: (408) 435-3720

Hamilton Hallmark
4545 Viewridge Avenue
San Diego 92123
Tel: (619) 571-7540
FAX: (619) 277-6136

Hamilton Hallmark
21150 Califa Street
Woodland Hills 91367
Tel: (818) 594-0404
FAX: (818) 594-8234

Hamilton Hallmark
580 Menlo Drive
Suite 2
Rocklin 95762
Tel: (916) 624-9781
FAX: (916) 961-0922

COLORADO

Anthem Electronics
373 Inverness Dr. S.
Englewood 80112
Tel: (303) 790-4500
FAX: (303) 790-4532

Arrow/Schweber Electronics
61 Inverness Dr East
Suite 105
Englewood 80112
Tel: (303) 799-0258
FAX: (303) 799-0730

Avnet Computer
9605 Maroon Circle
Englewood 80111
Tel: (800) 426-7999

Hall-Mark Computer
9605 Maroon Circle
Englewood 80111
Tel: (800) 409-1483

Hamilton Hallmark
12503 East Euclid Dr
Suite 20
Englewood 80111
Tel: (303) 790-1662
FAX: (303) 790-4991

Hamilton Hallmark
710 Wooten Road
Suite 28
Colorado Springs 80915
Tel: (719) 637-0055
FAX: (719) 637-0088

Pioneer Technologies
5600 Greenwood Plaza Blvd.
Suite 201
Englewood 80111
Tel: (303) 773-8090

Wyle Electronics
451 East 124th Avenue
Thornton 80241
Tel: (303) 457-9953
FAX: (303) 457-4831

Wyle Electronics
9525 Chesapeake Dr.
San Diego 92123
Tel: (619) 565-9171
FAX: (619) 365-0512

Wyle Electronics
3000 Bowers Avenue
Santa Clara 95051
Tel: (408) 727-2500
FAX: (408) 727-5896

Wyle Electronics
17872 Cowan Avenue
Irvine 92714
Tel: (714) 863-9953
FAX: (714) 263-0473

Wyle Electronics
26010 Mureau Road
Suite 150
Calabasas 91302
Tel: (818) 880-9000
FAX: (818) 880-5510

Zeus Arrow Electronics
6276 San Ignacio Avenue
Suite E
San Jose 95119
Tel: (408) 629-4689
FAX: (408) 629-4792

Zeus Arrow Electronics
6 Cromwell Street
Suite 100
Irvine 92718
Tel: (714) 581-4622
FAX: (714) 454-4355

CONNECTICUT

Anthem Electronics
61 Mattatuck Heights Road
Waterbury 06705
Tel: (203) 575-1575
FAX: (203) 596-3232

Arrow/Schweber Electronics
860 N. Main St. Ext.
Wallingford 06492
Tel: (203) 265-7741
FAX: (203) 265-7988

Hall-Mark Computer
Still River Corporate Ctr
55 Federal Road
Danbury 06810
Tel: (800) 409-1483

Hamilton Hallmark
125 Commerce Court,
Unit 6
Cheshire 06410
Tel: (203) 271-2844
FAX: (203) 272-1704

Pioneer Standard
2 Trap Falls Road
Shelton 06484
Tel: (203) 929-5600

FLORIDA

Anthem Electronics
5200 NW 3rd Avenue
Suite 206
Ft. Lauderdale 33309
Tel: (305) 484-0990

Anthem Electronics
598 S. Northlake Blvd.
Suite 1024
Altamonte Sprgs 32701
Tel: (813) 797-2900
FAX: (813) 796-4880

Arrow/Schweber Electronics
400 Fairway Drive
Suite 102
Deerfield Beach 33441
Tel: (305) 429-8200
FAX: (305) 428-3991

Arrow/Schweber Electronics
37 Skyline Drive
Suite 3101
Lake Mary 32746
Tel: (407) 333-9300
FAX: (407) 333-9320

Arrow/Schweber Electronics
4010 Boy Scout Dr.
Suite 295
Tampa 33607
Tel: (813) 873-1030
FAX: (813) 873-0077

Avnet Computer
541 S. Orlando Ave.
Suite 203
Maitland 32751
Tel: (800) 426-7999

Hall-Mark Computer
10491 72nd St. North
Largo 34647
Tel: (800) 409-1483

Hall-Mark Computer
13700 58th St. North
Suite 206
Clearwater 34620
Tel: (800) 409-1483

Hamilton Hallmark
3350 N.W. 53rd Street
Suite 105-107
Ft. Lauderdale 33309
Tel: (305) 484-5482
FAX: (305) 484-2995

NORTH AMERICAN DISTRIBUTORS (Cont'd)

Hamilton Hallmark
10491 72nd St. North
Largo 34647
Tel: (813) 541-7440
FAX: (813) 544-4394

Hamilton Hallmark
7079 University Blvd.
Winter Park 32792
Tel: (407) 657-3300
FAX: (407) 678-4414

**Pioneer Technologies
Group**
337 Northlake Blvd
Suite 1000
Alta Monte Spgs 32701
Tel: (407) 834-9090
FAX: (407) 834-0865

**Pioneer Technologies
Group**
674 South Military Trail
Deerfield Beach 33442
Tel: (305) 428-8877
FAX: (305) 481-2950

Wyle Electronics
1000 112th Circle North
St. Petersburg 33716
Suite 800
Tel: (813) 579-1518
FAX: (813) 579-1518

**Zeus Arrow
Electronics**
37 Skyline Drive
Bldg D., Suite 3101
Lake Mary 32746
Suite 800
Tel: (407) 333-3055
FAX: (407) 333-9681

GEORGIA

Anthem Electronics
2400 Pleasant Hill Rd
Suites 9 & 10
Duluth 30136
Tel: (404) 931-3900
FAX: (404) 931-3902

**Arrow/Schweber
Electronics**
4250 E Rivergreen Pkwy
Suite E
Duluth 30136
Tel: (404) 497-1300
FAX: (404) 476-1493

Avnet Computer
3425 Corporate Way
Suite G
Duluth 30136
Tel: (800) 426-7999

Hall-Mark Computer
3425 Corporate Way
Suite G
Duluth 30136
Tel: (800) 409-1483

Hamilton Hallmark
3425 Corporate Way
Suite G & A
Duluth 30136
Tel: (404) 623-5475
FAX: (404) 623-5490

**Pioneer Technologies
Group**
4250C Rivergreen Pkwy
Duluth 30136
Tel: (404) 623-1003
FAX: (404) 623-0665

Wyle Electronics
6025 The Corners Pkwy
Suite 111
Norcross 30092
Tel: (404) 441-9045
FAX: (404) 441-9086

ILLINOIS

Anthem Electronics
1300 Remington Road
Suite A
Schaumberg 60173
Tel: (708) 884-0200
FAX: (708) 885-0480

**Arrow/Schweber
Electronics**
1140 W Thorndale Rd
Itasca 60143
Tel: (708) 250-0500

Avnet Computer
1124 Thorndale Ave
Bensenville 60106
Tel: (800) 426-7999

Hall-Mark Computer
1124 Thorndale Ave
Bensenville 60106
Tel: (800) 409-1483

Hamilton Hallmark
1130 Thorndale Ave
Bensenville 60106
Tel: (800) 426-7999

MTI Systems Sales
1140 West Thorndale
Avenue
Itasca 60143
Tel: (708) 250-8222
FAX: (708) 250-8275

Pioneer Standard
2171 Executive Drive
Suite 200
Addison 60101
Tel: (708) 495-9680
FAX: (708) 495-9831

Wyle Electronics
2055 Army Trail Road
Suite 140
Addison 60101
Tel: (800) 853-9953

**Zeus Arrow
Electronics**
1140 W Thorndale Ave
Itasca 60143
Tel: (708) 250-0500

INDIANA

**Arrow/Schweber
Electronics**
7108 Lakeview
Parkway West Drive
Indianapolis 46268
Tel: (317) 299-2071
FAX: (317) 299-2379

Avnet Computer
655 West Carmel Drive
Suite 160
Carmel 46032
Tel: (800) 426-7999

Hall-Mark Computer
655 West Carmel Drive
Carmel 46032
Tel: (800) 409-1483

Hamilton Hallmark
655 West Carmel Drive
Suite 160
Carmel 46032
Tel: (317) 575-3500
FAX: (317) 575-3535

Pioneer Standard
9350 Priority Way W Dr
Indianapolis 46250
Tel: (317) 573-0880
FAX: (317) 573-0979

KANSAS

**Arrow/Schweber
Electronics**
9801 Legler Road
Lenexa 66219
Tel: (913) 541-9542
FAX: (913) 541-0328

Hall-Mark Computer
10809 Lakeview Ave
Lenexa 66219
Tel: (800) 409-1483

Hamilton Hallmark
10809 Lakeview
Avenue
Lenexa 66215
Tel: (913) 888-4747
FAX: (913) 888-0523

MARYLAND

Anthem Electronics
7168A Columbia
Gateway Drive
Columbia 21046
Tel: (800) 239-6039

**Arrow/Schweber
Electronics**
9800J Patuxent Woods
Drive
Columbia 21046
Tel: (301) 596-7800
FAX: (301) 596-7821

Avnet Computer
7172 Columbia
Gateway Drive
Suite G
Columbia 21045
Tel: (800) 426-7999

Hall-Mark Computer
7172 Columbia
Gateway Drive
Suite G
Columbia 21046
Tel: (800) 409-1483

Hamilton Hallmark
10240 Old Columbia
Road
Columbia 21046
Tel: (410) 988-9800
FAX: (410) 381-2036

**North Atlantic
Industries**
Systems Division
7125 River Wood Drive
Columbia 21046
Tel: (301) 312-5800
FAX: (301) 312-5850

**Pioneer Technologies
Group**
15810 Gaither Road
Gaithersburg 20877
Tel: (301) 921-0660
FAX: (301) 670-6746

Wyle Electronics
9101 Guilford Road
Suite 120
Columbia 21046
Tel: (301) 490-2170
FAX: (301) 490-2190

MASSACHUSETTS

Anthem Electronics
200 Research Drive
Wilmington 01887
Tel: (508) 657-5170
FAX: (508) 657-6008

**Arrow/Schweber
Electronics**
25 Upton Drive
Wilmington 01887
Tel: (508) 658-0900
FAX: (508) 694-1754

Avnet Computer
10 D Centennial Drive
Peabody 01960
Tel: (800) 426-7999

Hall-Mark Computer
10 D Centennial Drive
Peabody 01960
Tel: (800) 409-1483

Hamilton Hallmark
10 D Centennial Drive
Peabody 01960
Tel: (508) 531-7430
FAX: (508) 532-9802

Pioneer Standard
44 Hartwell Avenue
Lexington 02173
Tel: (617) 861-9200
FAX: (617) 863-1547

Wyle Electronics
5 Oak Park Drive
Bedford 01803
Tel: (617) 271-9953
FAX: (617) 275-3809

**Zeus Arrow
Electronics**
25 Upton Drive
Wilmington 01887
Tel: (508) 658-4776
FAX: (508) 694-2199

MICHIGAN

**Arrow/Schweber
Electronics**
44720 Helm Street
Plymouth 48170
Tel: (313) 462-2290
FAX: (313) 462-2686

Avnet Computer
41650 Garden Brk Rd
Suite 120
Novi 48375
Tel: (800) 426-7999

Hall-Mark Computer
41650 Garden Brk Rd
Suite 120
Novi 48375
Tel: (800) 409-1483

Hamilton Hallmark
44191 Plymouth Oaks
Blvd.
Suite 1300
Plymouth 48170
Tel: (313) 416-5806
FAX: (313) 416-5811

Hamilton Hallmark
41650 Garden Brk Rd
Suite 100
Novi 49418
Tel: (313) 347-4271
FAX: (313) 347-4021

Pioneer Standard
4505 Broadmoor S.E.
Grand Rapids 49512
Tel: (616) 698-1800
FAX: (616) 698-1831

Pioneer Standard
44190 Plymouth Oaks
Blvd.
Plymouth 48170
Tel: (313) 525-1800
FAX: (313) 427-3720

MINNESOTA

Anthem Electronics
7646 Golden Triangle
Drive
Eden Prairie 55344
Tel: (612) 944-5454
FAX: (612) 944-3045

**Arrow/Schweber
Electronics**
10100 Viking Drive
Suite 100
Eden Prairie 55344
Tel: (612) 941-5280
FAX: (612) 942-7803

Avnet Computer
9800 Bren Roaqd East
Suite 410
Minnetonka 55343
Tel: (800) 426-7999

Hall-Mark Computer
9800 Bren Road East
Suite 410
Minnetonka 55343
Tel: (800) 409-1483

Hamilton Hallmark
9401 James Ave South
Suite 140
Bloomington 55431
Tel: (612) 881-2600
FAX: (612) 881-9461

Pioneer Standard
7625 Golden Triangle
Drive
Suite G
Eden Prairie 55344
Tel: (612) 944-3355
FAX: (612) 944-3794

**Zeus Arrow
Electronics**
25 Upton Drive
Wilmington 01887
Tel: (508) 658-4776
FAX: (508) 694-2199

MICHIGAN

**Arrow/Schweber
Electronics**
44720 Helm Street
Plymouth 48170
Tel: (313) 462-2290
FAX: (313) 462-2686

Avnet Computer
41650 Garden Brk Rd
Suite 120
Novi 48375
Tel: (800) 426-7999

Hall-Mark Computer
41650 Garden Brk Rd
Suite 120
Novi 48375
Tel: (800) 409-1483

Hamilton Hallmark
44191 Plymouth Oaks
Blvd.
Suite 1300
Plymouth 48170
Tel: (313) 416-5806
FAX: (313) 416-5811

Wyle Electronics
1325 East 79th Street
Suite 1
Bloomington 55425
Tel: (612) 853-2280
FAX: (612) 853-2298

MISSOURI

**Arrow/Schweber
Electronics**
2380 Schuetz Road
St. Louis 63141
Tel: (314) 567-6888
FAX: (314) 567-1164

Avnet Computer
3783 Rider Train South
Earth City 63045
Tel: (800) 426-7999

Hall-Mark Computer
3783 Rider Trail South
Earth City 63045
Tel: (800) 409-1483

Hamilton Hallmark
3783 Rider Trail South
Earth City 63045
Tel: (314) 291-5350
FAX: (314) 291-0362

NEW HAMPSHIRE

Avnet Computer
2 Executive Park Drive
Bedford 03102
Tel: (800) 426-7999

NEW JERSEY

Anthem Electronics
26 Chapin Road, Unit K
Pine Brook 07058
Tel: (201) 227-7960
FAX: (201) 227-9246

**Arrow/Schweber
Electronics**
4 East Stow Road
Unit 11
Marlton 08053
Tel: (609) 596-8000
FAX: (609) 596-9632

**Arrow/Schweber
Electronics**
43 Route 46 East
Pine Brook 07058
Tel: (201) 227-7880
FAX: (201) 227-2064

Avnet Computer
1-B Keystone Avenue
Building 36
Cherry Hill 08003
Tel: (800) 426-7999

Hall-Mark Computer
1-B Keystone Avenue
Building 36
Cherry Hill 08003
Tel: (800) 409-1483

Hall-Mark Computer
10 Lanidex Plaza West
Parsippany 07054
Tel: (800) 409-1483

Hamilton Hallmark
1 Keystone Avenue
Building 36
Cherry Hill 08003
Tel: (609) 424-0110
FAX: (609) 751-2552

Hamilton Hallmark
10 Lanidex Plaza West
Parsippany 07054
Tel: (201) 515-5300
FAX: (201) 515-1601

MTI Systems Sales
43 Route 46 East
Pinebrook 07058
Tel: (201) 882-8780
FAX: (201) 539-6430

intel

NORTH AMERICAN DISTRIBUTORS (Cont'd)

PioneerStandard
14-A Madison Road
Fairfield 07006
Tel: (201) 575-3510
FAX: (201) 575-3454

Wyle Electronics
115 Route 46, Bldg F
Mountain Lakes 07046
Tel: (201) 402-4970

NEW MEXICO

**Alliance Electronics,
Inc.**
3411 Bryn Mawr N.E.
Albuquerque 87101
Tel: (505) 292-3360
FAX: (505) 275-6392

Avnet Computer
7801 Academy Road
Building 1, Suite 204
Albuquerque 87109
Tel: (800) 426-7999

NEW YORK

Anthem Electronics
47 Mall Drive
Commack 11725
Tel: (516) 864-6600
FAX: (516) 493-2244

**Arrow/Schweber
Electronics**
3375 Brighton Henrietta
Townline Road
Rochester 14623
Tel: (716) 427-0300
FAX: (716) 427-0735

**Arrow/Schweber
Electronics**
20 Oser Avenue
Hauppauge 11788
Tel: (516) 231-1000
FAX: (516) 231-1072

Avnet Computer
2 Penn Plaza
Suite 1245
New York 10121
Tel: (800) 426-7999

Avnet Computer
1057 E. Henrietta Road
Rochester 14623
Tel: (800) 426-7999

Hall-Mark Computer
2 Penn Plaza
New York 10121
Tel: (800) 409-1483

Hall-Mark Computer
1057 E Henrietta Road
Rochester 14623
Tel: (800) 409-1483

Hamilton Hallmark
933 Motor Parkway
Hauppauge 11788
Tel: (516) 434-7470
FAX: (516) 434-7491

Hamilton Hallmark
1057 E Henrietta Road
Rochester 14623
Tel: (716) 475-9130
FAX: (716) 475-9119

Hamilton Hallmark
3075 Veterans
Memorial Hwy.
Ronkonkoma 11779
Tel: (516) 737-0600
FAX: (516) 737-0838

MTI Systems Sales
1 Penn Plaza
250 West 34th Street
New York 10119
Tel: (212) 643-1280
FAX: (212) 643-1288

Pioneer Standard
68 Corporate Drive
Binghamton 13904
Tel: (607) 722-9300
FAX: (607) 722-9562

Pioneer Standard
60 Crossway Pk West
Woodbury, Long Island
11797
Tel: (516) 921-8700
FAX: (516) 921-2143

Pioneer Standard
840 Fairport Park
Fairport 14450
Tel: (716) 381-7070
FAX: (716) 381-5955

**Zeus Arrow
Electronics**
100 Midland Avenue
Port Chester 10573
Tel: (914) 937-7400
FAX: (914) 937-2553

NORTH CAROLINA

Anthem Electronics
4805 Greenwood
Suite 100
Raleigh 27604
Tel: (919) 782-3550

**Arrow/Schweber
Electronics**
5240 Greensdairy
Road
Raleigh 27604
Tel: (919) 876-3132
FAX: (919) 878-9517

Avnet Computer
4421 Stuart Andrew
Boulevard
Suite 600
Charlotte 28217
Tel: (800) 426-7999

Hall-Mark Computer
3510 Spring Forest Rd
Suite B
Raleigh 27604
Tel: (800) 409-1483

Hamilton Hallmark
3510 Spring Forest Rd
Suite B
Raleigh 27604
Tel: (800) 409-1483

Hamilton Hallmark
5234 Greens Dairy Rd
Raleigh 27604
Tel: (919) 878-0819

**Pioneer Technologies
Group**
2200 Gateway Ctr. Blvd
Suite 215
Morrisville 27560
Tel: (919) 460-1530

OHIO

**Arrow/Schweber
Electronics**
6573 Cochran Road
Suite E
Solon 44139
Tel: (216) 248-3990
FAX: (216) 248-1106

**Arrow/Schweber
Electronics**
8200 Washington
Village Drive
Centerville 45458
Tel: (513) 435-5563
FAX: (513) 435-2049

Avnet Computer
7764 Washington
Village Drive
Dayton 45459
Tel: (800) 426-7999

Avnet Computer
2 Summit Park Drive
Suite 520
Independence 44131
Tel: (800) 426-7999

Hall-Mark Computer
5821 Harper Road
Solon 44139
Tel: (800) 409-1483

Hall-Mark Computer
777 Dearborn Pk Lane
Suite L
Worthington 43085
Tel: (800) 409-1483

Hamilton Hallmark
5821 Harper Road
Solon 44139
Tel: (216) 498-1100
FAX: (216) 248-4803

Hamilton Hallmark
777 Dearborn Pk Lane
Suite L
Worthington 43085
Tel: (614) 888-3313
FAX: (614) 888-0767

MTI Systems Sales
23404 Commerce Pk
Road
Beachwood 44122
Tel: (216) 464-6688
FAX: (216) 464-3564

Pioneer Standard
4433 Interpoint Blvd
Dayton 45424
Tel: (513) 236-9900
FAX: (513) 236-8133

Pioneer Standard
4800 East 131st Street
Cleveland 44105
Tel: (216) 587-3600
FAX: (216) 663-1004

Wyle Electronics
6835 Cochran Rd.
Solon 44139
Tel: (216) 248-9996

OKLAHOMA

**Arrow/Schweber
Electronics**
12101 East 51st Street
Suite 106
Tulsa 74146
Tel: (918) 252-7537
FAX: (918) 254-0917

Hamilton Hallmark
5411 S. 125th E. Ave
Suite 305
Tulsa 74146
Tel: (918) 254-6110
FAX: (918) 254-6207

Pioneer Standard
9717 East 42nd Street
Suite 105
Tulsa 74146
Tel: (918) 665-7840
FAX: (918) 665-1891

OREGON

**Almac Arrow
Electronics**
9500 S.W. Nimbus Ave
Suite E
Beaverton 97008
Tel: (503) 629-8090
FAX: (503) 645-0611

Anthem Electronics
9090 SW Gemini Drive
Beaverton 97005
Tel: (503) 643-1114
FAX: (503) 626-7928

Avnet Computer
9750 SW Nimbus Ave.
Beaverton 97005
Tel: (800) 426-7999

Hall-Mark Computer
9750 SW Nimbus Ave.
Beaverton 97005
Tel: (800) 409-1483

Hamilton Hallmark
9750 SW Nimbus Ave.
Beaverton 97005
Tel: (503) 526-6200
FAX: (503) 641-5939

Pioneer Technologies
8905 Southwest
Numbus Ave.
Suite 160
Beaverton 97005
Tel: (503) 626-7300
FAX: (503) 626-5300

Wyle Electronics
9640 Sunshine Court
Building G
Suite 200
Beaverton 97005
Tel: (503) 643-7900
FAX: (503) 646-5466

PENNSYLVANIA

Anthem Electronics
355 Business Ctr Drive
Horsham 19044
Tel: (215) 443-5150
FAX: (215) 675-9875

Avnet Computer
213 Executive Drive
Suite 320
Mars 16046
Tel: (800) 426-7999

**Arrow/Schweber
Electronics**
2681 Mosside Blvd
Suite 204
Monroeville 15146
Tel: (412) 856-9490

**Pioneer Technologies
Group**
259 Kappa Drive
Pittsburgh 15238
Tel: (412) 782-2300
FAX: (412) 963-8255

**Pioneer Technologies
Group**
500 Enterprise Road
Keith Valley Bus.Ctr
Horsham 19044
Tel: (215) 674-4000

Wyle Electronics
1 Eves Drive
Suite 111
Marlton 08053-3185
Tel: (609) 985-7953
FAX: (609) 985-8757

TEXAS

Anthem Electronics
651 N. Plano Road
Suite 401
Richardson 75081
Tel: (214) 238-7100
FAX: (214) 238-0237

Anthem Electronics
14050 Summit Drive
Suite 119
Austin 78728
Tel: (512) 388-0049
FAX: (512) 388-0271

**Arrow/Schweber
Electronics**
Brake Ctr III, Bldg M1
11500 Metric Boulevard
Suite 160
Austin 78758
Tel: (512) 835-4180
FAX: (512) 832-5921

**Arrow/Schweber
Electronics**
3220 Commander Drive
Carrollton 75006
Tel: (214) 380-6464
FAX: (214) 248-7208

**Arrow/Schweber
Electronics**
19416 Park Row
Suite 190
Houston 77084
Tel: (713) 647-6868
FAX: (713) 492-8722

Avnet Computer
4004 Beltline
Suite 200
Dallas 75244
Tel: (800) 426-799

Avnet Computer
1235 North Loop West
Suite 525
Houston 77008
Tel: (800) 426-7999

Hall-Mark Computer
12211 Technology Blvd
Austin 78727
Tel: (800) 409-1483

Hall-Mark Computer
4004 Beltline Road
Suite 200
Dallas 75244
Tel: (800) 409-1483

Hall-Mark Computer
1235 North Loop West
Houston 77008
Tel: (800) 409-1483

Hamilton Hallmark
12211 Technology
Boulevard
Austin 78727
Tel: (512) 258-8848
FAX: (512) 258-3777

Hamilton Hallmark
11420 Page Mill Road
Dallas 75243
Tel: (214) 553-4300
FAX: (214) 553-4395

Hamilton Hallmark
8000 Westglen
Houston 77063
Tel: (713) 781-6100
FAX: (713) 953-8420

Pioneer Standard
1826D Kramer Lane
Austin 78758
Tel: (512) 835-4000
FAX: (512) 835-9829

Pioneer Standard
13765 Beta Road
Dallas 75244
Tel: (214) 263-3168
FAX: (214) 490-6419

Pioneer Standard
10530 Rockley Road
Suite 100
Houston 77099
Tel: (713) 495-4700
FAX: (713) 495-5642

Wyle Electronics
1810 Greenville Ave
Richardson 75081
Tel: (214) 235-9953
FAX: (214) 644-5064

Wyle Electronics
9208 Waterford Center
Blvd
Suite 150
Austin 78750
Tel: (512) 345-8853
FAX: (512) 345-9330

Wyle Electronics
2901 Wilcrest
Suite 120
Houston 77099
Tel: (713) 879-9953
FAX: (713) 879-9953

**Zeus Arrow
Electronics**
3220 Commander Dr
Carrollton 75006
Tel: (214) 380-4330
FAX: (214) 447-2222

UTAH

Anthem Electronics
1279 West 2200 South
Salt Lake City 84119
Tel: (801) 973-8555
FAX: (801) 973-8909

**Arrow/Schweber
Electronics**
1946 West Parkway
Boulevard
Salt Lake City 84119
Tel: (801) 973-6913
FAX: (801) 972-0200

intel.

NORTH AMERICAN DISTRIBUTORS (Cont'd)

Avnet Computer
1100 East 6600 South
Suite 150
Salt Lake City 84121
Tel: (800) 426-7999

Hall-Mark Computer
1100 East 6600 South
Suite 150
Salt Lake City
Tel: (800) 409-1483

Hamilton Hallmark
1100 East 6600 South
Suite 120
Salt Lake City 84121
Tel: (801) 266-2022
FAX: (801) 263-0104

Wyle Electronics
1325 West 2200 South
Suite E
West Valley 84119
Tel: (801) 974-9953
FAX: (801) 972-2524

WASHINGTON

**Almac Arrow
Electronics**
14360 S.E. Eastgate
Way
Bellevue 98007
Tel: (206) 643-9992
FAX: (206) 643-9709

Anthem Electronics
19017 120th Ave N.E.
Suite 102
Bothell 98011
Tel: (206) 483-1700
FAX: (206) 486-0571

Avnet Computer
8630 154th Ave, NE
Redmond 98052
Tel: (800) 426-7999

Hamilton Hallmark
8630 154th Avenue
Redmond 98052
Tel: (206) 881-6697
FAX: (206) 867-0159

Pioneer Technologies
2800 156th Ave S.E.
Suite 100
Bellevue 98007
Tel: (206) 644-7500

Wyle Electronics
15385 NE 90th St
Redmond 98052
Tel: (206) 881-1150
FAX: (206) 881-1567

WISCONSIN

**Arrow/Schweber
Electronics**
200 N. Patrick
Suite 100
Brookfield 53045
Tel: (414) 792-0150
FAX: (414) 792-0156

Avnet Computer
2440 South 179th St
New Berlin 53416
Tel: (800) 426-7999

Hall-Mark Computer
2440 South 179th St
New Berlin 53146
Tel: (800) 409-1483

Hamilton Hallmark
2440 South 179th St
New Berlin 53146
Tel: (414) 797-7844
FAX: (414) 797-9259

Pioneer Standard
120 Bishops Way
Suite 163
Brookfield 53005
Tel: (414) 780-3600
FAX: (414) 780-3613

Wyle Electronics
150 North Patrick
Building 7, Suite 150
Brookfield 53045
Tel: (414) 879-0434
FAX: (414) 879-0474

ALASKA

Avnet Computer
1400 W Benson Blvd
Suite 400
Anchorage 99503
Tel: (800) 426-7999

CANADA

ALBERTA

Avnet Computer
1144 29th Avenue NE
Suite 108
Calgary T2E 7P1
Tel: (800) 387-3406

Pioneer/Pioneer
560, 1212-31 Ave. NE
Calgary T2E 7S8
Tel: (403) 291-1988
FAX: (403) 295-8714

BRITISH COLUMBIA

**Almac Arrow
Electronics**
8544 Baxter Place
Burnaby V5A 4T8
Tel: (604) 421-2333
FAX: (604) 421-5030

Hamilton Hallmark
8610 Commerce Court
Burnaby V5A 4N6
Tel: (604) 420-4101
FAX: (604) 420-5376

Pioneer/Pioneer
4455 North 6 Road
Rochmond V6V 1P6
Tel: (604) 273-5575
FAX: (604) 273-2413

MANITOBA

Pioneer/Pioneer
540 Marjorie Street
Winnipeg R3H 0S9

ONTARIO

**Arrow/Schweber
Electronics**
36 Antares Drive
Unit 100
Nepean K2E 7W5
Tel: (613) 226-6903
FAX: (613) 723-2018

**Arrow/Schweber
Electronics**
1093 Meyerside, Unit 2
Mississauga L5T 1M4
Tel: (416) 670-2010
FAX: (416) 670-5863

Avnet Computer
Canada System
Engineering Group
151 Superior Blvd.
Mississauga L5T 2L1
Tel: (800) 387-3406

Avnet Computer
190 Colonade Road
Nepean K2E 7J5
Tel: (800) 387-3406

**Canada System
Engineering Group**
151 Superior Boulevard
Mississauga L5T 2L1
Tel: (800) 387-3406

Hamilton Hallmark
151 Superior Blvd.,
Unit 1-6
Mississauga L5T 2L1
Tel: (416) 564-6060
FAX: (416) 564-6033

Hamilton Hallmark
190 Colonade Road
Nepean K2E 7J5
Tel: (613) 226-1700
FAX: (613) 226-1184

Pioneer/Pioneer
3415 American Drive
Mississauga L4V 1T6
Tel: (416) 507-2600
FAX: (416) 507-2831

Pioneer/Pioneer
155 Colonnade Rd., S.
Suite 17
Nepean K2E 7K3
Tel: (613) 226-8840
FAX: (613) 226-6352

QUEBEC

**Arrow/Schweber
Electronics**
1100 Street Regis Blvd
Dorval H9P 2T5
Tel: (514) 421-7411
FAX: (514) 421-7430

**Gates Arrow
Electronics**
500 Boul.
St-Jean-Baptiste Ave
Quebec H2E 5R9
Tel: (418) 871-7500
FAX: (418) 871-6816

Avnet Computer
7575 Trans Canada
Suite 601
St. Laurent H4T 1V6
Tel: (800) 265-1135

Hamilton Hallmark
7575 Transcanada Hwy
Suite 600
Street Laurent H4T 2V6
Tel: (514) 335-1000
FAX: (514) 335-2481

Pioneer/Pioneer
520 McCaffrey
Street Laurent H4T 1N1
Tel: (514) 737-9700
FAX: (514) 737-5212